THE HISTORICAL RELIABILITY

of JOHN'S GOSPEL

Issues & Commentary

CRAIG L. BLOMBERG

IVP Academic

An imprint of InterVarsity Press
Downers Grove, Illinois

InterVarsity Press
P.O. Box 1400, Downers Grove, IL 60515-1426
World Wide Web: www.ivpress.com
E-mail: mail@ivpress.com

InterVarsity Press® *is the book-publishing division of InterVarsity Christian Fellowship/USA*®*, a student movement active on campus at hundreds of universities, colleges and schools of nursing in the United States of America, and a member movement of the International Fellowship of Evangelical Students. For information about local and regional activities, write Public Relations Dept., InterVarsity Christian Fellowship/USA, 6400 Schroeder Rd., P.O. Box 7895, Madison, WI 53707-7895, or visit the IVCF website at <www.ivcf.org>.*

Cover photograph: Symbol of St. John the Evangelist, Carolingian Northern Italy at the Albert Museum, London, UK/The Bridgeman Art Library

ISBN 978-0-8308-3871-4

Printed in the United States of America ∞

Library of Congress Cataloging-in-Publication Data

Blomberg, Craig.
  The historical reliability of John's gospel: issues and commentary / Craig L. Blomberg.
    p. cm.
  Includes bibliographical references.
  ISBN 0-8308-2685-8 (alk. paper)
    1. Bible. N.T. John—Criticism, interpretation, etc.—History. I. Title.
BS2615.6.H55 B56 2002
226.5'06–dc21

                                                                                2001051563

P	19	18	17	16	15	14	13	12	11	10	9	8	7	6	5	4	3	2	1
Y	27	26	25	24	23	22	21	20	19	18	17	16	15	14	13	12	11		

For Howard Marshall
in gratitude for both his scholarship and his godliness
for both his mentoring and his friendship

CONTENTS

PREFACE

Nearly a century ago, William Sanday gave a series of lectures in Union Seminary, New York, and Oxford University, England, which were subsequently published as *The Criticism of the Fourth Gospel* (1905). This book proves fascinating reading at the beginning of the twenty-first century. In some respects, the issues remain identical; only the names of the scholars have changed. Sanday wrote, believing that several recent publications had proved unnecessarily sceptical of the reliability of John, that they were based on faulty presuppositions and historical methodology, that they disregarded the majority of mainstream biblical scholarship which was more centrist in nature, and that in fact a strong case could be made on historical grounds alone for an even more conservative position.

In the past hundred years discussions of John have taken turns that could not have been anticipated a century ago, especially due to the discoveries just after the Second World War of the Dead Sea Scrolls and the Nag Hammadi library. We have made enormous advances in the understanding of first-century Mediterranean historiography and in the development of criteria for assessing the authenticity or historicity of the material concerning Jesus depicted in ancient sources both inside and outside the Christian canon of Scripture. But the spectrum of scholarly views today remains remarkably similar to what it was at the beginning of the twentieth century, and I find myself writing this book prompted by the identical four convictions that Sanday articulated.

Three successive Theological Books Editors at Inter-Varsity Press in the United Kingdom deserve my thanks. It was David Kingdon in the early 1990s who planted the seeds of the idea for this book, asking if I would use my chapter on problems in the Gospel of John in my book *The Historical*

Reliability of the Gospels (1987: 153–189) as a springboard for an entire volume on the historicity of John. It took me several years to decide I wanted to do it, and by that time David had moved on and Mark Smith had become my editor. I am grateful that he agreed to the project. Now he has in turn given way to Philip Duce, and once again I am extremely appreciative of his commitment. I must also thank Frank Entwistle, Inter-Varsity Press's Chief Executive in the UK, who has supported the project throughout, and Jim Hoover, Associate Editorial Director at the American InterVarsity Press, who enthusiastically agreed to co-publish this work in the US.

Some of the ideas in this book first took shape in much shorter formats. I am appreciative of opportunities to give papers on the historicity of John to the annual meeting of the Evangelical Theological Society in Boston in November of 1999 and to a group of students and professors in Ridley College, Melbourne, Australia, in August of 2000. I received extremely helpful feedback from participants in both gatherings in the discussion sessions following the delivery of the papers. By the time this book appears in print, some of my previous musings should likewise be published in a volume edited by Robert Fortna and Tom Thatcher with Westminster John Knox Press, provisionally entitled *Perspectives on John*. I appreciate the invitation to contribute to that highly eclectic volume. I must also acknowledge the invitation a decade ago from editors Robert Sloan and Mikeal Parsons to write on the historical reliability of John for an identically titled volume (1993), which was printed by a rather obscure press and received very little scholarly attention.

Closer to home, I remain profoundly indebted to Rick Scovel and Randy Kemp, whose work as research assistants helped me enormously in the identification, accumulation and synthesis of substantial amounts of secondary literature relevant to this project. Jeanette Freitag, assistant to the faculty of Denver Seminary, has again proved enormously helpful in numerous typing, editing and secretarial roles. Elodie Emig meticulously checked the final draft of my bibliography and my quotations from modern sources for accuracy. To both of them I offer my heartfelt thanks. I am grateful to the staffs of the libraries of Denver Seminary and the Iliff School of Theology for their judicious purchases of almost all the necessary literature for thorough, contemporary New Testament research and for their efficient use of inter-library loan services for the handful of items I needed that were not available here in Denver. I must also thank the Denver Seminary faculty and board of trustees for approving a July–December 2000 sabbatical term, which enabled me to complete the writing and revising of this volume. I am also grateful that our overall workload, while noticeably growing in recent years, still (though at times just barely) allows sufficient discretionary hours for those who are particularly judicious in time management to carry on research of this nature even when not on sabbatical!

Finally, I should like to dedicate this book to Professor I. Howard Marshall of the University of Aberdeen, now in partial retirement. It was his book *Luke: Historian and Theologian* (1970) that I discovered in my college library in the early 1970s when I was trying to decide how to respond to the claims of my religion professors that, if the Gospel writers were primarily theologians, then their presentations of material about Jesus could not be substantially historical in nature. Professor Marshall convinced me that this claim was almost entirely false and that both historical and theological motives dominated at least Luke's agenda and largely complemented one another. In many ways it was that *kairos* moment that set me down the path of expending considerable amounts of research and writing throughout my scholarly career to discussing the historicity of all four canonical Gospels. It became for me an extraordinary privilege, as well, when the University of Aberdeen accepted me for study under Professor Marshall from 1979 to 1982 for my PhD in New Testament. During those years I discovered that his keen scholarship was matched in quality by his adept mentoring and warm friendship. It has been a delight to keep in touch in the years since, primarily at academic conferences on both sides of the Atlantic; and it was a special privilege to have him as a guest lecturer on the Denver Seminary campus for the first time since shortly before I joined our faculty, in April of 2000. Recognizing that all the errors of this book are my own, I nevertheless dedicate it to Howard Marshall, with especial thanks for all that he has taught me over the years.

LIST OF ABBREVIATIONS

ABR	*Australian Biblical Review*
AJT	*Asia Journal of Theology*
BA	*Biblical Archaeologist*
BBR	*Bulletin for Biblical Research*
Bib	*Biblica*
BibTod	*Bible Today*
BTB	*Biblical Theology Bulletin*
BZ	*Biblische Zeitschrift*
CBQ	*Catholic Biblical Quarterly*
CTR	*Criswell Theological Review*
DR	*Downside Review*
EJ	*Evangelical Journal*
EJT	*European Journal of Theology*
EQ	*Evangelical Quarterly*
EstBíb	*Estudios Bíblicos*
ETL	*Ephemerides Theologicae Lovanienses*
ExpT	*Expository Times*
FN	*Filología Neotestamentaria*
HBT	*Horizons in Biblical Theology*
HeyJ	*Heythrop Journal*
HTR	*Harvard Theological Review*
IBS	*Irish Biblical Studies*
Int	*Interpretation*
ITQ	*Irish Theological Quarterly*
JBL	*Journal of Biblical Literature*
JETS	*Journal of the Evangelical Theological Society*
JSNT	*Journal for the Study of the New Testament*

JTS	*Journal of Theological Studies*
JTSA	*Journal of Theology for Southern Africa*
LouvStud	*Louvain Studies*
LXX	Septuagint
Neot	*Neotestamentica*
NESTTR	*Near East School of Theology Theological Review*
NIV	New International Version
NovT	*Novum Testamentum*
NRSV	New Revised Standard Version
NTS	*New Testament Studies*
PEQ	*Palestine Exploration Quarterly*
RB	*Revue Biblique*
RefRev	*Reformed Review*
RHPR	*Revue d'histoire et de philosophie religieuses*
RivBib	*Rivista Biblica*
RSR	*Recherches de science religieuse*
ScriptTheol	*Scripta Theologica*
SecCent	*Second Century*
SJT	*Scottish Journal of Theology*
SR	*Studies in Religion*
StVTQ	*Saint Vladimir's Theological Quarterly*
SEÅ	*Svensk exegetisk årsbok*
SWJT	*Southwestern Journal of Theology*
Theol	*Theology*
TrinJ	*Trinity Journal*
TS	*Theological Studies*
TU	*Texte und Untersuchungen*
TynB	*Tyndale Bulletin*
TZ	*Theologische Zeitschrift*
UBS	United Bible Societies
VT	*Vetus Testamentum*
WTJ	*Westminster Theological Journal*
ZNW	*Zeitschrift für die neutestamentliche Wissenschaft*
ZTK	*Zeitschrift für Theologie und Kirche*

PART ONE

INTRODUCTORY CONSIDERATIONS

INTRODUCTORY
CONSIDERATIONS

In his recent book *Is John's Gospel True?* Maurice Casey vigorously attacks more traditional studies, trying to demonstrate that there is precious little historical accuracy in John. He begins by arguing that John has misplaced Jesus' temple cleansing and altered the date of the Last Supper. These observations alone 'show that a conservative evangelical view of scripture is verifiably false' (Casey 1996: 29). Casey proceeds to present additional ways in which John's Gospel cannot be harmonized with the Synoptics, discussing its Christology, portrait of John the Baptist, style and content of Jesus' teaching, and passion narrative. Instead, this Gospel has fabricated its distinctive content in the light of the polemics between Christians and Jews at the end of the first century and in keeping with the pseudepigraphic tradition of much of Hebrew Scripture. Casey (1996: 229) concludes that John's Gospel 'is profoundly untrue. It consists to a large extent of inaccurate stories and words wrongly attributed to people. It is anti-Jewish, and as holy scripture it has been used to legitimate outbreaks of Christian anti-Semitism'. It is thus unworthy of inclusion in the Bible.

Casey's charges are hardly new. The Jesus Seminar in the US gained notoriety when it alleged that all but three of the sayings of Jesus in John's Gospel bore no resemblance to his authentic teaching (Funk and Hoover 1993: 401–470). Later, the Seminar coloured sixteen short excerpts of John's narrative material (from one line to a few verses in length) something other than black (Funk 1998: 365–440) – the colour that signifies an item bears no relationship to what the historical Jesus actually did or said. Much more irenic but only a little less sceptical is A. T. Hanson (1991: 318):

John is aware of an earlier historical tradition about Jesus which differs in certain important respects from his. He feels constrained by it at certain points even when it seems to conflict with his own. He has his own historical tradition, which appears to be inferior to that of the Synoptists, thought not without some value. But he allows himself a very wide licence indeed in altering, enriching, transposing and adding to his own tradition from his own resources, which were largely drawn from scripture as he understood it. He has therefore not provided us with a reliable historical account of Jesus. Could he have understood what we mean by 'a reliable historical account', he would probably repudiated [sic.] the suggestion that this is what he was giving us in his Gospel.

But most scholars have been less sweeping in their claims. More typical are the conclusions of C. K. Barrett (1978: 141–142):

> It is evident that it was not John's intention to write a work of scientific history ... John's interests were theological rather than chronological ... He did not hesitate to repress, revise, rewrite, or rearrange. On the other hand there is no sufficient evidence for the view that John freely created narrative material for allegorical purposes ... This means that the chronicler can sometimes (though less frequently than is often thought) pick out from John simple and sound historical material ... In the same way John presents in his one book both history and interpretation.

Similarly, Barnabas Lindars (2000: 103, 36, 45, 54) notes Clement of Alexandria's designation of John as 'the spiritual gospel' and warns of false expectations. 'The multi-dimensional character of the Gospel obviously precludes the idea that it is a straight historical record of what actually happened.' Instead of viewing fact and fiction as mutually exclusive categories, we must establish intermediate ones. Lindars himself opts for seeing kernel, authentic sayings having been midrashically expanded in the course of the Fourth Evangelist's own homilies on this material. Still, Barrett's and Lindars' approaches hardly inspire confidence in coming to the Fourth Gospel for a readily accessible source of historical information about the life and times of Jesus.[1]

1] Cf. Nordsieck (1998) for a quite recent restatement of the critical consensus with respect to authorship, origin and historicity of the Fourth Gospel. Like Barrett and Lindars, Nordsieck allows for some historical elements to emerge from uniquely Johannine material, but views a majority of it as later, theological overlay. Schnelle's recent commentary (1998) aptly reflects this 'consensus' perspective with respect to tradition and redaction in John.

The distinctives of John's Gospel have of course been observed throughout church history. They may be categorized under five headings (Blomberg 1987: 153–155). First, there is *John's selection of material.* Numerous prominent features of the Synoptics' portrait of Christ[2] are completely absent from John, most notably Jesus' baptism, the calling of the Twelve, exorcisms, parables, the transfiguration, and the institution of the Lord's Supper. Conversely, John includes information found nowhere in the Synoptics, including the miracle of turning water into wine, the resurrection of Lazarus, Jesus' early ministry in Judea and Samaria, his frequent visits to Jerusalem, and numerous extended discourses.

Second, *John's theological distinctives prove striking.* His is the only Gospel explicitly to affirm Jesus' divinity and to reflect a 'high Christology' throughout Jesus' life, without the synoptic plot development in which his disciples slowly come to understand his identity and in which his opponents more gradually increase in their hostility. Jesus' own claims more explicitly link him with God (8:58; 10:30; 14:6). In John, the Baptist denies being Elijah (1:21); the Synoptics affirm that he is (Mark 9:11–13). The Fourth Gospel emphasizes more the presence of eternal life; the Synoptics dwell more on the future aspect of the kingdom. And John ends with Jesus dispensing the Spirit after his resurrection and before his return to his Father (John 20:22), while Luke reserves this bestowal for Pentecost (Acts 2).

Third, *John's chronology appears to contradict the Synoptics' outline.* Everything described of Jesus' adult ministry in Matthew, Mark and Luke could have occurred within a few months; John's references to repeated Passovers (2:13; 6:4; 13:1) presuppose a ministry of more than two years (and maybe more than three years – cf. 5:1). In addition to the specific 'dislocations' stressed by Casey in his opening chapter, we may observe varying dates or times for Jesus' anointing by Mary of Bethany (John 12:1; cf. Mark 14:3), the call of the first disciples (John 1:35–42; cf. Mark 1:16–20) and the timing of the crucifixion (John 19:14; cf. Mark 15:25).

Fourth, *other apparent historical discrepancies appear.* John seems to think Christ was born in Nazareth rather than Bethlehem (7:52) and that Lazarus' resurrection, not the temple cleansing, was the catalyst for Jesus' arrest (11:45–53). He claims that Jews began to excommunicate Christians from their synagogues even during Jesus' lifetime (9:22), whereas other historical evidence suggests this was a late first-century development (the

---

2] Unless otherwise noted, I will use 'Jesus' and 'Christ' interchangeably throughout this book, solely for the sake of literary variety. I recognize that originally the latter was a title and not a given name!

'curse on the heretics' introduced into the synagogue liturgy).

Finally, *John's style of writing differs markedly from the Synoptics.* Jesus' teaching uses language and vocabulary indistinguishable from John's as narrator. Christ speaks in extended discourses rather than pithy aphorisms. His language merges with that of the narrator of the Gospel so that we are not sure where the one ends and the other begins (esp. John 3:1–21; cf. the same phenomenon with the words of the Baptist in 3:27–36). And, at several points, John's narrative seems out of sequence. In the farewell discourse, Jesus calls to his disciples, 'Come now; let us leave' (14:31), but he then continues talking for another three chapters. Similarly, John 21 appears to many as an appendix added by a later writer, because 20:30–31 reads like a fitting conclusion to the Gospel.[3]

It comes, then, as little surprise that contemporary historical Jesus research pays scant attention to John. Definitive tomes have been produced by focusing almost entirely on the Synoptics' portraits (Sanders 1985; Crossan 1991; Meier 1991, 1994; Theissen and Merz 1997). Evangelical counterparts have hardly differed from the critical consensus at this point (cf. Witherington 1990; Wright 1996).[4] But three observations suggest that the evidence for John's credibility may not be quite so sparse.

To begin with, we dare not overlook the numerous similarities between John and the Synoptics. I have spelled out several of these elsewhere (Blomberg 1987: 156–159) and shall mention each as it arises in the commentary section of this book. Second, over forty years ago J. A. T. Robinson (1959) identified what he called a 'new look on the Fourth Gospel', which viewed John as independent of the Synoptics, often preserving uniquely historical information, and thoroughly rooted in an early first-century Palestinian Jewish milieu. Not long afterwards C. H. Dodd (1963) penned what has become the classic, detailed expression of this perspective;[5] subsequent developments turned this 'new look' into a

---

3] A number of these phenomena are also conveniently summarized and elaborated in Mussner (1967), who concludes that John, unlike the Synoptics, portrays 'the essential identity of the Jesus of history with the glorified Christ' (86), i.e., that the entire Gospel reflects solely a unified post-resurrection perspective.

4] Cf. also the otherwise very helpful ecumenical conference proceedings on 'Jesus and the oral Gospel tradition' (Wansbrough 1991), which devotes only one essay to John (by an evangelical; Dunn 1991) and does not substantially advance our confidence in John beyond the Barrett-Lindars consensus approach.

5] This work, however, must be balanced with Dodd 1954, in which it was already made clear how many liberties the author of the Fourth Gospel felt free to take with the 'history' he narrated.

consensus in many quarters (Smalley 1978: 9–40). D. Moody Smith (1993) suggests that John's distinctive chronology, geography, portrait of the Baptist, vignettes of women and elements of the passion and resurrection narratives may all contain historical material. James Charlesworth (1996: 90) believes that the Dead Sea Scrolls have 'revolutionized the interpretation of John', enabling us to view it as a late first-century Jewish text relying on even earlier traditions rather than a late second-century Greek philosophical treatise. But sometimes the 'new look' simply favours John at the Synoptics' expense (cf. esp. J. A. T. Robinson 1985). And Gary Burge (1992: 27) is overly optimistic when he generalizes, 'The new look urges that we view the Gospel as Jewish and historically reliable.' The first predicate is true; the second would be more accurately worded as 'more historically reliable than previously thought' – which still leaves room for plenty of material to be viewed as relatively unhistorical.

Third, a spate of recent, article-length studies and fully fledged commentaries on John have appeared, all defending a substantial amount of historicity in the Fourth Gospel (articles: Carson 1981b; E. E. Ellis 1988; Silva 1988; García-Moreno 1991; Barton 1993; Blomberg 1993; E. E. Ellis 1993; Lea 1995; Thompson 1996; D. Wenham 1997, 1998; de la Fuente 1998; Moloney 2000; commentaries: Bruce 1983; Michaels 1983; Beasley-Murray 1987; Carson 1991; Pryor 1992a; Morris 1995; Witherington 1995; Borchert 1996; Ridderbos 1997; Köstenberger 1999; Whitacre 1999). A much larger number of exegetical studies of specific passages or themes in John points in the same direction, as the running commentary portion of this book will demonstrate. All of these works, however, have received little attention from the major studies of the historical Jesus, in part due to the high degree of compartmentalization in modern research and in part because many critical scholars continue simply to ignore most conservative scholarship. It is equally common for older, important studies of the historicity of John, not necessarily by evangelicals (esp. J. A. Robinson 1908; Askwith 1910; Holland 1923; Headlam 1948; Higgins 1960) to be neglected because of the curious methodological stranglehold of the latest and newest in much contemporary biblical study.

At the same time it remains patently obvious to any careful reader of the Fourth Gospel that John is more different from than similar to the Synoptics. One of the reasons that many stand unconvinced of the possibility of John being substantially accurate is that thematic studies of the Gospel's historicity still cover only representative problems that affect a minority of John's data. One may allow that this feature or that characteristic of the Fourth Gospel derives from historical tradition, but as one reads the text sequentially from start to finish there still seem to be just too many differences. The time seems ripe, therefore, for a study that discusses many of the standard introductory and background considerations, but which goes on to examine in some detail every passage in John, in order, with a view to assessing historicity.

One might argue that such a book ideally should be produced by a Johannine specialist, but I know of none currently being projected. One could equally argue, though, that fresh insights on a thoroughly debated topic like this might better emerge if a scholar who has devoted most of his research to synoptic and historical Jesus issues (like I have) would bring some of the distinctives of those disciplines to bear on the Fourth Gospel. At any rate, the last book to appear even to approximate the format I envision is more than a century and a quarter old (Sanday 1872), and the evangelical commentaries noted above devote only sporadic attention to the issues of historicity because of the other issues that a full-orbed commentary must discuss.

The rest of Part One will thus devote itself to introductory and topical concerns. Part Two will then proceed in commentary format, but restricting itself to questions that bear on the historical trustworthiness of the Fourth Gospel. A brief conclusion will gather together some of the most prominent results. Historicity is not necessarily the most important question that should be analysed for every gospel pericope, but it does have considerable implications for correct interpretation and, more indirectly, for biblical authority.[6] Exegetical and theological studies abound, assessing John's contributions to numerous themes. Increasingly, too, literary criticism is producing full analyses of the Fourth Gospel (for the most recent, extensive bibliographies of scholarship on John, see van Belle 1988; Mills 1995). The time is thus ripe for supplementing this fairly comprehensive coverage on other fronts with a consistently historical assessment of John.

AUTHORSHIP

The appropriate starting point in investigating the accuracy of any apparently historical narrative is to determine the author of that narrative, if possible. Was the author a credible witness? Did he or she depend on reliable sources of information? Data for determining authorship, in turn,

---

6] Theological truth may of course be communicated by literary genres across a spectrum from pure fact to pure fiction, but if Casey's harsh charges (above, p. 17) were accurate, it would indeed be difficult to continue to speak of John's truthfulness on any meaningful level.

subdivide into external and internal evidence – what others have said about the material in question and what clues may be reconstructed from the document itself. In the case of the Fourth Gospel, many modern commentators have begun with internal evidence, but nowhere does this Gospel make any explicit claim concerning the identity of its author. The number of different proposals generated by the internal data demonstrates how inconclusive that evidence is; one recent survey of scholarship discusses twenty-three different suggestions (Charlesworth 1995: 127–224)! On the other hand, every piece of ancient, external evidence, save one, agrees that the author was the apostle John, the son of Zebedee. So we must begin with this testimony and discuss its credibility.[7] Because there has been considerable renewed discussion of issues surrounding authorship, we shall go into more detail on this topic than on our other introductory considerations.[8]

EXTERNAL EVIDENCE

Critics of apostolic authorship make much of the silence of the earliest post-New Testament Christian writers in the first half of the second century (e.g. Barrett 1978: 102–103). Why, for example, does Ignatius, writing to the very Ephesians that tradition would come to associate with the Johannine community, and directly quoting Matthew and Luke, make no mention of the apostle John or his writing? Yet there are only a few direct quotes of any apostolic documents and Ignatius' epistles are primarily exhortational in nature, so that his quotations naturally draw on Paul's and Jesus' ethical teaching (the latter much more common in Matthew and Luke than in John). Polycarp's situation is similar. He was himself apparently a disciple of John, but his one extant epistle makes no

---

7] This is an important methodological point. Many scholars begin with internal data that raise doubts about Johannine authorship and come to the external evidence already prejudiced against it. Tellingly, those who defend John the son of Zebedee as author more often than not have begun with the external testimony. On the other hand, the pattern is not unvarying. R. E. Brown (1966, 1979) and Schnackenburg (1968, 1982) changed their minds over the years and rejected Johannine authorship on the basis of internal evidence, after having begun with the external evidence, while Westcott (1908: ix–lxvii) began with the internal evidence and still opted for apostolic authorship. Köstenberger (1996) notes how the shift in scholarship on this issue in the eighteenth and nineteenth centuries after the rise of the scientific Enlightenment occurred not on the basis of any new evidence but on a change of method.

8] For a robust defence of valuing the external evidence for the origins of all four Gospels more highly than the critical consensus does, see now Hengel 2000.

mention of the son of Zebedee. Although also exhortational in nature, it quotes 1 John 4:2 (in *Phil.* 7.1), suggesting that Polycarp may have known the other writings attributed to John as well.

Justin Martyr alludes to John 3:3–5 in his *First Apology* (61.4) and speaks of the Gospels as including 'memoirs of the apostles', in the plural, perhaps a reference to both Matthew and John since Mark and Luke were not apostles (67.4). Justin also seems to be familiar with John's logos Christology more generally (Pryor 1992b). Justin's (and others') reluctance to refer more explicitly to John may well derive from the growing use of his Gospel in Gnostic circles by the mid-second century (Dungan 1999: 24–26). Hippolytus (*Ref. Her.* 7.10) would write that the Gnostic Basilides quoted John 1:9 to support his system of thought, while Origen scatters references to the first known commentary on John, by the Gnostic Heracleon, throughout his writing. The Nag Hammadi library of Gnostic literature provides primary source material to corroborate this trend. Allusions to the Fourth Gospel are pervasive, especially in the *Gospel of Truth* and, to a lesser extent, in the gospels of *Philip* and *Thomas* and the *Apocryphon of John* (Morris 1995: 17). Epiphanius (*Her.* 51.3) would later write that the Gnostic *alogoi* (so-called because they denied the doctrine of the logos) attributed John's Gospel to the late first-century docetist teacher, Cerinthus.

By the latter portion of the second century, however, use of the Fourth Gospel appears explicitly in orthodox Christian writers. Tatian's *Diatessaron*, a harmony of the four Gospels, actually uses John as the base into which to fit the other three. Theophilus of Antioch (*To Autolyc.* 2.22) attributes to John the first verse of his Gospel ('In the beginning was the Word, and the Word was with God and the Word was God …').[9] The anti-Marcionite *Prologue to John* and the *Muratorian Canon* both attribute the Gospel to the apostle John, though in contexts of other information that may not be accurate.[10]

The most important second-century testimony comes from Irenaeus, who briefly describes the composition of all four canonical Gospels. After the first three were written, he recounts, 'John, the disciple of our Lord, who also had leaned upon his breast, did himself publish a Gospel during his residence at Ephesus in Asia' (*Ag. Her.* 3.1.1). Later in that same book

---

9] Unless otherwise indicated, Scripture quotations will follow the New International Version, Inclusive Language Edition (London: Hodder & Stoughton, 1996).

10] Numerous commentaries lay out the texts from the early Christian writers and discuss them in varying amounts. See, in increasing order of detail, Michaels 1983: xviii–xx; Bruce 1983: 6–12; Schnackenburg 1968: 77–91.

(3.11.1), Irenaeus quotes several verses from the Gospel to clarify the difference between orthodox and Gnostic doctrine, again attributing the words to 'John, the disciple of the Lord'. That Irenaeus has in mind the son of Zebedee is demonstrated from other texts in which he is specifically called an 'apostle,' and in which it becomes clear that 'disciple of the Lord' is merely synonymous language for John's apostolic office (e.g. 1.9.2; 3.3.4; cf. Lewis 1908: 18). In fact, the variety of contexts in which Irenaeus refers to John and/or his Gospel demonstrates that it was already commonly believed around the empire that the son of Zebedee authored this work (Lewis 1908: 24–32).[11]

No orthodox writer ever proposes any other alternative for the author of the Fourth Gospel and the book is accepted in all of the early canonical lists, which is all the more significant given the frequent heterodox misinterpretation of it. It is not until the early fourth century with the writings of Eusebius that any ambiguity appears. Eusebius, too, believes that the apostle John wrote the Gospel that had come to bear his name (*Eccl. Hist.* 3.24.5–13), but two other texts from his writing have led many scholars to wonder if matters were that straightforward. In 3.31.2–3 Eusebius cites the testimony of Polycrates, from the mid-second century, who refers to the death and burial of John in Ephesus along with the burial of the apostle Philip and his four daughters in Hierapolis. But Polycrates has confused the apostle Philip with the deacon by the same name, so one wonders if he has the right John in view. Polycrates also called the apostle John, 'who leaned on the Lord's breast', a 'priest, wearing the mitre, and martyr and teacher'. But nothing in the New Testament suggests John was a priest, and the word for 'mitre' (Gk. *petalon*) seems to refer to garb reserved for the Jewish high priest. Had the apostle come out of such a background, other early Christian writings would surely have stressed it. Richard Bauckham (1993b) thus argues that Polycrates must have confused two different Johns, probably on the basis of Acts 4:6, and that this second John wrote the Gospel (cf. also Winandy 1998).

A second source cited by Eusebius at first glance lends credence to this hypothesis. In 3.39.3–7 Eusebius describes the testimony of Papias from the first quarter of the second century, another individual with either direct or indirect ties to the apostle John.[12] Papias describes how 'if anyone came who had followed the presbyters, I inquired into the words of the

11] From approximately the turn of the (second to third) century, we may cite also Tertullian, *Ag. Marc.* 4.3; Clement of Alexandria (quoted by Eusebius, *Ecc. Hist.* 6.14.5–7); and Ptolemy (quoted by Irenaeus, *Ag. Her.* 1.8.5).

12] Eusebius describes how Irenaeus believed that Papias was a disciple of John in his

presbyters, what Andrew or Peter or Philip or Thomas or James or John or Matthew, or any other of the Lord's disciples had said, and what Aristion and the presbyter John, the Lord's disciples, were saying' (3.39.4). One natural interpretation of this text is that Papias is distinguishing two Johns, the original apostle, no longer alive, and a presbyter alive in Papias' day of whom he could directly enquire. When one notices that 2 and 3 John begin with greetings from one who simply calls himself the 'presbyter' (or 'elder' – Gk. *presbyteros*), one understands why scholars have from time to time suggested that this 'John the elder' may have been the author of one or more of the New Testament writings ascribed to John, and that later church tradition confused the two (for the greatest detail, see Hengel 1989).[13]

On the other hand, a case can be made that Eusebius in 3.24.5–13 is alluding to the writings of Papias there, too (Hill 1998), in which case Papias also would have believed that the son of Zebedee wrote the Fourth Gospel. If John were the sole living apostle, it is understandable that Papias should mention him twice, first in a list of apostles and then as one of the living elders of the church. As for Polycrates, it is difficult imagining *anyone* named John in the early church having been a former Jewish high priest without more reference to that fact. Polycrates may simply have confused the Jewish relative of Caiaphas named John (Acts 4:6) with the apostle, without any additional Christian 'John' in view. At any rate, even if there was a second early church leader named John, none of these testimonies links him with the Fourth Gospel *per se*. The external evidence must be deemed to opt overwhelmingly in favour of John, the son of Zebedee, as author of this document.

INTERNAL EVIDENCE
The early church Fathers have been shown at times to be wrong, however, on a variety of issues, so we must turn to the data within the Fourth Gospel itself to test the hypothesis of Johannine authorship.

---

younger years, but Eusebius believes that Papias's ambiguous testimony is best understood as removing himself one generation from the apostle, with otherwise anonymous 'elders' or 'presbyters' who knew the apostles as the direct source of Papias's information.

13] Bauckham (1993b) clearly distinguishes the two individuals but Hengel' (1989: 130–132) seems to fuse them, arguing that John the elder is the beloved disciple, a Palestinian Jew, an eyewitness to much of Jesus' ministry, and an old man writing to Ephesus at the end of the first century.

Evidence in support of John as author

The classic expression in modern scholarship of the internal evidence for Johannine authorship comes from B. F. Westcott almost a century ago (1908: ix–lxvii; cf. also Morris 1969: 218–256). Westcott mounts his case in five stages: the author was (1) a Jew, (2) of Palestine, (3) an eyewitness, (4) an apostle, and (5) St John. No full-scale refutation of Westcott has ever appeared, although important segments of his argument have been scrutinized. It would appear that his basic logic remains sound, even though each stage of the argument requires certain nuancing.

It is generally agreed today that the author of the Fourth Gospel was *Jewish*. The author accurately understands Jewish customs, is steeped in the Old Testament, is aware of finer points of distinctions among pre-70 Jewish sects, and is concerned to demonstrate Jesus as the true fulfilment of the Law and of the numerous rituals and institutions of Judaism. Indeed, the discoveries of the Dead Sea Scrolls have demonstrated affinities between Essene-Jewish thought and the distinctive milieu of John in ways that Westcott could not have anticipated (see esp. Charlesworth 1972). Thus the 'new look' on John has roundly rejected the dominant perspective of the first half of the twentieth century that saw the Fourth Gospel as mostly Hellenistic in background.

It is equally common to find current critics agreeing that the author was *from Palestine*. His knowledge of the geography and topography of Israel is excellent, particularly in Jerusalem and the surrounding Judean countryside (cf. esp. Albright 1956; Potter 1959; Schein 1980; Scobie 1982). The famous pools of Bethesda (John 5:2) and Siloam (9:11) have been excavated. Jacob's well at Sychar (4:5–6) remains today where it was located even in Old Testament times, while the 'Stone Pavement' corresponding to that described as 'Gabbatha' (19:13) has been discovered in Jerusalem, although the site is contested. Additional examples will be discussed as they come up in Part Two of this book. Aramaic terms are employed and explained, but only in Israel did Jews still widely use this language rather than Greek. In fact, John's Gospel regularly demonstrates Jesus and his Jewish opponents discussing 'halakhic' (legal) regulations relatively unique to Israel, and portions of the Gospel demonstrate affinity with distinctive Samaritan forms of thought.[14] It is of course possible that a Gentile Christian over numerous years could have become well enough acquainted with Palestinian Judaism to account for all of these phenomena under Westcott's first two headings,

---

14] For a succinct catalogue of parallels to Palestinian Jewish language, style and background in several of these categories, see Hengel 1989: 110–113; 208–212, nn. 6–45.

but this is not the first hypothesis one would naturally formulate.[15]

Whether 'John' demonstrates *eyewitness* touches has been more debated. It is extremely difficult to distinguish between historical realism employed in the service of a fictitious narrative and detail that can be explained *only* by eyewitness testimony to actual historical events (see esp. Tovey 1997; Byrskog 2000). Westcott (1908: xxxix–xliv) makes his case by examining details of persons, time, number, place and manner of action, many of which seem highly precise and theologically unmotivated. 'If it be said that we can conceive that these traits might have been realised by the imagination of a Defoe or a Shakespeare, it may be enough to reply that the narrative is wholly removed from this modern realism; but besides this, there are other fragmentary notes to which no such explanation can apply.' Among these appear 'minute facts likely to cling to the memory of one directly concerned (i. 40), though it is in fact difficult for us now to grasp the object of the writer in preserving them', details that appear to be in conflict with the Synoptics and thus not likely to have been invented (e.g. 1:21 with Matt. 11:14; and 3:24 with Matt. 4:12), and mysterious sayings left wholly unexplained (e.g. 1:29, 46, 48) (xliii-xliv).[16]

R. L. Sturch (1980) has examined many of these details and cautioned against immediately assuming an eyewitness source; they may mask hidden symbolism, reflect natural inferences, stress important details, satisfy readers' curiosity, stem from literary style, or be purely fictitious inventions (315–316). Nevertheless there remains 'a residue of items which resist … elimination', and which 'may suggest that eyewitness evidence could also lie behind some of the details where it cannot be proved' (324).[17] The use

---

15] Koester (1995) notes how the key locations in the Fourth Gospel not only enhance the credibility of the narrative but further the theological interests of the work. One should add, therefore, that the more the historical corroboration emerges as an almost tangential by-product of a narrative with other more central objectives, the more convincing it is.

16] Stauffer (1960a) compiled the most comprehensive catalogue of categories into which historically realistic elements of John may be divided: theologically irrelevant notices of geography or topography, historically corroborated details, parallels with the synoptic tradition, parallels with extracanonical Jesus-tradition, details that fit an early first-century Palestinian Jewish setting, proper order and sequence of the many Jewish festivals, juridical elements corresponding to legal customs of the time, general external and internal chronological coherence, and speeches based on historically verifiable kernels of Jesus' teaching.

17] On the other hand, Davies (1992: 276–315) surveys the geography, topography, flora, climate and cultural history depicted in the Fourth Gospel and thinks that, despite the general accuracy, most of these details could have been gleaned from a thorough knowledge of the Scriptures and the synoptic traditions.

of the first-person plural by the narrator of this Gospel in 1:14 and 19:35 also suggests that he views himself as a participant in the events described (though see below, p. 38).[18]

The fourth stage of the argument for those who follow Westcott is to affirm that the author was *one of the Twelve*. The claim of John 21:24 is that the individual referred to at several points in the Gospel as 'the beloved disciple' (or 'the disciple whom Jesus loved') was the author of the work or of at least a very substantial core of it. The passages in which this figure is so described are 13:23–25 (part of the Last Supper), 19:26–27, 34–35 (at the crucifixion), 20:2–5, 8 (at the empty tomb), 21:1–7 (fishing in Galilee) and 21:20–22 (the prediction of the possibility of the disciple living until Christ's return). Neither John nor the Synoptics ever demonstrably limits the disciples present in any of these contexts to the Twelve, but it has often been assumed that only these apostles would have communed with Jesus the last night of his life. If this is the case, then the beloved disciple must be one of the Twelve.

The very fact that the Fourth Gospel would describe a particular disciple as this intimate with Jesus also strongly suggests that we must think of one of the apostles. Indeed, the Synoptics on several occasions group Peter, James and John together as an inner core of three of the Twelve who participate in experiences like the transfiguration or Gethsemane to which the other nine are not privy. But Peter appears by name throughout John, even in the same scenes as the beloved disciple, so he cannot be this anonymous individual. James and John, however, never appear by name, though 21:2 contains a reference to 'the sons of Zebedee' as two of seven individuals (two others remain altogether unnamed) among whom the beloved disciple is numbered (cf. v. 7). But James, the brother of John, was martyred in AD 44 (cf. Acts 12:1–2), much too early for him to have authored this Gospel. That leaves John as the only likely candidate, precisely as early church tradition declared. The more difficult question to answer is if the logic just set out is the same as that which led to the early

---

18] Barrett (1978: 123) only partially agrees: 'The most the evidence that has now been surveyed can prove is that here and there behind the Johannine narrative there lies eyewitness material. It is certainly not proved, and is perhaps not provable, that the gospel as a whole is the work of an eye-witness. And the evidence already given of the Hellenistic side of John's thought suggests that the final editor of the gospel was not an eye-witness.' But this argument cuts both ways. If Barrett is correct in insisting earlier that a Gentile could have gained accurate knowledge of Israel and Judaism, then surely a Jew living and ministering for several decades in a Hellenistic context could gain accurate knowledge of the Graeco-Roman world as well.

church tradition (so, e.g. Casey 1996: 164–170) or if it is also based on actual historical information. The Fourth Gospel, after all, never identifies an inner trio as closer to Jesus than other disciples. Interestingly, as D. M. Smith (1999: 26) observes, this Gospel omits those episodes in which the Synoptics describe John playing a role (Mark 1:16–20, 29–32; 3:13–19; 5:35–43; 9:2–8; 10:35–41; 13:3; 14:32–42).[19]

A stronger argument leads to the fifth and final stage of the discussion. It involves *the complete absence from the Fourth Gospel of the name 'John' as a reference to anyone other than the Baptist.* Yet unlike the Synoptics, the Fourth Gospel never calls this John 'the Baptist', but simply 'John' (1:6, 15, 19, 26, 28, etc.). If the apostle by the same name were writing to a specific community who knew him well and knew that the Gospel came from him, this silence would be readily understandable. Then, as the Gospel circulated, and eventually became combined with the Synoptics in a fourfold collection, the title 'according to John' would naturally have been added.[20] But if the Gospel were written by anyone else named John (e.g. 'John the elder'), how could it introduce the Baptist without any qualification and expect people not to confuse him with the apostle by the same name? Or, with much modern scholarship, if the Gospel were penned partly or wholly by one or more of John's later disciples, surely they too would have wanted to distinguish these two Johns and highlight the involvement of their revered master (cf. Morris 1969: 277).[21]

It is also possible, however, that the author of this Gospel was one of the two anonymous disciples of 21:2. This hypothesis has often led to linking this individual with the anonymous disciple and companion of Andrew

---

19] Smith seems to think that this tells against Johannine authorship, but it is hard to be sure. None of these passages falls within the scope of the geographical and theological outline that governs the Fourth Gospel (see below, p. 55) and several do not really portray much at all about John.

20] It is normally assumed that none of the Gospel autographs would have contained the titles found later in the time from which relatively complete Gospel manuscripts have been preserved (beginning in the third century). After all, only as one Gospel began to be compared and combined with another would the need to distinguish them arise, and it is unlikely that all four documents independently would have been labeled identically: 'The Gospel according to —'. But see now Hengel (2000: 50–58, 78–106), who argues plausibly that Mark, or a very early copyist, may have coined the title, and that the other Evangelists consciously imitated this convention.

21] This argument has also at times been linked with the claim that John's modesty led him not to include his own name in the narrative, but Rese (1996) has correctly replied that calling oneself a disciple particularly beloved by Jesus is not a normal sign of modesty.

mentioned in 1:35, 40 and with the equally anonymous disciple and companion of Peter known to the high priest (18:15–18). These three passages, then, are often assumed to be further references to the beloved disciple, who is to be distinguished from the sons of Zebedee (cf. esp. R. E. Brown 1979: 31–34; Schnackenburg 1982: 383–387). If Johannine authorship be rejected, this is probably the strongest alternative. The author would still have been an intimate, eyewitness companion of Christ, possibly one of the Twelve not otherwise named in John (i.e. other than Jude, Judas Iscariot, Thomas, Peter, Philip or the sons of Zebedee) or possibly another close friend like Lazarus (see esp. 11:2 and cf. Eller 1987).[22] But the fact that the author goes out of his way to refer to one of Jesus' followers as 'beloved' in five different settings suggests that if he wanted his readers to link these other references about anonymous disciples to himself he could easily have used the same language in all eight passages. That he did not may well suggest that we are not meant to equate them. It would appear, then, that all five parts of Westcott's argument remain plausible, when appropriately nuanced, even today (so also Bruce 1983: 1–6; Carson 1991: 68–81; Morris 1995: 4–25).

Evidence against John as author

Why, then, is Johannine authorship almost universally rejected among more critical scholarship? The answer involves a sometimes lengthy list of objections as to why the son of Zebedee could not have penned this Gospel (cf. Parker 1962; Muñoz-León 1987 [who defends Johannine authorship against each objection]; Culpepper 1994: 74–76; Charlesworth 1995: 197–213). I have combined a number of them together and categorized them under nine headings. Other arguments belong elsewhere.[23]

1. Because so much of the synoptic portrait of Christ is missing in John, and what is included is so different, it is alleged that an apostle close to Jesus could not have written this Gospel. This argument, of course, presupposes that John did not have good theological and/or literary reasons for omitting much of what he knew and for including what he did, or that

---

22] Baltz (1996) has written a very short book, also defending Lazarus as author. But the vast majority of his arguments work for John as well, and he has not provided convincing evidence for rejecting this tradition. The same is true of the conservative apologetic for historicity that he believes results from his work.

23] For example, that John was martyred too early to have authored this Gospel, which will be dealt with under the discussion of dating below, or that the 'beloved disciple' passages are interpolations, which belongs under source criticism.

the only way a credible Gospel could be compiled was by including certain episodes lacking in John. We shall see below that both of these presuppositions are unfounded (pp. 54–56). Indeed, the argument is more pertinent to the issue of historicity than to authorship. The more one inclines to attribute the Fourth Gospel to a 'lesser light' than the apostle John, the *more difficult* it is to explain that author's willingness to paint a portrait that differed from central and widely known details of the earliest Christian proclamation of the gospel.

2. That John the apostle appears by name nowhere in the Fourth Gospel is frequently believed to count against Johannine authorship. This may be combined with the charge that no apostle would dare to refer to himself as a disciple especially beloved by the Lord. But the 'beloved disciple' passages are all in the third person and read more naturally as the work of a final redactor separate from the author of the bulk of the work (see below, pp. 37–38). And we have already seen that there is no reason for John's name to appear in the text if he were already well known to his original audience. It is more difficult to imagine someone other than John willing to compile a work that could easily lead to the assumption of Johannine origin and yet say nothing more explicitly about that apostle.

Casey (1996: 144–149), thinking he is arguing against apostolic authorship and for pseudepigraphy, highlights the extensive Hebrew tradition (in both Scripture and intertestamental literature) of documents whose authors' real names never appear in the text. But in fact Casey assumes what has never been conclusively demonstrated – that any of the ancient Hebrew canon *was* pseudepigraphical (cf., e.g. Beckwith 1985: 346–358). Demonstrable examples of pseudepigraphy appear only in the intertestamental literature, while numerous examples of *anonymous* authorship appear in the Hebrew canon. This is precisely the situation one finds with the four Gospels, which should thus not cause surprise. When later writers wanted to garner authority for Old or New Testament apocryphal documents they usually attributed them to a key Jewish or Christian figure *within the text of that document itself.* One would have expected this, were the Fourth Gospel penned by a later follower of the apostle John; as it stands, the silence of the Gospel is more consistent with apostolic authorship.

3. Some argue that because John's Gospel is written in a serene tone, emphasizing key themes of love and unity, it could not have come from one of the 'sons of Thunder' (the nickname for James and John in Mark 3:17), who are thus believed to have been wrathful and emotional. John was interested in apocalyptic, they say, hoping to call down fire from

heaven on the Samaritans (Luke 9:54) and wanting to sit at Jesus' right hand in his coming kingdom (Mark 10:35–45). If the beloved disciple were John, then he would not be portrayed as more passive than Peter, as a quiet bystander at the cross, and so on. But this argument has so many holes in it that it is difficult to believe that it is still seriously promoted! Nicknames do not demonstrate constant personality traits; the Synoptics provide far too little information for one to pontificate as to how a disciple could or could not behave in any given situation, and Acts regularly portrays John as Peter's less obtrusive 'right-hand man' (Acts 3:1, 3, 11; 4:13, 19; 8:14; cf. also Gal. 2:9). John had decades to mature as a Christian before writing this Gospel, so that two or three unrelated synoptic texts describing potentially impetuous behaviour are meaningless for determining the identity of an author of a later biography that centred on a different individual altogether – Jesus.

4. A variety of arguments compare the Fourth Gospel with the other putative Johannine literature – 1, 2 and 3 John, and Revelation. Only in Revelation does the name John actually occur (1:1, 4, 9, etc.); but some find the style of the Gospel too different from the apocalypse to have been written by the same person. Yet large numbers of critical scholars think the 'John' of Revelation to be an otherwise unknown prophet or seer. Others still defend apostolic authorship but are more impressed by the linguistic similarities with the Gospel. So, too, some find the anti-Gnosticism of the epistles clearer than in the Gospel and thus give more credence to the external testimony about the circumstances of the apostle John writing 1, 2 and 3 John than to that same testimony about him authoring the Gospel. Others point to the title 'elder' in the opening verses of 2 and 3 John as proof that 'John the elder' wrote the epistles. Debate then proceeds as to whether the Gospel is stylistically similar enough to warrant a similar ascription of authorship there. Sooner or later every one of these arguments is cancelled out by another. None makes it any more or less likely that the son of Zebedee wrote the Fourth Gospel.[24]

5. Equally unfounded are allegations that John the apostle was illiterate or too uneducated, culturally backward, or philosophically unsophisticated as a Galilean fisherman to have written the Gospel that now bears his name. Acts 4:13 implies only that the apostles did not have the advanced,

---

24] For elaboration on and representatives of each of these various positions, see any of the standard New Testament introductions. Particularly helpful now is R. E. Brown 1997, especially because he built on a lifetime of Johannine research and commentary writing.

theological education that prepared one to become a rabbi (see Witherington 1998: 195–196). Jewish boys for the most part *did* learn to read and write Hebrew and/or Aramaic and studied Scripture intensively in a primary school education from roughly the ages of five to twelve (Riesner 1980). Alan Millard (2000) has recently demonstrated how pervasive reading and writing were in Jesus' world, even in Greek, contrary to the claims of many. It is entirely credible that John the apostle could have learned considerable Greek, with or without formal education, over a possible seventy-year period of multicultural ministry in several parts of the Roman empire. On the other hand, the Greek of the Gospel of John ranks among the simplest of the New Testament Greek texts – precisely what one might expect from someone who learned it as a second language and never mastered it with the fluency of a native Greek speaker.

6. The detailed knowledge of geography and topography in the Fourth Gospel appears most clearly with respect to Judea and Jerusalem. Therefore, some argue that the author of this work must have been Judean not Galilean. This argument might carry some small weight if one had already determined that the Gospel were a literary fiction. As it stands, it professes to be a historical account of the ministry of Jesus, in which the author accompanied Jesus most of the time and would have been told about other events that he did not witness. Accuracy of narration demonstrates nothing about the geographical origin of the author, but merely about his access to reliable sources, including perhaps his own memory.[25]

7. The Synoptics claim that all the disciples forsook Jesus in the Garden of Gethsemane (Mark 14:50 par.), whereas the Fourth Gospel depicts the beloved disciple present with Mary, Jesus' mother, at the crucifixion (John 19:26). But the Synoptics also all recognize that Peter, at least, returned to follow Jesus to the high priest's courtyard (Mark 14:54 pars.), so who knows where else various apostles went after leaving Gethsemane? One may infer nothing about the presence or absence of any of the disciples from the crowds observing the crucifixion the next day simply because the Synoptics explicitly refer only to certain women there.

25] Casey (1996:172–174) scornfully dismisses Carson's and Morris's arguments for the Palestinian Jewish nature of the author of the Fourth Gospel based on his accurate knowledge of places and customs in Israel. To the extent that Casey's argument has any force, it boomerangs to undercut the critical consensus that precisely this same information demonstrates a Judean rather than Galilean home for the author.

8. The apparent rivalry between Peter and the beloved disciple in John 20 – 21 seems inappropriate if that disciple is John. But this way of putting things can mislead. It is true that many have deduced some tension in the church at the end of the first century (one wing supporting Peter and another John) to account for the inclusion of these episodes, but even this scarcely proves actual animosity between the two apostles sixty years earlier. And nothing in the text of John itself suggests any discord between the two men.

9. Probably the strongest argument (perhaps the *only* strong argument) involves the question of whether a Galilean fisherman could have been so well known and influential in Jerusalem to gain access to the high priest's courtyard and feel safe there while his master was on trial for his life (John 18:15–16). On the other hand, this objection plays down the evidence that the family of Zebedee may have been more well-to-do than is often imagined; they at least have 'hired men' – in the plural (Mark 1:20). Given that Jerusalem relied on its fish supply from Galilee, it is only natural to assume that the wealthier fishermen would have had the most access to the homes of the elite in Judea (cf. Charlesworth 1995: 56). It is also at least suggestive to observe that if one be permitted to 'harmonize' the list of women standing by the cross in the various Gospels, the sister of Mary, the mother of Jesus (John 19:25) is equated with Salome, the mother of James and John (Matt. 27:56; Mark 15:40). But Luke 1:36 also calls Elizabeth, the wife of Zechariah the priest and herself a descendant of Aaron (v. 5), a relative of Mary. The upshot is that the sons of Zebedee were relatives to at least one priestly family in Judea (v. 39). It is not impossible that such connections led to some kind of acquaintance with the household of Caiaphas (cf. J. A. T. Robinson 1985: 119–122).

Moreover, *all* of this is predicated on the assumption that the anonymous companion of Peter in John 18:15–16 is the same as the beloved disciple, a premise we have already seen is by no means secure. If this person is a separate individual, then the entire objection collapses. Despite glib and even inaccurate generalizations to the contrary,[26] the internal evidence against Johannine authorship appears remarkably weak.

26] E.g. O'Grady (1982: 54): 'Gone forever are the days when Christians thought of John, the Son Zebedee [sic.], sitting down in his old age and composing in a coherent and detailed manner his reflections on the meaning of Jesus and his teaching.'

The case for Thomas

What, then, of the case for other prominent Christians (named, anonymous or ideal) who were portrayed as followers of Jesus? Charlesworth (1995: 127–224) thoroughly surveys the entire sweep of modern scholarship, pointing out how no single alternative commands more than a small minority following and how all are fairly readily dispensed with.[27] Charlesworth then mounts an elaborate case for an alternative almost never before suggested in church history, the apostle Thomas (225–437). Because his case is so extensive and has received only a few, brief critiques, we must take the time to interact with it here.

The heart of Charlesworth's argument may be summarized as follows: John 21:7 discloses that the beloved disciple is one of the seven men referred to in verse 2. The sons of Zebedee are excluded because of the various arguments noted above (pp. 31–35). The two anonymous disciples are excluded because the link between verses 2 and 7 suggests that one of the purposes of this passage is to *reveal* who the beloved disciple is. That leaves only Peter, Nathanael and Thomas. Peter is obviously not the person in question since he is compared and contrasted with the beloved disciple in chapters 13, 20 and 21. Thomas is far more plausible than Nathanael because his confession of faith in Jesus after seeing his resurrected body (20:28) perfectly fits the purpose of the Gospel (20:31). Thomas's response forms the paradigm desired of all who read this work, as in fact does his earlier willingness to follow Jesus and die with him if necessary (11:16). Charlesworth recognizes that the strongest argument against Thomas is the observation that the beloved disciple apparently comes to faith as soon as he sees the empty tomb (20:8) rather than eight days later. Charlesworth thus devotes extensive discussion to try to bolster the claim that this verse need not refer to full, saving faith, in the light of the inadequate faith of various other characters described as believing throughout the Fourth Gospel (cf. esp. 8:30 with 31–59). While this point is well taken, it is still difficult to see how the description of the beloved disciple's behaviour in 20:1–14 is not *in some way* distinguishing him from Thomas.

The most telling observation about Charlesworth's case is that if one does not begin with the premise that John the son of Zebedee is already excluded, all of his main points support John even more strongly than they

---

27] Against the view that the beloved disciple is an ideal, even unhistorical, literary device, see also Bauckham 1993a. The only newer suggestion of which I am aware that Charlesworth could not treat is that of Schneiders (1998), who argues that the Samaritan woman of John 4 is the 'alter-ego' of the Fourth Evangelist. But she is not making a claim for actual authorship by this otherwise anonymous person.

do Thomas. The same is true for several of Charlesworth's supporting arguments – that the author must have been one of the Twelve, a Galilean, close to Jesus, and so on. The other points that try to strengthen his argument seem much weaker. For example, while it is true that John refers only to the beloved disciple as observing the crucifixion and only to Thomas as knowing about the wounds in Christ's hands, feet and side (20:25), it is improbable that only one disciple would have heard of these details. It is difficult to imagine one of the Twelve who witnessed the crucifixion *not* describing it to his companions, if indeed they were not present for that event. Charlesworth thinks that the Fourth Gospel's love of dualism would lead him to name both Christ's arch-enemy (Judas) and his closest follower (the beloved disciple), but it could be that Judas and Thomas are both named because they share a certain notoriety yet end up with quite contrasting fates.

The argument that John was martyred and Thomas was not relies on minority voices in the external evidence in both cases. That Thomas is 'narratively framed' and therefore highlighted by the inclusios in 11:16 and 20:24, or by 1:40 and 11:16, appears artificial, since in both cases much material comes in between that is unrelated to Thomas. That the ambiguous reference to 'another' witness in 5:31–39 is misunderstood in 11:2, and subsequently clarified in the beloved disciple passages as Thomas, is an argument that similarly joins several parts of the Gospel otherwise unrelated to each other and skips over large amounts of intervening material. Once one hypothesizes that Thomas may have authored the Fourth Gospel, various parallels with the other literature attributed to him in Gnostic and apocryphal circles may be discerned, but John is well known to have numerous parallels with a wide variety of ancient Jewish, Greek and Christian literature (R. E. Brown 1966: lii–lxvi; Schnackenburg 1968: 119–152; Barrett 1978: 27–62), so these similarities scarcely provide *initial* support for Thomasine authorship. Charlesworth, therefore, has not mounted a persuasive case for Thomas and has, despite his intentions, offered strong arguments for reconsidering John the son of Zebedee.

Stages of redaction

Arguing for apostolic authorship, however, does not commit one to believing that John himself wrote (or dictated) every word in the final form of the Fourth Gospel as we know it. Even highly conservative commentators have often recognized that 21:24–25 suggests a final redaction of the Gospel that at the very least added these two verses (e.g. Michaels 1983: 349; Morris 1995: 775–777; Ridderbos 1997: 670–672). While ancient parallels can be adduced for one writer referring to himself in the third person and first-person plural, as well as the ordinary first-person singular (Jackson 1999), the natural reading of a passage that in three consecutive verses uses all three forms is that different individuals are in view. It is probable that the 'we' of verse 24 reflects the stamp of approval by a group of the beloved disciple's followers, probably within the community to which the Gospel was addressed, making explicit his authorship of the rest of the work. Verse 25 then contains the observation of one of those individuals – perhaps the actual writer or speaker.

Once we allow even this minimal amount of redaction, it becomes natural to see all of the passages that refer to the beloved disciple in the third person as phrased that way by the final editor(s). Whether John originally wrote them in the first person or whether they were the additions of these later editors seems impossible to determine. If 21:23, as part of one of those passages, comes in its current form from this final stage of editing, then it is worth asking if the entire passage comparing the destinies of Peter and the beloved disciple (vv. 15–23) does as well. But these comparisons run throughout chapter 21, and many scholars have taken the entire chapter as an appendix to a Gospel that was originally designed to end with 20:31, both because chapter 20 ends as if the entire work is being concluded and because of a variety of vocabulary and stylistic differences between chapter 21 and the rest of the work (cf., e.g. Lindars 1972: 618–624; Barrett 1978: 576–577). It has also often been suggested that the prologue of 1:1–18 was the later addition of a separate hand, possibly though not necessarily the same one responsible for chapter 21. Some have found a self-contained poem beneath these verses that strengthens the case for a separate origin (for both of these suggestions, see esp. Miller 1989).

On the other hand, John 1:1–18 introduces so many key Johannine themes that, at least in its current form, it seems inseparable from the body of the Gospel that follows. Just as many modern writers often pen their introductions last (cf. esp. Miller 1993), it, too, may have been composed last on the basis of those main themes. Numerous recent studies make the literary unity of all of verses 1–18 more plausible than detailed tradition-historical hypotheses that isolate pre-Johannine forms (rightly Culpepper 1980; Staley 1986; Booser 1998). The linguistic and conceptual links between chapter 21 and the rest of John's Gospel are also being increasingly recognized (see below, p. 273), so that it is best to attribute the entire canonical form of this work to the same hand. It is certainly still possible to see the son of Zebedee responsible for every one of its verses (e.g. Carson 1991: 682–685), but it is perhaps somewhat more likely that a separate editor has lightly touched up the document throughout. But this editorial reworking must be limited to verses 24–25, possibly the various 'beloved disciple' passages, and to stylistic improvements throughout the Gospel, if we are to take seriously the testimony of verse 24 that the beloved disciple *wrote* something corresponding to the contents of everything that precedes this verse.[28]

But why would one or more followers of the apostle John feel free to edit his Gospel even minimally? The answer may be that they knew it was not yet in the final form that the apostle desired, and because John had recently died he was unable to complete the project. The misunderstanding described in 21:23 is difficult to explain if the beloved disciple were still alive, though it is possible that he was simply elderly and close to death. Either way, it appears that a distortion of Jesus' teaching that was claiming that John would live until the parousia was creating a crisis of faith among some in John's community and that his followers felt the need to correct this distortion. Both of these points follow somewhat more naturally if John had in fact just passed away (Smalley 1978: 120; Beasley-Murray 1987: 412; Talbert 1992: 262).[29]

Attempts to identify additional stages of redaction, however, founder in a sea of subjectivity. Most widely touted are Raymond Brown's five stages (1966: xxxiv–xxxix): (1) material from the apostle, (2) developed over decades of preaching in the Johannine community, (3) organized into a consecutive Gospel, (4) thoroughly edited by an anonymous evangelist, and (5) given a final reworking by a later redactor. It is not that we have concrete historical evidence to disprove any of this, merely that the hypothesis depends on numerous judgments as to what does or does not cohere internally at either a theological or stylistic level, each of which has

---

28] 'The natural reading of the words must lead us to conclude that the BD [beloved disciple] had a direct hand in the composition of all that precedes 21:24. He is more than just the authority figure at the back of the Johannine theology. That theology and the gospel's narratives must reflect quite accurately his own perception of Jesus. It is difficult to see why 'wrote' would have been used if the BD had not been involved in the initiative to write the gospel, even though the pupil/amanuensis was also active in a more than scribal capacity' (Pryor 1992a: 94).

29] Believers in the inspiration of Scripture often wonder how hypotheses like these can be squared with their theological convictions. The simple answer is that inspiration is not tied to single rather than multiple authorship of any book. There is good evidence that a number of biblical documents, particularly in the Old Testament, underwent stages of redaction, sometimes over centuries. The criterion of apostolic authorship for New Testament documents has always allowed for followers of apostles to be authors, as is demonstrably the case with Mark and Luke. That an apostle and one of his followers jointly contributed to the production of a Gospel raises no additional problems: one simply affirms that God inspired *both* individuals.

been disputed and explained differently by various scholars. The same literary unity that we shall note below under an examination of the Gospel's sources makes it impossible to be at all confident about any hypothesis of multiple stages of the composition of John's Gospel beyond the minimal editing I have discussed above.

The same is true of theories about a Johannine school collectively responsible for the final form of John's Gospel. Alan Culpepper (1975), who first made this theory especially prominent, subsequently demonstrated even more convincingly the literary unity of this final form (Culpepper 1983). But Culpepper does not seem to recognize how irrelevant his second work has made his first (though see his comments on 49, n. 85), especially when his depiction of John's 'school' was virtually indistinguishable from a sect or religious community, except in the one key area of teaching and writing – precisely the area that needed to be proved rather than assumed (see 261–290).

CONCLUSIONS

Despite widespread assumption to the contrary, a strong case can still be mounted for John the son of Zebedee as author of the Fourth Gospel.[30] If this case be rejected, then the next most likely alternative may be to see the author as one of the unnamed disciples of 21:2 (cf. esp. Boismard 1998). Third in probability seems to be the hypothesis about 'John the elder' as a disciple of John the apostle.[31] Even with these last two options, the author of the Fourth Gospel is no further removed in the chain of witnesses from the material he narrates than are Mark or Luke on the traditional assumptions that each of them travelled with and/or interviewed apostles

---

30] In addition to the sources already cited, one should consult Schulz (1994), who ably defends the early church's tradition about authorship for each of the four canonical Gospels, and E. E. Ellis (1999: 143–145), specifically concerning John.

31] Capper (1998) builds on the links between such a John and a priestly background, noted above, to argue that the author of the Fourth Gospel, not the son of Zebedee, came from Jerusalem and had an Essene background. Capper provides a wealth of evidence to connect the thought of this Gospel with such a background, but almost all of his evidence does nothing to disprove Johannine authorship. If Jesus did begin his ministry in close conjunction with the Baptist, who himself may have had contacts with Essenes, and if he did frequently minister in and around Jerusalem, then all of Capper's evidence fits equally well with the hypothesis that Jesus consciously taught in ways that would be compared and contrasted with Essene convictions and that John, as a companion of Jesus, faithfully recorded those teachings and may well have been influenced by them in his own thought.

and eyewitnesses of Jesus' ministry.[32] If Johannine authorship be accepted, of course, then the connection is even closer, comparable to traditional beliefs about the apostle Matthew penning the Gospel attributed to him. Given John's particularly close position to Jesus, we should have at least as much confidence in discovering accurate historical information as with any of the other three Gospels and perhaps even more.

On the other hand, short of postulating theological a prioris about the inspiration or inerrancy of Scripture that prevent a full-orbed assessment of the historical possibilities (cf. also below, p. 292), we must admit that much could have happened in the years between Jesus' ministry and the production of John's Gospel to modify the traditions he records. Aged apostles could also have had faulty memories! Conversely, the strong influence of memorization of oral tradition in ancient Judaism and the surrounding cultures, especially that held to be sacred, makes it entirely possible that accurate information could have been preserved down to the end of the first century even in completely non-apostolic Christian circles. And such memorization was also often combined with sufficient degrees of freedom and flexibility in each 'performance' of the tradition to account for the variations among the several Gospels (cf. esp. Gerhardsson 1961; Riesner 1984; Bailey 1991; Byrskog 2000). Millard's evidence (2000: 197–211, 223–229) makes it conceivable that certain members of Jesus' original audience could even have used a kind of shorthand to take notes concerning the outlines of his addresses, particularly memorable sayings and/or the overall contours of his ministry. This would then reduce virtually to nil the period of exclusively oral tradition! Thus our consideration of authorship creates some presumption in favour of the historical reliability of John, but that presumption might be present even on other theories of authorship. We must therefore move on to the question of the dating and the place of writing of John's Gospel.

DATE AND PROVENANCE

We have been presupposing the dominant early church tradition that John wrote his Gospel near the end of the first century to churches in and around Ephesus in western Asia Minor. This location seems relatively secure and commands a fair consensus among scholars from diverse theological traditions.[33] The strong Palestinian Jewish elements in the

---

32] Modern scholarship, of course, has doubted these traditions almost as frequently as those surrounding the composition of the Fourth Gospel. But see now Hengel 2000: 8–47.

33] Occasional attempts to locate the Johannine community elsewhere, e.g. in Alexandria, Syrian Antioch, Egypt or Jerusalem, have not garnered much of a following.

Gospel are often attributed to a previous stage in the life of the Johannine community, in which many of the Christians addressed lived in Israel or even Jerusalem. John Ashton (1991) has gone as far as to postulate eight discrete stages in the life of this church, divided between Palestine and Asia, discernible from the Fourth Gospel; others suggest similar but less segmented hypotheses (e.g. Painter 1993). But as with hypothetical stages of editing, these hypotheses are by definition virtually impossible to demonstrate and are probably unnecessary. The letters to the seven churches of Revelation (Rev. 2 – 3), which include a letter to Ephesus (2:1–7), demonstrate intense hostility between the churches and certain local synagogues in Asia Minor (2:9; 3:9), so that all of the seemingly anti-Jewish polemic in John can be accounted for by the situation his church faces at the end of the first century (cf. Witherington 1995: 7, 37–41).

The external evidence seems secure, as Eusebius cites Clement of Alexandria to the effect that John remained with the Asian elders in Ephesus until the time of Trajan (AD 98) (*Eccl. Hist.* 3.32.3–4). Irenaeus (*Ag. Her.* 2.22.5; 3.3.4) recounts this exact information. This provenance would account for the Hellenistic or Gentile flavour to John's Gospel as well as its Jewish background. Sjef van Tilborg (1996) has demonstrated how the entire Gospel proves thoroughly intelligible in the light of the specific political and religious backgrounds of Ephesus at the end of the first century (more briefly, cf. Kalantzis 1997).

Debate over the absence of direct quotations of John and over the presence of allusions to his Gospel in second-century Christian literature related to Asia Minor proves even more inconclusive for dating than it did for authorship (Barrett 1978: 110–115, 123–125). Of greater significance are the John Rylands Papyrus and Papyrus Egerton 2. The former is a scrap of a copy of John's Gospel with portions of John 18:31–33, 37–38 from about AD 130, the oldest known portion of any of the New Testament still in existence. The latter is a composite fragmentary narrative of stories about Jesus that quotes or alludes to several passages from John and the Synoptics and probably dates to the mid-second century. Few scholars today would thus want to date John much later than about AD 100.

A significant minority of scholars, however, has tried to push the date back to a considerably earlier period, particularly into the 60s before the fall of Jerusalem to the Romans (see Cribbs 1970; J. A. T. Robinson 1976: 257–258, 267–278; Kemper 1987; Berger 1997). However, most of their arguments stem from silence: John does not refer to the destruction of the temple; he does not know the Synoptics or Paul's letters; he does not focus on the sacraments as the later church did; there are no references to Peter as the foundation of the church, to the Lord's Prayer, the Gentile mission, the Sadducees, and so on. None of these points carries much weight. A document from the late 90s would be far enough removed from the events of AD 70 that no mention of the temple's destruction or of Sadducees need have occurred. We shall see below that John probably *is* familiar with the Synoptics even if he does not depend on them literally (pp. 47–49). His silence on the sacraments may be a protest against their growing institutionalization (see pp. 79, 187), and he does have texts that give Peter and the disciples authority to bind and loose (20:22–23), that enunciate many of the principles of the Lord's Prayer (ch. 17), and that foreshadow a Gentile mission (12:20–36).

An interesting grammatical observation that has convinced some of a pre-70 date is the use of the present tense in 5:2 – 'Now there *is* in Jerusalem near the Sheep Gate a pool, which in Aramaic is called Bethesda, and which *is* surrounded by five covered colonnades.' After Jerusalem's destruction, these statements would no longer be true; one would expect past-tense verbs. On the other hand, John frequently uses the historical present tense and that may be all he is doing here, to mark out the scene more vividly. Daniel Wallace (1990: 197–205) responds that he can find no other use of the historical present with the verb 'to be' (Gk. *eimi*), but it is difficult to know how much significance to attach to this observation. After all, most historical presents occur in narrative where a specific verb of speech or action is highlighted.

Other arguments involve the author's accuracy and the careful knowledge of the customs and topography of Israel already noted. But this hardly proves anything about John's date, unless one assumes such information could have been preserved accurately for only thirty rather than sixty years. Proponents of an early date often point out that supporters of a late date tend to bolster their position by assuming a slow, evolutionary hypothesis concerning the development of New Testament theology, so that only after this long a period of time could the high Christology of John have emerged. While correctly pointing out the fallacies of this argument (cf., e.g. the high Christology of the potentially pre-Pauline creed in Phil. 2:6–11), they often reinstate the same fallacy by pointing to signs of 'primitive' Christology in John. Early, undeveloped views of Jesus in the Fourth Gospel may have some bearing on questions of historicity but they demonstrate nothing about the date at which those views were recorded.[34]

It is also possible to support an early date for John by combining

---

34] Hengel (1989: 119) commits a similar fallacy in arguing that the 'unique and idiosyncratic terminology' of John shows that the Johannine church 'had long since parted company with the synagogue'.

apostolic authorship with the traditions that hold to an early martyrdom for the son of Zebedee. But these are much later and less reliable traditions than those I have cited, and they comprise a tiny minority voice within the early church (Barrett 1978: 103–104, with the relevant texts presented). Hans-Joachim Schulz (1994: 373–391) offers a novel argument that the comparisons and contrasts between Peter and John in chapter 21 may suggest that *Peter* has just died, pointing to a date in the late 60s. It is far more likely, however, as I noted above (p. 39), that the peculiar ending of chapter 21 is to be explained at least by John's advancing age if not his actual, recent death. There may have been something of a gap between the draft of the Gospel that John actually penned (which itself could have circulated locally in and around Ephesus) and its final redaction (possibly designed for more widespread use; see esp. Bauckham 1998b), especially if that editing took place posthumously. This would allow for the epistles of John and/or Revelation to intervene between the two stages of the publishing of the Gospel.[35] Yet, while it is true that the external evidence focuses primarily on John's age and location of ministry rather than explicitly tying the authorship of his Gospel to that late date, the subsequent conviction of the church that became the 'traditional' position should probably be accepted, dating the Fourth Gospel either to the late 80s or to the 90s.

It is an attractive apologetic for conservative scholars to opt for an earlier date, but the evidence is not nearly strong enough to do so with any confidence. As we have already seen, there were enough factors in the first-century Mediterranean world to make it possible for historical traditions to be preserved accurately for sixty years, along with enough impediments to that preservation for traditions to be distorted within thirty. What is more, any historian is only as good as his or her sources. It may be, too, that the finished Gospel of John has a late date but that its underlying sources take us back to a much earlier time. So it is to the question of Johannine source criticism that we must now turn.

SOURCES
HYPOTHETICAL DOCUMENTS
Rudolf Bultmann (1971) set the agenda for modern source analysis of John

---

35] R. E. Brown (1979: 109–144) makes a persuasive case that John's Gospel lent itself to incipient Gnostic misuse on several theological fronts, which the epistles, esp. 1 John, then sought to correct. Of course, almost every conceivable order of the five documents ascribed to John has been suggested at one time or another in scholarship; see the standard introductions to the New Testament.

by postulating a 'signs' source, a 'discourse' source and a 'passion' source to account for a sizeable percentage of John's unique material. Only the signs-source ever commended itself to a large number of scholars, especially due to the two books by R. T. Fortna (1970, 1988), which capitalized on the tension in the Gospel between the importance of miracles as a reason for belief (esp. 20:31) and the emphasis on believers not having to need miracles to support their faith (esp. 4:48; 20:29). The Jesus Seminar postulates the existence of a signs Gospel underlying John as an accepted datum of scholarship and dates it to somewhere between AD 50 and 70 (Funk and Hoover 1993: 16–19). However, scholarship at the beginning of the twenty-first century is moving away from this direction. While it is quite plausible to believe that the Fourth Gospel utilized written source material, as did the Synoptics (and most other ancient historians for that matter), it is quite another matter for us to declare with any confidence that we can determine what they are.[36]

Literary studies of John are increasingly offering plausible reasons for the so-called *aporiai*, or seams, in John's text that do not require us to imagine slipshod redaction of sources (van Belle 1985; Bjerkelund 1987; Ruckstuhl 1987). Some of the seeming inconsistencies of John most likely reflect the loose weaving together of orally preached material (Lindars 1977, 1981a).[37] Few today would adopt the radical displacement theories of Bultmann, as he frequently rearranged the sequence of passages in the Gospel to make it read more smoothly.[38] After all, a good redactor would have smoothed out the very breaks and awkwardnesses that are usually used as a pointer to his presence (cf. Hengel 1989: 107). Pierson Parker's famous tongue-in-cheek dictum (1956: 304) has proved prophetic: 'Unlike the various parts of Matthew and Luke, the writings supposed to underlie John exhibit the same theology *and the same language and style* throughout. It looks as though, if the author of the Fourth Gospel used documentary sources, he wrote them all himself.'

Gilbert van Belle's exhaustive survey of scholarship on a signs-source summarizes five arguments supporting its existence and five reasons that make him conclude the hypothesis to be improbable (1994: 366–376). In its favour are (1) the fact that the first two signs are numbered (John 2:11; 4:54), as if John were relying on a source containing all seven signs that he presents (the rest without numbering); (2) the possibility that John 20:31

36] Cf. already the survey of Carson 1978, who reaches similar conclusions.

37] To which one should add Thatcher's important dissertation (1996) on the *oral* nature of John's Gospel and its putative sources, esp. with respect to thirty 'riddles' of Jesus.

38] Haenchen (1984a: 51) declares flatly, 'The time of theories of displacement is gone.'

reads like the end of a Gospel because it formed the end of the signs-source (and thus it highlights the positive value of these *sēmeia*); (3) certain stylistic peculiarities in John's miracle narratives; (4) the homogeneity of the form of these narratives, which is distinct from the synoptic miracle stories; and (5) the seemingly different theology and Christology of these texts.

On the other hand, (1) John could have numbered his first two signs as easily as a source could have; the lack of further numbers does not really count for or against a separate source document. (2) Chapter 21 should be viewed as an epilogue designed to be an integral part of the Gospel. (3) There are more stylistic affinities between the miracle accounts and the rest of the Gospel than there are differences. (4) The form-critical homogeneity is equally attributable to John. (5) Why appeal to a source at all, especially when there are other explanations of the theological tensions? If the final editor of John were really correcting the theology of his source(s), why did he not simply remove all trace of it, or at least radically subordinate the strand of thought he inherited to his own? While it might seem to bolster the case for historicity to appeal to an early written source on which the fourth Gospel drew, the evidence is too slight for us to do so with any confidence.[39] But perhaps we can make more headway with the issue of John's knowledge of the Synoptics.

JOHN'S RELATIONSHIP TO THE SYNOPTICS
Here one may discern three phases of research in the modern period. Until the 1930s it was usually assumed that John knew the Synoptics, borrowed from them at places, but primarily chose to go his own way by supplementing or even contradicting them at numerous points (see esp. Windisch 1926). But while authors may rely on written sources even when they so rework their material and integrate it with their own that their redaction is hard to detect, the only way one can confidently declare a literary relationship between two documents without explicit external or internal statements about the author's procedure is when exact verbal parallels in the language of two texts recur. This is precisely what is extremely rare as one proceeds through a synopsis comparing John with all its synoptic parallels. Rarely do more than two or three words appear in the exact form in the same place in parallel accounts, and almost always these are the words one would expect an author to use, in view of the contents of the episode at hand, regardless of sources. Parallels in order of events can

---

39] One might more profitably speak of 'a variety of relatively small units that are well integrated by John into the larger whole ... understood better as traditions than as sources'. But even then John may have authored some of these himself (E. E. Ellis 1999: 182).

almost always be explained on the assumptions that the order recounted is historical and that both John and the Synoptics had access to historical information. And even where John and the Synoptics both narrate the same stories, the versions found in the Fourth Gospel typically include different portions of those stories than those that occur in the earlier Gospels.

Percival Gardner-Smith (1938) is usually credited with being the pioneer in breaking from the tradition of believing in John's literary dependence on the Synoptics. The pendulum eventually swung to viewing John as entirely independent. This left the door open for the rehabilitation of a significant minority of his unparalleled material as historical and the possibility of his differences from the Synoptics within paralleled passages as at times reflecting better historical tradition (again, classically, see Dodd 1963; cf. R. E. Brown 1966, 1970).

Since the 1980s the pendulum has begun to swing back, though claims of a new consensus that agrees that John knew at least Mark (Denaux 1992: viii) are probably premature. On the one hand, detailed exegetical studies have tried to demonstrate again the fine points in paralleled passages that can be attributed only to literary dependence (see esp. Neirynck 1979; for a counterpart at the theological level, cf. Dowell 1990), but it is doubtful these will convince those who were not convinced before.[40] On the other hand, Bauckham (1998b) has edited an important work that demonstrates the probability that all four of the Gospels would have circulated quite widely quite quickly and may even have been written with a broad or general audience in mind.[41] The probability of one or more of the Synoptics (esp. Mark) making it to an urban, Christian centre like Ephesus during an approximately thirty-year period (from the 60s to the 90s) is high. Bauckham himself (1998c) writes perhaps the most important chapter of the volume on 'John for Readers of Mark'. He does not argue

---

40] Even more idiosyncratic and less convincing is the attempt of Brodie (1993), often based on very vague 'parallels', to argue for John's systematic use of all of Mark, much of the sermons in Matthew, some of Luke–Acts, and numerous excerpts of the Pentateuch and Ephesians! One thinks of the similarly ingenious but now discredited lectionary hypothesis of Guilding (1960), in which Old Testament readings, especially related to the Jewish festivals, accounted for the contents and sequence of most of John's pericopae.

41] The latter of these two points I find less persuasive. Too many of the redactional distinctives in each of the Gospels align themselves with specific circumstances in specific early Christian communities to be coincidental. But it is entirely plausible to combine the two approaches: the Evangelists had specific communities foremost in view, but expected their writings to be copied and passed on, and eventually to be read widely.

that all of John's audience must have known Mark, but that some of them would have. Nothing in the Fourth Gospel requires knowledge of any other document in order to understand John's text, but numerous features of his narrative read as if he is trying to allude to events in Mark for those who are familiar with them.

For example, in the middle of the account of Jesus' and John's ministries of baptism, the parenthetical comment appears that 'this was before John was put in prison' (John 3:24). Nowhere else does John ever mention the Baptist's imprisonment, but Mark gives a detailed account (Mark 6:14–29). It would seem that John is explaining to people familiar with Mark's account that what he has narrated thus far in his Gospel is to be located chronologically before Jesus' 'great Galilean ministry', during which that imprisonment took place. John 5 describes Jesus' first trip to Jerusalem after the start of his ministry in Galilee, and the absence of any references to his disciples suggests that he may have travelled to Judea while the Twelve were sent out on their first missionary journey without him (cf. Mark 6:7–13, 30). John 5:33–35 also seems to locate this discourse after the Baptist's public ministry is over and thus after his imprisonment. And Mark 6:54 – 9:50 may well be summarized by John 7:1.

Again, John 11:2 explains that Lazarus' sister Mary 'was the same one who poured perfume on the Lord and wiped his feet with her hair'. This could simply be literary foreshadowing of 12:1–8, but it reads somewhat more naturally as if the narrator knows that his audience will have learned of more than one Mary in the gospel tradition and that he is clarifying which one is in view by referring to a well-known event associated with her. That is, in fact, exactly what Mark implies when he has Jesus declare, 'I tell you the truth, wherever the gospel is preached throughout the world, what she has done will also be told, in memory of her' (Mark 14:9). John 11:56–57 may be intended to help the person familiar with Mark's outline insert all of John 11 in between Mark 10:31 and 32. The abbreviated references in John 18:24 and 28 to Jesus' trial before Caiaphas also seem to presuppose knowledge of something like Mark 14:53–65. In addition to Mary, John introduces other characters without the explanations we would expect if his audience were not already familiar with them: John the Baptist (John 1:6, 15, 19), Simon Peter (1:40), the 'Twelve' (6:67), Judas Iscariot as the 'betrayer' (6:71) and Pilate (18:29). Even John's 'I am' sayings seem to presuppose or build on such texts as Mark 6:50 and 14:62.

Bauckham's argument proves largely persuasive (cf. also Dvorak 1998), though methodologically it is probably impossible to distinguish between John's presupposing knowledge of Mark's finished Gospel, a pre-Markan source or core oral tradition proclaiming the major contours of the life of Christ (thus esp. de Solages 1979; Borgen 1987). We may thus assume that

John was familiar with many if not all of the contents of the Gospels that preceded him even if he did not borrow from them in a strict, literary fashion. We may assume that he knew that at least some, if not many, in his audience would be familiar with the basic stories about Jesus and that he did not want to repeat many of these accounts. Combining our hypotheses about apostolic authorship, the possibility of separate sources underlying John (even if they may no longer be recoverable),[42] and his lack of literary dependence on the written form of the Synoptics, we can fairly speak of John as an important, independent witness to the words and works of the historical Jesus.

JOHN'S OMISSIONS

When John leaves out material found in the Synoptics, we may assume that he does so deliberately. The older approach that spoke of John as consciously supplementing Matthew, Mark and Luke thus remains valid, even if it may no longer be tied to theories of direct, literary dependence. As redaction criticism of the Synoptics has repeatedly demonstrated, it is always more difficult to explain why a Gospel writer left something out than to give reasons for his inclusion of distinctive material. But we may make some plausible suggestions.

PARABLES

Not a single narrative parable of the form common to approximately forty passages in the Synoptics appears in John. John certainly knows that Jesus characteristically spoke in metaphors; he uniquely speaks of the *paroimiai* (10:6; 16:25, 29; NIV 'figures of speech') of Christ. Kim Dewey (1980) translates this term as 'proverbs' and finds no less than thirty-four of them in the Fourth Gospel (cf. 1:46; 2:10; 3:8, 20, 27, 29, 30; 4:35, 37, 44; etc.). Many of these are closely parallel to the imagery used in synoptic parables and aphorisms. Dodd (1963: 366–387) had already identified six of these passages in John as examples of short narrative parables embedded in larger discourses that even more closely resemble synoptic forms (12:24; 16:21; 11:9–10; 8:35; 10:1–5; 3:29).[43]

42] These two hypotheses are not as incompatible as some would allege. Given the almost universal use of written sources by ancient historians, even those who had access to eye-witness testimony or were personally involved in some of the events narrated, it is not at all unlikely that John the son of Zebedee would be interested in seeing what others had written down and in following them where he deemed it appropriate, as he composed his Gospel.

43] Dewey (1980: 94) separates 10:1–5 into two separate proverbs (vv. 1–3a, 3b–50); otherwise the verse divisions are identical. Cf. also Schweizer 1996.

Still, no passages in John appear in the exact form of the major synoptic narrative parables. It is also significant that while more than two thousand parables appear scattered throughout the rabbinic literature, more than two hundred of which are attributable to the earliest (Tannaitic) period (roughly the first to the third centuries), no exact analogy to Jesus' or the Jewish parables has ever been found in the Graeco-Roman literature of the time (see Blomberg 1990: 58–68 and the literature there cited). That John was writing to a predominantly Hellenistic Christian audience in a strongly Graeco-Roman environment probably has a lot to do with his omission of this specific form. Given that there was an element of opacity to the parables even for Jewish audiences (Mark 4:11–12 pars.), that the details which were most immediately intelligible typically involved life in rural Galilee, and that John omits almost all of Jesus' Galilean ministry during which the vast majority of these parables were spoken, we should not be quite as surprised that he omits all of the major, narrative parables.[44]

John's omission of the parables probably relates as well to the infrequency of his use of 'kingdom of God' (only in 3:3, 5; cf. also 'kingdom' three times in 18:36) despite 103 uses in the Synoptics (including 'kingdom' and 'kingdom of heaven'), inasmuch as parables were designed to conceal and reveal Jesus' message of the kingdom. But Mark 10:24 and 30 demonstrate that Jesus could use 'kingdom of God' and 'eternal life' synonymously, and John's Gospel employs the latter expression considerably *more* often than do the Synoptics (Matt. twice, Mark twice, Luke twice, John seventeen times). In this instance, then, it is demonstrable that John is contextualizing the Gospel for a Graeco-Roman world that frequently discussed the nature of life after death but was unfamiliar with the uniquely Jewish forms of theocracy (cf. Ladd 1993: 290–295). So it is likely that his omission of the parables of the kingdom flows from similar motives.

Exorcisms

In the Synoptics another central feature of Jesus' ministry that demonstrates the arrival of the kingdom is his ability to perform exorcisms (see esp. Matt. 12:28 par.). Like the parables, exorcisms are absent from John. Again it is scarcely conceivable that John does not know about them. The Fourth Gospel recognizes that Jesus' entire life and death mean the

---

44] Perhaps more surprising is Luke's inclusion of so many, on the assumption that his Gospel was also written particularly to Gentile Christians, but the vast majority of Luke's parables are peculiar to his central section, which probably depends largely on an early Jewish-Christian source (Blomberg 1983).

overthrow of Satan (12:31; 14:30; 16:11). Unlike the parables, exorcism stories were well known in the Graeco-Roman world, in which the boundaries between miracle and magic were much fuzzier than in Judaism. That may be one reason for John's omission; another probably involves the Jewish polemic that his community confronted. From the days of his public ministry onwards, the exorcisms caused Jesus' enemies to charge him with demon-possession (esp. Matt. 12:24 pars.). Eric Plumer discusses all these points and concludes (1997: 368), 'In this way John clarifies both the scope and the nature of Jesus' conflict with evil. But this type of interpretation was already present in the teaching of Jesus himself, so that here, as in so many places, the Fourth Gospel may be viewed as a return to first principles.' One thinks especially of Luke 10:18, in which even the disciples' ministry of preaching, healing and exorcising leads Jesus to proclaim, 'I saw Satan fall like lightning from heaven' (cf. further Twelftree 1999: 223).

Pronouncement stories

A third literary form common in the Synoptics is what has alternately been called a pronouncement story, a conflict (or controversy) story, or a chreia (e.g. Mark 2:13–17, 18–22, 23–28; 3:1–6 pars.). This is a Graeco-Roman form of stylizing epitomes of individuals' deeds and sayings into short narratives that climax in a key proverb or pithy saying, often sufficiently radical or shocking in nature to generate opposition. Jesus finds himself embroiled in such controversy in almost every chapter of John; all that is missing is the identical form in which the conflicts are narrated. Even then, a passage like John 5:1–15 mirrors almost exactly the hybrid form of miracle plus controversy story illustrated by a synoptic text like Mark 2:1–12 and parallels. That John consistently records longer accounts of the controversies Jesus' teaching generated may suggest that he is closer to preserving the outline of an entire dialogue rather than condensing the material into such short and stylized forms as do the Synoptics.[45]

Discourses

The same conclusion may be drawn from the fact that John has Jesus teaching in extended blocks of material more generally. While the Synoptic Gospels, especially Matthew, present lengthy 'sermons' of Jesus (esp. Matt. 5 – 7, 10, 13, 18, 23 – 25), these are generally viewed as the composite creations of the Evangelists, who gathered together shorter independent

---

45] Millard's discussion of how listeners in Jesus' audience may have taken notes regarding the overall outlines of his longer addresses (above, p. 41) supports this proposal.

teachings of Jesus, especially from the hypothetical Q-source (material common to Matthew and Luke but not in Mark). Ancient historians and biographers did indeed at times create such 'speeches' for the main characters of their narratives in this fashion; long before the rise of modern biblical criticism, John Calvin (1555: 204–205) suspected this was how the Sermons on the Mount (Matt. 5 – 7) and Plain (Luke 6:20–49) were put together. On the other hand, while it is not often acknowledged, a strong case can be made for sermons like Matthew 5 – 7 and 24 – 25 being stylized abridgments or digests of much longer originals (see, respectively, Kennedy 1984: 67–69; D. Wenham 1984). As we proceed through the commentary section of this book, we shall see that a case for the literary unity of each of the extended discourses of Jesus in John is stronger than sometimes believed. It may be, therefore, that these are similar abridgments of longer conversations that in fact reflect the gist of the debates and discourses of Jesus on precisely the occasions to which they are attributed (cf. Westcott 1908: cxv).

At the same time, there is no question that John has written up his material with distinctive and characteristic linguistic style and vocabulary. This, too, was standard convention among ancient writers in a world without quotation marks or any felt need for them. The Synoptics no less than John paraphrase, select, abbreviate, omit, add and interpret the teachings of Jesus according to their theological and literary purposes.[46] But none of these practices necessarily calls into question their accuracy *according to the historiographical standards of the first century* (cf. Bock 1995; Byrskog 2000), which are of course the only standards by which we may fairly judge them. On the other hand, it is interesting to note as one proceeds through the Gospel how often stylistic peculiarities of John appear on Jesus' lips first and only afterwards in John's narrative material (e.g. 2:4; 3:15; 5:17–23; 6:39; 7:33), suggesting that John's own style may at times have been influenced by Jesus' manner of speaking. And it is not quite true that the discourses of Jesus in John are wholly indistinguishable from John's narrative style elsewhere. No less than 145 words spoken by Jesus in John appear nowhere in the Evangelist's narrative material, and many of these are general enough in meaning that we might have expected them elsewhere (Reynolds 1906: cxxiii–cxxv).[47]

46] Ensor (1996: 27–47) categorizes authentic Jesus sayings into (1) original speech; (2) a close translation; and (3) looser representations, including paraphrases, summaries and interpretative clarifications.

47] For theological omissions, including the question of John's approach to baptism and the eucharist, see the commentary section of this book under the key passages involved. Further

INTERLOCKING BETWEEN JOHN AND THE SYNOPTICS

I have already discussed places where John seems to presuppose knowledge of synoptic-like kerygma. There are at least as many examples of the reverse phenomenon, in which information that John provides helps to clarify enigmas in the Synoptics on the assumption that he has access to historical information. Leon Morris (1969: 40–63) has developed the lengthiest list of examples of this 'interlocking' (cf. Carson 1991: 52–55). Not all of his items prove equally persuasive; however, I list some of the more convincing examples. The additional ministry of Jesus in Jerusalem that the Fourth Gospel describes helps to account for the extent of the Jewish leaders' hostility, especially in Jerusalem, that the Synoptics narrate, and for the enthusiasm of the crowds on 'Palm Sunday'. Mark 14:49 ('Every day I was with you, teaching in the temple courts, and you did not arrest me') makes better sense if Jesus has taught there frequently at festival times, not just on the Monday and Tuesday of Passion week, as in the Synoptics. Previous time in Jerusalem would also explain Jesus' ability to prepare a room for his Passover celebration somewhat clandestinely (Mark 14:12–16 pars.) and his lament in Matthew 23:37 and parallel, 'O Jerusalem, Jerusalem, you who kill the prophets and stone those sent to you, *how often* I have longed to gather your children together, as a hen gathers her chicks under her wings, *but you were not willing*' (my emphasis). Luke in fact gives hints, too, that Jesus may have been in Jerusalem prior to the Passover at which he was executed (Luke 4:44; 6:17; 10:38–42 [cf. John 11:1; 19:44]).

Why did Jesus make his final fateful journey to Jerusalem when he did (Mark 10:1 pars.)? The Synoptics give no historical explanation, but John does: Lazarus was ill (John 11). How did Peter gain entrance to the high priest's courtyard (Mark 14:45 pars.)? Only the Fourth Gospel tells us: an unnamed disciple was well known there and allowed in, with Peter (John 18:15–16). Why were the false charges against Jesus before the Sanhedrin framed as accusing him of threatening to destroy the temple (Mark 14:58–59)? Only John offers an answer: because Jesus had predicted the temple's destruction early in his ministry in Jerusalem (John 2:19). The fact that two or three years had elapsed in between makes it that much more intelligible how his teaching had become so garbled. Why did the Jews feel compelled to send Jesus to the Roman governor, Pilate (Mark 15:1–3 pars.)? Again, John alone replies: the Jewish people were not permitted to carry out the death penalty in this instance (John 18:31).

comments relevant to this discussion of omissions appear below under 'The outlines of the four Gospels' (pp. 54–56) as well.

Additional examples of this kind of interlocking appear. Mark 1:16–20 and parallels describe an abrupt call by Jesus to his first disciples; they immediately leave their fishing nets and follow him. But John 1:35–42 makes their response more intelligible: several of them have already met and been impressed by Jesus earlier. The messianic secret motif in the Synoptics, especially Mark, has long puzzled readers. Why does Jesus so often tell people not to talk about him or disclose his identity? John 6:15 confirms what commentators have often suspected, that at least part of the answer is because of Jewish hopes for a political or military messiah (cf. esp. Dunn 1970a). But only John explicitly describes how after the feeding of the five thousand, the crowds 'intended to come and make him king by force'.

THE OUTLINES OF THE FOUR GOSPELS

These examples of interlocking between John and the Synoptics remind us that Matthew, Mark and Luke, no less than John, are highly selective in what they record and are theologically motivated in structuring their Gospels. One important answer to the question of why John and the Synoptics are so different, therefore, is that each Evangelist has determined what he wants to include via various theological, geographical and literary criteria. Whatever does not fit into the structures determined by those criteria is simply omitted, however crucial later readers of the four Gospels might come to think it was.

This procedure can be observed among the Synoptics themselves. Matthew 1 – 2 and Luke 1 – 2 differ from each other in roughly the same ways as John does from the Synoptics overall. Literary dependence of either on the other is unlikely, even though both agree on numerous historical details surrounding Christ's birth. But Matthew focuses exclusively on information that sets up his five quotations from the Old Testament, while Luke follows an outline that compares and contrasts the conceptions, births and significance of John the Baptist and Jesus (Blomberg 1997: 199–208). Matthew and Mark each follow primarily topical outlines for the first 'halves' of their Gospels and then turn to more strictly chronological outlines for the material leading up to and including Christ's passion. Luke adds and deletes material from Mark's basic outline to set up a geographical progression of the story of Jesus from its setting in Roman history to Galilee, to Samaria and Judea, and to Jerusalem, all of which is inversely parallel to his outline for Acts – from Jerusalem, to Judea and Samaria, to the uttermost parts of the earth (Acts 1:8; cf. Blomberg 1997: 115–117, 126–129, 140–145). Thus Luke's 'Great Omission' of Jesus' withdrawal from Galilee (Mark 6:45 – 8:26) does not mean that Luke did not know or use Mark, but merely that this material did not fit into his geographical-theological outline.

The same is true for John. Although the particulars of their outlines vary, many commentators recognize that the first main 'half' of the Fourth Gospel (2:1 – 11:57)[48] presents seven main signs and seven related discourses (see, e.g. Morris 1995), all designed to inculcate belief in Jesus as the Messiah. Chapters 12 – 21 further the identical aim by means of the testimony of Christ's death and resurrection (Blomberg 1997: 159–161). Theologically, a major emphasis for John is to present Jesus as the true fulfilment of the meaning of the major Jewish festivals and institutions. Thus chapters 2 – 4 present four episodes from Jesus' earliest period of ministry, not found in the Synoptics, in order to stress four ways in which Jesus' ministry brings something new: a new joy, a new temple, a new birth and a new universal offer of salvation (Blomberg 1997: 224–231). John 5 – 11 focuses exclusively on the relationship between Jesus and various Jewish festivals: the Sabbath, Passover, Tabernacles and Dedication. Thus John includes accounts of Jesus' pilgrimage to Jerusalem at festival times – an obligation incumbent on all Jewish males when possible, which we have no reason to doubt Jesus would have kept. The only exceptions, in which Jesus is back in Galilee, are the paired accounts of the feeding of the five thousand and the walking on water, which include Passover typology (cf. 6:4) and 'I am' Christology (6:20), both crucial to John's purposes (Blomberg 1997: 295–303). The last major section of John that presents material entirely unparalleled in the Synoptics is Jesus' farewell discourse and final prayer (14 – 17), and these contain the most concentrated cluster of distinctive Johannine themes anywhere in this Gospel (Blomberg 1997: 334–340).

I shall make more comments about each portion of John in the commentary section of this book, but this should suffice to demonstrate the central point of our discussion here: John and the Synoptics alike omit and include material according to relatively clear theological and literary criteria. What does not fit those criteria is not included, however much we might have thought it should be. Thus the resurrection of Lazarus does not appear in the Synoptics because it takes place in Judea prior to the last of Christ's trips to Jerusalem, of which the Synoptics wish to record only one. The transfiguration does not appear in John because it occurs in the middle of the ministry, but does not take place in or around Jerusalem or directly tie in with one of the Jewish festivals. And so we might continue. We may not be able to guess the reason for every omission in a given Gospel, but

---

48] Common alternatives include beginning the section at 1:19 and ending it at 10:42 or 12:50.

enough examples are clear that such omissions cannot be used to argue that a given Evangelist did not know of an event he omits, much less that it is not historical.

OTHER INDICATIONS OF HISTORICITY

Conversely, there are a variety of additional pointers not yet discussed that support the general historical trustworthiness of John. These will receive more detailed treatment in Part Two but may be mentioned briefly here. To begin with, the issues Jesus discusses in his extended discourses and debates with Jewish leaders (and others) reflect key issues within pre-70 Judaism: ritual purification (13:8–9; 18:28; cf. 2:6), the status of the Samaritans (4:9), Sabbath regulations (5:1–18, ch. 9); and the value of testimony about oneself (5:31–47; 8:13) (Thomas 1991b). Jesus' form of argumentation and biblical exegesis regularly parallels ancient Jewish approaches more generally (see esp. Reim 1983; Manns 1985). Indeed, John's work is steeped in the Old Testament throughout, not only via direct quotation but also by allusion and background.[49]

Second, various passages from the Pauline epistles support the historicity of Johannine events and the authenticity of Jesus' words in John, because they reflect knowledge of the Jesus-tradition already in the 50s, almost a half-century before the final redaction of the Fourth Gospel. 1 Thessalonians 2:13–16 demonstrates the hostility of Jews against Jesus and the first disciples, so often reflected in John, at a very early date in Christianity. Also, 1 Corinthians 1 – 4 discloses early Christian debate about the concepts of revelation and knowledge, two of John's distinctive emphases, well before the rise of the more developed Gnosticism that can account for John's emphases but not their creation. Philippians 2:5–11 and Colossians 1:15–20 may reflect pre-Pauline creeds that closely match John's high Christology (cf. also Gal. 4:4 and Rom. 1:3–4) (for these and other examples, see D. Wenham 1997: 155–170).

Third, several passages show how John differentiates what was understood before the cross from insights gleaned only after the resurrection, thus militating against the view that sees later Johannine interpretative insights so intertwined with nuggets of historical information as to be inextricable (cf. esp. John 2:22; 7:39; 12:16; 16:12–13). This phenomenon is closely related to the broader theme of misunderstandings in John's Gospel more generally, a sufficiently frequent feature of his narrative to suggest that John is not trying to further his

---

49] See esp. Hanson 1991, though he does not recognize how often these backgrounds argue for rather than against authenticity; more briefly, cf. Westermann 1998.

apologetic by falsely describing greater levels of belief in Jesus during his ministry than were actually present, or by blurring distinctions between the varying responses to the words and works of the historical Jesus (see esp. Carson 1982). Thus while it is true that John presents the role of the Holy Spirit or 'Paraclete' as teaching about the significance of Jesus' person and ministry (esp. 14:26; 15:26), thus explaining the freedom John felt to select and stylize the episodes that he records in the manner he did, these verses by no means support a view that John imposed later theological developments on the historical Jesus in ways that find no precedent in authentic data about Jesus' earthly ministry (cf. the good balance on this in Ridderbos 1997: 15–16).[50]

Finally, while it is certainly the case that many kinds of theological truth may be taught by fictitious genres, it is hard to square the uniquely Christian (and strongly Johannine) themes of God's incarnation in Jesus at a definable point in space and time with fictitious descriptions of precisely that event. Combine this with the observations that John regularly stresses the themes of 'witness' and 'truth' (see esp. Trites 1977: 78–127), that part of the purpose of his Gospel is to combat an anti-historical, anti-incarnational docetism (see esp. Schnelle 1992), and that he frames much of his Gospel as a prophetic lawsuit (Heb. *rîb*) against those who would deny all this (Harvey 1977; Lincoln 2000), and it is difficult not to agree with F. F. Bruce (1980: 18) that

> John presents the trial and execution of Jesus, as he presents everything else in his record, in such a way as to enforce his theological *Leitmotiv.* Jesus is the incarnate Word, in whom the glory of God is revealed. But the events which he presents in this way, and pre-eminently the events of the passion, are real, historical events. It could not be otherwise, for the Word became flesh – the revelation became history.

LITERARY GENRE

Everything discussed thus far supports the conclusion that John, no less than the Synoptics, was writing in a historical and biographical genre. The shift in synoptic criticism away from claims of the absolute uniqueness of the Gospel genre back in the direction of stressing its general affinities with ancient history and biography seems substantiated (Blomberg 2001:

50] Rahner (2000) elaborates, balancing the Spirit's role in enabling historical reminiscences with his inspiration of contemporary relevance. But he does not illustrate how his understanding would play out in assessing the historicity of specific texts.

273–277). To be sure, what qualified as good or reliable history in antiquity involved a broad range of literature with varying degrees of factual accuracy. Over the years, several short studies have argued that the Fourth Gospel's distinctives *vis-à-vis* the Synoptics can be explained in part by postulating that John adopts a more 'dramatic' form of presentation akin to styles observable in the Greek theatre (Bowen 1930; Muilenburg 1932; Connick 1948; E. K. Lee 1953; Flanagan 1981; Domeris 1983; Pilgaard 1987), though they differ as to the implications of this identification for historicity.[51] Even drama can recount history in a fashion that is faithful to the essential facts of its characters' lives, though obviously it can relate pure fiction, too. [52]

Observing the differences between John and the apocryphal gospels is instructive at this juncture. Four broad genres may be discerned within this later literature. (1) Some 'gospels' exist in such fragmentary form or are known only from excerpts cited by early church Fathers that we simply cannot pronounce on their overall genre. What little does exist may suggest that these were simply amalgamations of material from the canonical Gospels with some additions and alterations, but we cannot be at all sure. In this category appear what Wilhelm Schneemelcher (1991: 92–109, 134–178) labels 'fragments of unknown Gospels' and 'Jewish-Christian Gospels'. (2) Most of the 'gospels' from Nag Hammadi appear as post-resurrection dialogues (or monologues) of the risen Christ, teaching explicitly Gnostic theology, and bear little resemblance in either form or content to their canonical namesakes. Here one thinks of the gospels of *Philip* and of the *Egyptians*, and most of what Schneemelcher (1991: 228–413) labels 'dialogues of the Redeemer' and 'other Gnostic Gospels and related literature'. (3) The *Gospel of Thomas* is formally unique in collecting together 114 relatively unconnected logia attributed to Jesus. Roughly one-third of these find at least partial canonical parallels; that every one of the four Gospels, including those sections typically ascribed to distinctive sources (Q, M, L, John's 'sign-source', and the small amount of uniquely Markan material), is cited strongly suggests their dependence on the fourfold Gospel canon in relatively finalized form (cf. esp. Blomberg

---

51] The recent commentary by Schnelle (1998) likewise identifies John's genre as drama (398–400). It largely limits its discussion to literary rather than historical questions.

52] E. K. Lee (1953: 174) thinks that 'the plan of the writer is therefore historical even if his object is doctrinal,' while Domeris (1983: 33) concludes that 'these speeches, like those of Herodotus and Theucydides [sic.], represent an imaginative reconstruction of traditional material making use of *key-themes drawn* [sic.] *the realm of Greek and Jewish philosophical thinking*'.

1985 and the literature there cited). (4) Finally, there are gospels that supplement the 'gaps' in the canonical accounts of Jesus, fictitiously trying to satisfy curiosity about these periods in Jesus' life and to bolster certain later doctrinal developments. Here appear the so-called Infancy Gospels, the gospels of *Peter, Nicodemus* and *Bartholomew,* and the Abgar legend. A straightforward reading of the documents in all four of these categories readily demonstrates that none is a close or helpful parallel to the genre of the Fourth Gospel.

Particularly important for their analyses of John with respect to the fact–fiction spectrum are the studies by Samuel Byrskog (2000) on oral history in the ancient Mediterranean world and by Derek Tovey (1997) on narrative criticism and the Fourth Gospel. Byrskog surveys in detail the statements of ancient historians, biographers and rhetoricians about oral history or story telling, noting a recurring concern to anchor their accounts in accurate, even eyewitness, testimony. At the same time, the very act of recounting events in narrative form depended on ideological motives, required principles of selectivity, and blurred any absolute distinction between fact and interpretation. Nevertheless, many historians recognized the dangers inherent in this process, which at times challenged them 'to insist more clearly and emphatically on the importance of truth' (180). An apologetic text that sought to persuade an audience to a particular belief or action was in fact most effective 'when it could be shown to relate as closely as possible to the factual truth of the past' (210). In the light of the eyewitness claims of John 19:35 and 21:24, Byrskog identifies the Fourth Gospel as an example of 'history as authorial legitimation' and favours an approach to the genre of John that sees at the very least a substantial core of credible history (235–238).

Tovey embarks on a quite different study but with complementary results. Seeking to bridge the common divide between literary and historical criticisms, he focuses on the close connection between the Gospel's implied author and its story world, the distinctions within John between the time of Jesus and the time of the Gospels' composition, and the combination of history and theology that interact with each other throughout. Details that some modern scholars have taken as fictional in the light of modern parallels may have been understood by John's audience as more historical. Overall, for Tovey, the form of John's narrative falls about one-quarter of the way across a spectrum from pure history as an 'accurate record of the memory of what happened' to pure myth as 'narrative which is neither true nor does it approximate to actual events' (273). It is slightly freer in style than the Synoptics, which resemble 'memoirs' or 'personal reminiscences', but not as disinterested in factual reporting as aretalogy or a historical novel.

The two most extensive recent treatments of John's genre are both embedded in larger works on the literary form of the Gospels. Richard Burridge (1992: 220–239) notes that when the title 'according to John' was added to the early manuscripts of this Gospel, a literary equation was being made with the form of the Synoptics. Numerous common features of Graeco-Roman biography recur here: a prologue, the introduction of the subject of the work, the protagonist as the primary subject of the main verbs of the book, a structure (similar to Mark) with disproportionate emphasis on events leading up to the death of the protagonist,[53] continuous prose narrative, comparable length and scale, a combination of chronological and topical outlines, self-contained episodes (including stories, dialogues and speeches), probable use of sources, deeds and words as vehicles for characterization, reference to the hero's ancestry as semi-divine, and early years treated briefly with greater emphasis on later events and on the consequences of the hero's death. Burridge concludes by citing J. D. G. Dunn (1983: 338–339) to the effect that for all the differences between John and the Synoptics, John still resembles Matthew, Mark and Luke more than any other ancient documents we know.

On the other hand, Lawrence Wills (1997: 23–52) points out significant parallels between both Mark and John and the *Life of Aesop*, some of which overlap with Burridge's list. Wills observes that this largely if not wholly fictitious novel about the famous fable-teller begins with Aesop's adult life; describes a physically unattractive protagonist who teaches wisdom and calls for justice, using pithy proverbs, fictitious stories and longer discourses; is episodic in structure; includes miracles; and describes the hostility that the protagonist engenders, leading to his death but also to his establishment as a cult hero.

Would ancient readers of John have recognized any features in his Gospel that would have predisposed them to thinking he was writing a more historical biography than the *Life of Aesop*? Against those scholars who have argued that the ancients would not even have asked such a question, Lucian (*On Writ. Hist.* 39) clearly distinguishes between texts that reflect what essentially happened and was spoken at the times and places to which given events and words are assigned and those that do not. In an analysis of Luke's historiography, W. C. van Unnik (1979) suggests ten criteria that, to varying degrees, may help to make such distinctions. Some of the most significant include writing fearlessly and independently as a friend of truth, avoiding flights of fancy and rhetorical exercise,

---

53] R. F. Collins (1986) also pairs John and Mark, as both fitting Martin Kähler's famous description of the earliest Gospel as a passion narrative with extended introduction.

displaying good selection of events – dwelling at length on important details and passing quickly over less significant items, a clear order of events, touches of vividness but not overdone, the use of topographical details for clarity's sake, and appropriately placed speeches not merely for rhetorical flourish.[54] It would seem that John would hold up reasonably well when judged by such standards.

Similarly, Colin Hemer (1989: 100), in a massive defence of the historicity of Acts, notes eight elements of a reliable historian that were acknowledged in antiquity, six of which seem directly applicable to John: eyewitness participation, eyewitness interview, limiting coverage to material to which the writer had privileged access, the prospect of checking details with contemporary documents, the use of sources for speeches, and 'the vigour of the concept of "truth" in history "as it actually happened"'.[55] Again, none of this is to argue for the *ipsissima verba* (the literally translated words) of the Gospel's speakers but merely for the *ipsissima vox* (the authentic voice).[56] As D. A. Carson (1991: 47) clarifies:

> So far as John's understanding of his task goes, we may speak of the liberty he felt to use his own language, of the principles of selection that governed his choices of material, of the nature of the audience (and now the readership) that he envisioned, of the focus of his interests, of his remarkable habit of getting at the heart of an issue. But we may not glibly suppose that one who felt so strongly about the importance of fidelity in witnesses (*cf.* 10:40–42) could simply invent narrative and dialogue and pass it off as history.[57]

JOHN'S UNIQUE AUDIENCE AND PURPOSES

Speaking of the nature of John's audience leads us to a prominent approach to reading the Fourth Gospel based on the pioneering work of J. Louis

---

54] The other criteria are less helpful in sifting historical from non-historical material: a noble subject pleasing to one's readers, material that contributes to character formation, and a fitting beginning and ending.

55] The other two criteria are not as obviously applicable to John – a distinctive and rigorous theory of historiography and a stress on travel to the scene of events.

56] For the presumption in favour of finding authentic sayings in John, at least in the category of 'looser representations' (recall above, p. 52, n. 46), see Ensor 1996: 48–84.

57] Lincoln (2000: 369–397), while agreeing that John's theological emphases require at least basic contours of Jesus' life, esp. in the passion narrative, to be historically accurate, interacts primarily with a different set of authors than I have cited in this section and thus allows for substantially more 'fiction' to be interwoven into the Fourth Gospel.

Martyn (1979). This approach has assumed that the characters and issues highlighted in John refer (at least much of the time) not to the historical Jesus and his contemporaries but to the Christians in the Johannine community and their opponents (or other, more interested outsiders). As a perspective that impugns John's historicity, this approach could be justified only *after* a detailed examination of the Fourth Gospel's contents with repeated examples of information that contradicts what we can otherwise know about Jesus and his milieu. Martyn and his followers of course believe they have done precisely that, but our verdict will have to await an examination of the major texts involved in the debate. We can nevertheless affirm a priori that John's distinct audience and its unique circumstances certainly account for a major portion of his *selection* of narratives and the emphases they contain. To the extent that the Synoptics address different communities under different conditions, we have every reason to expect their contents to differ as well.

Second, if we try to pinpoint John's distinctive purposes, we have noted that we discover a fair consensus that agrees that his church was con- fronting the twin obstacles of rejection by local Jews and infiltration by proto-Gnostics, or at least by docetists (cf. also esp. D. M. Smith 1992). John's explicit purpose statement (20:31), however, is more ambiguous than might appear at first glance. Textual criticism reveals two different tenses used with the subjunctive mood for the verb 'believe'. John is writing either that people might 'keep on believing' (*pisteuēte* – present tense), and hopefully grow in their faith, or that they simply might 'believe' (*pisteusēte* – aorist tense). The textual evidence is fairly evenly balanced; if one opts for the latter, then the door is left open for an evangelistic dimension to John's purposes. Combine this with one possible translation of the preceding clause – 'that the Christ is Jesus' and one can view the Gospel as particularly directed towards non-Christian Jews who are look- ing for a Messiah, showing them who he is (Carson 1987). This would obviously impinge on John's selection of material as well.

On the other hand, John's sharp polemic against Judaism seems more understandable if it is addressed to Christians, some of whom come from Jewish backgrounds, trying to reassure them and others who may wonder about such intense Jewish opposition that they have made the right choice. The harsh tone works well to warn 'insiders' against their opponents; it is less plausible as a direct evangelistic appeal to those very opponents. The grammar of 20:31 does not require Carson's translation and is perhaps more naturally rendered, with the standard translations, as 'that Jesus is the Christ' (Brownson 1995). What is more, even if the textual evidence is divided, the scribes who opted for the present tense may have recognized the correct interpretation of John's words: an aorist need not mean anything as specific as 'come to faith for the first time'. Ben Witherington (1995: 2, 11) may be on the right track when he suggests that John is writing to Christians to help them, among other things, become more effective in evangelizing non-Christian friends and relatives, with a special focus on Jews.

THE BURDEN OF PROOF AND THE CRITERIA OF AUTHENTICITY

All of this introductory discussion has created a climate favourable to John's historical trustworthiness. But the most difficult question remains: can one credibly defend historicity passage by passage as one proceeds through the Gospel, carefully analysing its contents? Of course, there will be places where no comparative evidence remains. Some scholars would argue in such instances that the burden of proof always resides with the person making a case, either for or against authenticity. But this approach is not that which is commonly used in studying ancient history more generally. In fact, it would lead to much more widespread agnosticism about vast portions of that history than normally obtains. A historian who has been found trustworthy where he or she can be tested should be given the benefit of the doubt in cases where no tests are available (Goetz and Blomberg 1981).[58] Of course, if enough evidence of John's unreliability emerges as we proceed through Part Two, this presumption in John's favour will have to be reversed.

The 'third quest of the historical Jesus' has offered extremely important refinements of the classic criteria of authenticity. There has always been a tension between the dissimilarity criterion (material is authentic when it differs from both conventional first-century Judaism and post-Easter Christianity) and the criterion of Palestinian environment (material must cohere with what is conceivable in an early first-century Palestinian Jewish context). Both N. T. Wright and Gerd Theissen have thus created more nuanced criteria. Wright speaks of a double similarity and dissimilarity criterion (1996: esp. 131–133). It is not realistic to expect Jesus to have differed completely from his Jewish background or to have been completely misunderstood by his followers. Yet he clearly taught and acted in distinctive ways compared with his contemporaries, ways that were also difficult for others to imitate. Thus a combination of similarities and

---

58] Ensor (1996: 38–40) would limit the application to John of this presumption to the category of 'looser representations' of Jesus' teachings – i.e. we cannot presume a close verbal correspondence with the actual words of Jesus, but only a broader conceptual correspondence.

dissimilarities from both Judaism and Christianity in any given passage will probably support authenticity.

Theissen equally rejects the classic dissimilarity criterion in favour of what he calls the criterion of historical plausibility (Theissen and Winter 1998). This also breaks down into four parts. The saying or deed in question must be plausible in its historical context and demonstrate some influence in earliest Christianity, while at the same time disclosing Jesus' individuality within his original context and with some tendency to cut against the grain of later Christian theologizing (Theissen and Merz 1997: 115–118). It would appear that both Theissen and Wright have independently formulated equivalent criteria.

In addition, multiple attestation provides an important criterion of authenticity, since John remains independent, at least at a literary level, from the Synoptics. However, multiple attestation includes not merely the same saying or episode repeated in more than one independent historical source, but the recurrence of similar teachings, events, themes, motifs, or literary forms across those sources. So, too, singly attested material that coheres with passages authenticated by either the double similarity and dissimilarity criterion or by multiple attestation may be considered part of our database for authentic material as well (Theissen and Merz 1997: 116–117).

Of course, there remain large areas of subjectivity in the application of these criteria. We know only a small portion of ancient Jewish and Christian thought because so much literature has not survived to the present day. On the other hand, we already have a vast amount of data on which to build, and the discoveries of the Dead Sea Scrolls and Nag Hammadi literature have greatly added to our understanding of both Jewish and Gnostic backgrounds – crucial for interpreting John's Gospel. These two bodies of literature have also confirmed that previous generalizations about both Judaism and Gnosticism were not wildly inaccurate, even while they have provided significant items of new information. Thus it is not terribly likely, if we had access to considerably more ancient sources, that they would radically change our picture of the religious movements of the day.

On the other hand, especially due to the vast accumulation of writings by Jacob Neusner,[59] New Testament scholars regularly give at least lip

---

59] Because Neusner has written over seven hundred books, it seems presumptuous to cite any one or two of his works here, though arguably it was his three-volume study of Pharisaic traditions before 70 CE (1971) that first widely alerted the scholarly world to the perspectives noted here.

service to the notion that one's understanding of Jesus' Jewish background must rely on sources that probably contain traditions going back to pre-70 Judaism: the Old Testament apocrypha, most of the pseudepigrapha, the Dead Sea Scrolls and selected rabbinic traditions attributed to the oldest rabbis or to the Tannaitic period. But with the rabbinic literature, even these oldest traditions are often second and third century in their written form. Nevertheless, the oral tradition was relatively conservative, and they are at least more likely to reflect the Judaism of Jesus' day than the vast corpus of later Jewish material.

Thus the classic compendium of rabbinic parallels to New Testament texts by Strack and Billerbeck (1922–61) desperately needs to be updated or replaced with a comparable collection of texts that probably reflect traditions known in Jesus' day. Remarkably, even the most recent commentaries on John continue to cite almost all of the same Jewish traditions as their predecessors did, without weeding out the late material unlikely to be relevant to first-century Judaism. I shall try in the course of my discussion to avoid this anachronism as much as possible by citing post-Christian sources relatively rarely. Among the rabbinic sources, even when I do refer to them, I shall focus almost exclusively on the oldest: certain targums, the Tannaitic midrashim and the Mishnah.

Limited space and sound methodology combine to justify another omission. While I shall point out some of the most crucial, characteristic and/or distinctive examples of John's style, vocabulary and theology as we look at each passage, I shall not infer inauthenticity merely from the presence of demonstrably Johannine style or thought. If we had reason to believe that John had translated Jesus' mostly Aramaic speech as literally as possible into Greek, this procedure might be justified. But a comparison of Josephus' *Jewish War* with his *Antiquities of the Jews* demonstrates that Josephus felt free to so paraphrase his material, even when he was relying on his own written work in Greek as a source for his later Greek writing, that we cannot always reconstruct the original. How much more when translating from Aramaic into Greek might John have used his preferred vocabulary, including that mediated through decades of homiletical use. 'Greek vocabulary statistics cannot determine the authenticity of Jesus' *Aramaic* sayings' (Payne 1980: 178).

I shall also deal very little with Hellenistic backgrounds in Part Two of this book. Students of the history of religions have demonstrated parallels between numerous portions of the Fourth Gospel and numerous non-Jewish writings.[60] The broadly applicable nature of Jesus' teaching and

---

60] The most recent summary of the state of the discipline appears in de la Fuente (1998).

John's theology leads one to expect such parallels. However, again the question for a study of historicity is not whether Jesus' behaviour and teaching at times resembled that of his counterparts in other world religions, but whether anything John attributes to him is implausible or unlikely in a first-century Palestinian Jewish context, including one that at least in part had been increasingly permeated by Greek culture and influence in the time of Alexander's conquest of Israel in 331 BC onwards.

THE WAY FORWARD

The questions I shall raise of John's text in the next section thus essentially boil down to two: (1) What positive evidence via the recently nuanced criteria of authenticity do we have that the actions or words of the characters in John's narratives are indeed historical (i.e. factually accurate within the range of literary and historiographical freedom recognized in the ancient Mediterranean world)? (2) Is there anything in the text at hand that is implausible within the historical context to which it is attributed, particularly if we assume the general historical trustworthiness of the Synoptics?

In other words, I shall not assume, with the Jesus Seminar and like-minded scholars, that only a small percentage of even the Synoptics can be accepted, in part because I am convinced that this assumption is false and in part because it has often created a vicious circle: Why is a certain portion of the Synoptics not accepted as authentic? Because it resembles the Gospel of John, which we know to be unreliable. How do we know that? Because John is so different from the authentic portions of the Synoptics![61] This is not to say that one cannot distinguish layers of tradition in the Synoptics and make stronger cases for the authenticity of some parts over against others, but merely that it is methodologically inadmissible to address the question of 'Can we trust John when his Gospel is so different from the Synoptics?' by a priori excluding any portions of the Synoptics that may resemble John.

It is even more inadmissible to insist that the only legitimate form of historical investigation is one that knows in advance that it will find material to exclude as unhistorical (e.g. Crossan 1998: 154–155). The bias of such a perspective should be as patently obvious as that of an approach that from the beginning rules out the possibility of discovering such

---

Helpful older overviews can also be found in Barrett (1978: 27–41) and Schnackenburg (1968: 119–152).

61] Casey (1996), e.g., regularly rejects Johannine material, loosely paralleled in the Synoptics, by precisely such reasoning.

material.[62] Individual interpreters obviously build up over years of research presumptions in various directions that they must work hard to bracket if they are seriously going to allow for new data or new investigations to change their overall perspectives. I can freely admit to wrestling with this as much as anyone, but it is simply false to say that less conservative authors than me have any inherent advantage in approximating objectivity![63] Moreover, with modernists and against postmodernists, investigations about the historicity of ancient texts will prove utterly inconclusive unless one believes that such objectivity can be approximated, even if never fully attained.

The vexed question of historical harmonization will have to be faced *en route* as well. It is probably impossible in advance to describe which kinds of harmonizations of apparently discrepant texts are plausible and which are not. These will have to be treated on a case-by-case basis in conjunction with the other criteria already discussed. Historians of other ancient periods and events regularly use even 'additive harmonization' (two ac-counts each provide a partial description of a larger whole) on a regular basis, though this method is often mocked by various New Testament scholars. To be sure, numerous forms of harmonization have been overused and even abused, but we dare not throw the baby out with the bathwater and declare all harmonizing invalid before examining the evidence in more detail (cf. further Blomberg 1986a).

With these introductory remarks, I am now ready to proceed with my investigation of the historicity of John on a text-by-text basis. Afterwards, we will summarize my major findings and briefly discuss their implications.

62] This would be somewhat akin to my announcing to my students before an exam that none of them will be able to achieve a 100% score. No matter how accurate their answers, I shall count something wrong just to prove I have been objective! On the other hand, it is fair to ask scholars to point to counter-examples of unhistorical passages (and the criteria used to identify them) in ancient historical sources more generally; *somewhere* one's method must be able to identify fiction. See, e.g. my analysis of parables attributed to Jesus in the *Gospel of Thomas* (Blomberg 1985).

63] Over the years, reviewers of my work have sometimes written it off or believed that my conclusions were determined from the outset because I teach in a confessional context and affirm certain theological tenets about the nature of Scripture in order to do so. In reply, I must stress that (1) I came to the historical convictions that I hold prior to teaching in my current position, in a far more pluralistic environment without such confessional restraints; and (2) I would hope that I would have enough integrity to resign my position if ever my historical work led me to affirm positions incompatible with my institution's confession.

PART TWO

COMMENTARY

COMMENTARY

PROLOGUE (1:1–18)

The first eighteen verses of the Gospel of John form a self-contained unit. Before beginning the historical narrative of the life of Jesus, John explains the theological significance of the story he is about to recount. In so doing, he introduces numerous key themes that will recur throughout the Gospel: Jesus' pre-existence and divinity, Jesus as the source of eternal life, light versus darkness, belief and unbelief, God's glory and Christ's glorification, grace and truth, the rejection of the gospel by Israel as a whole, the supersession of the Jewish Law, and the role of John the Baptist as a witness to Jesus (Valentine 1996). John may be following the convention of a prologue in a Graeco-Roman drama by creating this kind of introduction (E. Harris 1994: 12–16).

More disputed is the tradition history of the prologue. Ed Miller (1989) has surveyed most of the proposals for a pre-existing poem or hymn that the final editor of John may have redacted and supplemented, creating the existing introduction to the Gospel, and has himself suggested one of the most plausible theories of composition, focusing primarily on verses 1–5. At the same time, several proposals for the structure of verses 1–18 make a strong case for their unity in their existing form (e.g. van der Watt 1995; Coloe 1997; Viviano 1998). The most compelling of these sees the prologue arranged chiastically, with the one section that deals with proper human response to the gospel (v. 12 or vv. 12–13) as the climactic centre (Culpepper 1980; Staley 1986; Booser 1998). Theories about stages of tradition history, of course, do not exclude the possibility of a final editor weaving his traditions together into a tightly knit unity, although the task may have proved more challenging than if he were not working with disparate traditions.

Elsewhere Miller (1993, 1999) also suggests that the prologue may have been composed last, after the rest of the Gospel, as a summation of key Johannine themes. Thus we cannot automatically assume that, because a key theme appears in the prologue, it is John's own unhistorical creation. He may introduce it here precisely because he recognizes it as a dominant element of the historical Jesus tradition. We can neither assume this nor rule it out, but we must proceed on a case-by-case basis as we move through the Gospel.

In terms of historicity, *per se*, there is actually little in John's prologue to examine. Most of this introduction involves theological affirmation that is not directly susceptible to historical confirmation or disproof – Jesus' pre-existence, the significance of his ministry, proper human response, and the like. On the other hand, historic Christianity has always alleged that if the main contours of the life of Jesus as presented in the New Testament could be disproved, traditional formulations of the faith could no longer stand.[64] There is no danger of that occurring from examining the modest historical claims of John's prologue. Clearly John is affirming the real humanity of Jesus as a historical figure, a claim not contested today by any serious scholarship (see esp. van Voorst 2000: 6–16). He speaks of Christ's rejection by 'his own' (v. 11), which may derivatively apply to the majority of humanity but first of all refers to the general response of the Jewish people (Pryor 1990), a fact that permeates the synoptic accounts and that ultimately leads to the crucifixion.

There is actually more potentially historical information in the prologue about John the Baptist than about Jesus. He is introduced as if he is already known.[65] John was 'sent from God' (v. 6), standard language for referring to a prophet, an opinion of John in harmony with everything else claimed for him by the Synoptics and Josephus (see esp. Webb 1991). His fundamental role involved testifying to Christ (vv. 7–8), a motif that reflects both the major way in which the Evangelist portrays the Baptist

---

64] G. N. Stanton (1974: 189) elaborates: 'at least some aspects of the portrait of Jesus are essential to faith, for if historical research were ever able to prove conclusively that the historical Jesus was quite unlike the Jesus of the gospels, then faith would certainly be eroded. The gospel is concerned with history: not in that it stands if its claims could be verified by the historian, but in that it falls if the main lines of the early church's portrait of Jesus of Nazareth were to be falsified by historical research.'

65] And as if he will not be confused with any other John. 'The traditional explanation of the non-mention of any other John in this Gospel is that the only other John in Jesus' circle, John the son of Zebedee, had a major responsibility for the production of this work. It is difficult to think of a better one' (Bruce 1983: 34–35).

throughout John 1 and 3 and one apt summary (out of several) of his ministry as portrayed in other sources (see below, pp. 75–76). Verse 15 goes so far as seemingly to cite a specific teaching of John's, though coming in the prologue as it does it may be more a Johannine formulation of a central tenet of the Baptist's teaching. It nevertheless parallels in part the specific saying of verse 30, which refers to John having said something similar on a previous occasion (see below, p. 79). Whether quotation or précis, it thus captures an important theme of John's ministry.

What can be stressed from John's prologue is how at home its theology is in the world of both the Hebrew Scriptures and the Hellenistic Judaism of the first century. Gone are the days when scholars can plausibly argue that John's Christology must have been produced only at a very late stage of a slow, evolutionary development of Christian faith, removed from its Jewish roots within a dramatically different Greek milieu. John 1:1 is clearly intended to call to mind Genesis 1:1. The role of the 'Word' (Gk. *logos*) being with God and being God (vv. 1–2) parallels the function of God's speech at creation. Interestingly, the Aramaic targums explicitly speak of the 'word' (*memra*) of the Lord as God's agent in creation.[66]

A fuller discussion of Jesus as God will have to await my treatment of the specific words and deeds of the historical Jesus, but two general remarks are in place here. First, Larry Hurtado (1988; cf. Segal 1977) has demonstrated that the monotheism of first-century Judaism allowed for diversity within the unity of the Godhead in ways that later forms of Judaism did not. Reflection on the mysterious reference in Daniel 7:9 to two thrones in heaven led to talk of angels and exalted humans in categories closely resembling deity. Bauckham (1998a) rightly stresses that the New Testament equation of Jesus with Yahweh goes beyond this Jewish 'mutation' of monotheism, though it is not clear that the evidence Hurtado cites is as irrelevant as Bauckham thinks it is in providing at least partial parallels and important conceptual background to the New Testament development. Bauckham does correctly demonstrate, though, that New Testament substitution of Jesus into roles previously reserved for Yahweh comes early and often (e.g. Mark 12:36–37; 1 Cor. 8:6; Phil. 2:6–11; and pars.) and is by no means unique to the Fourth Gospel.[67]

God's word as agent of creation, and hence bringer of life (vv. 3–4), is a

---

66] Evans (1993: 114–121) presents the parallels in detail. For excellent discussion, cf. Hayward 1978.

67] Cf. also D. M. Smith (1999: 50–51): 'Early Christianity did not begin with a low Christology and move by degrees to a higher one.' Smith then refers to 1 Cor. 1:24 and 8:6.

concept well known from Jewish wisdom literature. Indeed Wisdom herself is often personified as God's spokesperson, revealing God to humanity. Parallels to the pre-existence of the logos and Wisdom being with God and being God, an instrument of creation, a source of life, unable to be overcome by darkness or evil, continually coming into the world, appearing on earth and living among humans, rejected by a majority of them, creating a relationship with God for those who believe, and possessing unique glory all find Jewish parallels, especially in Proverbs, Sirach, Wisdom of Solomon and Philo.[68]

The contrast between light and darkness (v. 5) was long held to be due to Gnostic influence until the discovery of the Dead Sea Scrolls demonstrated the pervasiveness of this dualism within Essene Judaism (see, e.g. 1QS 3:20–25; 1QM 1:1; cf. esp. Bauckham 1997). *Katelaben* at the end of verse 5 should probably be translated 'mastered', to capture the dual sense of 'understood' and 'overcome' (Carson 1991: 138). That the darkness has not mastered the light will then refer both to the misunderstanding that led to the crucifixion and to the triumph of the resurrection. That the light would illuminate all humanity (v. 9) is of a piece with the numerous hints of a Gentile mission in the Synoptics (esp. Mark 7:24 – 8:26 par.), culminating in the 'Great Commission' of Matthew 28:18–20. Verses 10–11 reiterate the themes of Jesus as Creator, yet unrecognized and rejected. Still, some believed (a key synoptic theme; cf. Blomberg 1994) 'in his name' – a very Jewish reference to his person and authority (cf. Pss. 5:11; 20:1) – and were enabled to become God's spiritual children (vv. 12–13). Even the odd plural behind 'not of natural descent' (lit. 'not of bloods') finds a precedent in Wisdom of Solomon 7:1–2.

John's prologue may be designed to counter Gnostic theology intruding into his community as well (Talbert 1992: 74; cf. Pagels 1999), in which case verse 14 will form the climax of his disagreement with the opposition (Grappe 2000). Here is no docetic Jesus: 'the Word became flesh and made his dwelling among us'. The word for 'made his dwelling' comes from a verb that in the Septuagint translates the Hebrew *šākan*, used for the Israelites' dwelling in tents during their wilderness wanderings. One then thinks of the cognate *š^ekinâ*, used by the later rabbis to describe the presence of the 'glory of God' that accompanied them. It is precisely that glory that John claims to have seen in Jesus, possibly alluding to the transfiguration. 'We have seen his glory' is most naturally understood as a reference to earthly followers or disciples of Jesus observing his historical

---

68] For a convenient listing of some of the most striking examples in each of these categories, see Talbert (1992: 68). For a fuller discussion, cf. Ashton (1986).

ministry (D. M. Smith 1999: 59) and thus to eyewitness testimony behind the production of the Gospel (Byrskog 2000).[69] Exodus 33 – 34 contains a rich harvest of parallels to the language and concepts of these verses, as God passed before Moses revealing his glory (see esp. Mowvley 1984).

Verses 16–18 have been taken as sharply anti-Jewish polemic, but this is probably not their intention. 'One blessing after another' in verse 16 is literally 'grace instead of grace'. The contrast in verse 17 is thus relative, not absolute. The Mosaic Law came through grace, even though the grace of the gospel far surpasses it (R. B. Edwards 1988). Even the combination 'grace and truth' in this verse reflects the standard Hebrew pairing of *hesed* and *'emet*. The continuity and discontinuity between Gospel and Law implied here closely mirrors that found in the Sermon on the Mount (Matt. 5:17–20; cf. Carson 1991: 133). The prologue ends as it began, with a strong affirmation of the deity of Christ (v. 18),[70] but described in very Jewish language as Jesus being literally 'in the Father's bosom' (*kolpon*), the identical word used of Abraham's bosom as the place next to God where Lazarus, the beggar in Jesus' parable, resided after his death (Luke 16:23). And the assertion that God the Father is essentially invisible reiterates a fundamental tenet of the Hebrew Scriptures (see esp. Exod. 33:20).

THE BAPTIST'S TESTIMONY (1:19–34)

The historical portion of John's narrative properly begins in 1:19. As do all three Synoptics, the Fourth Gospel introduces the adult ministry of Jesus by starting with the testimony of the John the Baptist. In this Gospel, it is 'testimony', especially to Jesus, that most characterizes the portrait of the Baptist. Numerous commentators find this contrary to the 'oldest' and 'most primary' function of John according to the Synoptics, which present him as a baptizer or purifier of the people of Israel.[71] But to the extent that John preached as the Synoptics and Fourth Gospel alike suggest – to

---

69] Contra, e.g. Ashton (1994: 32–35), who still defends 'myth' as the right term to use here.

70] The textual variant 'the One and Only God' is clearly the more difficult reading, and has enough external evidence in its favour to be preferred. On this as the correct translation of *monogenēs*, classically rendered 'only begotten', see esp. Pendrick 1995.

71] Casey (1996: 63–79) gathers together the fullest set of historical objections to John's portrait of the Baptist. Cleary (1988) presents a typical tradition-historical reconstruction – from the historical John through the synoptic portraits to the Fourth Gospel. F. E. Williams (1967) proposes that John composed 1:19–28 as an expansion of Luke 3:15–16. For an overview of Johannine distinctives concerning the Baptist, see Ernst 1994: 57–58. For an exploration of the 'witness' theme, esp. in 1:29–34, see Charles 1989.

prepare the way of the Lord (Mark 1:3 pars.; John 1:23) – then his ministry could hardly have avoided testifying to the coming one.

Verses 19–28 discuss John's testimony about himself. 'Jews of Jerusalem sent priests and Levites to ask him who he was' (v. 19). Mark 1:5 agrees that Jews from Jerusalem came to hear Jesus; Matthew 3:7 refers specifically to Pharisees and Sadducees. No synoptic account mentions priests or Levites, but these are two groups that would have had particularly vested interests in John. He came from priestly lineage (Luke 1:5) and he spoke of purification (with which those two groups were particularly concerned). In the light of the numerous self-styled prophets and Messiahs in first-century Judaism, the official leadership needed to keep a close eye on every new movement (cf. Schnackenburg 1968: 288). Moreover, 'there is certainly no point after A.D. 70 stressing the opposition of chief priests or Levites to Jesus since the Temple was destroyed and their power base ceased to exist, *unless there really is some interest on the part of the evangelist in getting the historical facts straight about the opposition to Jesus*' (Witherington 1995: 376, n. 16).

The upshot of John's reply to his questioners (vv. 20–21) is to deny that he is the Messiah, Elijah (the anticipated forerunner of the Messiah – Mal. 4:5), or the eschatological prophet (of Deut. 18:18 – either a forerunner or the Messiah himself). The same conjunction of titles appears in the disciples' reply to Jesus about how people are labelling him (Mark 8:28). In the Synoptics Jesus declares that John is Elijah (Mark 9:11–13 par.; cf. Matt. 11:14), and Luke 1:17 depicts Gabriel predicting that John would go before the Lord 'in the spirit and power of Elijah'. But none of these texts implies that John was the literal Elijah returned from heaven, which may be precisely what John is denying in the Fourth Gospel (Burge 2000: 72). Closely related is the concept that the Messiah would remain hidden until Elijah would reveal him.[72] It is also probable that the Fourth Evangelist's community had encountered sectarians who worshipped the Baptist, so that part of John's purpose in depicting the Baptist is to play down his role *vis-à-vis* Jesus. Such a group existed in Ephesus both in the 50s (according to Acts 19:1–7) and in the mid-second century (Justin, *Trypho* 80; *Clem. Recog.* 1.54, 60), so it is plausible to posit that Christians at the end of the first century may have encountered such people there as well (D. M. Smith 1999: 55).

Who then is John the Baptist? Verses 22–27 supply the positive answer.

72] We find the concept of a hidden Messiah already in first-century Jewish texts (explicitly in *1 En.* 62.7, implicitly in *2 Ezra* 12.32, *2 Bar.* 29.3 and 39.7). By the end of the second century, Elijah's role becomes explicit (Justin, *Trypho* 8.49; cf. *Sot.* 9.15, *Eduy.* 8.7). Cf. esp. de Jonge 1973.

He is the famous voice of Isaiah 40:3 crying in the wilderness, and he is baptizing with water to point forward to a coming figure of much greater significance. With verse 23 we come to the first formal parallel to the synoptic tradition (cf. Mark 1:3 pars.). Most of John's differences are minor; the main one is that the Baptist himself utters these words. But it is no less probable that the Synoptics got part of their summary of the significance of the Baptist from his actual teachings than that the Fourth Evangelist has put on to the Baptist's lips narrative excerpts from previous Gospels.[73] Since the Qumran Essenes had used the same passage from Isaiah to refer to their entire community (1QS 8:12–14), it would not be surprising for John to use it self-referentially as well (Burrows 1974: 246). John 1:26–27 introduces a second saying of the Baptist with synoptic parallels. Verse 26a reflects the first half of the contrast between water and spirit baptism found in Mark 1:8 and parallels. The ignorance of the people in verse 26b appears also in the narrative of Luke 3:15, while the sandals saying of verse 27 closely mirrors Mark 1:7b and parallels. There is little thus far to justify the claim that we have to choose between John and the Synoptics in their portraits of the Baptist.

John 1:28, however, poses more of a challenge. We are told that all this has happened at Bethany beyond the Jordan. Most commentators take this to be an otherwise unknown location in Perea on the east bank of the river, across from the Judean wilderness where the other Gospels portray the Baptist ministering. Rainer Riesner (1987), however, has made a plausible case for identifying this site with Batanea, considerably further north, in which case we could postulate that John's two points of verbal contact with the synoptic tradition reflected central tenets of the Baptist's teaching likely to be repeated on more than one occasion. But without more information it is impossible to be sure; charges that John is probably mistaken (Casey 1996: 70) are as unjustified as claims that we have successfully confirmed his topography at this point.

Verse 29a supplies the first reference to chronology in John's Gospel. But because verses 19–28 refer to an incident in John's ministry that could have happened before or after Jesus' baptism, we have no way of securely correlating this information with the synoptic portrait (or of corroborating claims of contradiction). Verses 29b–34 read most naturally, however, as the Baptist's after-the-fact reflection on Jesus' baptism, suggesting that all of John's episodes about the Baptist may have occurred after that event, and thus after Jesus' temptations as well (cf. Mark 1:12–13 pars.). That one can add together the references to consecutive days in 1:29, 35, 43 and 2:1 has

---

73] For a detailed analysis of the quotation and its parallels, see Menken 1985.

suggested to many commentators that John is describing a 'week' in Jesus' ministry, with the wedding in Cana on the seventh day typologically corresponding to the resurrection and hence to new creation. This would probably prove more plausible if John had numbered the days throughout, so that it was obvious that by the 'third day' of 2:1 we had arrived at the seventh day in the larger sequence.[74] In any event, John regularly finds double meanings in genuine historical events, so such an interpretation does not exclude a literal chronology.

Verses 29b–34 focus on the Baptist's testimony about Jesus and raise perhaps the most difficult historical questions encountered thus far. Did the Baptist recognize who Jesus was before his baptism (so apparently Matt. 3:13–15) or not (so apparently John 1:32–34)? Only in the writings of the Fourth Evangelist does the term 'Lamb of God' ever appear in the New Testament (only in 1:29 and 36 in John but 27 times in Revelation). Did the Baptist actually use it of Jesus and what did he mean by it? In the light of the slow, synoptic progression of Christological understanding among even those closest to Jesus, are we seriously to imagine the Baptist articulating a full-blown doctrine of the atonement here at the very outset of Jesus' ministry (v. 29)? And what of his later doubts about Jesus' identity (Matt. 11:2–3 par.)?

The last of these questions can be dealt with most easily. Surely John never expected to be imprisoned and would have increasingly questioned why Jesus' teaching was not echoing, much less implementing, John's highly apocalyptic message of judgment (cf. Blomberg 1992: 185). Regarding the timing of the Baptist's insight, Jesus could well have already walked into the Jordan river to be baptized when John came to the conviction that this was indeed a specially anointed person and uttered his temporary protest. It is interesting that all four Gospels use simile for the Spirit coming 'like' or 'as' a dove (Matt. 3:16; Mark 1:10; Luke 3:22; John 1:32), which may suggest a more subjective, spiritual experience rather than an actual vision of a bird that could be pinpointed to a precise moment (cf. Blomberg 1992: 81–82). As for the 'Lamb of God', while the Fourth Evangelist almost certainly saw a constellation of Old Testament images in the background – Passover sacrifice, Isaiah's suffering servant and apocalyptic ram – it may well be the conquering judge pervasive in Revelation of which the Baptist first thought (see esp. Dodd 1963:

74] Somewhat more plausible, though equally difficult to prove, is the suggestion of Moloney (1998: 50–51) that with all of the allusions to Sinai in John 1 we are meant to think here of Moses' preparation for the third day (of revelation) in Exod. 19, supplemented by the early Jewish exegetical tradition of four additional days of preparation.

270–271; Sandy 1991). In that event, taking away the world's sins would refer to the avenging of injustice by the Messiah. But interestingly, the synoptic accounts all agree that a heavenly voice at Jesus' baptism used language allusive of the Isaianic servant songs (Is. 42:1; cf. Mark 1:11 pars.). And the case for at least a minority strand of pre-Christian Jewish messianic interpretation of Isaiah 52 – 53 has been considerably strengthened by Martin Hengel's recent study (1996).[75] Given the unique births of John and Jesus, relatives themselves (Luke 1:36), even if they grew up in different provinces and had little contact afterwards, one would think that John would have been told some of the stories about his special cousin. Doubtless, he did not know what to make of them and required the extra-ordinary events surrounding Jesus' baptism to confirm for himself that Jesus truly was God's anointed. John 1:31 suggests not that the two had never before met, but merely that John did not clearly understand Jesus' significance until this occasion. But if John could characterize his own ministry as producing forgiveness of sins (Mark 1:4; Luke 3:3), is it that unlikely that he would have recognized the Messiah's role as doing at least as much?

Verse 30 forms an otherwise unparalleled saying of John (but recall 1:15). Dodd (1963: 274) was convinced it should be rendered, 'There is a man in my following who has taken precedence of me, because he is and always has been essentially my superior.' This, in turn, suggests that Jesus began as a follower of John, for however long or short a period of time. This claim was not likely to have been invented by early Christianity, and especially the Fourth Evangelist, in its climate of de-emphasizing John and magnifying Jesus (see further Meier 1994: 116–120).

The reference to the Spirit coming and remaining on Jesus (v. 33) confirms that we have here the Fourth Gospel's equivalent to the synoptic accounts of Jesus' baptism. Here, too, appears the other half of the contrast between water and spirit baptism, begun in verse 26. But perhaps the most striking distinctive in John's account is what is missing – no actual narration of the baptism of Jesus – perhaps because John wanted to play down a growing institutionalization of the sacraments prevalent in the Christian church at the end of the first century.[76] Verse 34 rounds out this section with an allusion to the words of the heavenly voice (Ps. 2:7; cf. Mark 1:11 pars.). Jesus is not only suffering servant but messianic Son. Whatever else John did or did not understand at this stage, he will have

---

75] Citing esp. 1QIsaA, 4Q491, *Test. Levi* II, *Test. Benj.* 3.8 and the LXX *ad loc.*

76] See Paschal (1981) for a good overview of the major positions and their various advocates with respect to baptism and the Lord's Supper in John.

meant at least a victorious warrior. In the light of the discovery of 4Q246 at Qumran, 'Son of God' has now clearly been shown to be a messianic title in pre-Christian Judaism with no necessary overtones of divinity.[77] And nothing in all of this is inconsistent with John's overall message as portrayed in the Synoptics (cf. further Schnackenburg 1968: 306). John's ministry of baptism admirably satisfies the double similarity and dissimilarity criterion. One can trace an unbroken thread of immersion, from Jewish ritual lustrations, through John's and Jesus' baptisms, to the practice of the early church (see esp. Taylor 1997). But over against his predecessors, John gave his ministry a unique eschatological meaning, yet stopping short of claiming the exalted role that some would give him later. His baptism is not yet fully fledged Christian baptism, and even the Fourth Gospel's more 'theological' portrait has not blurred this distinction.[78]

THE FIRST FOLLOWERS OF JESUS (1:35-51)

All of 1:35 – 4:42 clearly belongs in the period skipped over by the Synoptics between Jesus' baptism and temptations and the beginning of his 'great Galilean ministry' (Mark 1:14–15 pars.). It is sometimes alleged that Jesus' gathering his first disciples here conflicts with the synoptic call narratives (Mark 1:16–20 pars.), but this is the case only if one reads into the latter accounts the unstated assumption that Jesus was there meeting these men for the first time. This suggestion seems improbable. It is far more likely that these Galileans would have been willing to follow Jesus as immediately as the Synoptics suggest, precisely because they had had prior exposure to him (R. E. Brown 1966: 77; Schnackenburg 1968: 306). Nothing in John indicates that this early encounter was as formal or permanent as the explicit calling of the Twelve that would occur later on (Mark 3:13–19 pars.), and the criteria for replacing Judas given in Acts 1:21–22 demonstrates that Christ had followers from the days of his baptism by John onwards (J. A. T. Robinson 1985: 168). That Jesus' first followers were originally the Baptist's disciples further corroborates the suggestion that Jesus, too, had begun his ministry as a follower of John, for a long enough period of time to have made a

---

77] A handful of important manuscripts attest the textual variants 'chosen one' or 'chosen son' rather than 'Son of God' in v. 34. 'Chosen one' is clearly the more unusual title, so that the internal evidence strongly favours this as the original reading. But it is hard to be very confident, because the external evidence is weighted strongly against any use of 'chosen'.

78] For a representative 'centrist' position on the most historically secure information concerning John the Baptist in the Gospels, see Theissen and Merz 1997: 196–211.

substantial impression on these men (Meier 1994: 120).[79]

The three names of the men called in verses 37–44 (Andrew, Simon and Philip) match names that we know from the synoptic call narratives. One of Jesus' first four followers is anonymous; he is thus often equated with the beloved disciple, though we cannot be certain of this equation (see above, pp. 30–31).[80] 'In typical fashion of potential disciples seeking out a famous sage or teacher, the question is raised about where Jesus' teaching house is, where he is staying' (v. 38). The recurring command, 'Come and see' (vv. 39, 46), parallels Wisdom's call to the people in texts like Wisdom of Solomon 6 (cf. Prov. 8; Sir. 51:23, 25–27; Witherington 1995: 69–70). That it was about the tenth hour (4.00pm) is a seemingly unmotivated detail that could reflect eyewitness recollection (v. 39).

The only particularly unusual feature in verses 35–51 is the collection of titles that these first followers of Jesus apply to him. Can we really believe that such 'exalted Christology' emerged this early in Jesus' ministry? Doubtless, the key to a correct answer is to realize that none of the titles applied here to Jesus (with the possible exception of John's 'Lamb of God' in v. 35; on which see above, pp. 78–79) necessarily implied anything in these disciples' minds beyond conventional Jewish hopes for a nationalistic and even militaristic Messiah, hopes that would have been raised by the heavenly voice and its declaration at Jesus' baptism. 'Rabbi' was not yet a formal title before AD 70 and meant simply 'Teacher' (v. 38; Köstenberger 1998). 'Messiah' itself was used in numerous ways in pre-70 Judaism, more often than not implying nothing that could not be predicated of a mere mortal (see esp. Charlesworth 1992). Philip's testimony in verse 45 employs classic Jewish language for describing the Messiah and identifies Jesus by his residence and father.[81] Not only is this standard Jewish style, but a later Christian writer would probably not have called Jesus the 'son of Joseph', potentially suggesting a merely human origin. At the same time, 'it is unlikely that the disciples would have taken long to begin wondering whether Jesus were the Messiah, but John, agreeing with the Synoptics, allows that they had to grow in their understanding of who Jesus really is' (Whitacre 1999: 72–73).

In addition to these titles, we read, too, of Jesus calling Simon by the name Peter (v. 42). That he uses the future tense verb 'will be called' meshes

---

79] On the continuity between John's and Jesus' baptisms, and on John encouraging his disciples to transfer their allegiance to Jesus, see Badke 1990.

80] John and James do appear in the early synoptic call narratives along with Peter and Andrew, so one of the sons of Zebedee is a natural inference.

81] On the 'Law and Prophets' cf. esp. Matt. 5:17.

well with his later dramatic dialogue with Peter on the road to Caesarea Philippi (Matt. 16:16–19). It is impossible to determine when Jesus first used Peter ('Rock') as a nickname for Simon. Matthew 16 does not preclude Jesus having used the name without explanation earlier, though it probably reads more naturally as the time at which he began to employ the term. Earlier references by the Evangelists to Simon as Peter (as in John 1:40 here, or in Mark 3:16) may simply reflect their retrojection into their narratives of the name by which this disciple had come to be known. That Simon is also 'son of John' formally conflicts with many English translations of Matthew 16:17 ('Simon son of Jonah'). Still, the underlying Greek (*Bariōna*) is merely Aramaic in transliteration and could just as easily be an abbreviation for 'son of Johanan' (Aramaic for John) as 'son of Jonah' (Bruce 1983: 58; cf. Barrett 1978: 182). Jesus' command to Philip 'Follow me' (v. 43) exactly matches his frequent synoptic calls (e.g. Matt. 8:22; 9:9; 19:21).

In John 1:45–51 a character appears whose name is found in no other New Testament book – Nathanael. Numerous suggestions throughout church history have tried to link him with one of the Twelve named in the Synoptics (see the survey in Hill 1997), but given the larger pool of followers of Jesus who come and go throughout his ministry (including Joseph Barsabbas and Matthias – Acts 1:23), such an equation is by no means necessary. On the other hand, the fact that Philip is paired with Bartholomew in all three synoptic lists of the Twelve (Mark 3:18; Matt. 10:3; Luke 6:14), coupled with the observation that Bartholomew (*bar Tholomais*) is a patronymic (meaning 'son of Talmai'), not a proper name, makes the frequent equation of Bartholomew with Nathanael defensible (Leidig 1980). That we are now in Galilee (v. 43), apparently one day after Jesus and John were together in Bethany beyond the Jordan (v. 28), would support an equation of that Bethany with Batanea (see above, p. 77), much closer to Bethsaida (v. 44) than to the Judean wilderness.[82]

That Jesus is said to be from Nazareth agrees with synoptic teaching (Mark 1:9, 24; 10:47; 14:61; etc.). The disparaging attitude Nathanael reflects in John 1:46 for this tiny 'backwoods' village may explain Matthew 2:23. There Jesus' living in Nazareth fulfils 'what was said through the prophets: "He will be called a Nazarene".' But this is not an identifiable Old Testament quotation. The unique, plural reference to 'the prophets'

82] For a plausible case in favour of John the Baptist having travelled up and down the Jordan River valley, see Murphy-O'Connor 1990. The Synoptics do not give us the precise villages of origin for these disciples, though Bethsaida does appear in other contexts (see Matt. 11:21 par.; Luke 9:10), but they do agree that most of the Twelve came from Galilee.

may suggest that Matthew is citing instead a general theme and is referring to the same disparaging attitude described in John. In this case, he may have the suffering servant passages of Isaiah mostly in mind, including their references to the Lord's servant as despised, with no human features or background to commend him (Is. 52:14 – 53:3; France 1985: 89).[83]

The most difficult interpretative questions in John 1 surround Jesus' dialogue with Nathanael (vv. 47–51). Verse 47b involves a play on words that requires knowledge of Hebrew to understand. In the Old Testament, Israel was another name for Jacob ('the deceiver'). 'A true Israelite, in whom there is nothing false,' might thus be paraphrased, 'An Israelite in whom there is no Jacob'! When Jesus explains that he knew Nathanael because he saw him under the fig tree (v. 48b), he may be invoking those passages that portrayed the coming age of blessing as one when every Israelite would sit in peace under his own fig tree (e.g. 1 Kgs. 4:25; Mic. 4:4; 1 Macc. 14:12). Especially pertinent is Zechariah 3:10, appearing in a seemingly Messianic context (Koester 1990).[84] In verse 49 Nathanael adds to the catalogue of titles ascribed to Jesus in John 1. Once again, 'Son of God' is immediately rephrased as 'King of Israel'; in its original context it probably meant nothing more than a triumphant, nationalist Messiah.[85] Not surprisingly, when Jesus' mission turns out to be quite different, the acclamations die down. Even in John they are replaced by statements about the disciples' misunderstanding (see esp. 6:68–69; 14:1–9). By the end of the first century, of course, John himself will have seen deeper meanings in all of these titles, but that is a separate matter unrelated to the historicity of the original dialogues.

The most enigmatic verse of all comes as Jesus promises Nathanael he will see even greater things, namely 'heaven open, and the angels of God ascending and descending on the Son of Man' (v. 51). This is the first of

---

83] Söding (2000) uses John 1:46 as a springboard from which to discuss how thoroughly Jewish the Johannine Jesus is, a feature that must moderate numerous charges concerning John's anti-Semitism.

84] Nicklas (2000b) lists five main interpretations of the fig tree of 1:48 – a place to study the Law, a parallel to the tree of knowledge of good and evil, a figure of speech for knowing everything about someone, a sign of the Messianic age, and an allusion to Hos. 9:10 – and argues that the narrative is deliberately ambiguous and polyvalent.

85] Cf. Ridderbos (1997: 91): 'The notion that here and elsewhere (cf. 20:31) "Son of God" completely overshadows "King/Messiah", thus proving that in Johannine christology the typically Jewish categories are blurred, is in conflict with all that has preceded in vss. 35ff ... which in fact depicts all these initial encounters in colours derived from Old Testament and Jewish future expectations.'

twenty-five times in John's Gospel that a saying of Jesus is introduced by the solemn formula, 'I tell you the truth' (literally, *Amēn, Amēn*). 'Amen' is a Hebrew word that is both distinctive and characteristic of the synoptic Jesus and is regularly held to be an indicator of his authentic teachings (Witherington 1990: 186–189). Lindars (1972: 48) believed that synoptic-like sayings play a crucial role in the discourses of Jesus in John and that 'very often John draws attention to this with the formula "truly, truly, I say to you", which is not merely a stylistic device; in nearly every case it points to the use of a traditional saying'.[86] In the synoptic texts one finds only a single introductory 'Amen'; in John, only a double one. The doubled form, however, appears at Qumran; in both John and the Dead Sea Scrolls it may be due to 'liturgical usage' (Schnackenburg 1968: 320).

Verse 51 also provides the first of a dozen 'Son of Man' sayings of Jesus in John. This title, too, is regularly recognized as both distinctive and characteristic of the synoptic Jesus and hence probably authentic (see esp. Kim 1983; Caragounis 1986). What exactly Jesus meant by the angels ascending and descending upon himself is disputed, although the general allusion to Jacob's ladder (Gen. 28:12) is clear. Perhaps the saying is an early, and thus appropriately cryptic foreshadowing of the cross and resurrection – angels accompanying Jesus to bear his body to heaven, in keeping with typical Jewish belief, and returning to announce his resurrection (as in Matt. 28:2 par.).[87] Some of the Johannine 'Son of Man' sayings present distinctive twists (see esp. Burkett 1991) but this one is completely at home in the apocalyptic world of approximately one-third of the synoptic 'Son of Man' texts (Morris 1995: 151).[88]

The criterion of double similarity and dissimilarity yields important results for this early period in Jesus' ministry. As in the Judaism of his day, Jesus functions as a rabbi gathering disciples, but instead of sifting through 'applicants', he calls them directly or they respond directly to John's testimony about Jesus. This teacher-disciple relationship would continue in subsequent Christianity, most notably with Paul and his co-workers, but

---

86] Culpepper (1993) accepts this generalization as frequently accurate and as almost always pointing to John's use of tradition, but he stops well short of declaring all the double-'Amen' sayings as authentic.

87] Cf. Bruce 1983: 62–63. For a slightly different but equally plausible approach, see Rowland 1984. The most recent survey of views is Walker (1994), though his own conclusions seem less likely.

88] None of the 'Son of Man' sayings in John, however, is incompatible with this apocalyptic background, even when dimensions of humanity (Ezek.) and suffering (Is. 52 – 53) are combined. All of these sayings should be considered authentic (Ham 1998).

without the same sovereign authority to command and receive instant obedience that is reflected here. We thus have reason to believe that John 1 presents substantially authentic material about the calling of the first followers of Jesus.[89]

WATER INTO WINE (2:1–11)

Quite a few scholars grant that John 1 may preserve independent, accurate traditions about the early days of the Baptist and Jesus. The situation is different when one turns to John 2. Immediately, we confront the first miracle ascribed to Christ. The format of this book precludes discussion of the complex scientific, philosophical, and historical questions surrounding the possibility of miracles in general.[90] Suffice it to say that, if one takes the position of Casey (1996: 52) that they are impossible, then further discussion proves fruitless. On the other hand, John Meier (1994: 509–1038) has demonstrated in massive detail not only that the overall miracle tradition of the Gospels is as credible as the most securely attested elements of Jesus' life but also that the vast majority of people in our scientifically sophisticated world nevertheless believe in miracles (520–521).[91] And this book is merely comparing John with the Synoptics to see if the two are too different for both to be simultaneously credible.

With this mandate, one immediately observes that the miracle at Cana is a 'gift-miracle' (Theissen 1983: 103–106), closely parallel in form and function to the feedings of the five thousand and four thousand in the Synoptics (Mark 6:30–44 pars.; 8:1–10 par.). In each case, more than acute human need is at stake.[92] Rather, these miracles are pointers to the in-breaking kingdom. In John 2:1–11 several details of the narrative remind the reader of Jesus' little 'parable' of new wine requiring new wineskins

---

89] Cf. in Wright 1996: 297–301 the more general observations regarding Jesus summoning his followers.

90] I have dealt with the issue elsewhere (Blomberg 1987: 73–112) and refer the reader to that treatment and the literature there cited, to which should be added esp. Latourelle 1988; Geivett and Habermas 1997; and Twelftree 1999.

91] Indeed, scientists, philosophers and historians in general are often making much more modest claims today about what their disciplines can and cannot adjudicate than are biblical scholars! Meier (1994: 949) does, however, conclude that the issues are too complicated with respect to this specific miracle account to come down in favour of its historicity.

92] Derrett (1963) and R. H. Williams (1997) both discuss the relevant ancient Jewish wedding customs that demonstrate how the honour of the host of the banquet (and perhaps of Jesus and his family) would have been greatly impugned if he had failed to provide enough wine.

(Mark 2:22 pars.). The newness and joy of the kingdom's arrival are vividly depicted. The account thus admirably satisfies the criterion of coherence with the central tenets of Jesus' authentic teaching (cf. further Blomberg 1986b: 333–337).[93] Jesus' enjoying festive food and drink meshes with the core truth beneath the caricature created by his opponents in Luke 7:34, who call him a glutton and drunkard. Given the early Christian tendencies towards asceticism, it is unlikely that a story of Jesus deliberately producing large amounts of wine, with which at least some of the guests could have become quite drunk, would have been fabricated without a strong historical basis.

Historical verisimilitude appears in numerous details in the passage as well. John 21:2 states that Nathanael came from Cana, so it would be natural for Jesus and his small group of followers to go there (2:1). Weddings were common, public events in which entire villages often participated. That John calls Mary simply 'Jesus' mother' fits ancient practice in referring to well-known figures and presupposes some knowledge of her within the Johannine community – the church or churches to which John was writing and among whom he had ministered in and around Ephesus (T. W. Martin 1998; Ridderbos 1997: 104). The interchange between Jesus and Mary in verses 3–5 shows that she has some understanding of her special son, exactly what we would expect if even the core of the synoptic birth narratives (Matt. 1 – 2; Luke 1 – 2) is true.[94] Jesus' reply (v. 4a) is not quite as rude in the Semitic original that it reflects (cf. Judg. 11:12; 1 Kgs. 17:18; 2 Kgs. 3:13; 2 Chr. 35:21) as in some English translations, but it clearly distances him from his mother (Morris 1995: 158–159; cf. Mark 3:34–35 pars.). The unflattering portrait that results is probably not the product of early Christian invention (Witherington 1984: 81).

In verse 4b Jesus employs the first of several references to 'his time' (lit. 'hour') in this Gospel, an important distinctive Johannine motif (cf. 7:6; 8:20; 12:23; etc.). But it is an expression that the Synoptists know, too (see

---

93] Indeed all of the so-called nature miracles can be seen to be parabolic in significance. This approach is to be distinguished from that which sees the passage created largely *de novo* on the basis of such parallels. That this miracle story was created on the basis of Hellenistic parallels like the legends of Dionysus is increasingly a minority position. Sabourin (1977: 129) demonstrates how vastly different the two accounts are. Even in antiquity there was considerable scepticism over the truth of the reports concerning water becoming wine in the Dionysiac temple.

94] Whitacre (1999: 79) notes in particular the similarities with Mary's humble response to the annunciation (Luke 1:38) and the spirituality of the Magnificat (Luke 1:46–55).

esp. Mark 14:35, 41 pars.). Archaeology has confirmed the use of the stone water jars described in verse 6 (Reich 1995). Verses 7–9 are striking in what they omit – no description of the miracle itself, precisely what later free invention would probably have created. The term for the 'master of the banquet' may have been coined on the basis of the stories of feasting in Esther, but many ancient weddings did have this kind of official (cf. Aus 1988:15–17). The proverb in verse 10 does not correspond to any known custom of the day, but it is inherently plausible (cf. Theissen 1983: 105).

Indeed, the major Johannine distinctives in this account appear where we would expect them: in John's narrative conclusion in verse 11. In the Fourth Gospel, miracles are primarily signs (Gk. *sēmeia*), intended to generate belief in Jesus (v. 12; cf. 20:31; see esp. Kysar 1976: 67–73). This creates a formal 'contradiction' with the Synoptics, in which Jesus refuses to work signs on demand (e.g. Mark 8:11–13 pars.). But the conflict is only apparent; both in John and the Synoptics, Jesus never produces a miracle simply to satisfy a sceptic, while Luke's second volume recognizes that 'signs and wonders' do have positive effects among unbelievers (e.g. Acts 4:30; 6:8; 7:36; etc.). The themes of revelation and glory as characteristics of Jesus' historical ministry are also more common in John than elsewhere (recall 1:14), though scarcely absent from the Synoptics (cf., e.g. Luke 2:32; 9:32). Once again our text fares well by the double similarity and dissimilarity criterion: the miracle is firmly rooted in a recognizable early first-century Galilean setting and coheres with key synoptic themes, but it reflects Jesus' distinctive, even scandalous, attitudes over against traditional Judaism. The main point of the passage – the joy surrounding the newness of what Jesus is offering – meshes with the broader new creation themes pervasive in early Christian theology, even as this particular example of festive eating and drinking has often scandalized the church (or led to elaborate allegorical reinterpretations).[95]

CLEARING THE TEMPLE (2:12–25)

John 2:12 stands somewhat unconnected to its immediate context. Theologically unmotivated, it describes Jesus' family and disciples moving on to Capernaum for 'a few days'. Perhaps it is a precursor to what the Synoptics depict as Jesus later leaving Nazareth to live in Capernaum (Matt. 4:13), an understandable move to a larger town on the shores of the lake and thus a better centre for Galilean ministry.

Verses 13–22 comprise the Johannine account of Jesus clearing the

---

95] For a good summary of arguments for the authenticity of this passage and rebuttals to objections to its historicity, see Latourelle 1988: 212–217.

temple. Apparent parallels appear in Matthew 21:12–13, Mark 11:15–17, and Luke 19:45–46, all in the context of the last week of Christ's ministry. Here emerges one of the most difficult questions facing a study of the historicity of John. Has John thematically relocated this passage as a kind of headline to the meaning of Jesus' ministry and to the mixed response Christ would receive (so most commentators today)?[96] Or did Jesus in fact clear the temple twice, once toward the beginning and once near the end of his public ministry (so most commentators throughout church history)?[97]

In favour of the former approach is the observation that this is the first pericope in John's narrative that is not unambiguously introduced with a reference to time that requires it to have occurred shortly after the previous episode. Nor does 3:1 contain any indication of a specific time that would require Jesus' conversation with Nicodemus to have followed 2:12–25. My introduction noted that the Synoptics regularly arrange material thematically with only vague temporal links between successive pericopae, so we should not be surprised if we found John doing the same thing (see above, p. 54). Moreover, the second main section of John's Gospel also opens with a passage that appears in a different context than in the Synoptics (John 12:1–11). Perhaps John began both major sections of his work with similar relocations (Michaels 1983: 32–33).[98] One can in fact imagine 2:12 originally leading directly to verses 23–35, with verses 13–22 as a later insertion (Lindars 1972: 135). On the other hand, we would expect a leading Pharisee on the Sanhedrin to reside in Jerusalem, so that it is natural to take Jesus' dialogue with Nicodemus (3:1–21) as the sequel to all of 2:13–25. And that dialogue *is* followed by an explicit temporal

---

96] For two good, recent studies that adopt this approach and go on to focus, respectively, on John's literary and theological concerns, see Schlosser 1990 and Schnelle 1996. Recall above (p. 17) on how Casey (1996: 8–14) thinks John's treatment of this incident almost singlehandedly disproves this Gospel's accuracy. In replying to my discussion of this passage (Blomberg 1987: 170–173), Casey (1996: 11–13) fails to note that I give equal credence to both approaches.

97] For a good survey, see F.-M. Braun 1929. Many of the apparent 'doublets' in the Gospels have been variously interpreted over the centuries, but this seems to be one in which relatively uniform agreement prevailed until the 1900s.

98] Kreitzer (1998) likens the account to the 'flash-ahead' of Mohandas Gandhi's murder early in the otherwise largely chronologically sequenced film *Gandhi*. Draper (1997) thinks this location reflects the importance of the supersession of the temple after AD 70 paralleled in Qumran and other Jewish literature reflecting on 2 Sam. 7, and its teaching that the temple was not God's will to begin with.

link: 'After this, Jesus and his disciples went out into the Judean countryside' (3:22).

Not a few scholars, therefore, think that John is claiming that this event happened at the outset of Jesus' ministry and that he is actually more historically accurate than the Synoptics at this point (see esp. Campbell 1982; cf. Moloney 2000: 55). J. A. T. Robinson has defended this perspective consistently for numerous contexts in which John and the Synoptics seem to be at odds. Here he points particularly to the evidence from Josephus (*Ant.* 15.380) that would identify the forty-sixth year since Herod began to have the temple rebuilt (John 2:20) as AD 28, two full years before AD 30, the most probable date for Jesus' crucifixion (1985: 127–131).[99] The 'false testimony' later at Jesus' trial alleging that he said he would 'destroy this temple made with human hands and in three days ... build another, not made with hands' (Mark 14:57–58 par.) corresponds to nothing Jesus ever uttered to the crowds or to his opposition in the Synoptics. (The closest parallel would be the Olivet discourse given privately to the disciples – Mark 13 pars.) The charge makes much better sense as a garbled recollection of John 2:19 two years later. Raymond Brown (1966: 118–120) suggests a hybrid solution: early in his ministry Jesus uttered a prophetic warning against the temple, at the end of his life he physically cleared it, and John has conflated the two episodes (cf. also Beasley-Murray 1987: 39). Jerome Murphy O'Connor (2000) reverses this sequence, thinking that Jesus could have acted against the money changers based on the Baptist's programme of radical religious reform. But his temple sayings, if authentic, must come from much later when his perception of his role in providing salvation had changed.[100]

It seems likely that John is independent of the Synoptics here (see esp. Campbell 1982: 111; cf. E. E. Ellis 1999: 157). The words the two accounts have in common are those one would expect in a description of an incident involving the protest of corruption in the Jerusalem temple, even if two different events are in view: 'sellers', 'tables', 'doves', 'money changers', 'drove out', 'temple' and 'house'. Otherwise, one is struck by the differences. Only John speaks of cattle, sheep, a whip of cords, and coins.

99] Contra Casey (1996: 20), nothing in the text requires the interpretation that John thinks the temple's reconstruction was completed within that forty-six-year period. And Casey's claim that the crucifixion itself could have occurred in 27 or 28 flies in the face of all the evidence that points to only 30 or 33 as the years in which Passover occurred on either a Friday or a Saturday.

100] Another intermediate approach is defended by Trocmé (1996), who finds John altogether independent of the Synoptics here but relating the same event as they do.

The key sayings attributed to Jesus are entirely different – a protest against commercialism (v. 16) and a cryptic prediction of his death and resurrection (v. 19). A different Old Testament passage is cited (v. 17 – Ps. 69:9) and different questions on the part of the Jewish leaders appear (vv. 18, 20). The synoptic accounts, in contrast, focus on the combination of quotations from Isaiah 56:7 and Jeremiah 7:11 (a house of prayer vs. a den of robbers).

On the one hand, as Paul Trudinger (1997) has demonstrated, these two accounts do not contradict each other at any point and can be combined to form a plausible, harmonious whole, despite frequent but unsupported claims to the contrary (cf. also Burge 2000: 94–95).[101] And the synoptic versions have regularly been viewed as reflecting a core, authentic episode that largely explains the timing of Jesus' arrest and the nature of the charges against him (see esp. Sanders 1985: 61–76; Evans 1989). On the other hand, it does seem odd how reluctant some are today to consider the possibility of two separate events.[102] A key question is whether or not the temple authorities would have taken action after one such demonstration to prevent its repetition. Morris (1995: 168) plausibly replies: 'At the time indicated in John Jesus was quite unknown. His strong action would have aroused a furor in Jerusalem, but that is all. The authorities may have well been disinclined to go to extremes against him, especially if there was some public feeling against the practices he opposed. It was quite otherwise at the time indicated by Mark.'

A protest merely against corrupt trade (an enacted fulfilment of Zech. 14:21 mg?) fits better early on in Christ's ministry; the synoptic account, in contrast, seems to threaten the destruction of the entire sacrificial system (Neusner 1989). The latter, more serious threat almost certainly would

---

101] Köstenberger (1999: 76–78) also supports two cleansings and notes that, if the unnamed feast of 5:1 is *not* Passover, Jesus thus acted consistently the only two times he did attend Passover during his public ministry.

102] Even as conservative a commentator as Borchert (1996: 160) pours scorn on such an approach, calling it 'a historiographic monstrosity that has no basis in the texts of the Gospels', because no Gospel contains more than one temple 'cleansing'. But, to take just one example of many that could be cited, by this logic one would have to equate Jesus' arrest with Stephen's, because the only place Luke locates a charge about threatening to destroy the temple is in the latter narrative (Acts 6:13–14), even though Matthew and Mark relate it to Jesus' temple clearing. In essence, Borchert is ruling out any form of 'additive harmonization', precluding two different writers from ever describing separate but similar events, each unattested by the other writer. But no credible historian ever adopts this approach a priori.

have led to Jesus' arrest (Mark 11:18). John's characteristic comments about what the disciples came to understand only after Jesus' resurrection (vv. 17, 22) further supports the idea that John is not blurring historical distinctions between separate periods in Jesus' ministry here (cf. Carson 1991: 183).

Barring the discovery of new information, we shall probably not be able to settle the debate among the various approaches to this passage surveyed here (similarly Whitacre 1999: 82). Suffice it to conclude that the entire account in John stands on its own with numerous allusions to the Hebrew prophets as a plausible, authentic episode from the life of Jesus (Mathews 1988). Of course, sacrificial animals and the coinage with which to buy them had to be available, but it is quite possible that Caiaphas, the high priest, had only recently introduced this commerce into the temple precincts themselves rather than using the nearby Kidron valley as previously. This could further explain Jesus' protest and the fact that the authorities initially tolerated it (Eppstein 1964). And it is interesting that, as with the miracle in Cana, the most overt Johannine theology comes only after the story itself. Verses 23–25 repeat the reference to the Passover and speak of additional 'signs' that lead many to believe (v. 23). But as will become clearer as John's narrative unfolds, not all who apparently believe continue in that faith, and Jesus recognizes that fact already at this stage in his ministry (vv. 24–25).[103]

JESUS AND NICODEMUS (3:1–21)

In response to Jesus' ministry in Jerusalem, a leading Pharisee engages in dialogue this upstart teacher. The interchange partially resembles those found in the synoptic controversy stories, although the climactic pro-nouncement (3:3, 5) appears early on, rather than at the end of the account. Given the Jewish leaders' penchant for signs, independently attested in 1 Corinthians 1:22, this passage forms a natural and plausible outgrowth of 2:23–25.[104] We cannot unequivocally equate Nicodemus with any character known to us from independent Jewish sources, but there are two men by that name who appear, respectively, in Josephus (*Ant.* 14.37) and the Babylonian Talmud (see esp. *b. Gitt.* 56a). The first was

---

103] Both the miracle at Cana and the temple-clearing also demonstrate John's key supersessionist theme – Jesus, not the Torah, provides the new wine and becomes the new temple. But, as we noted in the context of John 1:17, this understanding is present already in synoptic texts like Matt. 5:17.

104] Schnackenburg (1968: 364) declares matter-of-factly, 'There is no reason to doubt the historicity of the nocturnal scene.'

alive in 64 BC; the latter was a wealthy man in Jerusalem during the war
with Rome (late 60s AD). Both were part of the Gurion family, in which
only a handful of 'first' names reappear over the generations. Bauckham
(1996) demonstrates how the portrait of Nicodemus in the Fourth Gospel
corresponds to what we know of this family – part of the Jewish ruling
elite, Pharisees, teachers of the Law and extremely rich – and suggests
Nicodemus may have been the uncle of the Naqdimon ben Gurion of the
rabbinic literature.[105] There is thus no credible reason for doubting the
historicity of verse 1.

That Nicodemus should come to Jesus by night (v. 2) has regularly been
seen as motivated by a desire for secrecy, but it may have been simply the
natural time for study of Torah (1QS 6:7; cf. Witherington 1995: 94).
Nicodemus' opening gambit is entirely plausible and Jewish in content; he
calls Jesus a teacher (rabbi) who has come from God and is thus able to
perform miracles. There is no lofty Christology here. The first-person
plural may indicate the presence of disciples (Bruce 1983: 86). Jesus does
not acknowledge the compliment but redirects Nicodemus' attention to
the need for a new birth (v. 3). This double-'Amen' saying closely parallels
Matthew 18:3 (cf. Mark 10:15) and has often been viewed as the historical
kernel of the passage, even by those who find much later Christian
elaboration in the rest of the dialogue (Bultmann 1971: 135, n. 4; Lindars
1972: 150; Pryor 1991). 'Kingdom of God', so central to the Synoptics,
appears in John only here and in verse 5.

Being born *anōthen* can mean 'from above' or 'again', and John probably
intends a double meaning in the Greek. Whether one Aramaic expression
could generate both senses is more debated, but Lindars (1981b) points
out that Jesus need only have meant 'from above'. Once Nicodemus
misunderstands this as a second, biological birth, the sense of 'again' is
introduced into the conversation anyway. At any rate, becoming like a little
child is a frequent metaphor for conversion in the later rabbinic literature,
while 'birth from God' appears frequently in the Old Testament, especially
with respect to the nation, king, Wisdom and Torah (see Mounce 1981:
292–333 for a detailed list of texts in each category). Roland Bergmeier
(1995) acknowledges that the metaphor of rebirth goes back at least to
early Jewish-Christian baptismal theology. But there is no reason not to

---

105] Bauckham thus improves on the suggestion of J. A. T. Robinson (1985: 284–287) that
equated Gurion son of Nicodemus with John's Nicodemus. He also discusses the rabbinic
traditions that speak of one of Jesus' disciples as Nakkai or Buni (a Hebrew equivalent to
Nicodemus) and concludes that they also reflect reliable, independent testimony for the
man described in John 3.

attribute it to the historical Jesus himself, given the Jewish background applied in a novel way that baffles Nicodemus (not unlike the Baptist's requirement that all *Jews* repent), and given the coherence of the concept with the later Christian emphasis on 'salvation' despite the infrequency of the use of the metaphor itself.

Nicodemus' misunderstanding leads Jesus to explain his point slightly differently (vv. 4–5). 'Born from above' is the same as 'born of water and the Spirit'. This notorious crux is probably best explained as a metaphor of the cleansing power of the Spirit in the age of the new covenant, in keeping with Ezekiel 36:25–27 (Belleville 1980). Verse 6 introduces the *sarx–pneuma* (flesh–spirit) contrast, so well known in Paul. But in John it appears only here, and in the Synoptics only in Gethsemane (Mark 14:38 par.), both times in contexts in which 'flesh' means merely 'frail humanity', not 'sinful nature', so it is probably not the product of later Christian invention.[106] In verse 7, for the third time Jesus begins a saying with the solemn introductory formula that may well indicate authenticity. Here, too, is a little parable or metaphor embedded in the larger dialogue, this time clearly based on a Semitic double meaning. The Hebrew *ruah* can mean either 'wind' or 'spirit'; hence, like the wind, the Spirit blows where it wills (cf. Eccles. 11:5).

Verse 9 concludes Nicodemus' contribution to the conversation as he disparagingly dismisses Jesus' teaching. Jesus rightly chastises this leading teacher who should understand better (v. 10). Setting aside the question of Nicodemus' later two appearances in John (7:50–51; 19:39), it seems clear that, at this stage of the Gospel, the Fourth Evangelist wishes to portray Nicodemus as still outside the community of Jesus' followers (Blomberg 1995). In the light of the more positive references later in the Gospel, one would have expected free creation by a later writer to have generated a less negative portrait of Nicodemus here and a clearer witness to Christian truth.

Verses 11–15 round out Jesus' comments in this context. Johannine theology begins increasingly to shape the remarks attributed to Jesus: themes of knowledge and testimony, earthly and heavenly contrasts, 'lifting up' as both crucifixion and exaltation, and belief that leads to eternal life. But the concepts that underlie the Johannine vocabulary fit the ministry of the historical Jesus: opposition and misunderstanding by key Pharisaic leaders (vv. 10–11; pervasive in the Synoptics), parables or metaphors and their misunderstanding (v. 12; cf. esp. Mark 4:10–12

106] Lindars (1972: 153) notes parallels in the Dead Sea Scrolls' doctrine of the contrasting spirits of truth and deceit (see esp. 1QS 3:19).

pars.),[107] the apocalyptic Son of Man (v. 13; accounting for about one-third of the synoptic 'Son of Man' sayings), the 'prophet like Moses' typology (v. 14; particularly prominent in Luke),[108] and experiencing 'eternal life' as interchangeable with entering the kingdom (v. 15; cf. esp. Mark 10:17, 25 pars.). The cryptic reference early in Jesus' ministry to his later death (v. 14) calls to mind the equally ambiguous reference in Mark 2:20 ('But the time will come when the bridegroom will be taken from them, and on that day they will fast').[109] Together, verses 13–15 find several close parallels in ancient Jewish exegetical tradition (esp. *Mek. Exod.* 19.20; Ps. 68:17–19; and Dan. 7:13–14; see Borgen 1977).

With the NIV marginal note, verses 16–21 should probably not be viewed as words ascribed to Jesus (Morris 1995: 202). The final first-person pronoun in 3:1–21 appears in verse 12.[110] Verses 13–14 use the 'Son of Man', the one title almost always used by Jesus himself in all four Gospels, and verse 15 cannot be separated grammatically from verse 14. Verses 16–21, however, contain virtually nothing but a collage of major Johannine motifs: God's love for the world, references to his one and only Son, belief, eternal life, God's sending his Son, issues of judgment, contrast between light and darkness, good and evil deeds, conviction, truth and revelation (and recall the emphases of 1:1–18). As John Pryor explains (1992a: 20), 'In vv. 1–15, the categories and concerns are Jewish: who is the true teacher of Israel; Jesus as the only one who has descended from heaven; the Mosaic serpent tradition; Jesus as the exalted Son of Man. But from v. 16 to v. 21 the claims of Christ are now universalized: the message is about the only Son of God who is sent into the world (*kosmos* occurs x 5) for its salvation.' If this is correct, then we need not linger over these verses in a study of the historical Jesus, because John did not intend them as words of Jesus in the first place.

Although John 3:1–15 (or 21) is often considered the first of seven major discourses in John 1 – 11, the label is somewhat misleading. If Jesus' words last only until verse 15, then he speaks in three segments, none longer than nine lines of Greek text in the UBS New Testament. Each

---

107] For particularly close linguistic and conceptual parallels to v. 12 in earlier Jewish literature, see Wis. Sol. 9:16 and *4 Ezra* 4.2 (Barrett 1978: 212).

108] For close formal and conceptual parallels to v. 14 in the Synoptics, see Matt. 12:40 par. (Michaels 1983: 41). The Old Testament background is, of course, Num. 21:9.

109] For important Jewish background to the metaphor of 'lifting up', see Beasley-Murray 1987: 50.

110] Indeed, some interpreters end the quotation after v. 12 (e.g. Beasley-Murray 1987: 50; Talbert 1992: 100).

subsequent statement by Jesus is longer than his previous one, just as each successive remark by Nicodemus gets shorter. Peter Cotterell (1985) has shown how this kind of discourse structure, combined with Jesus' refusal to limit his conversation to the topics broached by Nicodemus, fits the way ancient speakers in a superior role (Jesus) would often treat their inferiors (Nicodemus). Such treatment of a leading teacher and ruler in Israel by an untutored upstart would have proved shocking, but it characterizes the sovereign freedom Jesus demonstrates in the Synoptics even *vis-à-vis* the Hebrew Scriptures (see esp. Matt. 5:17–48). The overall description of this encounter between Jesus and Nicodemus thus seems authentic. The latter is portrayed in a credible Jewish role and fits what we know about the Gurion family in Jerusalem, but he is not yet turned into a full-fledged believer, as in later Christian apocryphal tradition (see esp. the *Gospel of Nicodemus*). Jesus speaks enigmatically, as so often in the Synoptics, and as is appropriate for this early stage of his ministry. While Johannine wording intrudes somewhat into his language, enough of a separation remains between verses 1–15 and the thoroughly Johannine verses 16–21 to suggest that John is not deliberately blurring the distinction between the words of Jesus and later Christian theologizing.[111]

THE BAPTIST GIVES WAY TO JESUS (3:22–36)
John now offers a further glimpse into the earliest ministry of Jesus, while Jesus still overlapped with the Baptist. As in 1:19–34, the Fourth Gospel's theological emphasis seems to counter an over-exaltation of the Baptist (Burge 2000: 120). Here John recedes in importance even as Jesus flourishes. But there are reasons for finding historically accurate information in this passage as well. Like 3:1–15, verses 22–30 partly resemble the synoptic pronouncement stories (Talbert 1992: 105). Further paralleling the preceding parts of chapter 3, verses 22–36 seem to fall into two halves: the narrative of a dialogue (this time between the Baptist and his disciples), followed by the Fourth Evangelist's own summary remarks (vv. 31–36, NIV mg.).[112]

In verse 22 Jesus and his disciples leave Jerusalem and go into the

---

111] Morris (1995: 202, n. 73) notes three Johannine distinctives in vv. 16–21 not found anywhere in the words attributed to Jesus in the Fourth Gospel: *monogenēs* (one and only), 'believing in his name', and 'doing the truth'.

112] Wilson (1981) notes additional structural parallels between 3:1–21 and 22–36 in arguing for the integrity of the latter 'half' of this chapter, although not all of his 'parallels' are equally self-evident. E. E. Ellis (1999: 173–174) observes that 3:1–14 has features of a *yelammedenu rabbenu* (let our master teach us) midrash that supports its traditional character.

Ioudaian gēn (which could mean either the 'Jewish' or the 'Judean land'). Almost certainly the NIV is correct in interpreting this as 'the Judean countryside' (Bultmann 1971: 170, n. 3; Borchert 1996: 188). Here we are told in passing that Jesus conducted a ministry of baptism, too. Witherington (1995: 108) elaborates: 'It seems plausible that some of the disciples of John who had become followers of Jesus may have continued John's baptizing practices, and perhaps Jesus endorsed or even encouraged this. It is clear enough from a saying like Mark 11:27–33 (and par.) that Jesus believed that John's ministry and baptizing was of God.' Indeed, given the later Christian conviction that only baptism from Pentecost onward conveyed the Spirit in all his fullness (Acts 2), and given how little John makes of Jesus' practice here, this detail is almost certainly authentic (cf. Dodd 1963: 279–287; R. E. Brown 1966: 155; Meier 1994: 120; Taylor 1997: 294–299).

The location of Aenon, where the Baptist was currently ministering (v. 23), is disputed but was probably somewhere in Samaria not too far from the Jordan River, another incidental detail that even as sceptical a scholar as Bultmann (1971: 170, n. 9) assumed to be accurate. Samaria and Judea would provide separate settings for the two baptizers so that they would not immediately come into direct competition with each other. This geography may further support the conjecture that John the Baptist travelled up and down the entire Jordan valley (see above, p. 82). Verse 24 presupposes knowledge on the part of John's audience of the subsequent fate of the Baptist. In Mark 6:14–29 and Matthew 14:1–12 John's imprisonment and execution are narrated in some detail as occurring after the start of Christ's public ministry. Luke 3:19–20 drastically abbreviates the account and thematically relocates it earlier in his Gospel to keep it with the rest of his material about John. Carson (1991: 209–210) explains that the purpose of John's 'remark is not to state the obvious (after all, John could scarcely have been baptizing if he had already been incarcerated) but to explain that what is related here (and probably in all of chs. 2 – 4) takes place earlier than any ministry recorded in the Synoptic Gospels'. Again, 'apparently the Evangelist is aware that such a construction had circulated widely, and he does not want his credibility diminished by failing to explain the apparent discrepancy'.

Verse 25 is puzzling in what it does not explain. Who was the Jew (or Jews) who debated John's disciples? What was the debate about? All the Fourth Evangelist is interested in is providing an introduction to verse 26. But that makes the incidental setting of the Baptist's ministry as one of purification that much more likely to be historical, especially since the Synoptics and not John stress that aspect elsewhere (cf. Barrett 1978: 219). Verse 26 explains the heart of the problem: despite their geographical separation, Jesus is outstripping the Baptist in gaining adherents. The specific description 'everyone is going to him' resembles the synoptic narration of the initial impact of John's ministry (Mark 1:5 pars.).

In verse 27 John's reply presents the first of several instances in the Fourth Gospel of a theology of predestination. Interestingly, the closest ancient Jewish equivalents are found at Qumran (e.g. 1QS 3:13 – 4:26; cf. Carson 1981a: 75–83), the very site scholars have often suspected may have influenced the Baptist. The use of 'heaven' as a euphemism for 'God' clearly grounds John's saying in a Jewish milieu (Barrett 1978: 222). Verse 28 finds John echoing his teaching of 1:20. His addition in this context takes the form of a short metaphor or parable about a bridegroom and his friend (v. 29), which he then applies to Jesus and himself (v. 30). Here is now the third parallel of sorts in these opening chapters of the Gospel to teaching ascribed to Jesus in Mark 2, this time to verse 19: 'How can the guests of the bridegroom fast while he is with them?' Had the Baptist already heard Jesus use these wedding metaphors in a different context? They are common enough throughout Christ's teaching (cf. esp. Matt. 22:1–14; 25:1–13) that it is certainly possible.[113] But John's point is sufficiently different from Jesus' to stand on its own: the Baptist is no more than what we would call today the 'best man' (Lindars 1972: 167, who notes the Jewish background to this custom as well). Thus Christ 'must become greater', while John 'must become less' (v. 30), a distinction that almost exactly matches Jesus' own testimony about John in the Synoptics: 'Among those born of women there has not risen anyone greater than John the Baptist; yet whoever is least in the kingdom of heaven is greater than he' (Matt. 11:11).

At the same time, Johannine language again intrudes into the dialogue. Most notable is the Baptist's reference to his joy being complete (v. 29; cf. esp. 1 John 1:4). But it is not until verses 31–36 that this language becomes pervasive. Once again, no further first-person pronouns appear, so that this final paragraph of the chapter should be understood as the words of the Fourth Evangelist and not those of the Baptist (Bruce 1983: 96). Now we can see what John's theology stresses and what his writing looks like when he is not constrained by reporting historical facts or the teachings of John and Jesus. In highly condensed prose, he reiterates issues of pre-existence, earthly and heavenly contrasts, the superiority of the man from heaven, testimony that is often rejected but when accepted certifies its truth, the

---

113] Alternately, both may have drawn independently on the rich reservoir of Old Testament wedding metaphors (on which see esp. Morris 1995: 213), or Jesus may first have heard John use the comparison (Witherington 1995: 109).

love of the Father for the Son, belief leading to eternal life, and rejection leading to God's abiding wrath. Indeed, in so generalizing, John introduces a formal tension between verse 32 ('no-one accepts his testimony') and verse 26 ('everyone is going to him'). But both are obvious exaggerations – the latter referring to reaction to Jesus in one locale early in his ministry; the former, to the response of a majority of humanity throughout time. Once again the situation-specific circumstances of material ascribed to first-century characters distinguish it from John's free theological summaries that reflect a more cosmic perspective.[114] Wholesale rejections of the historicity of an account about a period of time in which both John and Jesus baptized, even as Jesus increased in popularity at John's expense (e.g. Backhaus 1991: 263–264), are thus unjustified (rightly, Schnackenburg 1968: 411).

JESUS AND THE SAMARITAN WOMAN (4:1–42)

John 4:1–3 resumes the narrative where we last left Jesus, involved with his disciples in a ministry of baptism in the Judean countryside (3:22). By putting Jesus in the same category as John the Baptist, the Evangelist is probably drawing on 'ancient tradition, if not a historical fact, that the Synoptics have suppressed or ignored' (D. M. Smith 1999: 110). As in the Synoptics (Mark 3:6 pars.), early in Jesus' ministry the Pharisees prove hostile. The antagonism here is merely implicit, but it causes Jesus to leave the region, just as he will later leave Galilee in response to opposition there (Matt. 13:15; Mark 3:7; Luke 5:16). In this context, John offers a clarifying remark that Jesus did not personally baptize people; instead, his disciples acted as his agents (v. 2). This clarification scarcely deserves to be called a contradiction. Paul will insert a similar kind of caveat into his discussion in 1 Corinthians 1:14–17. Bruce (1983: 100) observes that 'he who acts through a duly appointed agent is the real author of the act performed'. But John 4:2 may suggest that John is editing a source here and does not feel free to omit altogether reference to Jesus' baptismal ministry. And, in keeping with his concern to avoid an overly sacramental theology (see above, p. 79), he qualifies his source's remarks. A redactor not constrained by traditional data could surely have written more smoothly (cf. Whitacre 1999: 94). The silence of the Synoptics concerning this ministry is explained by their omission of the entire period of time described in John 2:1 – 4:42. Nothing, even in John, suggests that this

---

114] Beasley-Murray (1987: 53) notes that v. 33 itself immediately demonstrates that v. 32 cannot be absolutized. Contra Wink (1968: 93–95). The other contradictions Wink finds in this material are treated elsewhere in this commentary.

baptizing lasted beyond a very initial stage of Jesus' public ministry (Morris 1995: 223, n. 6).

Verses 4–6 set the stage for the next major incident John narrates: a special encounter between Jesus and a Samaritan woman. That Jesus would travel through Samaria to go from Judea to Galilee was natural enough (*Ant.* 20.118). Sychar probably corresponds to modern-day Askar, while Jacob's well is one of the best-attested archaeological sites in Israel (Beasley-Murray 1987: 580). Jesus' fatigue and thirst are entirely natural, providing as 'human a picture of Jesus' presence at the well as possible' (Ridderbos 1997: 153).[115] This is not the nearest supply of fresh water to Askar, but it may have been better than what was locally available (Lindars 1972: 179). The arrival of the Samaritan woman at noon, however, may suggest that she was trying to avoid both the more normal times (in the cool of the evening) and places (closer to home) for drawing water, and thus to avoid other people who could remind her of her shameful sexual history.

Jesus' conversation with the woman spans verses 7–26. This material naturally subdivides into two sections, verses 7–15 and 16–26. Each section begins with a short, simple request from Jesus (vv. 7–8, 16), followed by the woman's reply (vv. 9, 17a). Then Jesus offers a surprising response (vv. 10, 17b–18), which the woman does not fully understand (vv. 11–12, 19–20). Next Jesus provides a fuller explanation (vv. 13–14, 21–24). This far the structure of these two sections closely parallels Jesus' discourse with Nicodemus (3:1–15), except that there Nicodemus took the initiative. The parallels nevertheless suggest a definable pattern of Jesus' interacting with these two individuals. Since this pattern does not recur in the later 'speeches' of Jesus in John, it is more likely historical than redactional. Here, additionally, the woman has one last comment in each case (vv. 15, 25), and Jesus has the last and climactic word in the entire dialogue (v. 26).[116]

Verse 7 begins naturally enough, with Jesus asking for a drink from the only person there, and who had a bucket with which to draw water from the well. Verse 8 explains why Jesus was alone with the woman and reminds the reader of his proposed solution in the Synoptics to another need for food (Mark 6:36 pars.). The woman correctly recognizes that Jesus'

115] For the fullest recent theological study of the humanity of Jesus in John, see Thompson 1988.

116] And unlike Nicodemus, the woman holds her own as an equal conversation partner with Jesus, one of numerous ways in which the two characters contrast with each other, with the portrait of Nicodemus proving surprisingly negative and the picture of the woman appearing surprisingly positive. See Blomberg 1995.

behaviour is radically counter-cultural (v. 9). Ancient sources amply document the hostility between Jews and Samaritans (e.g. Josephus, *War* 2.232; *Life* 269). If verse 9b is to be translated as in the NIV ('Jews do not associate with Samaritans'), it will have to be recognized as a relative rather than an absolute statement. But perhaps we are to follow the margin's alternative ('Jews do not use dishes Samaritans have used'; see esp. Daube 1956: 375–379). This translation finds historical corroboration at least as early as the Mishnah (see esp. *Sheb.* 8.10; on the uncleanness of Samaritans more generally, cf. *Nid.* 4.1). Jesus, however, eschews all such ritual distinctions. His refusal to be put off by his conversation partner because of her gender, ethnicity, and moral reputation meshes perfectly with that strand of the synoptic tradition almost universally acknowledged to be authentic – Jesus as a friend who eats with outcasts and notorious sinners (see esp. Mark 2:15–17 pars.; Luke 7:36–50; for Samaritans in particular, cf. Luke 10:29–37; 17:11–19).[117]

In contrast to the literal water he has requested, Jesus now offers the woman spiritual or 'living water' (v. 10). The metaphor finds ample Old Testament precedent (Ps. 36:9; Prov. 13:14; 18:4; Is. 55:1; Jer. 2:13; 17:13; Ezek. 47:1–12; Zech. 14:8), but the woman does not catch the allusion and refers instead to the biblical story surrounding Jacob's well (vv. 11–12). Witherington (1995: 120) perceives similarities to Martha's response to Jesus in Luke 10:38–42. Jesus echoes further Jewish traditions as he explains that this 'water' leads to eternal life (vv. 13–14; cf. Is. 44:3; 49:10; Sir. 24:21). But verse 15 shows that the woman is still thinking of literal thirst-quenching. That Jesus would have been steeped in the Hebrew Scriptures, while the Samaritan woman would have had little occasion formally to study them, makes this give and take entirely plausible. And there are various parallels with the synoptic story of the tenacity of the Syro-Phoenician woman, who also overcomes ethnic distinctions to receive her request from Jesus and to demonstrate great faith (Mark 7:24–30 par.).

In verses 16–18 Jesus redirects the conversation to the woman's marital background. Whatever his motives for doing so, he demonstrates the same kind of insight reflected in synoptic accounts of his 'supernatural knowledge' (cf. esp. Mark 11:2–3; 14:12–15 pars.). The woman replies that he must be a prophet (v. 19). Luke 7:39 likewise demonstrates popular belief that prophets would have insight into a person's character, again in the context of an encounter between Jesus and a disreputable woman. A

117] Neyrey (1994) demonstrates how the woman would have been seen as the consummate deviant by the social conventions of honour and shame in her day and how Jesus' behaviour matches his 'radical inclusivity' elsewhere.

prophet should also be able to settle the centuries-old debate between Jews and Samaritans concerning the proper place to build the temple – Mount Gerizim in Samaria or Mount Zion in Jerusalem (v. 20; on which see esp. Bull 1975, who includes relevant archaeological observations). But Jesus' reply (vv. 21–24) classically enshrines his 'already but not yet' theology of the arrival of the kingdom so pervasive in Matthew, Mark and Luke: 'a time is coming ... and now has come' when the location of worship will prove irrelevant, because the external cultus of the temple(s) will have passed away. One thinks, too, of Jesus' synoptic discourse on the Mount of Olives concerning the Jerusalem temple's coming destruction (Mark 13 pars.).

Verse 22 should be accepted as authentic even if one rejects the bulk of this account, precisely because it cuts against the grain of John's tendency to criticize the official Judaism of Jesus' day (contra, e.g. Bultmann 1971: 189–190, n. 6, who rejects it as a later gloss). Jesus' positive attitude to his Jewish heritage here is also in keeping with the 'ethnocentrism' of texts like Matthew 10:5–6 and 15:24. This passage should help give the lie to charges against John of anti-Semitism. As Stephen Motyer (1997: 213) observes, both the positive statement here about salvation coming from the Jews and the nuanced portrait of Nicodemus in John 3 'serve to unmask as a caricature the picture of unrelieved hostility often drawn' of the relationship between the Fourth Gospel and Judaism.

Still, Judaism will not remain unchanged. 'God is Spirit, and his worshippers must worship in spirit and in truth' (v. 24). It is possible that this second clause should be interpreted as 'in spirit, that is to say, in reality' (C. J. Collins 1995). Jesus is ushering in an age when corrupt external, ritual practices will give way to purified internal, moral emphases in keeping with the prophesied new covenant of the Hebrew Scriptures.

Whether or not we are to think of the Samaritan woman's 'prophet' of verse 19 as 'the eschatological prophet' of Deuteronomy 18:18, Jesus' claims clearly have her thinking about the coming Messiah. The Samaritans actually looked for a 'teacher', 'restorer' and 'converter' figure called the *Taheb*, but John has provided the dynamic equivalent translations in both Hebrew (transliterated) and Greek.[118] There seems to have been less of an emphasis on his role as a military or nationalistic Saviour in Samaritan thought, so the major incongruity of this passage *vis-à-vis* the Synoptics can actually be explained in a straightforward fashion. Jesus feels freer to reveal himself to the Samaritans as the Messiah than he

118] For the fullest presentation and discussion of the relevant texts from the (admittedly later) Samaritan literature on the *Taheb*, see Kippenberg (1971: 276–305); on the eschatological prophet like Moses, see esp. 306–327.

does to the Jews precisely because of their differing expectations that less radically diverged from Jesus' own self-understanding. Even in the Synoptics 'Jesus is far more likely to encourage public testimony of those who have experienced his transforming power if they live in Gentile territory (e.g. Lk. 8:26–39)' (Carson 1991: 227). It is also important to remember that, while the Synoptics seem to present a Christ who only gradually discloses himself over the course of his public ministry, even as early as his baptism lofty Christology is being predicated of him (see esp. Wright 1996: 536–537).

In verses 27–38 the Samaritan woman departs the scene and goes home, even as Jesus' disciples return from their errand. They marvel that he has been alone with a woman, engaged in conversation with her (v. 27a). Certainly rabbinic Judaism is replete with references that would confirm the potentially scandalous nature of this behaviour (Morris 1995: 242–243, n. 67), scruples it is easy to imagine would already have been in force in Jesus' day, given the conservative nature of ancient patriarchy more generally. But Jesus has already made enough of an impression on his first followers that they do not question him (v. 27b). The verb 'surprised' is literally 'marvelled' (from Gk. *thaumazō*) and reflects a common synoptic reaction to Jesus' ministry as well (e.g. Matt. 21:20; Mark 5:20; Luke 4:22).

Meanwhile, the woman returns to her village and naturally shares the story of her encounter with Jesus (v. 28), much like the reaction of the witnesses to the exorcism of the Gadarene demoniac in the Synoptics (Mark 5:14a pars.). John phrases the question that she poses with the Greek negative particle *mē*, suggesting she is still somewhat sceptical about Jesus' claims to be the Messiah (v. 29). A free creation by a later Christian writer would surely have omitted this hesitancy.[119] Again paralleling the response of the Gadarenes in the Synoptics (Mark 5:14b pars.), the townspeople come out to see Jesus for themselves (v. 30).

The disciples are understandably eager for him to eat some of the food they bought (v. 31). But, as with his discussion with the woman about water, Jesus redirects the conversation to the topic of spiritual nourishment (v. 32). Like the woman, at first the disciples do not understand (v. 33), so Jesus explains that his 'food' is 'to do the will of him who sent me and to finish his work' (v. 34). The contrast between two kinds of food closely parallels Jesus' teaching and the disciples' misunderstanding about bread

---

119] On the negative aspects of the woman's faith, see esp. Danna 1999. At the same time, her openness to the possibility of the truthfulness of this claim, 'by reason of his revelation of her past life is consonant with the Samaritans' understanding of the role of the "Taheb" as restorer and revealer of the truth' (Beasley-Murray 1987: 63).

after the feeding of the four thousand in Mark and Matthew (Mark 8:14–21 par.). As narrator, John is clearly contrasting the misunderstanding of the disciples with the growing understanding of the Samaritan woman (Cuvillier 1996; cf. Mark 7:24–30 par., with its similar contrast between the disciples and the Syro-Phoenician woman), an unflattering comparison not likely to have been invented by one of those very disciples. Metaphorical bread also appears in a key synoptic context in the temptation narratives (Matt. 4:4 par.).

Verse 34 introduces three key Johannine concepts: Christ's doing the will of the Father, as one who is sent, and completing his work; nevertheless, all three also find synoptic precedents. Mark 3:35 provides a crucial parallel to Jesus doing the will of God in the context of redefining who comprises his family. Matthew 10:40, Mark 9:37 and Luke 10:16 all offer close parallels to Jesus speaking about the one who sent him.[120] Luke 12:50 and 13:32 both use the verb *teleioō*, as here, for the completion of Jesus' task, even if John describes that task using one of his favourite words – *ergon* (work).[121]

Speaking of work leads Jesus to unpack verse 34 in the light of the metaphors of sowing and harvest (vv. 35–38). Verse 35a appears to quote a popular proverb. 'The existence of such a proverb cannot be proved, but it is not impossible,' comments Rudolf Schnackenburg (1968: 449). He continues, 'Even though six months were normally counted between sowing and harvest, the interval could also be given at four months, counting from the farmer's last sowing till the beginning of the harvest, that is, the shortest period of waiting between his labours.' That the fields are ripe for spiritual harvest (vv. 35b–36) calls to mind Jesus' imagery in Matthew 9:37–38 and Luke 10:2, along with the parables of the sower (Mark 4:13–20 pars.) and the labourers in the vineyard (Matt. 20:1–16). Verse 37 alludes to another saying of unknown origin, yet one finds partial parallels in sources as diverse as Joshua 24:13, Ecclesiastes 2:18–21 and Matthew 25:24 (cf. further Watson 1970). The contrast between one sowing and another reaping (v. 38) calls to mind Micah 6:15 and finds a close parallel in the principle Paul enunciates in 1 Corinthians 3:6. Dodd (1963: 405) determines that John is not directly dependent on the Synoptics in any of these verses, 'but he has nevertheless taken from the common tradition sayings which presuppose the mission, and so

---

120] Only John uses the verb *pempō* for this kind of sending. The Synoptics use *apostellō*, but there is no significant difference in meaning in these contexts.

121] For a detailed defence of the authenticity of John 4:34 virtually verbatim, see Ensor 1996: 135–149; 2000.

incidentally provides independent confirmation of the synoptic report that
Jesus did associate his disciples with his own work by sending them out to
carry his message to the public at large'.

Verses 39–42 complete this narrative by describing widespread belief on
the part of the Samaritan villagers. The woman has become an apostle to
her people, a detail not likely to have been invented in a highly patriarchal
world. Given that John's theology of signs blesses those who believe
without first-hand evidence (20:29), the need for these Samaritans to hear
the word directly from Jesus is not likely to have been invented. 'Saviour of
the world' does not recur elsewhere in the Fourth Gospel but does resemble
the claims made by the Roman emperors for themselves. Because the
Samaritans were as frustrated with Roman occupation as the Jews were,
they may deliberately have chosen a title for Jesus to show their preference
for Christ over Caesar (Cassidy 1992: 34–35; cf. Koester 1990).[122] For both
of these reasons, then, this title is probably authentic in this context.

But we must not overestimate the amount of belief implied in this story.
John speaks only of one Samaritan village. 'Many' of a probable population
of a few hundred need not have implied more than a couple of dozen
adults. And John will later describe 'believers' who do not persevere in their
commitment (esp. in ch. 8), so we really have no way of telling how many
of these followers proved faithful. Commentators who find a contradiction
here with the more widespread, apparently inaugural Samaritan mission of
Philip the deacon, in Acts 8:4–25, usually ignore these observations. As for
Jesus' later restrictions to ministry among the Jews (Matt. 10:5–6; 15:24),
these are situation-specific even within the Synoptics (contrast Mark 7:21
– 9:1 par.; Luke 9:51–56).[123] Once again Schnackenburg (1968: 420)
seems correct to conclude that there is 'no reason for doubting the
historicity of the narrative'.

HEALING AN OFFICIAL'S SON (4:43–54)

At John 4:42 we seem to have reached the end of the material in the Fourth
Gospel that chronologically preceded Christ's 'great Galilean ministry'. As
with the temple incident in 2:12–25, we next encounter a passage that
closely resembles a synoptic episode (Matt. 8:5–13; Luke 7:1–10), yet with
just enough differences to make traditional commentators unsure as to

---

122] Talbert (1992: 40–42) also cites key passages in Josephus that describe towns
welcoming emperors, which provide partial parallels to the welcome given Jesus here.

123] For both of these charges, see Lindars 1972: 175. For a rebuttal of these and related
charges and a fuller defence of the authenticity of the episode in general, see Okure 1988:
188–191.

whether we are dealing with a variant account of the same healing or with a separate event altogether. This time, however, the synoptic and Johannine narratives are placed in compatible time periods: at the beginning of Jesus' public ministry in Galilee. Most commentators agree that John's account is literarily independent of the versions in Matthew and Luke; many imagine John to have relied on his putative signs-source here (Landis 1994).[124] There are not even two significant, consecutive Greek words parallel between John and either Matthew or Luke in this pericope. Only the words 'Capernaum', 'asked', and 'about to' utilize the same roots, while 'die' appears in both accounts via synonyms. That is the entire extent of the verbal parallelism. Curiously, though, there is greater diversity of opinion as to whether we are dealing with one or two incidents here than with the temple clearing,[125] even though the variant accounts are easier to harmonize.[126]

Verses 43–45 introduce this second miracle story in the Fourth Gospel. After two days of 'follow-up' ministry among the fledgling Samaritan 'converts', Jesus completes his trip to Galilee (v. 43). Verse 44 intrudes as an awkward parenthetical observation by the narrator. It closely parallels a proverb Jesus himself uses in the Synoptics (Mark 6:4 pars.). But there the homeland in which Jesus is dishonoured is Galilee, and even more narrowly the village of Nazareth. While there have been numerous attempts to make that understanding of the proverb fit here in John (most recently see van Belle 1998), it is better to recognize that in the Fourth Gospel, Jesus' 'own country' is all of Israel, with the official opposition from Jerusalem most central. Proverbs can be applied in numerous ways in different contexts, so there is no 'contradiction' in John using it to explain Jesus' withdrawal from Judea to Galilee (cf. Moloney 1998: 152; D. M. Smith 1999: 122). The Synoptics also know that Jesus originally commanded widespread support (cf. v. 45 here), even in his home town of Nazareth (Luke 4:15), although it would soon dissipate.

John 4:46a creates an inclusio with 2:1. The miracle of the wine and the healing of the official's son are the only two events any Gospel associates

---

124] For a dissenting argument in favour of direct dependence on the Synoptics, see Neirynck 1995.

125] Sample proponents of two different events include Bruce (1983: 117); Michaels (1983: 65); Carson (1991: 234); Morris (1995: 254–255); and Ridderbos (1997: 174–175). In favour of the same event are Dodd (1963: 188–195); Schnackenburg (1968: 471); Bultmann (1971: 204–205); Lindars (1972: 198–199); and Meier (1994: 718–726).

126] For a detailed presentation of the major approaches to each of the apparent discrepancies, see Siegman 1968.

with Cana. The device is clearly literary, employed to call attention to this material as a theologically homogeneous unit. John 2 – 4 stresses the newness of what Jesus is bringing: a new joy, a new temple, a new birth and a new universal offer of salvation (cf. further Blomberg 1997: 224–230). Verses 46b–53 can then be seen as occurring in Capernaum, as in the synoptic versions, even though it is not John's concern to clarify this. The 'royal official' (v. 46b; Gk. *basilikos*) could be either Jewish or Gentile,[127] but in conjunction with the story of the Samaritan woman we are probably meant to view him as a Gentile. A. H. Mead (1985) provides evidence for taking the term to refer to a Roman commander of auxiliary troops, thus entirely compatible with Matthew's and Luke's 'centurion'. John calls the sick boy both 'son' and 'servant' (vv. 46b, 49, obscured by the NIV's 'child' in the latter text), thus inadvertently harmonizing his account with the references to a servant in the 'Q' passage. Verse 47 contains material that matches both Luke (the boy is at the point of death; cf. Luke 7:2) and Matthew (the man is described as speaking directly to Jesus; cf. Matt. 8:6). The tensions between Matthew and Luke at this point are best explained by assuming that the terrible distress of the boy implies an illness on top of his paralysis (cf. the 'fever' of John 4:52) and that the Jewish intermediaries Luke describes (Luke 7:3) are the explicit agents by which the centurion initially communicates with Christ (Blomberg 1987: 134).

Verse 48 contains the most obvious Johannine emphasis in the Fourth Gospel's version – Jesus berating a faith based merely on miracles. From reading only certain English translations, this might appear flatly to contradict the synoptic, and especially Matthean, emphasis on praising the faith of the official (Matt. 8:10–12). But the verbs in the Greek are second-person plural: 'Unless you people see … you [pl.] will never believe.' If indeed Jewish elders did initially appeal to Jesus on behalf of a Gentile centurion, it would be natural for Jesus to use this occasion once again to criticize their unstated motives. And because the rebuke of a purely signs-based faith forms John's major emphasis, he first passes over the more exemplary faith of the official in relative silence.[128] Still, the requests of verses 47 and 49, even after Jesus' rebuke, presuppose considerable confidence in Christ. And Jesus does perform the miracle, which suggests the presence of belief beyond the scepticism of the Jewish leaders.[129] John

---

127] See Wegner (1985: 57–72) for detailed documentation of both possibilities.

128] The Synoptics agree with John that requests for miracles designed merely to satisfy scepticism are inappropriate (Matt. 16:4; Mark 9:19). Jesus can also berate Galilean cities for not having responded in belief to his signs and wonders (Matt. 11:20–24).

129] For this whole approach to this passage, see esp. Whitacre 1999: 115–116.

then explicitly mentions the officer's faith (v. 50). Verses 51–53 stress what Matthew 8:13 treats much more briefly – that the boy was healed at a distance at the very moment Jesus spoke the word. That saying – literally, 'your son lives' (vv. 50, 53) – also closely parallels Elijah's promise to the widow of Zarephath in 1 Kings 17:23. Verse 54 concludes the episode, highlighting John's focus on the true nature of the miracle as a 'sign', that is, designed to generate more mature, genuine faith in Jesus.

Whether or not we take John's healing story here as the same event as the one recounted in Matthew and Luke, arguments for its authenticity appear. If these are separate events, and one accepts the authenticity of the synoptic incident,[130] then the striking similarities between the two events support the historicity of the Johannine episode. If they are variant accounts of the same event, as I have tentatively favoured, then on the one hand we have a good example of the freedom that John felt to bring out different details and emphases in stories already commonly known from early Christian oral tradition, if not from the final form of the Synoptics themselves. This measure of freedom will recur in subsequent passages in John that are demonstrably describing the same events as their synoptic counterparts. Indeed, in this case, the dissimilarity between Matthew and Luke is at least as great as that between John and either Matthew or Luke. On the other hand, scrutiny of a synopsis also demonstrates that there are no necessary contradictions among the variant accounts. This conclusion should inspire confidence that, in the majority of Johannine pericopae for which we have no synoptic parallels to use for comparison, John is not freely inventing 'history' incompatible with the actual words and deeds of the historical Jesus.[131]

130] Or at least of a fundamental core of that incident, on which see Wegner 1985: 408–428; Latourelle 1988: 132–139; and Twelftree 1999: 296.

131] On either approach, it is also interesting to note a close conceptual parallel in the later rabbinic literature (*b. Ber.* 34b). Hanina ben Dosa, a charismatic Jewish miracle-worker after the time of Christ, is said to have healed the son of Gamaliel II at a distance by praying to God and then simply speaking a word of healing, at which time the boy was instantaneously cured. The episode is too late to account for the origin of the biblical story, but the way in which it was narrated may suggest a specific rhetorical form in which such healings were couched. If this form influenced John and either Matthew or Luke, or the traditions they inherited, one could further explain the similarities between the otherwise literarily independent accounts by the use of this stylized and perhaps even standardized form.

HEALING THE INVALID BY THE BETHESDA POOL (5:1–18)

Here appears the first of several literary seams that led Bultmann (1971) frequently to rearrange the order of John's text so as to create what he thought was a more coherent narrative flow. But commentators today have largely and rightly abandoned this approach.[132] From chapters 5 to 11 John is concerned primarily to add material not found in the Synoptics, associated with Jesus' numerous trips to Jerusalem at the time of the various annual festivals. John passes over whatever other ministry Jesus performed in Galilee after the healing of 4:43–54 and describes him going 'up' to Jerusalem for an unnamed feast (5:1). The description is accurate because pilgrims ended their journey climbing the ascent to Mount Zion, irrespective of the direction from which they came.

It is also exactly what we should expect, that Jesus, a faithful Jew, should join the Galilean throngs in Jerusalem during the various festivals mandated by the Mosaic Law (Fredriksen 1999: 239). Nothing in either John or the Synoptics suggests that Jesus ever violated the written Law; his conflicts revolved around 'oral Torah' (cf. esp. Westerholm 1978). We are not told which feast this is. The most common suggestions have been Tabernacles or Passover in AD 28, but apparently John does not think we need to know. Most of the episodes in chapters 5 – 11 will relate to Jesus fulfilling the true intention of one of the annual festivals of Israel, but in 5:1–18 the focus is on the weekly celebration of Sabbath (cf. Moloney 1998:167).

Commentators have often divided the account of the miracle in two (vv. 2–9a, 9b–15; most recently see Labahn 1998),[133] thinking that the latter half was an add-on in that nothing about the Sabbath appears in the first half. But John as narrator elsewhere reserves information about time and place for the end of a pericope (most notably in 6:59), each 'half' of the story is less meaningful without the other, and healings on the Sabbath are frequently attested in the synoptic tradition (Mark 1:21–29 pars.; 3:1–6 pars; Luke 13:10–17; 14:1–6). The text should be allowed to stand as John presents it (cf. further Latourelle 1988: 218–222; Ensor 1996: 166–170).[134] There is also general agreement (contra Lindars 1972: 209) that this is a separate event from the healing of the paralytic described in

---

132] See Ridderbos (1997: 183) for a good discussion of the logical and chronological flow of thought from chapters 4 to 7 as they currently stand.

133] For more complex tradition-critical dissection, cf. Witkamp 1985.

134] Thatcher (1999) identifies as deliberately ironic John's withholding information about healings occurring on a Sabbath here and in ch. 9.

Mark 2:1–12 and parallels: among other things, the settings are entirely different.

Nevertheless, there are striking similarities between the two passages that support the authenticity of the Johannine story. In each case Jesus heals an invalid, afflicted at least in part because of some sin, in a deliberately provocative way that ensures the Jewish leaders will charge him with blasphemy. Most notably, Jesus' command in John 5:8 ('Get up! Pick up your mat and walk.') matches Mark 2:9 verbatim in the Greek (minus a *kai* – 'and'). Given the number of sick people in Jesus' world, we should not be surprised to find him healing people with similar maladies in similar ways.[135] I shall now comment on other details in the passage in sequence.

John 5:2 was dramatically corroborated by archaeological discoveries in the 1890s, as the site of the pool of Bethesda was located in Jerusalem. Reconstruction showed how two juxtaposed rectangular enclosures would have created five porticoes (NIV 'covered colonnades') – the four sides forming the perimeter of the entire area combined with the dividing wall down the middle.[136] Identification of the name of the site was later made possible by the reference in the Copper Scroll from Qumran (column 11, line 12) to *Bet ešdataîn*. The Sheep Gate was the name of one of the entry points into the walled-in city, attested as early as Nehemiah 3:1 and 12:39. The four categories of people lying around the pool (v. 3) precisely match categories of the sick that Jesus regularly encounters and heals in the Synoptics. Isaiah 35:6 may well lie in the background, which includes among the signs of the Messianic age the promise that 'then will the lame leap like a deer'. After AD 135 the pool was used by Roman cults as a pagan healing sanctuary, sacred to the god Asclepius, making plausible that even in Jesus' day among the more unorthodox similar superstitions might have been in vogue (Michaels 1983: 72; cf. the later textual variant that

---

135] Meier (1994: 680–681) proves more pointed: 'It hardly strains credulity [sic.] to suppose that during Jesus' ministry there was more than one person in Palestine suffering from some form of bodily paralysis. In fact, if one holds that Jesus' ministry lasted for more than one year and that – as most religiously inclined Palestinian Jews would – Jesus regularly went up to Jerusalem for the great pilgrimage feasts, one would be surprised if the famed miracle-worker from Nazareth performed no miracles in and around the Holy City.'

136] There is general agreement that the twin pools of St Anne's are on or near the correct site of first-century Bethesda, though a few have disputed whether they form the structure John describes or whether he has in mind a number of nearby small grottoes, complete with washing basins (Morris 1995: 267, n. 13). Less probable are the suggestions of Boismard (1999) and Devillers (1999) that a previous version of this account referred to the pool of Siloam rather than to Bethesda.

comprises vv. 3b–4 and v. 7). That this man had been suffering for thirty-eight years (v. 5) corresponds to synoptic passages in which we are given the length of an illness or disorder (e.g. Mark 5:25; Luke 13:11).

Jesus now addresses the man he is about to heal (v. 6). The question 'Do you *want* to get well?' uses the same verb (*thelō*) employed in the leper's comment to Jesus in Mark 1:40 – 'If you are *willing*, you can make me clean.' As in the majority of the synoptic healings, the cure comes instantaneously when Jesus speaks the word (vv. 8–9). The ensuing controversy stems from Jewish Sabbath laws already in place in Jesus' day. Conceivably, even Old Testament prohibitions against carrying a load on the Sabbath (Jer. 17:21; cf. Neh. 13:15) could be seen to have been violated, though it is not clear that one's own mat (vv. 10–11) necessarily constituted a 'load'. Nevertheless, later more petty Sabbath restrictions (see, classically, *Shab.* 7.2; cf. 10.1–5, 11.1–2) had already begun to form part of the oral laws that Jesus regularly combated (see *Jub.* 2.25–30; 50.6–13; cf. also Thomas 1991b: 169–172). The Jewish leaders would have reasoned that if the man had been disabled for so long, one more day until the Sabbath was past could hardly have mattered. Jesus obviously had deliberately chosen this timing for his miracle to provoke additional controversy (Witherington 1995: 134).

'The Jews' – as often in John a shorthand for 'key Jewish leaders' – understandably inquire about who commanded the man to carry his mat, but he cannot tell them (vv. 12–13). When he does find out, he reports simply that it was Jesus (v. 15). Free invention by a later Christian hand would surely have put loftier titles into the man's mouth or used this climax of the miracle story as an opportunity for the man to testify more explicitly on behalf of Christ. Instead, we read only that Jesus charged the man to 'stop sinning or something worse may happen to you' (v. 14). Here Christ mirrors the common Jewish theology of the 'Deuteronomistic historian' that the man's suffering was a punishment for sin. That is not the only explanation for illness in the Old Testament, and in John 9 Jesus will make quite different pronouncements concerning a man blind from birth. But it is one explanation that Christians have alternately ignored or abused throughout church history, and one that is entirely conceivable as part of the teaching of Jesus the Jew.[137]

Verses 16–18 are best taken as the conclusion to this miracle story. Verse 17 contains a climactic declaration that makes verses 1–18 not only a healing miracle but also a pronouncement story, exactly as in Mark 2:1–12. At the same time, verses 16–18 prepare the way for the lengthy discourse

---

137] For a balanced approach to the theological implications, see Thomas 1995.

that occupies the rest of John 5. The structure of verses 19–47 sets that section off from this earlier material (see below, p. 113). As the aftermath of the miracle, the authorities begin to persecute Jesus (v. 16), seeking an opportunity to kill him (v. 18a). One recalls the Pharisaic plot against Jesus' life mentioned early in the synoptic chronology (Mark 3:6). But instead of calming his critics, Jesus troubles the waters further by claiming, 'My Father is always at his work to this very day, and I, too, am working' (v. 17). John regularly refers to Jesus' ministry as his 'work', but a strong case can also be made for the authenticity of this saying. Already in the first century, rabbis were discussing how God could constantly work and yet not violate the Sabbath (e.g. Philo, *Cherub.* 87–90; *Ep. Arist.* 210), making probable that similar discussions in later sources reflect earlier conversations as well (esp. *Gen. R.* 11.10; cf. *Exod. R.* 30.9). Behind this discussion 'is the rabbinic awareness that since people are born and die on the Sabbath, God cannot be said to be idle on any day, for the gift of life and the work of judgment are divine prerogatives' (Pryor 1992a: 26–27).[138]

At first glance, verse 18b comprises that portion of this text that least fits into an early first-century Jewish milieu. In fact, it seems to be incompatible with Jewish monotheism altogether. On closer inspection, this proves not to be the case. 'Calling God his own Father' in a uniquely intimate sense corresponds to Mark's portrayal of Jesus addressing God as *Abba* (Mark 14:36). But if God is Jesus' Father, then Jesus is God's Son, a title that could be used in Judaism simply as a synonym for Messiah (see above, p. 80). To the extent that Jesus has already been acknowledged as the Messiah in the titles scattered about the second half of John 1, then we may follow the logic of J. C. O'Neill (1995: 54–55):

> Jesus is not being charged with being equal with God in all respects but with making himself equal with God in the one respect, in respect of claiming that he was the Messiah. That was a prerogative that the Father had reserved to himself. The Father, it was assumed, did have a Son, the Messiah. Human beings were allowed to speculate about whether John the Baptist or Jesus was that Messiah, but no human being was allowed to say that he was himself the Messiah. To do so would be to usurp the Father's prerogative and to arrogate to oneself equality with the Father in a prohibited respect.

With Darrell Bock (1998: 25), we may need to add that it was not merely because Jesus 'dared to make a messianic claim, when he needed to

---

138] For a detailed defence of authenticity, see Ensor 1996: 170–184.

be silent, but because his messianic claim was perceived for clear reasons to be false and risky' (cf. *Sanh.* 11.5). But this is still a kind of equality with God that stops well short of later Christian reflection about the second person of the Trinity, which did clearly transcend the boundaries of Jewish monotheism. The Fourth Evangelist, of course, sees a fuller sense of divine Sonship in Jesus as he writes at the end of the first century. But the account as it stands is also fully intelligible within Jesus' world some sixty years earlier.[139]

THE SON'S TESTIMONY (5:19–47)

The charge against Jesus leads him to reply with an uninterrupted discourse that occupies the rest of John 5. In fact, it is the only discourse of Jesus in the Fourth Gospel that is completely without interruption, notwithstanding common scholarly references to seven major sermons or discourses in chapters 2 – 11 alone. The passage falls logically into two parts. In verses 19–30 Jesus explains that as the divine Son he is merely imitating his Father; in verses 31–47 he provides corroborating testimony to the truth of his claims.[140] Neither the contents nor the form of the passage has exact parallels in the synoptic tradition, although Jesus does of course speak in extended 'sermons' at five key points in Matthew's narrative (chs. 5 – 7, 10, 13, 18 and 23 – 25). But those passages are regularly assumed to be composite; at least they break down into smaller, more numerous definable subunits than does John 5:19–47. On the other hand, as noted in my introduction (see above, p. 52), even the lengthier discourses in the Synoptics seem artificially short for what a popular teacher would say on a given public occasion: they may well be stylized abridgments of longer originals. This observation suggests that discourses like those in John, though perhaps equally stylized and abbreviated, may to some degree correspond more closely to the fuller details Jesus' original speeches would have contained.

John 5:19–30 forms a neat and elaborate chiasmus. Verses 19–20a and 30 articulate the thesis of this section, that the Son does only what he sees or hears the Father doing. In each case a subordinate clause gives part of

---

139] For more detail on the authenticity of vv. 1–18 overall, see Latourelle 1988: 222–223; Twelftree 1999: 297–298; and Meier 1994: 680–681.

140] Burge (2000: 179–180) separates off vv. 41–47 as a subsection in which Jesus prosecutes his opponents, figuratively speaking. 'This was not unusual in Jewish courts. Unlike today, defendants did not simply prove their innocence and thus end the trial. Jewish trials worked to uncover the truth, and accusers who made false claims in court could find themselves placed in the defense and subject to serious jeopardy.'

the rationale for this principle of imitation. Verses 20b and 28–29 present right and wrong ways to 'marvel' (NIV 'be amazed'; Gk. *thaumazō*). Verses 21–22 and 26–27a supply a pair of illustrations about life and judgment introduced with 'for just as' (Gk. *hōsper gar*) and 'so also' (Gk. *houtōs kai*) clauses. Verse 23 unpacks verses 21–22 with a further purpose clause; verse 27b offers an additional reason for verses 26–27a. Verses 24–25 thus form the climactic centre of the chiasmus with statements about salvation, each introduced with the solemn double-'Amen' formula (cf. Vanhoye 1970). In chart form, this yields:

Principle of imitation + rationale (vv. 19–20a)   (v. 30)
    Teaching about 'marvelling'   (v. 20b)   (vv. 28–29)
        Illustrations of life/judgment   (vv. 21–23)   (vv. 26–27)
            + purpose or reason
                Double-'Amen' saying on salvation (v. 24)   (v. 25)

Is this tightly knit unity traditional or redactional? If we accept the likelihood of the double-'Amen' sayings as reflecting substantially authentic teachings of Jesus, we could view verses 19–20a and 24–25 as the historical scaffolding on which the larger structure of this sermon was subsequently built (Lindars 1972: 221, 224). Proceeding through the remaining material sequentially, it could be argued that verses 21–23 are John's commentary on Jesus' words, just as we saw him append his own reflections to the words of Jesus and the Baptist in chapter 3. Nothing in these three verses is phrased in the first or second person to suggest that Jesus is still addressing his original audience. The same is true of verse 26. On the other hand, verse 27 contains the title 'Son of Man' that seems to be reserved for Jesus' own use, while verses 28–30 do contain second and first person language. So while it is surely possible that an editor combined disparate materials to compose the tidy chiastic structure of verses 19–30, it is certainly easier to argue that such unity was present from the outset. We should then be inclined to ascribe the entire passage to the historical Jesus.

But what of the contents of these verses? Do they sufficiently resemble synoptic material for us to consider them authentic? Clearly the themes of the relationship between the Father and the Son, eternal life and judgment, and the realized eschatology of this passage stamp it as thoroughly Johannine in both concepts and vocabulary. But 'redactional' and 'historical' are not mutually exclusive categories. There is in fact significant evidence that the ideas in this discourse, however they may have been rephrased, do go back to Jesus himself. Jesus has just been accused of wrongfully calling God his Father, so it is natural for his discourse to begin with the affirmation that he is nothing but an obedient Son (v. 19).[141] Verses 19–20a have often been viewed as a proverb or short parable that may originally have referred to any apprentice learning from his master, as sons regularly learned their trades from their fathers (see, e.g. Dodd 1963: 386, n. 2). And of course the Synoptics demonstrate that the heart of Jesus' teaching, recognized as authentic even by most critical scholars, involved speaking in parables (cf. further Blomberg 1990).[142]

Verses 21–22 refer to two major 'works' that Jews recognized God continued to perform on the Sabbath – giving life (as children were born) and exercising judgment (as people died).[143] As frequently in the Synoptics, Jesus associates himself with activity often reserved in the Old Testament for God, without making direct or explicit Christological claims.[144] The language of honouring and dishonouring the Father through the Son (v. 23) closely resembles Synoptic texts like Matthew 10:40, 18:5 and Mark 9:37.[145] Verse 24 may be the strongest statement of realized eschatology in the New Testament: eternal life and death begin in this life with the choices one makes with respect to Jesus. As such, the theology is distinctively Johannine. Yet the parable of the two builders in the Sermon on the Mount/Plain declares equally firmly that judgment, which cannot be limited to the future, is based on one's response to 'hearing Jesus' words'

141] McGrath (1998) understands the transition as follows: Jesus has in essence been accused of being a rebellious son because he equates himself with his Father. Jesus denies the charge by arguing that only if he did not do what his Father commanded would he be rebellious. The context is thoroughly Jewish; see Deut. 21:18 as developed in Sir. 3:6–16 and Philo, *Dec.* 118.

142] For a detailed defence of the authenticity of verses 19–20, see Ensor 1996: 201–216. Köstenberger (1999: 97) notes that Jesus' apprenticeship analogy 'may well be rooted in Jesus' own earthly experience of learning the trade of carpentry from his adoptive father Joseph'.

143] See Moloney (1998: 178–179), who also includes a detailed listing of Old Testament texts that generated this consensus understanding.

144] In the parables alone, one finds Jesus indirectly likening himself to the bridegroom, rock, director of the harvest, sower, shepherd, father, giver of forgiveness, vineyard owner and king. See further Payne 1981.

145] On the language about Son and Father in this passage more generally, Michaels (1983: 74) remarks, 'the kinship of Son with Son of Man and the firm testimony of John's gospel that Jesus was actually accused of claiming divine sonship (5:18; 10:33–36) make it more likely that language of this kind goes back to Jesus (cf. Matt. 11:27/Luke 10:22; also the voice at Jesus' baptism in the Synoptics and Jesus' address to God in prayer as "Abba," or "Father")'.

(Matt. 7:24–27; Luke 6:47–49; cf. Barrett 1978: 261). And verses 25–27 immediately balance out Jesus' realized eschatology with a recognition that much judgment and reward still does lie in the future. The exact phrase already used in John 4:23 recurs here in 5:25 ('a time is coming and has now come') to capture the 'already but not yet' sense of the 'presence of the future', so central to the Synoptics.

Verse 27 supplies a third eschatological or apocalyptic 'Son of Man' saying in John, again congruent with numerous similar synoptic uses, most notably Mark 8:38 and Luke 12:8–9 (Beasley-Murray 1987: 77). Links between the Son of Man and judgment also proliferate in *1 Enoch* (esp. 49.4; 61.9; 62.2–3; cf. Talbert 1992: 125). The reference to the coming bodily resurrection of just and unjust (vv. 28–29) finds its clearest Old Testament parallel in Daniel 12:2. Numerous intertestamental texts further developed this belief (see esp. Schnackenburg 1968: 106). In the Synoptics, one thinks especially of the enigmatic little story of the resurrection of certain saints in conjunction with Jesus' resurrection (Matt. 27:52–53). And 'the importance of human action as a litmus test of human commitment is a frequent message of the New Testament'. In the Synoptics one immediately recalls the 'parable' of the sheep and goats (Matt. 25:31–46; Borchert 1996: 242).[146]

Pryor (1992a: 27–28) rightly concludes that the significance of such a catalogue of parallels 'for the credibility of John's presentation is enormous. He is no theologian whose christological presentation emerges *ex nihilo*, but he works with and meditates upon authentic gospel traditions'. The idiom may be Johannine, but the concepts are thoroughly consistent with the synoptic portraits of the historical Jesus. In fact, the double similarity and dissimilarity criterion works well again here. Everything attributed to God in John 5:19–30 was commonplace in Judaism, yet Jesus' implicit association of himself with these divine functions proved scandalous. On the other hand, the overall emphasis in the text is on Christ's subordination to his Father (see esp. Keener 1999), rather than on the equality with God that became the preoccupation of early Christianity in general and of patristic exegesis of this passage in particular (Ensor 1996: 212–213, 222–225). It is not at all clear, then, that John should be accused of arbitrarily imposing later developments in Christian theology on to his historical narrative at this point.

John 5:31–47 turns to supporting testimony that substantiates Jesus' claims. Verses 31–32 introduce the need for independent witness. The rest

---

146] Dahl (1990) helpfully analyses the 'how much more' or 'from the light to the heavy' logic of John 5:28–29, a characteristic rabbinic hermeneutic.

of the chapter offers, in turn, the witness of John (vv. 33–35), of Jesus' work (v. 36), of the Father (vv. 37–38) and of the Scriptures (vv. 39–46).[147] The structure is not as seamless as in vv. 19–30, and it appears that the Fourth Evangelist may have put more of his own distinctive stamp on this material (cf. esp. von Wahlde 1981). The theme of witness, of course, is deeply embedded in Jewish tradition (cf. esp. 1QS 8:6), as are John's prophetic and forensic concerns more generally (Harvey 1977; Lincoln 2000). In fact, the very need for witness stems ultimately from the requirement of Deuteronomy 19:15 that 'a matter must be established by the testimony of two or three witnesses'.

Jesus begins by acknowledging the illegitimacy of self-witness (v. 31; cf. *Ket.* 2.9). Indeed, first-century rabbis agreed that in certain non-capital cases one could testify for oneself (*Yeb.* 15.1–2; *Ket.* 1.6–9; cf. Thomas 1991b: 174–177). But Jesus does not risk leaving it at that. The subordinationist nature of verse 31 speaks for its authenticity; later Christians would probably have affirmed that Jesus' own witness was indeed adequate. Verse 32 euphemistically alludes to the supporting testimony of the Father (Ridderbos 1997: 202), which will become explicit in verses 37–38. Likewise, God as witness appears throughout Isaiah 42 – 44 and in Wisdom of Solomon 1:6. Verses 33–35 hark back to the testimony of the Baptist in chapters 1 and 3, especially to the sending of the embassy to interrogate John (1:19). Verse 34a reminds the reader of 2:24–25, while verse 34b uses the verb 'save' (Gk. *sōzō*) for the first time in this Gospel in speech attributed to Jesus. One thinks of its prominence in Luke, especially in Jesus' summary statement that 'the Son of Man came to seek and to save what was lost' (Luke 19:10). That 'John was a lamp that burned and gave light' (v. 35a) runs parallel to Jesus' declaration in the Sermon on the Mount that his disciples were 'the light of the world' (Matt. 5:14). The Jews in general were quite attracted to John (v. 35b; cf. Mark 11:32, Josephus, *Ant.* 18.116–119). One thinks again of Matthew 11:11–12: John was greater than all who were born before Jesus, but one even greater is now present.

Still weightier testimony is to be found in Jesus' work (v. 36). This verse uses the language of 4:34, which we saw was probably authentic (cf. Ensor 1996: 222–232, 261). The witness of the Father (vv. 37–38) alludes first of all to the testimony at Jesus' baptism and provides another example of 'interlocking' with the Synoptics (cf. above, pp. 53–54). 'The readers of the

---

147] Alternately, the witness of the Father may be seen as unifying this entire section. The Father's witness, then, is manifested through John, Jesus' works (some would add 'and words'), and the Scriptures (cf., e.g. Whitacre 1999: 136).

Gospel were presumably sufficiently familiar with the story of Jesus' baptism by John to be able to fill in these details for themselves' (Bruce 1983: 136). That the Jewish leaders had never heard God's voice or seen his form (v. 37) contrasts with the experiences of Moses (Exod. 33:11) and Jacob (Gen. 32:30–31), respectively (Morris 1995: 291), who were viewed by these leaders as among their founding fathers. That God's word does not dwell in them (v. 38; from Gk. *menō* –'remain') illustrates Jesus' teaching in the parable of the sower about the seed that fell on rocky ground (Mark 4:5, 16 pars.).

Perhaps most pointedly of all, Jesus challenges their ability to read and understand the Scriptures. Verse 39 refers to the characteristic rabbinic activity of Torah-study. The Greek for 'diligently study' (*eraunaō*) corresponds to the Hebrew *dāraš* (Barrett 1978: 267), from which the concept of 'midrash' or Scripture commentary is derived. Audaciously, Jesus declares that these same Scriptures testify about him. This is the identical claim, made explicit, that resides implicitly in Matthew 5:17. He will later offer specific examples of how the Old Testament is fulfilled in him in Mark 12:10, 35–37 and parallels (R. E. Brown 1966: 228). The leaders' refusal to come to Christ (v. 40) recalls Jesus' plaintive lament in Luke 13:34 about how he longed to gather Israel together 'but you were not willing'.

In verse 41 Jesus repeats the point of verse 34. In verse 42 he charges his opponents of not having God's love in them, the very key, according to the Synoptics, to obeying the Law (Mark 12:28–34 par.). Verse 43a reiterates Jesus' dependence on the Father, again stressing his subordination. Verse 43b alludes to the numerous self-proclaimed first-century prophets and messiahs, about which Josephus writes so much (see esp. Horsley and Hanson 1985). The rest of the passage (vv. 44–47) sharply criticizes how these leaders reject Jesus while thinking they are pleasing God. The closest synoptic parallels are Jesus' lengthy woes in Matthew 23:1–36. If they were really following Torah, they would recognize Jesus for who he is. 'Moses as accuser' resembles Jewish teaching elsewhere about his intercessory role (see esp. *Test. Mos.* 11.17; 12.6; and *Jub.* 1.19–21; cf. Schnackenburg 1968: 129). The ironic conclusion to Jesus' parable of the rich man and Lazarus resounds in the background: 'If they do not listen to Moses and the Prophets, they will not be convinced even if someone rises from the dead' (Luke 16:31).

In the light of all these parallels, Barrett (1978: 258–259) understandably concludes:

> The whole passage ... is an independent rewriting, lit up by acute theological insight, of the historical situation disclosed by the earlier

gospel tradition. The Son of man did fulfil his vocation in obedience, obscurity and suffering (e.g. Mark 10.45) and came to his death in the midst of Jewish unbelief. The messiah was rejected; his ministry separated men into two groups (Mark 4.11f). John, employing in this chapter primitive Christian rather than any other terminology, and starting from the well-known fact of Sabbath disputes, hardly does more than develop, with attention to the question of Christology and the phenomenon of unbelieving Judaism, the historical situation to which the work of Jesus gave rise.

Or, with George Beasley-Murray (1987: 80), speaking of 4:43 – 5:47 more generally:

Every aspect of this Christology and Eschatology is foreshadowed in the synoptic Gospels (e.g. Matt 11:27//Luke 10:22; Mark 13:32; Luke 22:29; Mark 8:38 with its Q parallel; Luke 12:8–9; Matt 10:32–33; Matt 25:31–46). But what for the latter is latent is for the Evangelist patent: Christology is the root of eschatology; eschatology is outworking of the Christology of the only Son of the Father.

In short, while we may not have quite as literal a rendering of Jesus' words in John 5:31–47 as we have had for the most part thus far in the Fourth Gospel, and while there may be a composite nature to this material, John is scarcely indulging in free invention. All of the thoughts and concepts fit what we know from the Synoptics about the historical Jesus during his earthly ministry.

FEEDING THE FIVE THOUSAND (6:1–15)

Here we come for the first time since chapter 1 to an entire passage that has undisputed parallels in the Synoptic Gospels, indeed in all three of them (Mark 6:32–44 pars.). John 6 in fact contains an interesting series of parallels, some merely conceptual, to a sequence of events that spans Mark 6 – 8: the feeding of the five thousand, walking on the water, a request for a sign, discourse about bread, Peter's confession, and Jesus' anticipation of the passion (for details, see R. E. Brown 1966: 238).[148] Still, it is unlikely that we are to think of literary dependence here. Only isolated words appear the same in the Greek of John *vis-à-vis* the Synoptics and then

---

148] Likewise there are striking parallels between John 6 and Numbers 11 with the identical sequences of people grumbling, bread in the wilderness, flesh to eat, and a question about gathering the fish of the sea (R. E. Brown 1966: 233).

seldom in identical inflectional forms. These are words without which the story could hardly have been told: a large crowd, following, buying, eating, five loaves of bread, two fish, blessing, and the distribution. The references to 200 denarii not being adequate to supply food for the crowds and to twelve baskets of leftovers being gathered reflect the type of details that would readily have become fixed in the oral tradition (cf. further Dodd 1963: 196–222). Many of the parallels support independent eyewitness reportage behind Mark's and John's accounts (see esp. Barnett 1986). And John may once again presuppose some knowledge of this story on the part of his audience, thus allowing him to narrate it in such a streamlined fashion (for details, see Morris 1995: 303).

If one is open to a core of the synoptic accounts representing an actual historical event, then it should not be difficult to treat the Johannine narrative with similar confidence (see esp. Johnston 1962). The geography of John 6:1 at first glance proves puzzling. But if we assume that Jesus and his disciples, like all the Galilean pilgrims, would have returned home after the feast of chapter 5, then it makes sense to read of them crossing over to the 'far shore of the Sea of Galilee'.[149] This meshes with Luke 9:10, which situates the feeding near Bethsaida (-Julias) on the northeast shore of the lake. Only John names the Sea (Galilee) and adds its Greek counterpart (Tiberias), both to help his largely Gentile, Asian audience understand.

As throughout the Synoptics, great crowds follow Christ (v. 2). Here John seems to allude to the larger Galilean ministry of the Synoptics, of which he otherwise describes only a small portion (Witherington 1995: 151). As he does in order to preach his great sermon in Matthew 5 – 7, Jesus goes up into the hill country and sits down with his followers (v. 3). Verse 4 is John's unique addition and explains his inclusion of an event that otherwise does not fit his pattern in these chapters of focusing on Jesus in Judea: Passover typology is present even if Jesus is not attending the festival at this moment. Verses 25–71 will make it clear that John sees in this event Jesus behaving like a 'new Moses', who once again provides bread in the wilderness. As he was the fulfilment of the Sabbath in chapter 5, in chapter 6 Jesus fulfils the Passover (cf. Carson 1991: 269).

The description of the conversation in verses 5–7 identifies one key participant – Philip – who is not mentioned by name in the Synoptics. But

---

149] Against those who would try to rearrange John's sequence of chapters here, J. A. T. Robinson (1985: 195) observes, 'It seems better to conclude that in 6.1 John is introducing a new and disconnected incident with his vague and resumptive phrase: *meta tauta*, which the NEB here correctly renders "some time later".'

hailing from Bethsaida (1:44), he would be a natural to go on an errand to the nearby village. Only John phrases Jesus' words to Philip as a question (v. 5) and clarifies that this was a 'test' (v. 6). John agrees with Matthew and Luke against Mark in phrasing Philip's response as a statement (v. 7). All this 'is a clear illustration of how details can be fixed in tradition but function differently depending on the context' (Ridderbos 1997: 211, n. 67). Still, the gist of the interchange remains unaltered. In verse 8 John again clarifies which disciple made a comment and specifies that the loaves were made of barley. Barley loaves appear explicitly in Elisha's miracle of feeding one hundred men in 2 Kings 4:42–44, a passage with sufficient parallels to the Gospels' feeding miracles to suggest deliberate allusion.[150] In verses 10–13 John runs most closely parallel to the Synoptics, not surprisingly because here is the description of the miracle itself, the story's climax. How the crowd could be counted is explained only in Mark's version: they were arranged in companies of fifty and one hundred. This detail, like others in Mark, points to the earliest stage of the miracle story as containing eschatological overtones of Jesus as the coming messianic prophet whom Moses himself predicted (Deut. 18:15–18; cf. Blomberg 1986b: 337–340).[151] This prophecy proved important only in very early Christian preaching (cf. Acts 3:23; 7:37), so it is not the product of Johannine invention (cf. R. N. Longenecker 1970: 32–38).

When we then see this same 'prophet-like-Moses' typology in John's unique conclusion to the miracle story (vv. 14–15), our confidence in the historicity of these details grows. Expectation of a 'new Moses'-like Messiah (v. 14) appears explicitly in *2 Baruch* 29.3 and 8 and in several later rabbinic sources (Talbert 1992: 132–133). Numerous scholars are prepared to grant historicity to verse 15 (Pryor 1992a: 31). It fits the rising nationalist fervour of early first-century Israel, cuts against the grain of Johannine redaction in treating Jesus as a merely political king, and embarrassingly portrays Jesus as having to run away from the crowds, as it were (cf. further Dodd 1963: 215). It also explains what remains unclear in Mark's account: why Jesus dismissed his disciples so abruptly.[152] Raymond Brown (1966: 250) appropriately concludes of verses 1–15,

---

150] Kügler (1998) also compares and contrasts the story with the midrashic accounts of Joseph providing grain in Egypt in the pseudepigraphical story of Joseph and Aseneth.

151] John's distinctive use of *eucharisteō* versus Mark's *eulogeō* has suggested to many that John sees eucharistic significance to the miracle as well. That John is concerned about the Last Supper will become clear from the rest of ch. 6, but where he stands on the practice will have to be determined by his more specific teaching (see below, pp. 126–127).

152] For this and other 'indices of historicity', see Latourelle 1988: 76–77.

'There is nothing that is really implausible or that would weigh against the independent value of the Johannine tradition.'

WALKING ON WATER (6:16–21)

This miracle story, too, is paralleled in the Synoptics (Matt. 14:22–33; Mark 6:45–52). Again it is presented with a briefer amount of information. Conceptually, the accounts run parallel to each other with references to the arrival of evening, the disciples' getting into the boat and crossing the lake, the rise of the wind, and the encounter with Jesus. Verbal parallelism appears with the 'boat' (v. 17), 'beyond' (v. 17), 'walking on the water' (v. 19), and the climactic pronouncement, 'It is I; don't be afraid' (v. 20). As with the versions of the feeding of the five thousand, once this story was put into the stylized form of the oral tradition, this amount and kind of parallelism is exactly what one would expect. In neither instance can we prove that John was not literarily dependent on Mark. But, if he was, he has rephrased things to such an extent that we cannot demonstrate it. More likely the accounts are independent.[153]

John's concise form leaves few redactional distinctives. Only John has the disciples head for Capernaum (v. 17a), a natural improvement over 'Bethsaida' (Mark 6:45).[154] John arguably heightens the sense of the miraculous slightly by adding suspense (v. 17b) and stressing that the wind was 'strong' (v. 18) and that the boat 'immediately' reached shore after the storm was calmed (v. 21). A gale-force headwind kept the boat from progressing little more than three miles (v. 19), even though the disciples had rowed for many hours (Mark 6:48).[155] Perhaps a typological allusion to Psalm 107:30 is present in John's ending (Michaels 1983: 90).

As with the feeding of the five thousand, one's view of the historicity of this passage will largely be determined by one's view of Christ's 'nature miracles' overall. Again there are multiple allusions to the role of Yahweh in the Old Testament, the God who treads on wind and waves (see esp. Job 9:8 and Ps. 77:16–19; cf. Blomberg 1986b: 342–345). The Christological heart of the miracle is even clearer in the Markan form with its allusion to

---

153] Several scholars suggest that John is even closer to the original here than Mark (e.g. Lindars 1972: 238; Schnackenburg 1980: 25–28).

154] But the two can be harmonized, since a small bay at the north end of the Sea of Galilee would have allowed for the feeding miracle to occur in the hilly country northeast of Bethsaida and for the disciples to set off for home in the direction of Capernaum, with Bethsaida *en route*. See Blomberg 1997: 273, n. 33.

155] Barrett (1978: 280) declares that the references to time and distance in Mark and John 'correspond with sufficient accuracy' to the size of the lake.

God 'passing by' Moses on Mount Sinai (Mark 6:48). All three versions probably allude to the divine name 'I am' of Exodus 3:14 with Jesus' words *egō eimi* (NIV 'It is I'; cf. Ridderbos 1997: 218). The story is thus firmly grounded in Jewish backgrounds. And all of the circumstances of the story, apart from the miracle itself, are thoroughly realistic, including the frequent rise of sudden and severe squalls over the Sea of Galilee.

What is possibly most striking about John's version is how this brief narrative seemingly interrupts the rest of the chapter with its discussion of bread in the wilderness. Probably the two miracles were inseparably attached to one another in the tradition[156] (possibly even in a signs-source; thus Perry 1993; though see above, p. 46). All three versions of the walking on the water also suggest a tight chronological connection with the feeding of the multitude. If one is open to the possibility of a miracle behind the synoptic form of the story, then John offers no further obstacles to belief in its historicity (cf. further Latourelle 1988: 144–147).

THE BREAD OF LIFE DISCOURSE (6:22–59)

Verses 22–24, somewhat cumbersomely, explain how Jesus ends up addressing the crowds again back on the western shore of Lake Galilee in the Capernaum synagogue (v. 59). Does John think of the crowds as famished for the hearing of the words of the Lord, running 'from sea to sea' as in Amos 8:11–12 (so Kiley 1995)? That fishing boats could have carried only a fraction of the multitudes suggests a tiny overlap between the crowds that witnessed Jesus' feeding miracle and those he addresses here (cf. Mark 6:53 par.).[157] Nevertheless those who followed him now realize he has not taken the boat across the lake and wonder how he got to the other shore (v. 25).

As in the conversation with Nicodemus (3:1–15), Jesus does not reply to the opening gambit with which he is addressed. Instead he berates his audience for looking for physical rather than spiritual blessings (vv. 26–27). Verse 26 is odd, since John's theology regularly stresses the inadequacy of faith based merely on signs. Yet here apparently the crowds should have been focusing on the sign rather than on their full stomachs.

156] Barrett (1978: 279) comments, 'It is probable that John included the narrative (a) because it was firmly fixed in the tradition along with the miracle of the five thousand, and (b) in order to bring Jesus and the disciples back to Capernaum, where the discourse on the Bread of Life was held (6.50).'

157] 'This "crowd", of course, is not to be identified with the entire multitude that had been present at the feeding miracle; it was not an armada that crossed the Lake to find Jesus!' (Beasley-Murray 1987: 90).

What Jesus must mean is that they did not discern the spiritual symbolism of the feeding miracle (Beasley-Murray 1987: 91; recall above, p. 119).[158] That this saying cuts against the grain of John's redactional emphases, is introduced with the double-'Amen' formula, and remains somewhat cryptic, all speak for its authenticity. Verse 27 elaborates by returning again to the theme of work, discussed already in the contexts of 4:34 and 5:36. Just as Jesus could offer the Samaritan woman living water (4:10), he can speak here of spiritual 'food that endures to eternal life'. Jesus refers to himself again as the Son of Man, in an apocalyptic context, a hallmark of authenticity. The one on whom 'God the Father has placed his seal of approval' may be technical Jewish language for being 'accredited as an envoy' (Borgen 1993: 273).

Because Jesus has mentioned 'work', this Jewish audience understandably raises the question of what kind of works God requires (v. 28). There is a close parallel to this concept of God's works in the Qumran Manual of Discipline (1QS 4:4). Paradoxically, however, Jesus defines the appropriate work in terms of belief in the one whom the Father has sent (recall 5:30). This statement passes the double similarity and dissimilarity test with flying colours. It is grounded in Judaism's fascination with 'works' but offers a stunning redefinition. It coheres with later Christian emphases on belief, but uniquely continues to speak of faith as a good deed.

At first glance, verses 30–31 seem completely incongruous. The crowds now ask for a sign to legitimate Jesus' claims, alluding to Moses' provision of manna for the Israelites in the wilderness. But Jesus has just worked a miracle intentionally reminiscent of that very event! Part of the solution undoubtedly lies in the fact that this is primarily not the same crowd as that which witnessed the miracle (cf. the Jewish leaders' request for a sign in Matt. 16:2–4 and Mark 8:11–13 on the heels of the feeding of the four thousand). Perhaps, too, they were looking for a phenomenon that was not a one-off event but an ongoing miracle, as the manna had been in days of old (Morris 1995: 321).[159] In citing the apparently scriptural quotation 'He gave them bread from heaven to eat' Jesus' audience may be alluding to any or all of Exodus 16:4, Nehemiah 9:15 and Psalm 78:24–25 (for details, see Menken 1988b).

158] Borgen (1993: 278) thinks that Jesus had legitimated himself as the prophet-like Moses, but now needed to legitimate further his stronger claim to be the Son of Man, the Father's heavenly commissioned envoy. But it is not clear that one can drive that much of a wedge between the two claims.

159] For Jewish background, again recall 2 Bar. 29.5–8. Cf. also Philo, Mut. 44–45; Sir. 24:19–23. For a thorough discussion, see Balfour 1995.

Jesus replies by again contrasting literal and metaphorical bread (vv. 32–33). Another introductory 'Amen, Amen' suggests authenticity. Jesus' approach follows the classic Jewish hermeneutical principle of *'al tiqrî* ('Do not read … but rather …'); in this case, 'do not read Torah as saying "Moses will give" the bread but rather that "God has given" it' (cf. Barrett 1978: 290). The contrast implied between Moses and Jesus reminds the reader of the antitheses in the Sermon on the Mount (Matt. 5:21–48). Jesus' distinctive and characteristic use of 'my Father' rather than 'our Father' also stands out.[160] Like the woman at the well (4:15) the audience responds by clamouring for this spiritual nourishment, though they obviously do not grasp its true nature (v. 34).

Verse 35 brings us to the beginning of the more 'sermonic' part of this dialogue. Here John introduces the first of the seven famous 'I am' sayings of Christ in this Gospel, which have no direct counterpart in the synoptic tradition. Before jumping to the conclusion, however, that they are purely Johannine invention, we must notice that the 'I am' sayings with a predicate all depend on metaphor and would not have sounded nearly as blunt or explicit as Christians today sometimes interpret them – that is, as direct affirmations of Jesus' deity. Moreover, the Synoptics do have parallels to the more sweeping 'I am' statements without a predicate (e.g. Mark 6:50; 13:6; 14:62), though each of these could also be translated simply 'I am he' or 'It is I.' Divine Wisdom, personified in Proverbs 9:5 and Sirach 24:21, could speak in similar first-person language, as could Qumran's Teacher of righteousness.[161] *Joseph and Aseneth* several times describes the 'bread of life' as that 'which yields eternal life' (e.g. 8.5, 11; 15.5; 16.16; cf. Talbert 1992: 136). The synoptic Jesus, finally, can also speak of metaphorical bread in both positive (Luke 11:5–8; Matt. 13:33 par.) and negative (Mark 8:11 par.) contexts. Perhaps John is responsible for the specific 'I am' form of these sayings, but the concepts are not foreign to either Jesus or Judaism elsewhere.

Still, his audience does not believe (v. 36, perhaps harking back to a previous statement resembling 5:38; Michaels 1983: 102). That Jesus will protect all those who are his introduces the important themes of

---

160] Lindars (1972: 258) finds here 'a remarkable echo of a petition of the Lord's Prayer', taking the petition for bread to be eschatological (the food of the coming age), which is already available to those who belong to Christ.

161] E. E. Ellis (1999: 180) thus thinks that the 'I am' sayings could 'represent primitive traditions of a type of Jesus' teachings that John's allied apostolic missions did not include in their Gospels. Otherwise, they represent a more explicit wording by John of Jesus-traditions similar to some found in less direct forms in the Synoptics.'

predestination and the security of the believer (vv. 37–39). One hears clear echoes of the 'Johannine thunderbolt' of Matthew 11:25–27 and parallel (vv. 37, 39), sandwiched around an affirmation of Jesus' obedience in language reminiscent of Gethsemane (v. 38). On 'not driving anyone away', contrast Luke 13:28; on 'not losing anyone', compare Matthew 18:14. Verse 40 emphatically repeats the promise of eternal life as the Father's will for all who believe in the Son, life defined in terms of coming bodily resurrection on 'the last day', a concept deeply embedded in first-century Judaism.

Some in the audience naturally begin to 'grumble' at Jesus' claims (v. 41). John undoubtedly employs this verb to allude again to the Israelites' repeated behaviour in the wilderness. The complaint in verse 42, that Jesus and his family are well known and thus ordinary people, closely resembles the complaints of the villagers in Nazareth in Mark 6:3 and parallels. Jesus tells them to stop grumbling (v. 43) and then describes his followers in a third way. Not only has the Father given them to the Son (v. 39), even though they of their own free will believe (v. 40), but also the Father must 'draw' them to himself (v. 44). This language calls to mind Jeremiah 3:3 (LXX) and Hosea 11:4. A more remote echo is heard in Mark 10:27, where what is impossible for humans is possible for God.

Jesus next directs the assembly's attention to a second scriptural text (v. 45a) – Isaiah 54:13. *Psalms of Solomon* 17.32 demonstrates that at least some pre-Christian Jews understood this text in a Messianic sense: 'He will be a righteous king over them taught by God. There will be no unrighteousness among them in his days, for all shall be holy, and their king shall be their Lord Messiah' (cf. Barrett 1978: 296). Just as correct interpretation of the Scriptures leads one to Christ (5:39, 45–47), so also proper listening to what the Father says and learning (the standard rabbinic sequence) points people to Jesus (v. 45b). Precisely because no-one can see the Father directly, they must learn of him from the one who has seen him (v. 46; recall 1:18). Jesus' words in this sermon increasingly take on the flavour of characteristic Johannine terminology but remain coherent in the context in which they are placed.

With verse 47 we come to the third double-'Amen' saying of this chapter and to the simplest of the three. No new concepts appear here (recall v. 35b) nor in verse 48, where the claim of v. 35a is reiterated. C. H. Talbert (1992: 135–136) sees not only an inclusio but also an elaborate chiasmus, accounting for the structure of all of verses 35–48, but not all of his supposed parallels are nearly as obvious as they were in 5:19–30. Verses 49–50 return to the text about 'bread from heaven', while verse 51 introduces a new thought that subsequent paragraphs will unpack: Jesus' spiritual bread is his 'flesh', which he will give 'for the life of the world'. 'By the time we get to v. 51 we are left in no doubt: it is not manna, Torah or Wisdom which is the true, eschatological bread of God and which nourishes his people, but Jesus himself' (Pryor 1992a: 33). Presupposed in verse 51, too, is the notion of eating Christ's flesh (cf. the question raised in v. 52). Talbert (1992: 138) believes this language is understandable in the light of an (admittedly later) rabbinic teaching that speaks of 'eating the Messiah' (*b. Sanh.* 99a).[162]

Verses 53–58 form the most difficult portion of this discourse to ascribe to the historical Jesus. To begin with, most commentators understand it as explicitly eucharistic in nature, and, as Casey (1996: 42–51) correctly stresses, Jesus could not have expected Galilean crowds a year before his death to have understood the significance of teaching not articulated until the last night of his life. But it is not at all clear that we should take this passage as John's equivalent to the Last Supper. There Christ offers his *body* (Gk. *sōma*) and blood; here he speaks of eating his *flesh* (Gk. *sarx*) and drinking his blood. In chapters 13 – 17, while giving us more detail about Jesus' last meal with his followers than all three Synoptics combined, John assiduously avoids the 'words of institution' of the Lord's Supper. As in my discussion of Jesus' baptism (above, p. 79), it is more probable that John is playing down references to the sacraments, which by the end of the first century have become too institutionalized for his liking (cf. Burge 2000: 214–215).[163] So we should understand Jesus' graphic language here in John 6 as vivid metaphors for identifying with him in his death, not commands to celebrate the Lord's Supper (see further, below, p. 187).[164] The metaphors are rooted in Jewish thought but go beyond it in dramatic fashion; they are preserved in later Christian discourse but quickly misinterpreted as supporting sacramental regeneration. What Jesus claims will result from eating his flesh and drinking his blood – an experience of true life, resurrection on the last day, remaining in him, and living for ever – are exactly the experiences he has just promised to all who believe (vv.

162] The standard English translations render 'enjoying the Messiah' but the Hebrew verb employed is from '*ākal* ('to eat').

163] Barrett (1978: 284) elaborates, 'John is not in any crude sense anti–sacramental, but he does appear to be critical of sacramental tendencies prevailing in his day, and to lay such stress on the fundamental sacramental fact of the incarnation that the partial expressions of this fact, baptism and the eucharist, are relegated to a subordinate place.'

164] J. A. T. Robinson (1985: 209) recognizes that the eucharistic overtones come from a later sacramental reading of the event, but that John accomplishes this, 'not by developing the theology at the expense of the history but by being faithful to the history and all its temporal, geographical and political detail'.

35–51). So it is unlikely that he is now contradicting himself and replacing faith with partaking of the sacraments (cf. further Ridderbos 1997: 235, 241, citing both Calvin and Augustine for support). Thus Casey's criticisms prove irrelevant.

What, then, shall we conclude about the authenticity of Christ's discourse (or dialogue) in John 6:25–59? Peder Borgen (1965) has demonstrated that the bulk of this material (vv. 31–58) forms a unity following the Jewish rhetorical and literary form known as a *proem midrash*.[165] A text of Scripture is introduced for discussion (v. 31), which is then exegeted and paraphrased (vv. 32–40). Certain considerations of this discussion lead to a second, related Scripture (vv. 41–44), which is then expounded (vv. 45–47). Finally, attention returns to the first passage, with further exposition (vv. 48–58). Clearly the theme of Jesus as the bread from heaven unifies this material to such a degree that we do not need to parcel it out into various stages of tradition and redaction, not even the 'troublesome' material of verses 51–58 (contra, e.g. Temple 1961; Painter 1989). This homiletical form is paralleled in shorter synoptic parables (e.g. Luke 10:25–37; Mark 12:1–12 pars.; cf. Blomberg 1990: 231, 251; E. E. Ellis 1977: 105–106) and in various speeches in Acts (Bowker 1967), so it is well within the range of the historical Jesus to have uttered something substantially similar to what John 6 presents here.[166] We do not find a midrash of this length in the Synoptics, no doubt because there we are *never* given in detail the contents of any of Jesus' preaching *in the synagogues*, precisely where we should expect such an exegetical and homiletical device to flourish. But we are told that Jesus did frequently preach there (see esp. Mark 1:21–22 pars.; cf. Luke 4:16–21, with a brief resumé). We may once again readily concede that John has written up the material with his distinctive style and emphases; the original sermon doubtless lasted substantially longer. But there are no reasons to deny the substance of the remarks attributed to Christ in John 6 to the historical Jesus, despite frequent claims to the contrary.

165] Borgen's discussion has been affirmed and supplemented by Muñoz-León (1977) with examples from early targumic material.

166] Borgen himself does not make quite so ambitious a claim, content to see the unity more at a redactional level, though he does argue strongly against separating off verses 51–58 and attributing them to a different source than the rest of the discourse. But cf. Carson (1991: 280): 'there is no entailment from such a position to the conclusion that the discourse is inauthentic: if the four canonical Gospels bear witness to anything about Jesus, it is that he himself was a gifted, telling and creative exegete of the Old Testament Scriptures'.

A TURNING POINT IN JESUS' MINISTRY (6:60–71)

Jesus' insistence that people eat his flesh and drink his blood is so 'hard' a teaching that many in the crowds of those otherwise favourable to Christ cannot accept it (v. 60). This rejection is sufficiently disrespectful that it was unlikely to have been invented. Jesus becomes aware of their grumbling (v. 61). Is this, like Mark 2:8, an example of his knowing what people are thinking and saying 'behind his back', as it were? He asks them if his teaching offends them. The Greek verb for 'offend' (*skandalizō*) is more common in the Synoptics than in John (Barrett 1978: 303); one thinks especially of Matthew 18:5, 7, 8 and 9. In verse 62 Jesus speaks again of the ascent of the Son of Man (recall 1:51; 3:13), with another clear allusion to his pre-existence. This kind of language does not appear in the Synoptics, but Matthew's and Luke's understanding of Jesus' virginal conception concords with it.

The climax of Jesus' reply, however, comes in verse 63. Here is the key to recognizing that Christ has not just articulated a doctrine of 'sacramental regeneration'. It is the Spirit, through Christ's words, not the Lord's Supper, that gives life (cf. Carson 1991: 301).[167] The concept is thoroughly rooted in the Hebrew Scriptures. Genesis 1:2 and Ezekiel 37:1–14 describe the Spirit giving life. Proverbs 8:35 does the same with hypostatized Wisdom. Jeremiah 15:16 declares:

> When your words came, I ate them;
> they were my joy and my heart's delight.

In Acts 7:38 Stephen echoes the Jewish belief that Moses received the living words of God and gave them to the people. Raymond Brown (1966: 297) suggests that 'Jesus might be challenging the type of Jewish thought we find later exemplified in the Midrash Mekilta on Exod xv 26: "The words of the Law which I have given you are life for you."' The 'spirit'/'flesh' contrast in this verse differs from what we saw in John 3:6, but resembles characteristic early Pauline usage.

Verse 64 discloses Jesus' first stated awareness that not all of his apparent followers were genuine. John adds a narrative aside about the coming betrayal, which verse 70 will address more directly. Jesus repeatedly predicts the treachery of his disciples in the Synoptics, too (see esp. Mark 14:18–21, 27–31 pars.), but not this early in the sequence of events. Verse 65 com-

---

167] Jesus may be intentionally foreshadowing the Last Supper, but he cannot expect any of his followers to understand that foreshadowing until they reflect back on this event after his death and resurrection (recall the distinctions made in 2:19–22).

bines the thoughts of verses 39 (those who have been given to Jesus) and 44 (those whom the Father draws) to restate the point that only those whom the Father 'gives' to Jesus (from Gk. *didōmi*; contra NIV 'enabled') come to him. Hence, we should not be surprised that some would fall away.

We are seeing a pattern in the Fourth Gospel of Jesus speaking comparatively cryptically or briefly on key issues that are addressed more directly or in more detail only at a later stage in his ministry in the Synoptics (calls to discipleship, Simon's second name, criticism of the temple, Messiahship, the Last Supper, and now betrayal). Given the highly selective nature of what the Synoptics include and given John's obvious interest in supplementing the core kerygma, it seems historically plausible that Jesus would have earlier on foreshadowed themes that would loom larger as his ministry unfolded (cf. Morris 1995: 343–344, n. 161). That John is presupposing and building on commonly understood tradition is again clear from the fact that (1) he never completely explains Jesus' 'hard teaching'; (2) the reference to the betrayal assumes some understanding of that later event; (3) a larger group of 'disciples' is mentioned that has not earlier been described; and (4) the 'Twelve' are introduced in verse 67 without explanation (cf. Barrett 1978: 306).

Verses 66–71 repeat the pattern of verses 60–65: a negative reaction by disciples (vv. 60, 66), discussion of the 'words of life' (vv. 61–63, 67–69), and teaching on betrayal (vv. 64–65, 70–71) (Talbert 1992: 140).[168] Verse 66 makes explicit what is merely implicit in the Synoptics: as Jesus increasingly turns his attention to the cross, the huge crowds dissipate. Dodd (1963: 222) elaborates:

> If John's account is to be taken seriously, we can see a reason why, at an early stage, this particular part of the Ministry impressed its sequence of events on the memory of the followers of Jesus: it was a crisis and a turning point. The vast assembly, gathered about Jesus on the east side of the Sea of Galilee, somewhere between the shore and the hills, represented a high point in his popularity. But this popularity took a disastrous turn when an attempt was made to force his mission into a political channel. When Jesus firmly resisted the attempt, separating his immediate followers from the crowd and withdrawing to the hills, the result was widespread defection, and the Twelve emerged from the crisis as the faithful remnant with which a fresh start was to be made.

168] Broadhead (1995) implausibly argues that John has transformed an account originally about an exorcism in these last subsections.

Verses 66 and 67 are again both sufficiently uncomplimentary so as not to have been invented. With verses 68–69 we come to the climax of the chapter, as Peter confesses Jesus as the only source of eternal life and the 'Holy One of God'. Historically, commentators have divided over whether to see this as the Johannine reworking of Peter's confession on the road to Caesarea Philippi (Mark 8:27–30 pars.) or as a separate event.[169] Because John supplies no setting for verses 67–69, the former is possible without introducing any necessary contradictions between John and the Synoptics (Cipriani 1967: 109). If it is a separate event, the remarkable congruence with Peter's (later?) confession supports the authenticity of the Johannine account. But perhaps a third alternative is better still. In Matthew 14:33 the disciples respond to Jesus' walking on the water by acclaiming him 'Son of God'. Even in Matthew, this cannot mean as much as Peter means in 16:16 on the road to Caesarea, since there Jesus praises his response as uniquely God-given (v. 17). Is it not possible that John's description of Peter's confession is more of an equivalent to this earlier acclamation, especially since we have just read of the walking on the water in John 6 as well (cf. Borgen 1993: 285–287)? William Domeris (1993) has shown that 'Holy One of God' is steeped in the Old Testament and more akin to the divine sense of 'Son of God', attested also in the Synoptics (on the lips of demons – e.g. Mark 1:24), than to 'Messiah'.[170] It would be natural if here, after the walking on the water, the disciples are finally getting an inkling that their remarkable teacher may be more than merely a conventional human deliverer. As in Mark 8:30 (contra Matt. 16:17–19), Jesus does not affirm Peter's confession but turns again to predict his betrayal (John 6:70–71). As the Synoptics more fully detail, Jesus has chosen each of his twelve closest followers (Mark 3:13–19 pars.). But one will commit such treachery that he can be called a 'devil'!

Paul Anderson's study of John 6 (1996) is essential reading for anyone grappling with either the historicity or the theology of this chapter. It is impossible to summarize in short compass and defies categorization into the standard 'conservative-to-liberal' spectrum. On the one hand, Anderson acknowledges that detailed homiletical and midrashic reflection on the original core teachings of Jesus have combined with issues in the Johannine community to create a complex mixture of tradition and redaction. On the other hand, he does not find any of this unfaithful to the

---

169] Cipriani (1967: 103) observes that Protestants have been more inclined to the former; Catholics, to the latter.

170] It is also another title for Jesus used early in the preaching of Acts (3:14) but seldom elsewhere.

teachings of the historical Jesus and identifies numerous signs of eyewitness testimony still remaining in the final form of the chapter. My far briefer discussion suggests that we should agree.

JESUS LEAVES FOR THE TABERNACLES FESTIVAL (7:1–13)

Roughly six months elapse, as John passes over the rest of Jesus' 'great Galilean ministry' in silence. 'Though further adventures in Galilee are not described, clearly 7:1 indicates the evangelist knows of such' (Witherington 1995: 170). That Jesus wanted to avoid Judea because the Jewish leaders there sought to kill him harks back to 5:18. John 7:2 – 10:21 is all apparently put forward as part of Jesus' ministry surrounding the Feast of Tabernacles during the autumn of AD 29.[171] Jesus' brothers would naturally expect him to attend the festival as all faithful Jewish males were expected to do (vv. 2b–3a). As I noted above (p. 55), that Jesus should have engaged in extended teaching ministry in and around Jerusalem is inherently quite plausible. The Synoptics' silence on these earlier forays to Judea is based on the geographical nature of their outlines, not because Jesus had never gone up to Jerusalem prior to the Passover at which he was executed (see above, p. 54; cf. R. E. Brown 1966: 309).

Here Jesus' brothers seemingly taunt him into disclosing himself more plainly (vv. 3b–4) because, as John explains, they did not yet believe in him (v. 5). Hence, just like the crowds after the feeding of the five thousand, they demand some kind of sign that is even more foolproof, couched indirectly as if they are concerned that he more effectively convince those who had already begun to follow him.[172] John 7:3–8 contains the identical five elements present in Luke 13:31–33: an approach to Jesus, a command given to Jesus by those sceptical of his claims, its offering as if for his benefit, its rejection by Jesus, and his rationale for that rejection. At the very least, this suggests a traditional origin of the Johannine narrative

---

171] For the literary unity of all of John 7 – 10, see Schenke (1989), who nevertheless discerns earlier stages of tradition and redaction in this material. For the unity of chs. 7 – 8 as a subsection, see esp. Neyrey 1996. For detailed study of the historical and religious background to these two chapters in view of Jewish traditions about Tabernacles, see Camarero María 1997. The foundational Old Testament sources are Exod. 23:16; Lev. 23:33–36, 39–42; and Deut. 16:13–15. Cf. also esp. the Mishnaic tractate *Sukkah*.

172] Cf. Bruce (1983: 171): 'What the brothers did not realize was that those disciples' faith was imperfect precisely because it was based on the outward signs about proper appreciation of the inward truth they were intended to convey; that kind of faith would not be strengthened by the sight of greater or more numerous wonders.'

(Dodd 1963: 322–335; contra Rochais 1993). The contrast between Jesus' private and public teaching calls to mind synoptic texts like Mark 4:22/Luke 8:17, Luke 12:2 and Matthew 10:26 (Barrett 1978: 311). That his brothers remain sceptical of Jesus until after the resurrection is corroborated by Mark 3:21 and 1 Corinthians 15:7 (cf. D. M. Smith 1999: 168). At the same time, their remarks have been phrased in characteristic Johannine language, especially with their references to 'seeing his works' and 'showing himself to the world'.

In verses 6–8 Jesus replies with language particularly reminiscent of the miracle of turning water into wine (2:1–12). As also in 4:46–54 and 11:1–44 there is a pattern of a request to Jesus by someone else, an apparent response of rebuke, and an action of Jesus in granting the request nevertheless (cf. esp. Giblin 1980). As at the wedding in Cana, here Jesus specifically refers to his 'time' (for full disclosure and death) as not yet having arrived, though this time John uses *kairos* rather than *hōra*. *Kairos*, however, is frequent in the Synoptics in apocalyptic contexts, so John is probably again relying on traditional material. Mark 1:15, Matthew 26:18 and Luke 21:8 are important partial parallels to either the term or the concept (Lindars 1972: 283).[173] Jesus' reference to the world's hatred in verse 7 resembles his prediction of the persecution his disciples will experience in Matthew 10:17–39, while also recalling the thoroughly Johannine language of John 3:19. Thus Jesus for the moment appears to declare that he will not go up to the Feast at all (v. 9).

Verse 10, however, immediately explains that he did go up a few days later (cf. v. 14) but secretly, not as part of the festal throng of pilgrims. Despite numerous attempts to make this qualification a huge problem,[174] the text reads naturally as it stands. Jesus declares in the present tense (*anabainō*) that he is not going up with everybody else, but knows he will go to the festival in a different way and at a different time (cf., e.g. Morris 1995: 354, 356). As Herman Ridderbos (1997: 260) elaborates, 'Without meaning to harmonize the irreconcilable at any price, it must still be said that the Evangelist ... emphasizes the "wholly other" character of this "going up" compared to what Jesus' brothers wanted him to do and themselves did.' Or in J. R. Michaels' words (1983: 110), 'Only when Jesus has made very clear that what he is about to undertake is *not*

173] Numerous parallels emerge among the Dead Sea Scrolls to this kind of use of the 'right time', e.g. 1QS 8:4; 9:12–16, 19–20; 10:1–5; 1QM 1:5, 11–12; 14:13; and 15:5.

174] For the most recent survey of treatments, see Caragounis (1998), who implausibly argues against the more difficult textual variant ('not') in favour of the easier one ('not yet'; so also NIV – but see the mg.).

that final self-disclosure but a preliminary one is he free to go ahead and undertake it. His hand will not be forced by anyone, not even his own relatives. No one directs his movements but the Father, and when the time comes ...'

Thus the Tabernacles feast begins with the participants, remembering Jesus' impact in Jerusalem during previous festivals and wondering when he will appear again (v. 11). The division of opinion reflected in verse 12 is a recurring, unifying motif throughout chapters 7 – 10. Previously, the majority in Jerusalem have responded positively; from chapter 11 onward, increasing hostility will mount until it climaxes in Christ's execution. In a historically realistic fashion these chapters describe an intermediate stage – progressive polarization with many on each side. Those who think he is 'a good man' are scarcely asserting lofty Christology, an observation that supports John's historicity here. On the other side, those who claim 'he deceives the people' echo the charge found in Mark 3:20–30 and parallels, which persists as the most common Jewish explanation of Christ's ministry in the later rabbinic literature (see esp. Stanton 1994). That the debate is not yet as public as it will become (v. 13) also fits a credible progression of events, especially in the light of the earlier opposition to Jesus in Jerusalem on the part of key leaders.

JESUS BEGINS TEACHING AT TABERNACLES (7:14–36)

The 'discourse' of John 7 is a compilation of five segments of Jesus' words, none more than four verses in length, and each slightly shorter than the previous one. Verses 16–19 repeat the theme of 5:19–30 about Jesus doing nothing but his Father's will. In verses 21–24 Jesus defends his healing on the Sabbath. In verses 28–29 he summarizes the theme that his listeners do not know him because they do not know the Father. Verses 33–34 foreshadow the emphasis of the farewell discourse (chs. 14 – 16) that he will be with his listeners only a little while longer. Finally, verses 37–38 reflect his claim to be 'living water'. This claim is associated with a separate day of the feast, so I shall deal with it as a separate section of this commentary (vv. 37–52).[175]

That Jesus should appear in the temple to teach, midway through the week-long festivities of Tabernacles (v. 14), fits his consistent pattern of teaching in Jerusalem throughout John but also matches what the Synoptics describe him doing during the last week of his life (Mark

---

175] For a representative study employing tradition-critical dissection of this material, see Attridge 1980. For a more synchronic, holistic analysis, see Cory 1997.

11:27 – 12:44 pars.).[176] His audience understandably marvels at his teaching since he has had no formal rabbinic training (v. 15). A similar response follows the Sermon on the Mount (Matt. 7:28–29) and the preaching of the disciples in Jerusalem after Pentecost (Acts 4:13). Jesus' reply in verses 16–19 picks up the conversation exactly where it left off the last time he was in Jerusalem (ch. 5). Responding to those who find this unusual, Ridderbos (1997: 262) remarks, 'A reference back to earlier dialogues is no proof of displacement of materials originally belonging together. It rather suggests the modus operandi that characterizes the Evangelist.'[177] Jesus' words gather together characteristic Johannine emphases – the Father as the one who sent Jesus; doing God's will; knowing that Jesus and his teaching come from God, that he does not speak on his own or glorify himself, that this is the truth, and that if the audience truly understood the Law they would recognize him. Still, conceptual parallels to every statement can be found in the Synoptics, suggesting that John is editing tradition, not inventing *de novo* (see above, p. 118). In addition, we may note that the ancient targums on Genesis 32:8, 12 (*Pseudo-Jonathan*) and on Leviticus 19:3 (*Neofiti*) describe the dutiful son as the one who is concerned for the glory or honour of his father, and that Christ's overall argument resembles his challenge to the 'tradition of the elders' in Mark 7:1–13 and parallel (Lindars 1972: 289).

Not all of the current crowd would have been present for the events summarized in 5:18, so they naturally wonder about the alleged death threat against Jesus (v. 20). The charge of being demon-possessed again resembles Mark 3:22, which likewise occurs not long after a controversy over healing on the Sabbath, complete with its death threat (Mark 3:1–6). The Mishnaic laws concerning false prophets (*Sanh.* 11.5) make these threats credible, while it is improbable that any later Christian would have invented so insulting a charge against his or her Lord. As after John 3:2 and 6:25 Jesus does not respond to the comments directed to him. Instead, he

---

176] Bruce (1983: 174) suggests that Jesus went up to the temple secretively to avoid the kind of triumphal entry that was foisted on him six months later. Such a premature demonstration would have been especially embarrassing if the Tabernacles festival in the autumn of 29 took place only recently after the Galilean massacre in the temple courts by Pilate described in Luke 13:1.

177] Pryor (1992a: 38–39) further observes that six of the ten uses of the verb 'teach' in the Fourth Gospel occur in chs. 7 – 8; two of the three uses of 'teaching', here in vv. 16–17. He concludes that this accumulation of references compares favourably with the Synoptic Gospels, including Mark's frequent editorial references to Jesus' teaching (e.g. Mark 1:21–22).

continues to defend his behaviour in healing the invalid by the Bethesda pool (vv. 21–24; cf. 5:1–18). Here he employs the classic Jewish hermeneutical strategy of arguing 'from the lesser to the greater' (vv. 22–23).[178] In fact, the very issue of certain circumstances permitting one to override normal Sabbath laws is commonly discussed elsewhere. In the Synoptics one observes a particularly close parallel in Jesus' teaching, in the context of the Sabbath healings of Luke 13:10–17 and 14:1–6. In early rabbinic literature, the very case to which Jesus appeals here is regularly cited: circumcision on the eighth day *must* be carried out, even when that day falls on the Sabbath (*Shab.* 18.3; 19.1–2; *Ned.* 3.11). In earlier and later literature on this topic, even the a fortiori form is at times employed (*Mek. Exod.* 31.13b; *b. Yoma* 85b). With circumcision as one of the first-century Jewish 'badges of national righteousness', we would be astounded if Jesus did not allude to the practice somewhere; the Synoptics are more puzzling in their silence on the topic. Verse 24, finally, reminds the reader of Matthew 7:1–5 with its sequence of commands concerning right and wrong forms of judgment.

John 7:25–27 reflects the beginning of John's emphasis on the polarization of the crowds. Verses 25–26 speculate that some, even among the authorities, must have begun to believe in Jesus since they tolerate his teaching. But verse 27 represents the more sceptical counter-argument, related to the discussion in 1:19–28. The Messiah is to emerge more or less from nowhere, from an ordinary, obscure family in Galilee.[179] Again one thinks of the parallel objections in Mark 6:2–3 and parallels.

The reference to Jesus 'still teaching in the temple courts' (v. 28) may suggest that we have now jumped to a later time or day during the festival. At any rate, it reminds us that John is offering us the barest of summaries of what was surely far more extended dialogue. Jesus, ironically, perhaps even sarcastically, repeats the claims of his sceptics (v. 28a), though they know only his human origin. As in chapter 5 (esp. vv. 41–47), their lack of knowledge stems directly from their failure truly to know the Father (vv. 28b–29). The aborted attempt to arrest Jesus closely resembles the aftermath of his preaching in the Nazareth synagogue (Luke 4:28–30). John uses his favourite term to explain that Jesus' 'time' (lit. 'hour') has not yet come (v. 30). Still, many in the crowds believe, at least at some superficial level (v. 31). That this belief runs counter to the Fourth

---

178] Or, if one follows Derrett (1991), 'from the particular to the general'.

179] Cf. Carson (1991: 317), following Justin Martyr in his *Dialogue with Trypho* 8.7 'that the Messiah would be born of flesh and blood yet would be wholly unknown until he appeared to effect Israel's redemption'. Cf. further R. E. Brown (1966: 313).

Evangelist's redactional emphasis on the growing unbelief and opposition of the majority of the Jewish people, especially in Jerusalem, supports its historicity. That John elsewhere stresses the inadequacy of a merely signs-based faith (2:23–25; 3:1–3; 4:48; etc.) cautions us against assuming that this belief is necessarily profound or even genuine.[180]

Now the threats against Jesus resume (v. 32). Pharisees in Jerusalem would naturally consult with 'the chief priests', who were in charge of the temple precincts, even if they differed with them on many legal issues. The priests in turn would issue orders for their servants (probably, as in the NIV, the 'temple guard') to arrest Jesus, rather than attempting the feat themselves. Meanwhile, his address to the crowds continues, and he anticipates that his time is drawing short (vv. 33–34). But he speaks enigmatically and his audience misunderstands, thinking he is planning to escape to Gentile territory where the Jewish Sanhedrin has no jurisdiction (vv. 35–36). Even the crowds' misunderstanding is historically intelligible.[181]

THE LIVING WATER (7:37–52)

We now jump ahead to the last, climactic day of the Tabernacles feast (v. 37a). What began in Old Testament times as a seven-day festival had probably developed into an eight-day celebration by Jesus' day (Josephus, *Ant.* 13.372; Beasley-Murray 1987: 114).[182] For the first week, daily libations were offered in the temple with water drawn from the pool of Siloam in Jerusalem. On the final day, however, no such ceremony was performed (*Sukk.* 4.9; 5.1).[183] How poignant and provocative, then, for

---

180] 'The Fourth Gospel itself does not report many miracles, but this and other references to his "many miracles" (2:23; 3:1; 4:45) are indicators that the Evangelist assumes that his readers know more about Jesus' words and works than he tells of' (Ridderbos 1997: 269). As for the theological logic that led many to infer Jesus' Messiahship from his miracles, see Beasley-Murray 1987: 112.

181] Lindars (1972: 296) thinks there may be a play here on Jesus' well-known 'Seek and you will find' from Matt. 7:7 par. Schnackenburg (1980: 150–151) finds possible Old Testament background on seeking and not finding in Hos. 5:6 and Amos 8:12. On seeking and finding, cf. Is. 55:6.

182] Knapp (1997) gives full details of various developments in the celebration over time.

183] Since the Josephus reference describes other post-biblical additions to the Tabernacles ceremony attested in the Mishnah present as early as the time of Alexander Jannaeus in the early first century BC, it is reasonable to suppose that these other customs had also developed by this time, or at least by the early first century AD. That John goes out of his way

Jesus to offer spiritual water at precisely this moment in the festival (vv. 37–38). The first part of his invitation 'Let anyone who is thirsty come to me and drink' (v. 37b) matches the substance of his earlier offer to the Samaritan woman (4:10, 13–14).

Verse 38, however, creates a translation problem for Jesus' entire utterance in verses 37b–38. The NIV margin reflects a popular, alternate modern rendering that is more tightly parallel and poetic in form: 'Let anyone who is thirsty come to me. And let anyone drink who believes in me. As the Scripture has said, he will have streams of living water flowing from within.' This translation makes it possible for the 'he' of the last sentence to refer to Jesus, not to the believer (cf., forcefully, Burge 2000: 227–229). But the 'he' could also be generic, as it must be on the more traditional translation, and this is probably the most natural way to take the text (Carson 1991: 322–325; Morris 1995: 375). No one specific Old Testament quotation is unambiguously in view on either interpretation, but a cluster of possibilities lies in the background: Psalm 77:16–20, Isaiah 12:3, Ezekiel 47:1–11, Zechariah 14:8 and 16–19, portions of Nehemiah 8 – 9, and the whole Pentateuchal tradition of Moses providing water for the Israelites in the wilderness.[184] The Jerusalem Talmud explicitly associates Isaiah 12:3 with Tabernacles (j. Sukk. 5.1). If this association had already developed by the first century, John (or Jesus) may have been rereading the 'wells of salvation' as the 'belly of Jesus', simply by repointing the Hebrew consonants (Marcus 1998).[185] The Mishnah further attests to the tradition of praying for rain at this same festival (Taan. 1.1), a custom going back at least to the time of Rabbi Eliezer b. Hyrcanus in the late first century. The Tosefta later amplifies this tradition by describing prayers for the spiritual rains of the messianic age (t. Sukk. 3.3–12). There seems to be the possibility, thus, that a rich cluster of biblical and traditional water-motifs resides in the background as a foil for Jesus' remarkable claims (cf. further Grigsby 1986). It is unlikely that all this occurred coincidentally in a largely Hellenistic community rewriting Christian tradition at the end of the first century. When the Jewish backgrounds are combined with the

---

to stress what day of the feast it was further suggests that he saw significance in Jesus' words uttered at precisely this time in the festival.

184] Menken (1996) analyses the text form and possible sources in greatest detail. Carson (1991: 326–328) is relatively alone in proposing the Nehemiah references. Morris (1995: 376) lists numerous other Old Testament references to water symbolizing spiritual blessings. R. E. Brown (1966: 322) develops the theme of 'water from the rock' and lists numerous Scriptures for possible background.

185] This would then require the Christological reading of vv. 37–38, as in the NIV mg.

obvious awkwardness of having Jesus refer to a Scripture that cannot be identified, the case for authenticity appears strong.

In addition, verse 39 introduces another of John's historical distinctions between the time of Jesus and that of the early church, which supports the idea that he is not simply fusing the two horizons together. Of course, the Spirit was present throughout the Old Testament and in Jesus' day, but he 'was not given in the characteristically Christian manner and measure until the close of the ministry' (Barrett 1978: 329). It will be only after Jesus' resurrection, here described in John's characteristic language of 'glorification', that the Holy Spirit will permanently indwell all believers (see below, p. 267).

From this point onwards, John 7 narrates no additional words of Jesus. The rest of the chapter (vv. 39–52) focuses on the division among the people, and even among the Jewish leaders, that Jesus' ministry during Tabernacles has stimulated. The somewhat positive responses of those who speculate that Jesus may be the eschatological prophet-like-Moses or even the Messiah himself (vv. 40–41a; as we have seen, p. 76, these expectations had begun to coalesce) remind the reader of what the disciples in the Synoptics also reported the crowds were starting to suggest (Mark 8:28 pars.). They again cut against the grain of the Johannine pattern of growing opposition to Christ and are therefore that much more likely to be authentic. The confusion over Jesus' birthplace (vv. 41b–43) is a classic example of Johannine irony. By the end of the first century both John and his readers would have known of Christ's birth in Bethlehem (cf. Matt. 2:1–12; Luke 2:1–20), but many during Jesus' lifetime would not have known this. Jesus is generally identified as coming from Galilee because that is where he spent the majority of his childhood (cf. further Lindars 1972: 305; Barrett 1978: 330). Once again John's narrative reflects historical verisimilitude.

Verses 44–45 hark back to the orders given in verse 32 to arrest Jesus. Apparently the soldiers sent on the mission became so enthralled with Jesus' teaching that they refused to carry out their commission (v. 46). One recalls the response of the crowds after the Sermon on the Mount (Matt. 7:28–29) and of the centurion after Jesus' death (Mark 15:39 pars.). Certain Pharisees reply indignantly that the guards have been 'deceived' (v. 47), exactly the recurring charge against Jesus in the later rabbinic literature (see above, p. 133). Only the 'mob that knows nothing of the law' – a classic reference to the 'am ha-āreṣ – are 'believing' in Jesus (vv. 48–49). Even J. L. Martyn (1979: 103, n. 150), otherwise most noted for stressing all the ways that the Johannine narrative seems to correspond to a *Sitz im Leben* at the end of the first century instead of during Jesus' lifetime, concedes that we find here 'the most transparently accurate reference to the

Am ha-aretz in the whole of the New Testament'.[186]

After the protestation in verse 48 that none of the Pharisees has believed in Christ, it comes as something of a surprise to learn of Nicodemus' positive intervention in verses 50–51. But nothing in his actions yet suggests he is a true disciple (recall above, p. 95). As early as the Mishnah, Jewish law required witnesses to argue on behalf of an accused person and granted permission for the accused to speak for himself (*Sanh.* 5.4). What is more, 'Roman law agreed with Jewish law on this point, as is evident from the words of Festus in Acts 25:16. In both codes, the accused must have the opportunity to speak in his own defense before the verdict of the court is reached' (Bruce 1983: 186). Nicodemus is not portrayed here as a believer, but merely as an honest judge (cf. Gamaliel in Acts 5:34–39).

Verse 52 reiterates the misunderstanding concerning Jesus' birthplace. Various prophets, of course, had come from Galilee (most notably, Hosea, Jonah and Nahum) but the NIV margin is probably correct here in suggesting that the discussion continues to refer to the eschatological prophet or Messiah. Two very early papyri (P66 and P75) in fact include the definite article at this point ('the prophet'). This may well reflect John's original text (R. E. Brown 1966: 325; Schnackenburg 1980: 151; Beasley-Murray 1987: 52); if not, it probably supplies the correct interpretation in the light of the discussion begun in verses 40–42 (Carson 1991: 332; Talbert 1992: 151).[187] And a later, free Christian composition would surely have clarified this controversy surrounding Christ's origins.

As we look back on chapter 7 we can see that John's focus has been at least as much on the schism Jesus' teaching generated as on Jesus' actual claims themselves. Verses 1–13 highlight the unbelief of Jesus' brothers. Verses 14–36 and 37–52 each reveal a tripartite structure with a synopsis of Jesus' teaching (vv. 14–24, 37–39), divisive speculation among the people (vv. 25–31, 40–44), and the mission of the temple guard (vv. 32–36, 45–52) (cf. Lindars 1972: 286).[188] Along the way one reads of at least

---

186] Cf. *Aboth* 2.6, in which Hillel, an older contemporary of Jesus, is reported to have said that such boors cannot be 'sinfearing'. Numerous, more elaborate condemnations occur in the later rabbinic literature (cf. Barrett 1978: 330).

187] Whitacre (1999: 202), on the other hand, thinks that 'a prophet' is original and that the Jewish leaders in Jerusalem are thus disclosing their immense prejudice against Galileans by flying in the face of scriptural facts.

188] R. Brown (1966: 330–331) discerns a fivefold parallelism between vv. 25–36 and 37–52 that leads him to conclude that these may be duplicate Johannine accounts of the same scene. But not all of the supposed parallels are equally clear and, even if the structure be accepted, it might merely reflect John's stylizing of similar conversations that

superficial faith existing among those in the crowds and in some of the authorities, leading to the striking inability of Jesus' opponents to carry out their orders to arrest him. All of this demonstrates that John is not monolithically representing response to Jesus as negative, even among the Jewish leadership, despite his redactional concerns to highlight Jesus' ultimate, widespread rejection. Historical concerns to depict a nuanced response despite growing opposition complement John's theological emphases rather than competing with them.

[THE WOMAN CAUGHT IN ADULTERY (7:53 – 8:11)]

Contemporary textual critics almost unanimously agree that this famous pericope does not form part of what John originally wrote (see esp. Wallace 1993; contra Heil 1991). It is absent in all the oldest and most reliable manuscripts, and those that do include it sometimes have only 8:2–11 or 3–11 or insert the passage after 7:36, 21:24 or even Luke 21:38. It seems to have been transmitted in at least two somewhat different forms, one of them preserved by the apocryphal *Gospel of the Hebrews*.[189] Many scholars nevertheless suggest that it may reflect a genuine episode from Jesus' life, preserved in the oral tradition, and later added to the text by Christian scribes (see esp. Burge 1984). The incident passes the double similarity and dissimilarity test with flying colours. Neither earlier Judaism nor subsequent Christianity had a very good track record of treating female sex offenders with this magnanimity, despite principles in their Scriptures that make such forgiveness appropriate (see esp. James 1979). Christ's behaviour, however, comports well with the core of historical Jesus material, which so consistently paints him as compassionate towards the outcast, while rebuking the religious establishment of his day (cf. esp. O'Day 1992). But we cannot appeal to this passage in a study of *John's* historicity if it most likely did not form part of his autograph.

THE LIGHT OF THE WORLD (8:12–30)

If one reads John 8:12 immediately after 7:52, the narrative proceeds smoothly. Jesus is still speaking at Tabernacles[190] and now makes a second

---

undoubtedly recurred frequently in the context of Jesus' disputes with the authorities.

189] Ehrman (1988) thinks there were two dramatically different forms. McDonald (1995) questions this, while highlighting the numerous textual variants within even the received tradition. Young (1995) rather unconvincingly postulates that the original account lacked v. 6a and was intended to portray the Pharisees in a positive light.

190] Morris (1995: 386) and Michaels (1983: 130) think some time may have elapsed, so

claim that stands out in bold relief in the light of the rituals of the festival. Every night of the feast, four huge lamps were lit to accompany joyful singing and dancing. On the last night the main candelabrum was deliberately left unlit as a reminder that Israel had not yet experienced full salvation (cf. esp. *Sukk.* 5.2–4). But Jesus speaks up and declares himself to be that salvation, 'the light of the world'. The threefold structure of his words closely parallels that of his claim to provide living water in 7:37–38: the claim itself, a reference to the one who believes in or follows Jesus, and the results for that individual as sharing the characteristics Jesus himself manifests (Ridderbos 1997: 292). Moreover, the wilderness imagery continues. Just as chapter 6 revolved around the provision of manna in the desert, and Jesus' claim of chapter 7 harked back to the water from the rock, so also here the light is reminiscent of the pillar of fire that followed the Israelites of old by night.[191] In the Synoptics, Jesus declares his followers to be the 'light of the world' (Matt. 5:14); it is a small step from that declaration to Jesus' claim here to be the source of that light. The contrast between light and darkness, as we have seen (above, p. 74), is characteristically Johannine but also thoroughly Jewish, especially in the light of Qumran (see esp. 1QS 3:7).

In 8:13 the Pharisaic leaders challenge Jesus explicitly with the objection that his discourse in 5:19–47 implicitly assumed what was already lurking in people's minds. One's own witness is not valid; one must have corroborating testimony (recall *Ket.* 2.9). As we noted in conjunction with chapter 7, each time Jesus teaches in Jerusalem, it is historically probable to assume some overlap in the make-up of the crowds from his last public appearance, along with some newcomers. Hence he can refer back to issues previously addressed, yet he must also repeat himself in various places. Thus Jesus' interchange in verses 14–19 echoes themes we have heard before: his audience does not know his true origin, there is a difference between his judgment and that of others, the Father is his primary witness, and knowing Jesus and knowing the Father are intricately interconnected. But this time he challenges the principle of needing extra witness (v. 14), even while going on to provide it (vv. 17–18; citing Deut. 19:15). Since Jesus knows he speaks the truth, what he says remains true whether or not anyone else supports him (cf. Michaels 1983: 128; Morris 1995:

---

it is now shortly after the feast. While this view is not impossible, the continuation of imagery so tightly tied in with Tabernacles suggests otherwise.

191] For a succinct summary of this and other Old Testament and intertestamental texts employing light as a metaphor for spiritual realities, see Witherington 1995: 174–175.

390–391).[192] Jesus' statements about judgment (vv. 15–16) line up with two apparently contrary strands of teaching in John. Sometimes Christ does not pass judgment (cf. 5:30 and 12:47); sometimes he does (cf. 5:22 and 9:39). Barrett (1978: 339) observes that 'in both sets of passages however the stress lies on the complete unity of will and action that exists between the Father and the Son', and that when Jesus does judge it is in the name and as the agent of God. When he says he does not judge, he therefore means that he does not judge on his own, independent of the Father's will. All this makes good sense as part of the tradition of Jesus' frequently cryptic sayings, but, if a later redactor had felt free to rephrase material as radically as many scholars affirm he did, he would surely have smoothed things out to an extent here.

Perhaps the hardest issue in these verses for a study of historicity is Jesus' reference to the Torah in verse 17 as 'your own' Law (from the Greek reflexive pronoun *hymeteros*). It appears at first as if John thinks Jesus is not even Jewish! But this is impossible in the light of the number of times in both John and the Synoptics that Jesus cites the Scriptures as authoritative (but cf. a similar sovereign freedom in the antitheses of the Sermon on the Mount: Matt. 5:21–48). The language is best viewed as parallel to the manner in which Moses and Joshua frequently addressed the Israelites, speaking of 'the Lord your God', when clearly he was the God of these spokesmen as well (e.g. Deut. 2:30; 4:20, 21, 23, 24; 18:15; Josh. 1:11, 13, 15; etc.). It is *ad hominem* language calling on the listeners to remember the teachings of their Law (or their God), especially in contexts in which they are not observing it (cf. esp. Joel 1:14). It is not a disavowal of the authority of Torah (or Yahweh) by the speaker (see esp. Augenstein 1997; cf. Whitacre 1999: 213).

Verse 20 brings the first subsection of 8:12–30 to a close, as John again describes where a dialogue takes place only after narrating the gist of it (recall 6:59; 7:9). Morris (1995: 394) thinks that 'John adds another of those little notes which indicate an exact knowledge of the circumstances.' As in 7:30, Jesus remains free despite the plots to arrest him; John again explains that his hour had not yet come. Because of the numerous parallels between segments of 8:14–20 and 7:27–35, Raymond Brown (1966: 343) concludes that 8:12–20 'is a composite and must have had a complicated literary history before it took its present form'. But it can equally easily be seen as the necessary repetition and clarification that Jesus would have had

---

192] For early rabbinic debates on the legitimacy of father and son as combined witnesses, see esp. *Rosh Ha-Shan.* 1.7.

to make, teaching repeatedly in one place to ever-changing audiences.[193]

In 8:21 Jesus again refers to his coming death in language that is readily misunderstood (v. 22; recall 7:33–36). This time, however, his discourse turns more pointed: his opponents will die in their sins. This turn of phrase comes from Deuteronomy 24:16 and is amplified in numerous texts in Ezekiel (esp. 3:18–19 and 18:17–18). As for synoptic parallels, one thinks of the headline used to summarize Jesus' public ministry: 'Repent' (Mark 1:15 pars.), language that echoes the Baptist's earlier more explicit call to repent 'for the forgiveness of sins' (Mark 1:4 pars.). As frequently in both John and the Synoptics, Jesus does not directly resolve the controversy his enigmatic comments have generated, but goes on to claim that his opponents originate 'from below' and are 'of this world' – unless they believe in him (vv. 23–24). As in the parallel contrast in 3:11–15, the language is thoroughly Johannine, while the concepts are deeply embedded in Jewish apocalyptic.

Verse 24b introduces another of John's puzzling *egō eimi* texts. The Greek might literally be rendered, 'if you do not believe that I am, you will die in your sins'. The most natural way to interpret this is probably by inserting in English the personal pronoun, thus, 'if you do not believe that I am he' (as in 4:26 and 6:20; cf. NIV mg.), hence the NIV rendering, 'I am the one I claim to be' (cf. McKay 1996).[194] Even then most scholars suspect that there is a veiled allusion to Isaiah 43:10, in which Yahweh himself declares, 'I am he' (R. E. Brown 1966: 341; Morgan-Wynne 1980). But by 8:58 a clear reference to Exodus 3:14 will appear, so one wonders if Jesus (or John) is not already foreshadowing that language here. But, once again, the wording is sufficiently puzzling to be credible as the gist of an utterance of the historical Jesus, whatever his exact Aramaic may have been.

Obviously Jesus' audience is still baffled and so asks him directly, 'Who are you?' (v. 25a). Still Jesus does not give a direct reply (v. 25b)[195] and shifts the topic back to the reliability of his judgment because it mirrors that of the Father (v. 26). Verse 27 provides another narrative aside, showing that

---

193] Lindars (1972: 313) discerns the same tripartite structure in 8:12–30 as in 7:15–36 and 37–52, while admitting it is not as clear cut. Again, his conclusion that John has thus freely composed all this material out of a relatively small amount of tradition is by no means the only logical deduction.

194] Freed (1983) points out that the expression combined with an emphasis on judging could be just another way to make a messianic claim.

195] Miller (1980) surveys the various ways Jesus' words have been rendered in this half verse and convincingly opts for 'I am the One at the beginning, which is what I keep telling you.'

John continues to be concerned to preserve some distinctions between what was or was not understood during Jesus' lifetime and the insights to which his followers later came. Verse 28a provides another apocalyptic 'Son of Man' saying, but as in 3:14 using the phrase 'lifted up', by which John refers to the crucifixion as well as the exaltation.[196] In this half-verse *egō eimi* occurs again with all the options and ambiguities of verse 24. The rest of verses 28b–29 merely stress again how completely in harmony Jesus is with the Father. One hears at least distant echoes of the Matthean emphasis on Jesus as Emmanuel, 'God with us' (cf. Geiger 1992: 471).

Verse 30 completes the first half of John 8 by again reminding us that the response to Christ was not monolithically hostile. The next half chapter, however, will complicate matters considerably. As a summary of the structure of 8:12–30 we may agree with Neyrey (1987), who reads John's narrative against the Old Testament background of a lawsuit or court case. It seems that the Jewish authorities informally have Jesus on trial; by the end of the chapter it will be clear that Jesus, speaking for God, believes that it is these authorities who stand condemned. Even these initial verses can be subdivided into verses 12–20, in which the authorities are assembled to judge the plaintiff (Jesus), and verses 21–30, in which Jesus turns the tables on them and charges them with refusing to believe in who he really is. None of this requires the postulation of Hellenistic or Gnostic influence: it is thoroughly explicable in the light of the historical background of and competing claims within early first-century Judaism. Johannine language intrudes at numerous points, but we have no need to charge John with freely inventing material at any juncture.

JESUS AS THE 'I AM' (8:31–59)

With verse 31 Jesus apparently centres his attention on those Jews who had just put their faith in him (v. 30). By the end of this passage, these 'believers' want to stone him! Numerous suggestions have been put forward to explain this anomaly, most of them unconvincing.[197] Motyer (1997:

196] Cf. Beasley-Murray (1987: 131): 'In the synoptic predictions of the Passion (notably Mark 8:31; 9:31; 10:32), which are closely related to the Johannine lifting up sayings, the Son of Man suffers, dies, and rises as the instrument of the kingdom of God. This Christological, soteriological, and eschatological tradition is assumed in the Johannine counterparts.'

197] Swetnam (1980) surveys many of these, pointing out their inadequacies. His own proposal – that the perfect participle in v. 31, as equivalent to a pluperfect, suggests that these were people who once believed but believe no more – has been shown by Segalla (1981) to be equally implausible.

162–165) is more convincing in suggesting that the audience in verse 31 is larger than but inclusive of the group referred to in verse 30. Frequently throughout John superficial faith does not mature into genuine faith; so also here. But in verse 48 we are meant to see a narrowing of John's focus to those Jewish authorities who oppose Jesus.[198] The heart of Jesus' appeal at the outset of this section (v. 30b) is for his hearers to 'remain' or 'abide' in (NIV 'hold to'; Gk. *menō*) his teaching, a characteristic Johannine verb. But this need for perseverance exactly matches the thrust of the synoptic parable of the sower (Mark 4:3–9 pars.), even while using different language.

Verse 32 next offers one of the most memorable sayings ascribed to Jesus in John: 'Then you will know the truth, and the truth will set you free.' Considerable Jewish literature, some of it extant already in the first century, suggests that Jesus' contemporaries ascribed this role pre-eminently to the Torah.[199] The Tabernacles' celebration of the Israelites' release from Egyptian bondage provides further illuminating background. And to the extent that sporadic beginnings to the Zealot movement were already underway, Jesus' claim to be himself the dispenser of freedom would have stood out by contrast against several foils.

Not surprisingly, Jesus' audience protests that, as Abraham's 'seed' (NIV 'descendants'; going back to Gen. 12:2), they have never been enslaved in the first place (v. 33). Obviously they cannot be referring to political bondage. Israel was currently occupied by Rome, the latest in a series of foreign empires that had subjugated the nation off and on for centuries. Instead, for once, they recognize that Jesus must be speaking at a spiritual level, but they dispute their need for freedom even here. The verb 'set free' (Gk. *eleutheroō*) appears in the Gospels only in this passage (here and in v. 36), but the cognate adjective *eleutheros* is used in Matthew 17:26 in a similar context. There Jesus contrasts the freedom from taxation that kings' children have *vis-à-vis* the subjugated peoples of the empire and applies that concept of freedom to his disciples in the spiritual realm. Here verse 34 explains that Jesus' listeners are slaves to sin, a diagnosis similar to N. T. Wright's summary (1996: 443–474) of the synoptic Jesus claiming that slavery to Satan rather than Rome formed the real nature of Jewish exile. This verse also presents the first of the double-'Amen' sayings to have appeared since 6:53, a reminder that John is not just scattering them around liberally or indiscriminately within freely invented material.

198] Cf. also Morris (1995: 404) and Ridderbos (1997: 308), who both unpack this theme of superficial discipleship in helpful ways.

199] Barrett (1978: 344) gives references, particularly from Josephus and Philo. On the Targums, cf. Sabugal 1974. From the Dead Sea Scrolls, see esp. 1QS 4:20–21.

Verse 35 may reflect a little metaphor that could originally have had a tradition history of its own (see esp. Dodd 1963: 379–382). In context it contrasts the transience of slavery with the permanence of sonship in the family of God (v. 36). At any rate, we are scarcely far from the world of the synoptic parable-teller. In verse 37 Jesus returns to the crowds' observation that they are ethnically Jewish, pointing out how poorly this meshes with their readiness to kill him. If the larger group, including apparent follow-ers, is still present at this juncture in the dialogue, then we can readily grasp why they could not accept Jesus' charge. Yet all four Gospels will make it plain how even the vast majority of the once-sympathetic crowds in Jerusalem turn on Christ, even calling for his crucifixion, during the last hours of his life. These professed followers do not yet recognize the deep evil that still lurks within them. In the Synoptics 'shallow reliance on descent from Abraham is condemned by John the Baptist and by Jesus himself' (Matt. 3:9 / Luke 3:8; Matt. 8:11–12 / Luke 13:28–29) (Lindars 1972: 324–325). Verse 38 contrasts Jesus' father with the crowds' father, setting the stage for the intensifying polemic to come.

Of course, Jesus' listeners will claim Abraham as their 'founding father' (v. 39a). But Jesus points out that true spiritual offspring should then imitate the exemplary behaviour of Abraham (v. 39b). Jesus may have the specific hospitality of Genesis 18:1–19 in view, in which Abraham enter-tained divine visitors unawares (cf. Witherington 1995: 177). But far from treating Jesus this way, whether they yet realize it or not, most in Jerusalem will side with those who want to execute Christ (v. 40). Once again, a different father must be motivating them (v. 41a). Whoever the crowds take that father to be, they recognize that Jesus is disputing their lineage. 'We are not illegitimate children,' they protest and, besides, ultimately God is their true father (v. 41b). Early patristic commentary regularly saw an im-plied insult against Jesus here, too; perhaps *he* is illegitimate. If this slur is in view, it may reflect the ancient Jewish alternative explanation to the Chris-tian account of Jesus' virginal conception – that Jesus was the bastard child of Mary with someone other than Joseph (cf. van Voorst 2000: 117 for a discussion of the rabbinic texts). But it may simply represent a Jewish claim of faithfulness to God instead of an attack on Christ (Talbert 1992: 156).

Still, Jesus retorts that their behaviour belies their protestations (vv. 42–43). He then clarifies who this father of his opponents is, a father who is neither Abraham nor God. 'You belong to your father, the devil, and you want to carry out your father's desire' (v. 44a). This charge has often been called the most anti-Jewish statement in the New Testament.[200] More likely,

---

200] For recent polemic against this text, Casey (1996: 24–27) is representative.

it is one of the most *misunderstood* statements in Scripture. We must not generalize from the setting in which John places it. In fact, it is precisely those critics who assume that the words are not Jesus' but John's, addressing the entire Jewish community harassing Ephesus at the end of the first century, who risk overly generalizing the application of this verse and unwittingly proving anti-Jewish. In its putative historical context it refers to one small group of Jewish leaders, who execute Christ half a year later and not necessarily to anyone else, and it is important to realize that Jesus is making an ethical and not an ontological accusation (see esp. Motyer 1997: 185–190).

Here, too, is probably the best place to comment on John's use of 'the Jews' more generally (cf. v. 48). In John's narrative the expression has become a kind of shorthand for 'certain Jewish authorities', especially the most religious of the Jewish leaders in Jesus' day, who are also the most implacably opposed to him.[201] The reason he uses the term in a fashion so readily susceptible to later misunderstanding and charges of anti-Judaism may have to do with the escalating tensions at the end of the first century as both Christianity and formative (rabbinic) Judaism emerged as rival competitors for the legacy of pre-70 Judaism. The practice also owes much to the nature of rhetoric in the ancient Mediterranean world more generally (Johnson 1989). But it did not originate in the Johannine community. As for John's meaning, the context of each usage must be examined on its own (cf. further Reim 1984).

To charge would-be executioners with following in the devil's footsteps (v. 44b) would not have struck a Jewish audience as inappropriate, since Jewish tradition regularly attributed the first murder (Cain slaying his brother Abel) to diabolical motivation (cf. esp. Wis. Sol. 2:24). That their father, the devil, is the 'father of lies' (vs. Jesus' telling the truth – vv. 45–46)[202] proves scarcely more inflammatory than the Synoptics' portrait of John the Baptist labelling certain Pharisees as a 'brood of vipers' (Matt. 3:7 par.), which may likewise contain a reference to Satan as the serpent. The problem with such people is that they do not hear or obey Jesus' words (John 8:43, 47), precisely the behaviour that the synoptic Jesus attributes to the devil's temptations in the parables of the sower and of the wheat and

---

201] Motyer (1997: 46–54) succinctly surveys the other suggested explanations for this phenomenon before persuasively defending this one (54–56).

202] R. E. Brown (1966: 358) observes that 'the background of the tradition may be that of the Suffering Servant of Isa liii 9 in whom there was *no deceit.* The Testament of Judah xxiv 1 says: "No sin will be found in him [the star from Jacob]"; but we cannot be certain if this was a Christian interpolation.'

tares (Mark 4:19 pars.; Matt. 13:39). The synoptic Jesus, moreover, calls Simon Peter 'Satan' when he refuses to countenance the road to the cross (Mark 8:33 pars.). Such language may offend certain modern sensibilities, but that probably tells us more about the compunctions of the people offended than about the historicity of John's narrative!

With verse 48 the focus explicitly narrows to Jesus' sharpest antagonists. The charge of demon-possession is not new, either in John or the Synoptics (see above, p. 134). Here, however, appears the lone use of 'Samaritan' in the New Testament as a disparaging epithet rather than an ethnic identification. But a later rabbinic tradition will equate 'Samaritan' with 'magician' (*b. Sot.* 22a), and already in Acts 8 we read of Simon the Magician who led the Samaritans astray (by either Jewish *or* Christian standards) in the first century! In the light of the centuries-old hostility between Jews and Samaritans the pejorative use of the epithet is entirely believable. So also is the psychology of the situation: 'When their theological argument fails, Jesus' opponents turn to personal abuse' (Carson 1991: 354).

Jesus denies the charge and points out its implications for a culture steeped in conventions surrounding honour and shame (v. 49). A true criterion for evaluating Jesus is whether or not he seeks to glorify himself. Verse 50 thus reintroduces the subordinationist motif so prominent in 5:19–47; as there, it is unlikely to be the creation of a later Christian church concerned to glorify *Jesus*. It may also reflect an implicit claim to Messiahship (cf. Is. 16:5). As another double-'Amen' saying, it may well be authentic. On keeping Jesus' words (v. 51a), recall the parable of the two builders (Matt. 7:24–27 par.). 'Not seeing death' (v. 51b) is a classic Hebraism (Ps. 89:48; cf. Luke 2:26).

But how can Jesus promise people they will never die? Even Abraham died, like all the other Jewish luminaries. Is Jesus claiming to be greater than Abraham? If so, he must be mad (vv. 52–53)! John's readers know better. The synoptic Jesus likewise refers indirectly to himself as someone who is greater than key Jewish heroes and institutions: Solomon, Jonah, the temple (Matt. 12:39–42; Luke 11:29–32).[203] Again Jesus skirts the pointed question 'Who do you think you are?' and reiterates themes I have already discussed, including his subordination to the Father (vv. 54–55). But the conversation reaches a new level when Jesus claims that 'Abraham rejoiced to see my day' (v. 56; NIV's 'at the thought of seeing' seems less accurate here). A considerable body of Jewish literature built on the

---

203] Barrett (1978: 334) adds, 'The treatment of descent from Abraham, a privilege which Jesus minimizes in comparison with something greater, recalls his question about the Messiah and David's son' (Mark 12:35–37 pars.).

promises to Abraham in Genesis 12, 15 and 18, speculating about Abraham's opportunities to learn of heavenly secrets and know the future in more detail than the Bible explicitly discloses (Schnackenburg 1980: 221–223). Representative of this are *2 Esdras* 3.14, *2 Baruch* 4.4 and *Apocalypse of Abraham* 31.

The authorities, however, think Jesus is making an even stronger claim – to have been alive at the time of Abraham (v. 57). The reference to 'fifty years' probably 'indicates the common view of the end of a man's working life (see Num 4:2–3, 39; 8:24–25); Jesus has not yet reached seniority, and he claims to have seen Abraham!' (Beasley-Murray 1987: 139).[204] Jesus replies with arguably the strongest Christological declaration ascribed to him in any of the four Gospels, 'I tell you the truth ... before Abraham was born, I am' (v. 58). The authorities obviously interpret him to have crossed over a boundary in usurping divine prerogatives and thus feel he deserves to be stoned for blasphemy (v. 59; cf. Lev. 24:16).

If any of Jesus' *egō eimi* sayings in John alludes to Exodus 3:14 and the revelation of the divine name to Moses in the burning bush, this one surely does (Schnackenburg 1980: 224).[205] Still, Jesus stops well short of what countless charlatans in the history of religion have explicitly declared, namely 'I am God'! We recall that blasphemy before AD 70 was defined considerably more loosely than the mere ascription to oneself of the name Yahweh (above, p. 111). But recent studies of Jewish apocalyptic have demonstrated that angels or exalted humans could bear the divine name. Motyer (1997: 209) plausibly concludes that John 8:58 'would *not* be heard as a claim to *be God*. It *would* be heard as a claim to be a divine agent, anointed with the name and powers of God, and (in this case) active in the *genesis* of Abraham.'[206] And it is arguable that Jesus' *egō eimi* in Mark 14:62 in reply to the high priest's interrogation makes a loftier claim more explicitly than anything in John, as Jesus goes on to identify himself with the heavenly Son of Man ascending to the divine throne-room and returning to judge the cosmos over which he has been given complete authority (cf. Dan. 7:13–14).

204] Alternately, M. J. Edwards (1994) thinks the reference is to the fifty years of each Jubilee, used as a conventional round number for an average lifespan.

205] But there is continuing debate; see Harner 1970.

206] Michaels (1983:141) finds a synoptic parallel of sorts to the dispute with the Sadducees in Mark 12:18–27 pars., in which Jesus implies that the patriarchs are still alive as resurrected beings. D. M. Smith (1999: 190) comments, 'Apart from its polemical edges and thrusts, however, chapter 8 does not go beyond what has earlier been said of and about Jesus. It does not advance those claims but sets them over against the sharpest opposition.'

If one wishes to reject the historicity of this verse because of preconceived convictions about what Jesus could or could not have claimed, that is one's prerogative. But let all the 'anti-Jewish' rhetoric cease, for this entire passage presents a credible interchange among squabbling Hebrews in the world of pre-70 Judaism.[207] Verses 32–58 form a tightly knit unity, most noticeably with their fivefold cycle of statement, misunderstanding and explanation (Neyrey 1987), while the movement from verses 12–30 to 31–59 closely mirrors that of 6:14–50 to 51–59 (Carson 1991: 348). John 8:31–58 may on the one hand be fairly described as classic Johannine theology. But it is all held together by repeated references to Abraham, who does not otherwise appear in the Fourth Gospel, and we can trace reminiscences of Jewish tradition about the patriarch at almost every turn. Parallels of various kinds to the Synoptics appear regularly interspersed. For all these reasons Dodd (1963: 330–332), with his characteristic caution and understatement, concludes that John and the Synoptics alike drew from primitive tradition here. I suggest more boldly that the tradition reflects an authentic dialogue involving the historical Jesus (cf. esp. Ridderbos 1997: 306–307).[208]

HEALING THE MAN BORN BLIND (9:1–12)

We proceed to an illustration of Jesus' role as the light of the world. Presumably, Jesus is no longer teaching in the temple but is still in Jerusalem (v. 1). This could be later on during the last day of the feast or up to a few days afterwards, prior to the Galileans' return to the north (cf. Barrett 1978: 356 with Carson 1991: 361). Tabernacles imagery, however, is still pervasive. Not only does Jesus provide physical sight for a blind man against the festival's backdrop of rituals of light and darkness, but that man must wash in the very pool, Siloam, from which the water was drawn for the daily processions to the temple (recall above, p. 136).

The healing invites comparison and contrast with 5:1–18. In both cases, Jesus is working a miracle associated with the Messianic age, a relationship the Baptist stresses in the Synoptics (Matt. 11:5 par.). In both cases we learn somewhat belatedly that the healing took place on a Sabbath (5:9;

207] For a sane reply to the charges of anti-Judaism in John more generally, see esp. Lea 1994.

208] The fullest treatment of the (largely Jewish) background to 'I am he' texts is now C. H. Williams 2000. For the implications for interpreting John's Gospel, see 255–303, although Williams focuses exclusively on theological and literary issues and does not address the question of historicity. In defence of the likelihood of Jesus having used 'Christologically self-conscious "I am" sayings' before his death and resurrection, see esp. Maier 1981: 278.

9:14), in a fashion that suggests that Jesus went out of his way to challenge the oral Torah of the Pharisees. In both cases the healing is merely the prelude to the longer-lasting debate on the question of Jesus' identity. There are crucial differences here, however, that demonstrate that John is scarcely creating a doublet of the earlier narrative. This man has been blind from birth; one thinks also of the congenital illnesses the apostles will heal in Acts 3:2 and 14:8. Healing the blind in general is rare among the miracle stories of antiquity, but common for the synoptic Jesus. The healing of congenital blindness, however, seems unprecedented (Bruce 1983: 218).

Because of the common Jewish link between sickness and sin,[209] a theological dilemma emerges. Did this man sin *in utero* or is he being punished for the sins of his parents (v. 2)?[210] But if Jesus affirmed a direct relationship between sin and sickness in 5:1–19, here he stresses that it scarcely applies to all situations of personal illness. Rather, 'this happened so that the work of God might be displayed in his life' (v. 3).[211] This logic may well be based on Exodus 9:16 and God's rationale for dealing harshly with Pharaoh. It is paralleled in the Synoptics in Luke 13:1–5, in which Jesus makes plain that the disasters he describes are not due to the greater sinfulness of their victims. Jesus then explains that his work will accomplish this man's healing. Verse 4 recalls earlier uses of 'work' by the Johannine Jesus (esp. 4:34 and 5:36) and is again probably authentic (see esp. Ensor 1996: 108–122). Jesus' point is also 'exactly the same as the saying of R. Simeon ben Eleazar (c. AD 190): "Work so long as you can and it is possible for you and it is still within your power" (*B. Shabbath*, 151b)' (Lindars 1972: 342). The inherent limitations on Jesus implicit in verses 4–5 are not likely to have been invented (Ridderbos 1997: 335).

The method Jesus uses to heal this blind man (vv. 6–7) is unique in John's Gospel but resembles the use of spittle on the eyes of the blind in both Mark 7:33 and 8:23. The latter text occurs in the context of a two-stage healing just as we find here.[212] Saliva was often thought to have

---

209] Talbert (1992: 158) and Borchert (1996: 313) give the most important Old Testament background.

210] For further options, see the survey of opinions in Thomas 1998: 112–117.

211] Poirier (1996) repunctuates the text so that v. 3b goes with v. 4 rather than v. 3a. Burge (2000: 272–273) notes that four of the other eleven uses of *all' hina* in the Gospel of John go with what follows rather than with what precedes. If this is the correct interpretation here, then Jesus is not giving a reason for the man's condition at all, but merely describing the positive outcome that will eventually result.

212] For further structural parallels between 9:1–7 and synoptic healing miracles, see E. E. Ellis 1999: 159–160.

medicinal value in the ancient Mediterranean world; Jesus is probably playing on that belief here (Barrett 1978: 358, with documentation). John sees a wordplay in the similarity between the Hebrew for Siloam (*Šilōaḥ*) and 'send' (*šālaḥ*). Just as Jesus is the one the Father has sent, so now this once-blind man becomes a 'sent one'. Later rabbinic sources would link Isaiah 8:6 (on the Jews' refusing the gently flowing waters of Shiloh) with Genesis 49:10 ('The sceptre will not depart from Judah ... until Shiloh comes'; cf. NIV mg.), interpreted messianically. It is possible, therefore, that we are to understand an implicit messianic claim here, too (K. Müller 1969). Bruce Grigsby (1985) also postulates an allusion to rabbinic traditions about Siloam functioning eschatologically in the light of the life-giving water that will flow from the temple, as prophesied in Ezekiel 47. Less esoterically, one remembers Elisha's command to Naaman to wash in the Jordan river to be cured of his leprosy (2 Kgs. 5:10). Tellingly, archaeologists have even more confidence about having identified the pool of Siloam in Jerusalem than they do about the pool of Bethesda. Originally part of Hezekiah's tunnel (2 Kgs. 20:20; 2 Chr. 32:30), Siloam was excavated in 1880, complete with an inscription enabling its identification (Michaels 1983: 150).[213]

Having never witnessed such a miracle, the neighbours of the healed man naturally question whether they are seeing the same person or not (vv. 8–9a).[214] He assures them they are (v. 9b)[215] and then describes his cure in response to their inquiries (vv. 10–11). Unlike the blind man of 5:1–18, this man knows who healed him. He remains in the dark only concerning Jesus' present whereabouts (v. 12). Carson (1991: 366) aptly comments, 'Unlike the healed paralytic in ch. 5, this man appears sharp, quick-witted, and eventually quite sardonic toward religious leaders who would not face facts. The colour in the two personalities testifies not only to the Evangelist's stylistic versatility, but to the differences in people to whom Jesus ministered.' Not surprisingly, there are a fair number of scholars who accept the authenticity of the essence of this entire miracle story (e.g. R. E. Brown 1966: 379; Meier 1994: 694–698; Twelftree 1999: 302–303).

213] On the form and authenticity of vv. 1–7, esp. in the light of synoptic parallels, see Pryor 1992a: 41.

214] That blind men had to resort to begging is widely attested, not least in Mark 10:46.

215] The man's reply (*egō eimi*) demonstrates that 'I am [he]' does not have to have divine overtones in John! But see Parsons (1993), who finds a Johannine double meaning here nevertheless.

THE AFTERMATH OF THE MIRACLE (9:13–41)

The Pharisees would be particularly interested in interrogating the once-blind man, because Jesus went out of his way to break their oral laws in healing the man on a Sabbath (vv. 13–15). Making the mud mixed with spittle would have been considered 'kneading' (*Shab.* 7.2); Christ may have violated traditions about anointing the eyes as well (*j. Abod. Zar.* 14d; *b. Abod. Zar.* 28b). That the Pharisees themselves are divided in their response to this breach of tradition (v. 16) is historically credible and suggests that John is not merely inventing a unilaterally negative response to Jesus on the part of the Jewish leaders. The division in fact follows the approaches of Jesus' contemporaries Shammai and Hillel. 'The school of Shammai tended to argue from first principles (so here: anyone who breaks the law is a sinner); the school of Hillel tended to have regard to the established facts of a case (so here: Jesus has performed a good work). In a case like this, their conclusions were bound to conflict with each other' (Bruce 1983: 213). That the man's own testimony to Jesus' identity employs no higher a title than 'prophet' (v. 17) further suggests historical verisimilitude.[216]

Getting nowhere with the healed man, the authorities now turn to his parents. Are they sure he is the same person who had been blind and, if so, how can he now see (vv. 18–19)? The scepticism is completely credible, especially given the unprecedented nature of the healing. The parents' reply is appropriately restrained and equally plausible. They can no more explain the miracle than anyone else, but they can definitely confirm the man's identity. They 'serve the ball' back into their son's 'court' (vv. 20–21). The language, 'he is of age' (vv. 21, 23), suggests that the blind man may have been young enough to be mistaken for a minor.

Verse 22 explains the reluctance of the parents to say any more. It is also one of the most historically suspect statements in the entire Gospel (cf. also 12:42 and 16:2). Martyn's influential two-level reading of John (1979), which focuses primarily on what he believes was invented to address John's community at the end of the first century (see above, p. 62), takes its starting point from these texts. Numerous scholars have agreed with Martyn that the so-called *birkat ha-mînîm* (the 'blessing [euphemistic for 'curse'] against the heretics'), introduced into the eighteen benedictions of the synagogue liturgy, was developed at the council of Jamnia in about AD 85 and had Jewish *Christians* specifically in view. Prior to this, it is argued, excommunication from the synagogues simply did not occur

---

216] Borchert (1996: 318) thinks that the man might have put Jesus in the same 'wonder-working category of an Elijah or an Elisha'.

– what we read in John is blatant anachronism.[217]

On the other hand, a spate of studies since the 1980s has questioned whether anything like a uniform, much less empire-wide, curse on Christians was introduced at all this early. Even if it were, there is reason to question the claim that Christians were its primary target.[218] In other words, if what John is describing in 9:22 and elsewhere is understood as an empire-wide edict, then no such ban had occurred even by the end of the first century when his Gospel was published. But if John's text is taken at face value to refer to an informal policy not necessarily adopted anywhere outside certain synagogues in Jerusalem during Jesus' lifetime, then the practice becomes far more plausible (cf. Ezra 10:8 for Old Testament precedent). After all, here was the centre of the strongest opposition to Christ, the place where he would be arraigned by the Sanhedrin within six months and be sentenced to die. The synoptic Jesus predicted synagogue expulsion for his followers (Luke 12:8–9; Mark 8:37 pars.; Luke 6:22–23 par.). The consistent portrait of Acts is that hostility against the first Christians came from fellow Jews, starting from soon after Pentecost in AD 30. For those inclined to disbelieve Acts, Paul, in one of his earliest letters, speaks of past Jewish persecution of Jewish Christians in Judea (1 Thess. 2:14). If indeed at least a few secret supporters of Jesus had begun to appear, even among the Jewish leaders in Jerusalem (12:42), it is not incredible that the parents of a man so spectacularly cured could begin to

---

217] For a recent, vitriolic representative of this perspective see Casey (1996: 54–55). But his supporting arguments are less representative and noticeably weak: (1) Confessing a person is not a feasible cause of preventing people from attending the synagogue. (2) Confessing Jesus Christ as the trigger for excommunication makes sense only after AD 70. (3) If 'many' of the rulers had believed (12:42), they would have formed too powerful a group to be kept out of Jewish meetings. (4) There is no trace in any of the Gospels of the more formal Jewish disciples of Jesus being excommunicated. In reply, we may note that (1) and (2) are sheer affirmations that are by no means self-evident. Rom. 10:9–10 demonstrates that the confession 'Jesus as Lord' was one of the earliest marks of Christian identity, while the apostles and other followers of Jesus are rejected by numerous Jewish groups from the earliest pages of the Acts of the Apostles onwards. As for (3), the 'many' of 12:42 need by no means imply a majority, nor need they have been strong in their belief (esp. in the light of 8:30, followed by vv. 31–59). As for (4), if this was a local, informal practice merely involving certain Jerusalem synagogues, then there is no reason for the Galilean disciples of Jesus to have been affected.

218] Motyer (1997: 92–94) summarizes a number of these studies. Three of the most recent that sum up the current state of the question are Joubert 1993; van der Horst 1994; and Mimouni 1997.

display the seeds of faith but also fear reprisals for going too public with it. Not surprisingly, then, an impressive number of recent commentators accepts the possible historicity of John 9:22,[219] even if their arguments are still too often ignored by the critical 'establishment'.

Interestingly, Jesus has disappeared from the scene throughout 9:8–23. He will not reappear until verse 35. Once again we see that the idea of Jesus speaking in nothing but extended blocks of discourse in John 3 – 11 is a misleading generalization. For a majority of this chapter, in fact, the focus remains completely off Jesus and on the Pharisaic inquiry and debate that the healing generated. Verses 24–34 are unified by the authorities' further questioning of the formerly blind man. The entire exchange is thoroughly Jewish and credible. The expression 'Give glory to God' matches the command to Achan in Joshua 7:19 and mirrors the English idiom, ''Fess up!' That the man professes not to know whether Jesus is a sinner (vv. 24–25) 'is another sure sign that the evangelist is not portraying the man born blind as a model Christian' (Witherington 1995: 389, n. 49). All he can say for sure is what happened to him. Verses 26–27 suggest his annoyance with the repeated interrogation. 'Do you want to become his disciples, too?' is at least ironic, if not downright sarcastic.[220]

Not surprisingly, the officials reply in kind (vv. 28–29). Instead of being impostors they are truly 'disciples of Moses'. This is an unusual expression but fits Jesus' observation in Matthew 23:2 that the scribes and Pharisees 'sit in Moses' seat'. The man who has been healed finds it amazing that his questioners could think Jesus 'came' from anyone other than God (vv. 30–33). The man's logic is not entirely above reproach; we have already seen repeated allegations that Jesus got his power from the devil rather than from Yahweh. But it is exactly what one would expect of a believing Jew who had experienced so dramatic a cure. 'Without knowing it, the man anticipates a rabbinical maxim later expressed' as 'Every one in whom is the fear of heaven, his words are heard' (*b. Ber.* 6b; Bruce 1983: 218). The flip side, that God does not hear sinners, is well entrenched in Old Testament and intertestamental texts (Barrett 1978: 363, with references). The man uses no established Christological titles in his testimony, as we might

---

219] E.g. Bruce 1983: 215–216; Michaels 1983: 155; Hengel 1989: 114–115; Carson 1991: 366–367; Talbert 1992: 161; Pryor 1992a: 43; Morris 1995: 434, n. 36; Witherington 1995: 389, n. 48; Borchert 1996: 319–321; Motyer 1997: 94; Ridderbos 1997: 343; Burge 2000: 275. Even Bultmann (1971: 335, n. 5) noted that *aposynagōgos* corresponds to the rabbinic *mᵉnûḏeh*, and that such a person is to be distinguished from the one completely separated from the community (by *mᵉšûpāḏ*).
220] On the larger ironies in this exchange, see Derrett 1998a.

expect if John were inventing the dialogue. Once again, the interchange ends with the Jewish leaders abandoning logic and resorting to slander (v. 34). The conviction that Jesus earlier rejected – that the man was born blind because of someone's sin – re-emerges here in the retort of the authorities.

Jesus now takes the initiative to track down the man he has healed. Verses 35–41 complete this story with a final dialogue between the original two characters 'on stage' and with an aside to the Pharisees. Jesus' taking the lead in finding the man is consistent with the more formal calling of his disciples and resembles Wisdom of Solomon 6:16, in which Wisdom personified goes about in search of those to whom she wishes to appear. Jesus' use of 'Son of man' reintroduces his favourite and distinctive title (v. 35) and makes one think of Luke 18:8: 'However, when the Son of Man comes, will he find faith on the earth?'[221] That the healed man does not immediately recognize that Jesus is referring to himself speaks for historicity (v. 36). The way in which Jesus clarifies that he is using the title for himself is equally circumspect (v. 37). The man responds as John would have all readers respond to this Gospel – in belief – though the prostration (from Gk. *proskyneō*) referred to here may originally have been just that, rather than formal 'worship' (v. 38; cf. Beasley-Murray 1987: 159; Carson, 1991: 377; Witherington 1995: 389, n. 54). 'The fact that the former blind man's confession of faith comes only *after* his expulsion from the synagogue is strong evidence that the narrator's concern here is historical, not just theological or illustrative' (Michaels 1983: 158). And the action of a person bowing down to Jesus occurs frequently in the Synoptics, but remains otherwise unattested in John.

Jesus replies to the man's obeisance by declaring how his ministry will reverse the roles of the blind and the sighted (v. 39). The 'I have come' language here parallels numerous synoptic texts (e.g. Mark 2:17; Matt. 5:17; Luke 12:49, etc.). 'This paradoxical language is a stylistic device which also appears in synoptic sayings of Jesus' (e.g. Mark 8:38 pars.; Matt. 10:26 par.; Luke 12:51; 14:26 par.; Schnackenburg 1980: 255). The concept of judgment creating 'outsiders' out of would-be 'insiders' parallels Jesus' rationale for teaching in parables (Mark 4:10–12 pars.). As for the apparent contradiction with sayings in John in which Jesus claims not to judge, see above, page 142. In addition, even Bultmann (1971: 341–342) comments, 'This is the paradox of the revelation, that in order to bring

---

221] This is the first Johannine Son of Man saying to approximate to the common synoptic category of Jesus' humanity, a virtual circumlocution for 'I' (contra M. Müller 1991, who finds this usage distinctive to John).

grace it must also give offence, and so can turn to judgement. In order to be grace it must uncover sin; he who resists this binds himself to his sin, and so through the revelation sin for the first time becomes definitive.'

Thus, whether the Pharisees overhear this conversation in a public locale or learn about it later, they ultimately confront Jesus again. 'Since the metaphorical use of blindness was already familiar from the Old Testament (Is 42:16, 18ff; 43:8 etc.) and in later Judaism (Wis 2:21; Philo), they realize very well that he means spiritual blindness' (v. 40; Schnackenburg 1980: 256). Jesus confirms that he is speaking of them with this language (v. 41); one thinks again of Mark 3:29.[222] 'The judgment on the blind state of the Pharisees here in John was not very different from Jesus' judgment on the hypocritical Pharisees of Matt 23:16–19, who were condemned as pathetic, blind guides' (Borchert 1996: 326). A similar concept also lies behind the synoptic teaching that, from those who are given much, much shall be required (Luke 12:47–48; 16:10–12). Jesus also refers to Pharisees and other Jewish leaders as blind in Matthew 15:14 and 23:26.[223]

Thus while conventional tradition-critical studies of John 9 continue to be written,[224] the artistic and literary unity of the chapter proves increasingly obvious.[225] The double similarity and dissimilarity criterion again appears apropos. The entire chapter makes sense in an early first-century Palestinian Jewish framework, yet clearly promotes the Johannine (and Christian) agenda of belief in Jesus. At the same time, Jesus' actions and claims prove scandalous, even while the explicit Christology is far too muted throughout to be attributable exclusively or even primarily to later Christian invention. As throughout our study, historical tools do not allow us to pontificate on the historicity of every detail, and John has clearly written things up in his own idiom. But no reasons have emerged for doubting that the essence of the chapter reflects the deeds and words of the historical Jesus and those around him.

222] For the gift of sight to the blind, cf. Ps. 146:8; Is. 29:18; 35:5; 42:7, 18. For the blinding of those who see, cf. Is. 6:10; 42:19. Cf. further Barrett 1978: 366.

223] Dodd (1963: 327–338) deals with vv. 38–41 as a short epigrammatic dialogue reminiscent of numerous synoptic parallels.

224] Rein (1995) provides the fullest detail among recent studies, with a complex proposal about slow development in numerous stages. Reim (1978) sees an original miracle supplemented by a large block of discourse, with only minor additions by a final redactor.

225] Painter (1986) discusses the symbolism at the redactional level, while still (unnecessarily) assuming conventional tradition-historical dissections. Sabugal (1977) demonstrates the literary unity not only of ch. 9 but also of chs. 7 – 11 as a whole. He does not draw direct conclusions from this for historicity but does seem to favour it at numerous junctures.

THE GOOD SHEPHERD (10:1–21)

Despite the chapter break, Jesus apparently continues to address the Pharisees. Moloney (1998: 301) even places the major break at 9:40.[226] Links with Tabernacles continue. Jesus is not only living water and light for the world, but the messianic shepherd who will preserve his flock in ways that Moses could not. Interestingly, the author of *2 Baruch*, writing about the same time as John, reflected the conviction that the Law would function as the true shepherd, light and water (*2 Bar.* 77.11–16). Jesus in essence claims to provide what many Jews thought only Torah could (Moloney 1998: 307).

Verses 1–5 form a short parable. The word John uses to describe it in verse 6 (*paroimia*; NIV 'figure of speech') was at times interchangeable with the more common Greek word for 'parable' (*parabolē*), including in translation of the Hebrew *māšāl* in the Septuagint (see esp. Sir. 39:3; 47:17; cf. also Dewey 1980). This passage provides the closest parallel in the Fourth Gospel to the form and contents of any synoptic narrative parable. Conceptually, of course, it closely resembles the parables of the lost sheep in Matthew 18:10–14 and Luke 15:3–7. Structurally, it is most like the good Samaritan (Luke 10:25–37), in which a relatively helpless figure is able to discern between good and wicked authority figures on the basis of who offers help. Like the synoptic parables (see Blomberg 1990), the key characters in these verses carry the symbolic freight of the text: Christ is the shepherd; the current Jewish leaders, the robbers; and the sheep, the people of Israel (Simonis 1967: 193). Like its synoptic counterparts, too, this little parable is largely realistic by first-century Jewish standards (see esp. Bailey 1993), while setting the stage for a more surprising or uncommon meta-phorical statement in verse 11 – a shepherd sacrificing his life for his sheep (but cf. 1 Sam. 17:33–37 concerning David, the shepherd-king; Morris 1995: 453, n. 38). The rest of the details of the passage should not be allegorized.

Verse 1 leads off with another solemn 'Amen, Amen' saying, suggesting authenticity. In the light of the charges against the Pharisees in 9:40–41 a comparison between true (vv. 2–4) and false (vv. 1, 5) shepherds proves

---

226] Burge (2000: 286) apparently assumes that all of ch. 10 was uttered at the feast of the 'Dedication' (v. 22). But despite John's penchant for giving this kind of information about the setting of a sermon after it has already begun, and notwithstanding the textual variants in this verse, it is difficult to see v. 22 as not introducing a new episode within John's narrative. None of the sixteen other uses of *egeneto* in John's Gospel ever refers backwards rather than forwards when it means 'it was' in the sense of 'something happened at such-and-such a time'.

natural. Here Jesus draws on a rich tradition of Old Testament texts about sheep and shepherds.[227] Probably most foundational is Ezekiel 34, with its similar critique of the leaders of Israel in the sixth century BC and its promise of a coming, perfect messianic shepherd. The Synoptics, too, lament that the Jewish crowds in Jesus' day were like sheep without a (decent) shepherd (Mark 6:34; Matt. 9:36). Elsewhere Jesus speaks of 'the lost sheep' of the house of Israel (Matt. 10:6; 15:24) and likens his followers to sheep among wolves (Matt. 10:16; cf. 7:15), to be distinguished from goats (Matt. 25:31–46), but soon to be scattered (Mark 14:27 par.). A 'gatekeeper' (Gk. *thurōros*) reappears in the New Testament only in the little parable of Mark 13:34. Jesus thus implicitly claims to be the promised messianic shepherd. God's true people can then be expected to respond to his voice and not to the calls of competing leaders. The metaphorical significance of Jesus' illustration, as so often in the Synoptics, is nevertheless lost on his audience (v. 6).

Verses 7–10 form the first of two sections of application Jesus draws from his parable. Each is carefully structured and coherent in its own right; we need not postulate a tradition history in which two competing interpretations have become intermingled (rightly Pryor 1992a: 45; Bailey 1993; contra J. A. T. Robinson 1955; Dodd 1963: 382–385).[228] Although Jesus will call himself the good shepherd in verses 11–18, he first refers to himself, again with the double-'Amen', as the 'gate for the sheep' (vv. 7, 9). Modern readers might find these two identifications contradictory, but as E. F. F. Bishop (1960) pointed out, traditional Palestinian shepherds often slept in the (sole) entrance to the sheepfold to provide extra security for their flocks. Ancient listeners would have had no problems envisaging Jesus as both a metaphorical gate (cf. also Matt. 7:13–14) and a shepherd. The contrast remains with the false shepherds (vv. 8, 10a), still called thieves and robbers, who do not enter by the gate (much less lie down in it!), but climb in 'by some other way' (v. 1). It seems strange that Jesus condemns 'all who ever came before me' (v. 8). Surely he was not including the Old Testament prophets, but merely his most immediate predecessors among the Jewish leaders. The Greek present tense '*are* thieves and robbers' may support this suggestion (Morris 1995: 450–451; contra NIV 'were'). But

---

227] Beutler (1991: 18–32) gives a full listing, contra Turner (1991), who thinks Hellenistic parallels are more apropos. Tragan (1980: 243) provides a helpful verse-by-verse chart of the most relevant Old Testament backgrounds.

228] One of the few points of consensus that the anthology edited by Beutler and Fortna (1991) can claim is that 10:1–21 forms a literary unity. Whether or not this still allows for a previous complex tradition history continues to be debated.

from another angle, he who would refer to himself as 'the way and the truth and the life' (14:6) and who would call human loyalty to family 'hate' in comparison with 'love' for God (Luke 14:26) might well not have shrunk from distancing himself from all previous religious leaders in this way (cf. Carson 1991: 385). Jesus alone makes it possible for anyone to be 'saved' (v. 9a), a concept subsequently illustrated as 'coming in', 'going out', 'finding pasture', and experiencing the 'abundant life' (vv. 9b, 10b). One further recalls Luke 19:10 – 'For the Son of Man came to seek and to save what was lost.'

The final third of this passage finds Jesus now unpacking the theme of his role as good shepherd (vv. 11–18). Not only the specific imagery but the very nature of metaphor lends itself to this kind of multiple interpretation.[229] The primary, additional point that Jesus wants to make in this section is that he is prepared to lay down his life for his flock in order to save them (vv. 11, 15, 17, 18). The most important Old Testament background for this concept may be the role of Isaiah's suffering servant, who was slaughtered as a substitute for sinful 'sheep' (Is. 53:4–7). The most important synoptic parallel is probably Mark 10:45 ('For even the Son of Man did not come to be served, but to serve, and to give his life as a ransom for many'; Tragan 1980: 287). Now the contrast shifts to the true shepherd vs. the hired hand ('mercenary' – vv. 12–13). 'The Mishnah lays down the legal responsibility of the hired shepherd. An interesting provision is that if one wolf attacks the flock he is required to defend the sheep, but "two wolves count as unavoidable accident" ' (*Bab. Metz.* 7.9; Morris 1995: 454)! In verses 14–18 Jesus sets aside all comparisons and merely elaborates on his ministry as the good shepherd. He is intimately acquainted with his flock just as he is with the Father, and vice versa (v. 15; cf. again Matt. 11:27). He has future Gentile followers for which he must make provisions (v. 16; cf. the entire 'withdrawal from Galilee' in Matthew and Mark).[230] And his coming sacrificial death will be voluntary, not coerced (vv. 17–18; cf. the synoptic agony in Gethsemane). As in 7:43 and 9:15 Jesus' audience is divided. Some proclaim him mad and demonized; others are still so impressed by his curing the blind man that they sharply

---

229] 'That sheep farming was widespread in the largely agrarian cultures of the first-century Mediterranean basin ensures that *many* associations would commend themselves to both writer and readers. To demand that these constitute a single, self-consistent mental picture, or a story with a unified plot, is to be unnecessarily restrictive on the natures of both metaphor and parable' (Carson 1991: 382, n. 1).

230] On the Old Testament background of the 'one flock' theme, see esp. Ridderbos 1997: 363.

disagree (vv. 19–21). As before, one may isolate distinctively Johannine traits in the language of this section, most notably Jesus' fourfold use of 'I am' and the reference at the end of verse 18 to the command he received from his Father. But the conceptual parallels to the Synoptic Gospels for almost every verse make it impossible to sustain the claim that John is creating *de novo*. There is evidence for reliance on credible tradition for virtually every affirmation in the passage.[231]

THE FEAST OF DEDICATION (10:22–42)

Shortly after the Tabernacles feast in the autumn of AD 29 Jesus and his disciples would have returned to Galilee. Apparently some time before Hanukkah ('the Feast of Dedication' – v. 22a) that December, Jesus left Galilee for the last time to 'go on the road' with his itinerant ministry (Mark 10:1; Matt. 19:1; Luke 9:51). There is no obvious gap in John's sequence of events from 10:22 – 12:1 in which to place another return home to the north,[232] while Luke 9:51 – 18:14 shows that Jesus' final trip to Jerusalem lasted for a prolonged period, involving significant ministry not treated in Matthew or Mark. This leaves room for John to supplement Jesus' itinerary as well with the events of 10:22 – 11:57.

That Hanukkah fell in the winter creates the correct chronology in verse 22b. The Maccabean repurification of the temple, which the festival commemorated, occurred on 25 Chislev in 164 BC (1 Macc. 4:52–53). The season explains verse 23. 'When the cold wind sweeps in from the east across the desert, Jesus walks in the east portico of the Temple, the only portico whose closed side was protected from the east wind' (Talbert 1992: 69). This portico, known as Solomon's Colonnade, appears in several references in Josephus as well (*Ant.* 15.396–402; 20.221; *War* 5.184–185). References to the colonnade reappear during the ministry of the first apostles just after Pentecost in Acts 3:11 and 5:12. Here various Jewish leaders recall Jesus' earlier teaching in Jerusalem and challenge him to state plainly if he is the Messiah (v. 24). This verse provides an important reminder that, even limiting our focus to the Fourth Gospel, Jesus is not

---

231] Indeed, so detailed is the list of parallels that Sabbe (1991) argues for literary dependence on the Synoptics. But *verbatim* parallelism is too sparse to prove that case. Kowalski (1996) persuasively demonstrates the literary unity of vv. 1–18, despite presupposing a Martyn-like tradition history. Deeley (1997) points to numerous conceptual parallels in Ezek. 33 – 37 to the shepherd motif and related themes that run throughout John 8 – 11, although many of her emphases recur throughout the Old Testament prophets.
232] Unless, as discussed above (p. 77), 10:40 refers to Batanea in the northeast, in which case John may pass over in silence further ministry in Galilee, west of the Jordan.

being portrayed as having revealed himself as unequivocally as some later interpreters take his earlier remarks – most notably the 'I am' sayings. One thinks again of Mark's 'messianic secret' motif (Barrett 1978: 378). The authorities' question resembles that of John the Baptist's followers in Matthew 11:2–3 and parallel that of the high priest at Jesus' trial before the Sanhedrin (Mark 14:61 pars.).[233]

As consistently in the Synoptics, Jesus' answer remains somewhat cryptic (v. 25a). He has said and done enough that his interrogators should be able to answer the question for themselves; so he will not give them a direct response. Luke 22:67b affords a particularly close parallel: 'If I tell you, you will not believe me.' The rest of verses 25–30 simply reiterate themes we have encountered before with Jesus' teaching in Jerusalem: the witness of his miracles (v. 25b), his role as shepherd (vv. 26–27), the guarantee of eternal life for his followers (vv. 28–29), and oneness with his Father (v. 30). Verses 27–29 mirror the three-part structure of verses 14–16: the mutual knowledge of sheep and shepherd, the shepherd's gift of life to his sheep, and the shepherd's ministry to his sheep (Michaels 1983: 172). The themes of true leadership and salvation from God are as apt at Hanukkah as at Tabernacles, because the celebration focused on the warrior-deliverers of the Maccabean family. The language of verse 29 resembles Wisdom of Solomon 3:1 and Isaiah 43:13. The subordination of Jesus to his Father, first stressed in John 5:19–30, continues in this verse as well; again, no early Christian is likely to have invented such a statement of the superiority of the Father over 'all', presumably including the Son.[234]

Still, as in previous contexts in John, this subordination is immediately balanced by Jesus' oneness with his Father (v. 30). One recalls the blasphemous claim of the Seleucid tyrant Antiochus IV to be *Epiphanes* (God manifest); it was Antiochus' desecration of the temple that prompted the Maccabean revolt. But, as in John 5:18, Jesus is not directly equating himself with Yahweh by using the divine name; he is 'making himself as

---

233] Pryor (1992a: 46) notes a remarkable similarity between the forensic inquiry and defence in 10:24–33 and the synoptic trial tradition of Mark 14:53–65. 'First comes the question of Jesus' messiahship. In his response Jesus goes beyond messiahship to give an answer in terms of a unique relationship with God. This elicits the charge of blasphemy (indicated by the attempted stoning), for the Jews detect in Jesus' response a threat to the oneness of God.'

234] Indeed, so problematic was this saying for various Christian scribes that a hornet's nest of textual variants arose to try to make the text more palatable, most notably the option the NIV mg. includes: 'What my father has given me is greater than all.'

God' (Gk. *ōn poieis seauton theon* – v. 33; more literal than NIV's 'claiming to be God'). That is, he is arrogating to himself what Jews believed was Yahweh's sole prerogative – to point out who was the true Messiah (O'Neill 1995: 55–59; recall the caveats in Bock 1998: 25).[235] At the same time, we must not diminish the force of the claims Jesus *was* making:

> Jesus and the Father are *one* because they do the same work and stand in the same relation to the sheep. This is not the same as saying merely that Jesus imitates or obeys the Father. Their oneness is not an ethical oneness, or unity of will. They actually do the *same* work, that is, the Father accomplishes his work in the world uniquely through Jesus his Son. Jesus' statement is no less provocative to his audience than was 5:17 or 8:58. (Michaels 1983: 173)[236]

As the authorities pick up rocks for stoning, Jesus sarcastically asks them for which of his many good works they would execute him (vv. 31–32). When they explain that it is rather that he has blasphemed (v. 33), he replies by citing Psalm 82:6 and employing a 'from the lesser to the greater' kind of logic, standard among Jewish debaters (see esp. Neyrey 1989). If mere mortals (or possibly angels) in Old Testament times could be called 'gods',[237] how can it be blasphemy for him to claim that he is 'God's Son' (vv. 35–36)? The Hebrew for 'gods' (*'elōhîm*) could refer to various exalted beings besides Yahweh, without implying any challenge to monotheism, so if Jesus acknowledges that the Father has appointed him to be the divine Messiah, it is no crime to confess it (cf. Talbert 1992: 170). In verses 35–36 Jesus adopts thoroughly Jewish convictions about Scripture's unity and inviolability and refers to himself as one whom the Father 'sanctified' or 'dedicated' (Gk. *hēgiasen*; NIV 'set apart'). As with all of the preceding holy days on which Jesus has taught, he makes a direct link between

---

235] Cf., only slightly differently, R. E. Brown (1966: 408): 'In Johannine thought the error was not in the description of Jesus as divine ("the Word was God"), but in the assertion that he was *making himself* God. For John, Jesus never makes himself anything; everything that he is stems from the Father.'

236] Cf. the similar balance in Burge (2000: 296): ' "One" in Greek is neuter and does not refer to "one person." Therefore, Jesus is affirming a unity of purpose and will ... However, we must quickly say that this is not a denial of the ontological unity of the Father and the Son ...'

237] The interpretation of Psalm 82 in its original context is itself disputed and the subject of considerable discussion. For the two main views mentioned here see, respectively, Ackerman (1966) and Emerton (1966).

himself and the core meaning of the festival at hand (this time 'Dedication'). No previous text in John finds Jesus using the exact title 'Son of God' (v. 36), but his repeated contrasts between himself as Son and God as Father amount to the same thing. And we must again remember that 'Son of God' could be a virtual synonym for Messiah in first-century Judaism (above, p. 80); it certainly did not yet mean everything implied by 'the second person of the Trinity' as formulated by later creeds and councils. Verses 37–39 repeat earlier points,[238] creating a small chiasmus in verses 31–39: aborted attempts to seize or stone Jesus (vv. 31, 39), Jesus' appeal to the testimony of his works (vv. 32, 37–38), discussion of blasphemy (vv. 33, 36b), and the climactic, central focus on the significance of Psalm 82 (vv. 34–36a).

Jesus' teaching in the temple during Hanukkah aptly satisfies the double similarity and dissimilarity criterion. All of the points and counterpoints made in this debate resonate with Jewish background, Scripture and exegetical technique. Yet Jesus makes a sufficiently outrageous claim so as to provoke the authorities' hostility once again. Early Christianity regularly discerned important Christology in this interchange but frequently assumed Jesus' claims for himself were more unambiguous than they actually were (more cautiously, cf. R. E. Brown 1966: 404–405). Still, the threat against Jesus was severe enough for him to leave Jerusalem for the safety of a different location, east of the Jordan (v. 40). Wherever we identify 'Bethany beyond the Jordan' in 1:28 to be, that is the location to which Jesus returns. More people believe in him, following on from their enthusiasm for the Baptist (vv. 41–42). 'The historicity of this report can hardly be doubted; but it betrays hostility to the Baptist: only Jesus can lay claim to the witness of extraordinary works' (Schnackenburg 1980: 315; cf. Barrett 1978: 387).

THE RESURRECTION OF LAZARUS (11:1–44)

We now come to what is widely regarded as the most spectacular miracle in all of the four Gospels. As an account of reawakening to mortal life, it is paralleled in the Synoptics by the resurrections of Jairus' daughter (Mark 5:21–24, 35–43 pars.) and of the Nain widow's son (Luke 7:11–17).[239]

238] John 10:25, 32 and 37–38 all refer to Jesus' works and cohere with earlier, arguably authentic *ergon* sayings in John (see above, p. 103) as well as with Matt. 11:2–6 par.; 11:20–24 par. (Ensor 1996: 245–256).

239] Schnackenburg (1980: 341) notes five particularly close parallels with the account of the raising of Jairus' daughter: (1) the death of a sick person before Jesus arrives; (2) the metaphor of sleep for death; (3) Jesus' displeasure at the loud lamentation; (4) Jesus'

Likewise both Elijah and Elisha in the Old Testament were empowered to revivify recently deceased persons (1 Kgs. 17:17–24; 2 Kgs. 4:8–37). What makes the reanimation of Lazarus more notable is the length of time he has been dead (at least four days – vv. 17, 39; his body presumably would have begun to decay!). Of course, if one comes to these texts already convinced that resurrections are under no circumstances possible, no amount of evidence will persuade one of historicity (e.g. Casey 1996: 55–56). Others find themselves unable to believe that the Synoptics would have omitted such a story if it actually happened, but recall my introductory comments on how it does not fit into their outlines (above, p. 55; cf. Schnackenburg 1980: 345), and, as just noted, it is not as if they included *no* resurrection accounts. Commentators have frequently observed that Luke 16:19–31 contains a parable about the death of a poor man named Lazarus whom the rich man in the story would like to have resurrected, and some have gone on to speculate whether one story might have given rise to the other (e.g. Dunkerley 1959; Schneiders 1987). But the name, based on the Hebrew Eleazar ('God helps'), was far too common for such speculation to get us anywhere (cf. Pollard 1973: 435). Interestingly, the names of all three family members – Mary, Martha and Lazarus – were found in 1973 in ossuary inscriptions near Bethany. But for the same factor of the commonness of the names, this discovery cannot be labelled anything more than an interesting coincidence (Bruce 1983: 240).

John 11:1 introduces us to Lazarus by explaining that he was the brother of Mary and Martha, as if John's readers were more likely to have heard of the two women. This comports with the fact that Luke 10:38–42 narrates a visit by Jesus to these two sisters. Elsewhere in the Synoptics we learn of Jesus lodging in this same village of Bethany while he was ministering in Jerusalem (Mark 11:11–12 pars.; 14:3 par.). John further describes Mary as 'the same one who poured perfume on the Lord and wiped his feet with her hair' (v. 2). This descriptor obviously distinguished this Mary from the mother of Jesus, but it suggests in addition that Mary's action here was also previously well known, especially since John has not yet narrated his version of this episode (see 12:1–8; cf. Bauckham 1998c: 161–166). Such fame fits well with Mark 14:9 in which Jesus proclaims that 'wherever the gospel is preached throughout the world, what she has done will also be told, in memory of her'.

When Lazarus becomes ill, Mary and Martha send word to Jesus (v. 3). They refer to their brother as 'the one you love', leading a few

---

command with which he calls the dead girl back to life; and (5) Jesus' command after the resurrection.

commentators to speculate that Lazarus was the 'beloved disciple' behind the composition of the Fourth Gospel (e.g. Eller 1987; Baltz 1996). But Jesus obviously loved more than one person (cf. v. 5), and 'it would be a very curious procedure to speak of him by name 11 times in chapters 11 and 12 and to abandon the name in all subsequent references to him' (Morris 1995: 478, n. 13). Jesus' reply (v. 4) mirrors his description of God's purposes for the blind man in 9:3. On the heels of 10:36 it is not surprising that Jesus should now refer to himself as God's Son. What is more puzzling is that, despite his love for this family, he stayed where he was for two more days (v. 6). Once we know the end of the story, this becomes clearer. Had Jesus left immediately, he might have had only to heal Lazarus.[240] As it was, he was able to raise him from the dead (or raise him after a longer period of death) – an even greater miracle 'for God's glory'.

When the time is right, then, Jesus calls his disciples to accompany him back to Judea (v. 7). They remember the danger he found himself in the last time he was there and question the wisdom of the proposal (v. 8; cf. 10:31). Similar fear of going up to Jerusalem in the spring of AD 30 appears in Mark 10:32.[241] The negative light verse 8 casts on the disciples is unlikely to have been invented later by those very disciples. In verses 9–10 Jesus employs what may already have been a well-known proverb or short parable (Dodd 1963: 373–379), reminiscent of John 9:4. Barnabas Lindars (1972: 389) thinks of the similar parable in Luke 11:34–36 and parallel, while Raymond Brown (1966: 432) finds relevant Old Testament background in Jeremiah 13:16:

> Give glory to the LORD your God
>   before he brings the darkness,
> before your feet stumble
>   on the darkening hills.
> You hope for light,
>   but he will turn it to thick darkness
>   and change it to deep gloom.

240] This, of course, depends on the location of Bethany beyond the Jordan. If it is Batanea in the north, at least two days' journey from Bethany near Jerusalem, Lazarus would already have died by the time Jesus arrived. If Bethany were just across the Jordan from Jericho, a messenger could have arrived midday and Jesus could have made it to Lazarus' home by evening, perhaps while the sick man was still living.

241] Michaels (1983: 181) also notes significant parallels with Mark 14:42 / Matt. 26:46 in Gethsemane.

The contrast between light and darkness is of course also thoroughly Johannine.

In verse 11 Jesus announces to his followers that 'Lazarus has fallen asleep'.[242] The verb *koimaomai* denotes literal sleep four times and death fourteen times in its eighteen New Testament occurrences (Morris 1995: 481, n. 24). It was a standard metaphor for death in both the Jewish and Graeco-Roman worlds of Jesus' day (Lindars 1972: 394; Borchert 1996: 352; each with key texts). As in the story of the resurrection of Jairus' daughter, those who hear Jesus speak of 'sleep' take him too literally (v. 12; cf. Mark 5:39–40). Thus first John as narrator (v. 13) and then Jesus himself (v. 14) explain that Lazarus has actually died. Verse 15 repeats the idea that Jesus allowed this to happen for a specific reason – that the disciples might believe – a further reminder that in John initial faith is not always adequate faith.[243] He repeats his call to the disciples to follow him, and Thomas replies with what seems like a fatalistic resignation to the inevitable (v. 16). 'This conclusion comports with the later portrait of Thomas, in John 20, as skeptical and doubting' (Witherington 1995: 202).

Thus the little troupe arrives in Bethany near Jerusalem. As it turns out, Lazarus has been entombed for four days (v. 17). That it has taken at least a two days' journey (recall v. 6) for Jesus and the disciples to get there could support the identification of Bethany beyond the Jordan with Batanea (recall on 1:28; cf. Carson 1991: 408). Verse 18 clearly differentiates the Bethany in which Lazarus lived from the other Bethany and reminds us of its proximity to Jerusalem. An ominous note is sounded because of the hostility to Jesus already manifest there. The geographical reference again demonstrates John's historical accuracy. The NIV's 'less than two miles' is literally the Greek for 'fifteen stadia', not quite three kilometers or a mile and three quarters, precisely the distance between the site of ancient Bethany (modern El 'Azariyeh) and the capital (R. E. Brown 1966: 424).

That many Jews should be present at Lazarus' 'wake' (v. 19) is exactly in keeping with ancient custom in which almost an entire village could turn out to mourn the death of one of its families' members (cf. Wis. Sol. 19:3; *Ket.* 4.4). Recognizing the danger of over-psychologizing, it is nevertheless interesting to observe that John portrays Mary and Martha exactly like

---

242] Hanson (1973: 252–254) finds several elements of Job 14 inspiring this verse, confirming 'the view that there lies behind the story of the raising of Lazarus some historical element' (253).

243] Delebecque (1986b) thinks vv. 14–15 should be translated and punctuated as 'Lazarus is dead – and I rejoice for your sake – dead because you will come to faith, dead because I was not there.'

Luke does: Martha is the more active; Mary, the more restrained (v. 20; cf. Luke 10:38–42).[244] Verse 21 forms a credible complaint by a grief-stricken person aware of Jesus' healing ministry, but it remains enough of a rebuke so as not to be the natural creation by a later Christian writer. Verse 22 resembles Jesus' promise that those who ask shall receive (Matt. 7:7 par.). 'In the circumstances it is virtually a request that he should procure the restoration of Lazarus to life.' Yet 'it falls short of the faith required, because she does not see that Jesus is himself the divinely appointed agent of resurrection', as the rest of the story will demonstrate (Lindars 1972: 394). Martha's comments resemble Jesus' mother's approach to him in John 2:3 – a mild rebuke with an implicit request, followed by some level of confidence that Jesus can still act helpfully.

Jesus promises Martha that her brother will live again (v. 23), but she understandably interprets him as referring merely to the general resurrection of all people at the end of the age (v. 24). Notwithstanding Sadducean scepticism, the vast majority of all Jews by the first century looked forward to a coming bodily resurrection (Bauckham 1998d). Jesus replies by stressing that *he* is the resurrection and the life (v. 25a).[245] This is another one of his very dramatic 'I am' statements. As throughout John, it means that he promises his followers eternal life (v. 25b). But clearly the vast majority of believers are not resurrected before the end of the age, so Jesus' powerful metaphor still does not do anything to heighten Martha's expectation of Lazarus' immediate revivification.[246] Again, one wonders if a later writer who felt free to add fictitious details would not have made all this a bit clearer. Jesus asks if Martha believes all that he has spoken, a prime opportunity for her to illustrate full-orbed Johannine faith (v. 26). At first, it seems she provides precisely such a confession, calling Jesus both Messiah and Son of God (v. 27), just as in 20:31. But verse 39 will show that her faith has not advanced beyond conventional Jewish messianic expectation, while the rest of chapters 11 and 12 will suggest that Mary rather than Martha provides the exemplary model of faith (see esp. Moloney 1998: 327–331). Just as Peter uses the identical two titles in confessing Jesus in a fashion that only God himself could inspire (Matt.

244] Bruce (1983: 243) notes that the 'portrayal of the two sisters' character and temperament in this Gospel agrees in general with that in Luke's record, where Mary sits at Jesus' feet while Martha is busily engaged with housework'.

245] Malzoni (1999) wonders whether the shorter 'I am the resurrection', attested in the Syriac of v. 25 could be authentic, and taken as the 'messianic consolation' as in several later rabbinic traditions.

246] On the theology of the claims of v. 25, see esp. J. P. Martin 1964; Moule 1975.

16:16–17), yet immediately so fails to understand Christ's full mission that he is rebuked as an unwitting tool of the devil (v. 23), so also here we must not credit Martha's faith with being so rich that only a post-resurrection perspective can account for it (rightly R. E. Brown 1966: 433; Bruce 1983: 245; Witherington 1995: 199; Borchert 1996: 357; all contra a majority of commentators).

Jesus now turns his attention to Martha's sister, Mary (vv. 28–30). Mary's quick response to Jesus' overture fits her devotion to learning from him displayed in Luke 10:39. Those grieving with Mary follow her, thinking she is going to the tomb instead (v. 31).[247] John's reference to 'the Jews' here, as in verse 19, is qualified so as to make it clear that only one group of the family's companions is in view. It is still a little odd for John to refer to them by their ethnicity, but one upshot of the label is to create two references where people called 'the Jews' are portrayed in a relatively positive light. So again, we see that it is a caricature to say that the Fourth Gospel is unremitting in its negative portrait of 'the Jews'. But, to the extent that negative references still outweigh positive ones in reflecting John's redactional emphasis, these more complimentary passages are that much more likely to be historical (cf. R. E. Brown 1966: 428).

When Mary meets Jesus, she laments his 'late' arrival just as her sister did (v. 32). The implied rebuff to Jesus is unlikely to be fictitious. Jesus' response to Mary and her fellow mourners is to be 'deeply moved in spirit and troubled' (v. 33). The first of the two verbs in this expression is *embrimaomai*, a strong word referring to a vehement expression of emotion, sometimes including anger (Lindars 1992). Again, a later inventor of unhistorical tales would probably not have ascribed this attribute to Jesus.

But is Jesus upset that Lazarus died, that so much grief surrounds his death, or that his friends and family do not believe that Jesus can raise him? Perhaps a little of each, as Carson (1991: 416) explains: 'If sin, illness and death, all devastating features of this fallen world, excite his wrath, it is hard to see how unbelief is excluded.'[248] Jesus asks to see the tomb (v. 34); no supernatural insight about its location is attributed to him. Verse 35 is not merely the shortest verse in the Bible but another key indicator of Christ's genuine humanity and normal emotions. Jesus will likewise weep

---

247] Schnackenburg (1980: 516, n. 48) provides numerous scriptural background texts reflecting the practice of mourning at the tomb of a recently deceased person.

248] Much less convincingly, Story (1991) argues that Jesus is rebuking his own spirit (that was ruing the fact that he had not come sooner), though if this view were correct Jesus' humanity (and the probable historicity of the passage) would be that much more magnified.

over the entire city of Jerusalem just a few miles away in the not too distant future (Luke 19:41). The mourners attributed Jesus' weeping merely to his love for Lazarus (v. 36; recall v. 3); the positive use of 'the Jews' continues here. But 'some' (a minority?) remember his healing the blind man of chapter 9 and think he could have prevented this loss (v. 37). As previously, the criticism is not likely to have been invented, since it presupposes some level of belief on the part of his critics in Jesus' miracle-working ability.

Jesus again becomes indignant (from Gk. *embrimaomai*) as he arrives at the tomb (v. 38). The burial chamber is 'a cave with a stone laid across the entrance', exactly like some that have been discovered in modern-day Israel (cf. also *Bab. Bat.* 6.8). Jesus' body will later be placed in a similar tomb (Mark 15:46 pars.). Martha's protest against Jesus' command to remove the stone from the entrance proves that she is not thinking in terms of a bodily resurrection at this moment (v. 39). Verse 40 does not exactly correspond to anything John has previously narrated, while agreeing with the gist of verses 23 and 25–26. A narrator not constrained by historical information might have been expected to make a more precise match.[249]

Verses 41–42 contain the only prayer recorded in the Gospels by Jesus prior to his working a miracle. But Jesus explicitly plays to the crowd by telling God that he is praying out loud for the benefit of the bystanders. If any part of this passage reads like a Johannine insertion, this is it! On the other hand, Jesus' use of 'Father' recalls the synoptic *Abba* (cf. above, p. 114), Jesus' thanksgiving resembles Psalm 118:21 (on which, see esp. Wilcox 1977) and Matthew 11:25, and the audible prayer shows that Jesus does nothing on his own authority apart from the Father's will (Lindars 1972: 401; Barrett 1978: 402–403). Additionally, Bingham Hunter (1985) notes the similarity in form with numerous Jewish thanksgiving prayers or psalms (*hodayot*), the reference in John 6:11 that Jesus 'gave thanks' before feeding the five thousand, the unusual trauma Jesus himself was experiencing that could account for his exceptional behaviour, and the partially parallel, audible prayers of Jesus and Stephen just before their deaths. However John may have stylized the wording, it seems probable that Jesus did pray something like what these two verses record before he proceeded to raise Lazarus.[250]

249] Alternately, with Michaels (1983: 192), perhaps we are meant to see v. 4 as the word sent back to the two sisters, in which case v. 40 could be referring to v. 4 as well.

250] Even Bultmann (1971: 407–408) seems less embarrassed by this text than by many in John, explaining that 'Jesus directs his gaze to heaven for prayer, but he utters no request; he gives thanks for the hearing already granted (v. 41). It thus appears that the Son of God does not need to make a request in prayer; and precisely this appears to be stressed in v. 42:

Verses 43–44 bring us to the climax of the passage. With a loud cry Jesus calls Lazarus to come out of his tomb. The description of Lazarus' wrappings fits contemporary Jewish practice (Beasley-Murray 1987: 195, with details) and could suggest an accurate report. A writer of fiction might not have bothered with the coverings, assuming that Jesus could have freed Lazarus from them as well. Martha's fear of the body's odour (v. 39) implies that Lazarus had not been embalmed. 'Some have argued that v. 44 contradicts this assumption. However, what is described in v. 44 is much less than an embalming, and in any case aromatic spices were used in Jewish circles not to embalm bodies (as did the Egyptians) but to counter-act repulsive odours from bodily decomposition' (though never terribly successfully; Carson 1991: 417).[251] The concluding command to some of the onlookers to free Lazarus calls to mind Jesus' concern for giving Jairus' newly resurrected daughter something to eat (Mark 5:43).[252]

What then should we conclude about the historicity of this remarkable miracle story? We note once again that a majority of the account is neither miracle nor uninterrupted discourse, but a credible give-and-take between Jesus and his disciples and between Jesus and the two sisters in Bethany. Keith Pearce (1985) finds numerous similarities between the miracle itself and healings and resurrections in Luke's Gospel, which, contra his conclusions, should support historicity. More conventional dissections of the text into layers of tradition and redaction prove so diverse that they largely cancel each other out (see Marchadour 1988 for a detailed over-view): are we to divide the passage into competing traditions reflecting Mary's and Martha's respective roles (Burkett 1994), break it up into a historical core reflecting some kind of healing miracle overlaid with substantial theological redaction (Kremer 1985), or adopt a three-stage analysis based on an Old Testament origin, early catechetical expansion, and final theological emphases, with no historical core whatsoever (Rochais 1981: 113–146)? In keeping with general trends in the analysis of John's Gospel, Josef Wagner (1988) has demonstrated the literary and theological unity of the account in such a fashion that, while not excluding possible tradition-historical development, nothing in the chapter requires it. A

---

since the Son is constantly sure of the Father's hearing, he never needs to make requests; if he prayed on this occasion it was only for the sake of the people present, "that they might grasp faith" that God sent him.'

251] At the same time, there are possible theological overtones in the description of Lazarus' bandages. See esp. B. Osborne (1973) and Reiser (1973).

252] E. E. Ellis (1999: 170–171) presents numerous additional elements in common between these two resurrection accounts.

fairly impressive array of recent analysts of the miracles attributed to Jesus, along with studies of this text in particular, concludes that a substantial historical core does appear to underlie John's narrative (Sabourin 1977: 124–128; Latourelle 1988: 229–238; Hunter 1985; M. J. Harris 1986; Meier 1994: 798–832 [far more cautiously]; Twelftree 1999: 308–310). In the absence of convincing evidence to the contrary, this approach seems to be the best.

PLOTTING TO KILL JESUS (11:45–57)

Verse 45 recalls previous examples in John of a signs-based faith, not all of which have proved long-lasting (cf. esp. 8:30). But that many of the observers of Lazarus' resurrection would have begun to believe in some way is entirely credible. Others, however, report Jesus to the authorities (vv. 46–47a). Here is the first and only mention of the Sanhedrin in John (but cf. Mark 14:55 pars., 15:1; Matt. 5:22; and the use of the plural 'sanhedrins' for lesser courts in Matt. 10:17 and Mark 13:9). That it was composed primarily of chief priests (largely Sadducees) and Pharisees is historically accurate. All four Gospels agree by referring more to the priests and less to the Pharisees as the primary Jewish instigators of Jesus' crucifixion, from this time onward, even though the Pharisees (and scribes) were his primary opponents earlier in his ministry. This shift fits the fact that Sadducees dominated the Sanhedrin and Jerusalem in Jesus' day and further demonstrates that the Gospel writers are not simply lumping the religious authorities together indiscriminately (cf. Morris 1995: 501). The council described here may be a formally convened meeting of the Jewish high court, in which its members passed a resolution to pursue Jesus (Bammel 1970; J. A. T. Robinson 1985: 223–224). Inclusion of this account here could explain why John felt free to refer to Jesus' trial before Caiaphas later on in as abbreviated a form as he did (18:24, 28).

The catch-22 situation in which the authorities find themselves (vv. 47b–48) foreshadows a similar dilemma that the Synoptics describe when Jesus asks them whether John the Baptist was from God or not (Mark 11:29–33 pars.). The tenuous relation with Rome reflected here matches what we know from other ancient documents. 'There is evidence from Jewish sources that the authorities were rather nervous for some time before the Jewish War. Thus Josephus speaks of all manner of portents that occurred in Jerusalem (*Bell.* 6.288ff)' (Morris 1995: 502, n. 103). For earlier fears, compare *Antiquities* 14.163–184. The use of 'place' for 'temple' agrees with Old Testament usage, as in Jeremiah 7:14 and Nehemiah 4:7.

Verse 49a introduces us to Caiaphas, the 'high priest that year'. This information agrees with the Synoptics (Matt. 26:3, 57; Luke 3:2), Acts (4:6), and Josephus (*Ant.* 18.35, 95), from whom we also learn that he occupied the office from AD 18–36. What is odd is the reference to 'that year', as if he ruled for only twelve months or so. Prior to Caiaphas' long tenure, the Romans had installed and deposed high priests often enough that the office might have seemed to have become an annual appointment, even when extensions could be granted (Beasley-Murray 1987: 197).[253] Most commentators, however, follow Origen (c. AD 200) and understand 'that year' to mean something like 'that fateful year in which Jesus died'. Caiaphas' sentiments form a classic example of Johannine irony (vv. 49–50; Nicklas 2000a). But they, too, are historically believable; many governments throughout human history have been willing to execute outspoken critics when they have felt their national security at stake. In the synoptic tradition Jesus himself predicts the Roman destruction of Jerusalem (Mark 13:2; Luke 21:20); the Jewish authorities must have frequently contemplated the possibility of such an attack (R. E. Brown 1966: 444).[254]

John next refers to Caiaphas' words as unwitting prophecy (vv. 51–52). At least some Jews believed high priests were also prophets (based on Num. 27:21 and 2 Sam. 15:27). Josephus credited John Hyrcanus with prophetic powers (*Ant.* 11.327; 13:299), while later first-century sources seem to associate prophecy with the priesthood in general (Josephus, *War* 3.352; Philo, *Spec. Laws.* 4.192). What is more, 'prophecies made without the knowledge and intention of the speaker are often mentioned in the rabbinic literature' (Barrett 1978: 407, with references). Dying 'for the Jewish nation' harks back to the role of the Maccabean martyrs (cf. esp. 2 Macc. 7:37–38).[255] The 'scattered children of God' in John's mind could foreshadow the Christian mission to the Gentiles, which prediction, as we have seen (above, p. 54), is consistent with Jesus' own historical ministry (cf. also R. E. Brown 1966: 443). But Caiaphas undoubtedly was thinking only of the restoration to Israel of literal Jews from the diaspora (Moloney 1998: 344). John 11:47–53 is thus framed with two references to 'gathering' (from Gk. *synagō*) – first of the Sanhedrin and then of the dispersed Israelites. These correspond to the two contrasting themes of verses 47–53: the gathering of the mighty to maintain a rule of violence

---

253] Thus Witherington (1995: 205) thinks the reference is a beautiful stroke of sarcasm, inasmuch as Rome had the power to make or unmake a high priest in an instant.

254] Burge (2000: 322, n. 25) notes that Mark 3:6 likewise refers to a plot among the Jewish leaders to do away with Jesus, immediately after he has restored physical and spiritual health to various individuals.

255] More speculatively, Barker (1970) sees a foreshadowing here of later Jewish traditions about a Messiah ben Joseph who dies, as a predecessor to a Messiah ben David who reigns as king.

versus the gathering of humanity united by one who is a powerless victim (Beutler 1994). The literary unity suggests we need not attempt a tradition-critical dissection.

For John, the resurrection of Lazarus is thus the climactic catalyst for the plot that will eventuate in Christ's death (v. 53). Critics have sometimes complained that the disciples could not have known what occurred in the private sessions of the Sanhedrin, but the friendly roles played by Nicodemus, Joseph of Arimathea, and Gamaliel elsewhere in the Gospels and Acts suggest that several sources could have 'leaked' the information. More commonly, John's text is said to contradict the Synoptics, because for them it was the temple clearing that sealed Jesus' fate (Mark 11:18 pars.). Nevertheless, both John and the Synoptics know of multiple, previous plots to kill Christ (Mark 3:6 pars.; Luke 4:28–29; John 5:18; 10:31–33), so why should these later references be viewed as mutually exclusive? In fact, the Johannine account makes the synoptic narratives more credible. It was not merely one public demonstration that led to Jesus' arrest but a series of relatively recent events. Moreover, as we saw in conjunction with 2:19, there is an 'interlocking' between John and the Synoptics here – a reference to the destruction of the temple (John 11:48 – 'take away our place') which forms part of the garbled charge against Jesus in Mark 14:57–58 and parallels (cf. R. E. Brown 1966: 441–442). Ernst Bammel (1970) in fact finds four main features of John's account of the proceedings against Jesus particularly credible: the beginning of legal proceedings considerably before the crucifixion (cf. *b. Sanh.* 43a), this initiative undertaken solely by the Jewish authorities, the role of Caiaphas as a 'survivor' over so many years in office under Rome, and Jesus' subsequent flight from danger (cf. also Grundmann 1984; J. A. T. Robinson 1985: 223–229).

As frequently in both the Synoptics and John, Jesus thus withdraws from the growing hostility. Here he leaves Bethany near Jerusalem for a relatively small and isolated village in Judea called Ephraim (v. 54). Josephus (*War* 4.551) mentions it along with Bethel, so it may have been nearby that Old Testament site to the north of Jerusalem. That little is known about the site favours historicity, 'since an author writing at Ephesus late in the first century would scarcely be aware of, or interested in, an obscure Palestinian town, and any mysterious or symbolic meaning of the name is out of the question' (Dodd 1963: 243).[256] Jesus stays at Ephraim until it is time for the Passover, presumably in the spring of AD 30

256] Katz (1997) notes that all other references to specific towns in Israel in the Fourth Gospel stem from the fact that one of the characters in the Gospel lived or worked there. He thus speculates that the 'disciples' in v. 54 refer to other followers of Jesus besides the

(v. 55).[257] The reference to ceremonial cleansing is an authentic touch (cf. Josephus, *War* 1.229; *Pes.* 9.1; originally based on Num. 9:6–13), not normally stressed as much in John as in the Synoptics (cf. esp. Mark 7:1–20 par.). Because of the threat against Jesus, the crowds wonder whether he will make an appearance (vv. 56–57). The first main section of the body of John's Gospel has now come to a close (cf. Blomberg 1997: 161), and the stage is set for the last week of Christ's life and the dramatic events that unfold during it.

MARY OF BETHANY ANOINTS JESUS (12:1–11)

As we draw close to John's account of Christ's death and resurrection, parallels with the Synoptics increase. 'Six days before the Passover' (v. 1) brings us to the Saturday night before 'Palm Sunday'. John 12:1–8 parallels the anointing of Jesus by an unnamed woman in Mark 14:3–9 (= Matt 26:6–13), apparently in the context of the last night of Jesus' life. The latter account is almost certainly referring to the same event as John does here; it is unlikely that two separate women would anoint Jesus with identical bottles of costly perfume for the same reason – to anticipate his burial – leading to the same conversation about the poor, in the context of a meal with his disciples, all within five days of each other! When one looks at the Markan passage, however, several indications suggest that Mark has thematically relocated (and Matthew has simply copied him) what John narrates in its correct chronological sequence. Mark 14:1–2 begins by observing that the Passover was still two days away, as the authorities continued to plot how to arrest Jesus. Verses 10–11 flow naturally from verse 2 as the continuation of that plot. Not until verse 12 do we come to the Last Supper account itself. Mark 14:3, on the other hand, is linked with verse 2 merely by a *kai* (and) and goes on to describe an incident that takes place at some unspecified time while Jesus 'was in Bethany'. Once we observe that both Mark and John have Jesus interpreting the anointing as preparation for his burial, one can understand why Mark would insert the story immediately preceding a description of other foreshadowings of his death, including his last meal with the Twelve (cf. Blomberg 1987: 173 and literature there cited).[258]

Twelve who resided in Ephraim and with whom Jesus stayed while in town. This would then explain the choice of the village to which Jesus retreated.

257] A fair consensus of scholars today agrees on AD 30 as the year of Christ's crucifixion, but an important minority view opts for AD 33. The issue need not be settled for our purposes.

258] For a helpful list of the similarities and differences between John's and Mark's accounts, in chart form, see Burge 2000: 337.

At the same time Luke 7:36–50 is best taken as a separate event altogether. In this incident, explicitly described as at a different time and location in Jesus' ministry, an immoral woman pours part of a flask of ointment on Jesus' head, leading to an entirely different conversation – a controversy about Jesus permitting the scandalous action and a discussion of the woman's salvation. An alabaster container (cf. Mark) and wiping Jesus' feet (cf. John) afford the only significant verbal parallels between Luke and the other Gospels. Thus despite a critical consensus that all four Gospels narrate three independent versions of one original event, we should follow a strong, minority voice that does not treat Luke's account as relevant to an analysis of John 12:1–8.[259]

Returning to the accounts in John and Mark, I agree with the current consensus that these are not sufficiently parallel to demonstrate direct, literary dependence. As with previous episodes in John mirrored in the Synoptics, we cannot rule out such dependence. We must admit, however, that if John borrowed directly from one of his predecessors he has so reworded his material as to cover his tracks. The closest parallels come precisely where one would expect oral tradition to be the most fixed: the specialized terminology concerning the perfume and the climactic interchange between Judas and Jesus (cf. Ridderbos 1997: 412; for a detailed comparison, Wagner 1988: 371–384).

John 12:1–2 uniquely associates the anointing with the events of chapter 11. Mary, Martha and Lazarus are present with Jesus and his disciples at a festive meal in Bethany. The depiction of the two sisters, with Martha serving and Mary worshipping, 'is once again remarkably consistent with Luke's portrayal of the two in the one paragraph where he mentions them (Luke 10:38–42)' (Bruce 1983: 255). Mark 14:3 and parallel locate the meal at the home of Simon the leper. The Dead Sea Scrolls confirm that a leper colony lived on the outskirts of Bethany (11QTemple 46:16–18).[260] John does not say where the meal occurred, but the presence of Lazarus as 'among those reclining at the table' makes it sound as if we are not in Lazarus' home where he would have played the role of host (cf. Schnackenburg 1980: 366). Simon's past or present leprosy may have

---

259] Holst (1976) both describes the consensus and offers a long list of exegetes who have differed as we do. If anything, the minority position has grown in number of adherents in the last quarter century. It is possible that the two traditions, however, did cross-pollinate each other a little in the oral tradition, leading to certain similarities in form and wording. 260] It is unclear whether Mark means that the home was Simon's but he is no longer able to live there because of his disease or, perhaps more probably, whether he is someone who has been healed (by Jesus?) and is now able to host the party.

prevented him from marrying: in a culture defined by traditional gender roles we should not be surprised that a female neighbour like Martha helps to serve the meal.

Mary's behaviour in anointing Jesus (in Mark and Matthew she remains anonymous) includes letting down her hair to wipe Jesus' feet with it (v. 3a). This action could easily have been perceived as a sexual advance; its potentially objectionable nature means that no early Christian would readily have invented it (cf. Morris 1995: 512; Burge 2000: 345). That 'the house was filled with the fragrance of the perfume' (v. 3b) 'looks like the reminiscence of someone who was there' (Morris 1995: 513). In the Markan parallel, the woman anoints Jesus' head (Mark 14:3 par.), action perhaps inspired by Psalm 133:2. But in the Old Testament text, the 'precious oil poured on the head' also runs down on Aaron's beard and on to the collar of his robes. Like the 'dew of Hermon' that falls 'on Mount Zion' (v. 3), presumably the oil eventually falls to the ground, thus covering Jesus' feet as well. The cost of the nard indicates a large quantity of the perfume; breaking the flask at its neck suggests the jar was full. The analogy of anointing for burial would also imply a lavish amount of ointment in keeping with the huge quantities of spices with which corpses were wrapped. Both Mark and Matthew recognize that the liquid fell on Jesus' body as well as his head (Mark 14:8; Matt. 26:12). All these features combine to suggest that Jesus was moistened from head to foot, with each account bringing out various portions of the anointing (cf. esp. Carson 1991: 426–427). J. F. Coakley (1988: 246–248) provides numerous Jewish and Graeco-Roman parallels from antiquity to suggest that anointing the feet of a guest with oil or perfume, while uncommon, did at times occur as a special gesture of hospitality.[261] Theologically, John no doubt wants to foreshadow the footwashing of chapter 13, which he alone describes.[262]

John next makes explicit what Mark and Matthew simply attribute to unnamed disciples: Judas objects to the 'waste' of this perfume. Think how much money could have been raised for the poor by its sale (vv. 4–5)! The objection is credible enough; it has been repeated throughout church history by believers with robust social consciences against all kinds of more 'frivolous' expenditures. But John makes it clear that the remark stemmed

---

261] Coakley in fact argues for the historicity of John's account at the expense of the Synoptics. Casey (1996: 211–215) correctly points out the weakness of this approach but then also proposes, by his own admission, a highly speculative argument against John's trustworthiness.

262] For the theology of John's account, see esp. Giblin (1992), without endorsing his tradition-historical conclusions.

rather from hypocrisy; Judas was accustomed to raiding the disciples' money bags (v. 6). If some of the other disciples were more genuinely motivated in their concern, it is appropriate to note that 'unusual expense at a funeral was not regarded as unseemly; why should anyone object if the ointment which would otherwise have been used to anoint his dead body in due course was poured over him while he was still alive and able to appreciate the love which prompted the action?' (Bruce 1983: 257). As for Judas taking charge of the 'common pot', this information is unique to John but comports with Judas's financial interest in later betraying Jesus (Mark 14:11 par.). Verses 7–8 are similar enough to the synoptic parallels and to Deuteronomy 15:11 to provide no problems for historicity. The upshot of the analysis again yields a passage that well satisfies the criterion of double similarity and dissimilarity. The general meal scene, Mary's behaviour, Judas's objection, and Jesus' reply all fit an early first-century Jewish milieu, even while certain details prove sufficiently shocking to set Mary and Jesus somewhat apart from their culture's conventions. Nothing in the text contradicts later Christian theology, especially its concern for the poor (cf. Blomberg 1999), but the Christology here is at best implicit and Christians have always struggled with the right balance between spending on areas of social concern and lavish devotion to Christ.

Word understandably spreads quickly concerning Jesus' whereabouts, and crowds of Jews flock to see both Jesus and the man he raised from the dead (v. 9). No negative overtones sound in John's use of 'a large crowd of Jews' here, while verse 11 provides another reference to at least some level of faith on the part of many of the onlookers. Both features combine to provide another pointer to authenticity (cf. Talbert 1992: 184). Ironically, the authorities thus determine to do away with Lazarus as well as Jesus (v. 10). Treating these verses as introducing the 'triumphal entry' (vv. 12–19), Casey (1996: 208–209) lists four objections to historicity: (1) Lazarus plays so prominent a role that his omission from the Synoptics is inexplicable. (2) The plot to kill someone just raised from the dead is incredible. (3) Verse 16 finds the disciples remembering what they had not previously known. (4) Verses 17–19 contradict verses 9–11 by focusing exclusively on Jesus. None of these objections proves strong. Points (1) and (4) largely cancel each other out. Lazarus is not a primary focus of attention here; even in verses 9–11 he remains subordinate to Jesus. Point (2) demonstrates John's love of irony not incredulity. Of course, the Jewish authorities who sought to condemn Jesus would not have believed he genuinely raised Lazarus and would have assumed that killing him would deal with the problem. As for (3), the Greek verb *mimnēskomai* can be translated 'realize' (NIV) as well as 'remember', although in the context of recognizing a fulfilment of Scripture, even the sense of 'remember' (i.e. a previous Scripture they had already known) may be appropriate.

THE 'ATRIUMPHAL ENTRY'[263] (12:12–19)

Known throughout much of church history as the triumphal entry, this next passage actually plays down messianic fervour on the part of the crowds coming up to Jerusalem for Passover. There is no question that this is the same event recorded by all three Synoptics as happening on the Sunday before the crucifixion (Mark 11:1–10 pars.). John poses little difficulty for would-be harmonizers, but still manages to include more unparalleled than paralleled information. The only verbatim repetitions come with the name of the city, the fact that Jesus 'sat upon' a donkey, and portions of the two quotations from the Septuagint.[264] Entirely unique to John are the introduction (v. 12), the reference to the palm branches (v. 13), the clarification that the disciples did not at that time understand the fulfilment of prophecy (v. 16), the reference to Lazarus (v. 17), the nature of the miracle as a sign (v. 18), and the Pharisees' lament (v. 19). It is not as clear as elsewhere whether John is presupposing some knowledge of this event on the part of his audience, although Ridderbos (1997: 422) thinks this would account for the 'extreme conciseness' of the narrative. It is more clear that he is literarily independent of the Synoptics, however, as painstaking analyses of the details have repeatedly shown (Dodd 1963: 152–156; D. M. Smith 1963; Wagner 1988: 384–393; contra Freed 1961).

John 12:12 ties back in with 11:56 – the crowds discover that Jesus is indeed coming to the feast. Acclaiming Jesus by waving palm branches (v. 13a) harks back to the custom, attested during the Hasmonean dynasty, of celebrating military victories and welcoming national rulers with similar festivity (1 Macc. 13:51; 2 Macc. 10:7; cf. 14:4; Josephus, War 7.100–102; for further references, see Coakley 1995: 470–471). 'Palms appear on the coins struck by the insurgents during the Jewish wars against Rome (AD 66–70, 132–135); indeed, the use of the palm as a symbol for Judea was sufficiently well established that the coins struck by the Romans to celebrate their victory also sported it' (Carson 1991: 432). The crowds are clearly hoping that Jesus will be a nationalistic warrior–king (cf. Farmer 1952). As for the objections that palm trees are not found today in or around Jerusalem, we must remember that many of the pilgrims would have been coming up from Jericho, the city of palms, which still features

---

263] I have borrowed the term from Kinman 1994.

264] Even here, it appears that John has not relied on the forms of the quotations found in the Synoptics; see Menken 1989.

that plant to this day. Moreover, a letter from Simon bar-Kochba, hailed by some as Messiah in the Jewish uprising against Rome in the 130s, refers specifically to loading and sending palm branches to a camp near Jerusalem, probably for the celebration of Tabernacles (Yadin 1961). The crowds' use of Psalm 118:25–26 (v. 13b) supports a messianic interpretation of this episode. 'Hosanna' ('God save [us]') was used to address kings in 2 Samuel 14:4 and 2 Kings 6:26. The text was most likely taken as messianic by many Jews in Jesus' day, as was 'the King of Israel' (Coakley 1995: 473–476). The spirit of John 6:15 carries over to this new context.

But Jesus' riding on a donkey should have dampened the crowds' enthusiasm (v. 14). This action likewise fulfilled Scripture (v. 15; cf. Zech. 9:9). Jesus was probably making an implicit messianic claim, but his choice of animal, as opposed to, say, the white horse of the victorious Roman conqueror, suggests a peaceful, humble entry to Jerusalem (R. E. Brown 1966: 463; J. A. T. Robinson 1985: 230). Not even his closest followers understand all this (v. 16a), as the subsequent events of 'Passion Week' narrated in all four Gospels make plain. As before, John preserves an important historical distinction between what was recognized during Christ's life and what his disciples subsequently came to believe about him (v. 16b; recall 2:21–22; 7:39; 8:27–28; 10:6); he is not blurring pre- and post-Easter history here. The only unambiguous Johannine theology comes in the language of the narrator of this passage, exactly where we should expect it: Jesus' death as glorification (v. 16), the theme of witness (v. 17), and the reference to the sign (v. 18) that led to some level of discipleship on the part of numerous onlookers (v. 19). Lindars' conclusion (1972: 422) seems sound: 'In spite of the difference of terminology, John's understanding of the event is in striking agreement with what appears to have been its actual significance for Jesus.'

JESUS' DEATH AND THE MINISTRY TO THE GREEKS (12:20–36)

The rest of John 12 is unique among the Gospels, at least at this point in the 'Holy Week' narrative. Verses 20–22 describe a group of Greeks coming to celebrate Passover and the audience they request with Jesus. Verses 23–36 present Christ's reply, with appended dialogues, which does not appear directly to address the Greeks' request. On closer inspection, however, these verses are unified by further prediction of Jesus' death, which is necessary before the fully fledged Gentile mission can begin. In that respect, they explain why Jesus does not feel the need to meet with these particular inquirers at this time.

Despite recent debate, the work of Irina Levinskaya (1996) should now put beyond doubt the claim that numerous Gentile God-fearers populated various Jewish assemblies throughout the early first-century Roman empire (cf. Josephus, *War* 6.420–427; Acts 8:27–28). Attempts to refer to these *Hellēnes* (NIV 'Greeks') as Hellenistic Jews fly in the face of the conventional usage of the term (rightly Kossen 1970). It is entirely credible that at least a few Gentiles should have participated in the Passover festival; indeed Jesus' temple protest (Mark 11:15–19 pars.) in part centred on the court designed for Gentile worship ('a house of prayer for all nations') having been given over to trade (Mark 11:17). If John 12:20 refers to an event that happened just after this protest, these Greeks may even have recognized Jesus' action as undertaken on their behalf (Bruce 1983: 263). They may have approached Philip first because he was from the largely Gentile Bethsaida (recall 1:44), as was Andrew, who is again paired with his fellow townsman (vv. 21–22; cf. Ridderbos 1997: 427–428).

At first glance, Christ's reply sounds as if he did not even hear the request by these Greeks to see him! Instead Jesus employs a series of metaphors and proverbs to remind his disciples of his upcoming death (vv. 23–26). Verse 23 is largely Johannine in language – Christ's 'hour' has at last come and he will be 'glorified' (lifted up on the cross but then also in exaltation at the resurrection/ascension). Still the use of 'Son of Man' in this verse suggests that this saying, however reworded, is based in authentic Jesus-tradition. Verse 24 resembles the various synoptic seed parables (see esp. in Mark 4:1–34), with the twist that the focus here is on the appearance of death when the seed is planted and disappears in the ground, only to be followed by new life in abundance poking through the soil at a later time. Paul's use of the identical imagery in 1 Corinthians 15:36 may suggest a common tradition of sayings known to have come from Jesus. The 'I tell you the truth' introduction also favours authenticity. Verse 25 clarifies the spiritual lesson of the metaphor with a pronouncement that 'has close parallels in no less than five Synoptic passages' (Matt. 10:39; 16:25; Mark 8:35; Luke 9:24; 17:33) and contains characteristic marks of authenticity (Dodd 1963: 338–343; Lindars 1972: 429). Just as Jesus must die so that he and others can live, so also his followers must imitate and serve him (v. 26), a verse with consecutive parallels to Mark 10:43–45 and parallel; 8:34 and parallel; and Matthew 25:21 and 23 (Lindars 1972: 430). Isaiah's suffering servant may lie in the background of this verse, too, a motif that possibly unites all of verses 20–50 (see Beutler 1990).

A shift in time and place may occur before John 12:27. Verse 29 speaks of a crowd present, which may have been there all along if Andrew and Philip had approached Jesus in public in verse 23. Otherwise we are meant to understand that Jesus is once again teaching before a large audience, probably in the temple (cf. Mark 11:27 – 12:44 pars.). Verses 27–33 have often been seen as a drastic reworking of the synoptic Gethsemane narrative (e.g. Stanley 1980: 234–236). John 18 will include excerpts of Jesus' time in the Garden on the night of his arrest, but that chapter lacks any mention of his specific prayers. John may have intended 12:27–33 to compensate for that omission, but it is likely that this is a separate, prior event. It is inconceivable, if Jesus really did have even a faint premonition of his coming death, that he should not have struggled with that destiny more than once. The sentiments of verses 27–28 exactly match those of Mark 14:36 and parallels.[265] Hebrews 5:7 may reflect knowledge of a pre-Johannine version of verse 27, since it uses the same verb 'save', which the Synoptics do not employ here (R. E. Brown 1966: 467).[266] Jesus' prayer in verse 28a, like God's response in verse 28b, again involves the distinctive Johannine language of glorification. But it is not without good Jewish precedent; compare the *Testament of Levi* 18.6–7: 'The heavens will be opened, and from the temple of glory sanctification will come upon him [a new priest] with a fatherly voice, as from Abraham to Isaac. And the glory of the Most High shall burst forth upon him. And the spirit of understanding and sanctification shall rest upon him.' The crowd's divided response (v. 29) resembles elements from the accounts in Acts of the voice at Paul's conversion – Paul heard the words; his companions, a noise; and later speculation imagined that an angel had spoken (Acts 9:7; 22:9; 23:9). And, of course, the heavenly voice recalls God speaking from heaven in the synoptic accounts of Jesus' baptism and transfiguration (Mark 1:11 pars.; 9:7 pars.).

Jesus' reply echoes his words at the resurrection of Lazarus: the heavenly voice, like Jesus' earlier prayer, was solely for the crowd's benefit (v. 31; cf. 11:41–42).[267] Verse 31 summarizes the key Johannine theme of judgment as part of realized eschatology, but conceptually the thought is closely paralleled in Luke 10:18, in which Jesus declares, 'I saw Satan fall like

---

265] The end of verse 27 should probably be punctuated as an initial statement, not as a question. To make the prayer part of the question 'imparts to Jesus' words something of studied (not to say histrionics) artifice' (Bruce 1983: 266; cf. Beasley-Murray 1987: 212). Jesus' first impulse is to want to be saved from the hour of death, but he recognizes that he must do his Father's will.

266] Indeed R. E. Brown (1966: 471) thinks it quite probable that John's scattering of prayers and sayings of this nature (esp. vv. 23, 27 and 28) may 'actually be closer to the original situation than the more organized Synoptic scene'.

267] Tasker (1960: 152–153) discusses how unintelligible words could still be intended for the crowd's benefit. Most importantly, any kind of miraculous phenomenon in response to Jesus' prayer could suggest that God was looking favourably on it.

lightning from heaven.'[268] Verse 32 employs two key Johannine verbs in senses that we have seen before: Jesus must be 'lifted up' (cf. 3:14; 8:28) so that through him God can 'draw' people to himself (cf. 6:44). But the double meaning of 'lift' (v. 33) works in Aramaic as well as in Greek, and there are early creedal parallels to John's thought here in 1 Timothy 3:16, Philippians 2:9 and Hebrews 1:3. Luke 9:51 also recognizes a time in Jesus' ministry when he knew he soon must 'go up' – both to Jerusalem and to his Father. For all these reasons (cf. Beasley-Murray 1987: 214), we must be cautious about claiming that Jesus could not have uttered the gist of what John attributes to him here.

Objections from the crowd now revolve around how the Messiah can be said to die (v. 34). Some Jewish traditions taught precisely that (esp. 2 Esdr. 7:28, 30), but a larger number looked for an eternal reign (Morris 1995: 532, n. 94, with references).[269] The targum on Isaiah 52:13 may reflect an old enough belief to be particularly relevant, when it speaks of the *exaltation* of 'my servant Messiah' (Chilton 1980). The question 'Who is this Son of Man?' could reflect the ambiguity of Jesus speaking of himself in the third person, especially in such lofty terms, or it may be synonymous for 'what kind of Son of Man are you talking about?' Again Jesus exercises his sovereign freedom not to respond as directly as his audience would have liked. Instead he returns to his (and John's) favourite metaphor of light versus darkness to encourage his listeners to follow him while they still have time (vv. 35–36). Verse 35 offers a little parable of a traveller at sunset, 'which may be based on authentic tradition'. The man on the trip 'must make an effort to finish the journey before the darkness overtakes him, or he will lose his way. This is obviously a parable of crisis, comparable to the parables of watchfulness in Mt. 24.42–51' (Lindars 1972: 435). The expression 'children of light' in verse 36a recalls the frequent use of 'sons of light' or 'sons of darkness' at Qumran (e.g. 1QS 1:9; 2:16; 3:13, 20–21; 25; 4:11; 1QM 1:1).[270] The synoptic Jesus uses the identical contrast to distinguish his followers from the rest of the world at the end of the parable of the unforgiving servant (Luke 16:8). As frequently in both the Synoptics and John, especially in the presence of danger, Jesus proceeds to leave the

---

268] Michaels (1983: 212) finds additional similarities to Jesus' parable of the binding of the strong man and related teachings (Matt. 12:29; Mark 3:27; cf. Luke 11:21–22).

269] 'The Law' may very well be the oral Torah here, although Morris (1995: 532) also discusses Old Testament passages from which the notion may have derived, esp. Pss. 89:36; 110:4; Is. 9:7; and Dan. 7:14.

270] For more on Jesus' use of 'light' as a metaphor in John and the Synoptics, see above, pp. 74 and 141.

public arena and 'hides' (v. 36b). John 12:20–36, in keeping with contemporary apocalyptic tradition – see especially *1 Enoch*, *Testament of Moses*, and Qumran's *Manual of Discipline* and *War Scroll* (Kovacs 1995, with numerous texts cited), has presented a unified view of a cosmic battle going on behind the scenes. It is a battle that will eventuate in Jesus' death but only at the exact moment the Father has planned.

SUMMARIES OF JESUS' MINISTRY (12:37–50)

Verses 37–43 summarize the variegated responses to Jesus' teaching that the Gospel of John has thus far presented. As an overall generalization, especially by this late date in Jesus' ministry, John can declare that, despite the 'miraculous signs', most of the Jewish nation did not believe in Jesus. This may be further confirmation, not just in 8:30 but elsewhere in the Gospel, that when various groups are said to believe, such belief may never have turned into mature, abiding faith (e.g. 9:22; 10:21, 42; 11:45). John's summary may be modelled on Moses' words to Israel in Deuteronomy 29:2–4 that charged the Israelites as a whole with unbelief despite the signs God had worked in their midst (Michaels 1983: 216). At any rate, John sees the response in Jesus' day as typologically fulfilling two passages from Isaiah (53:1, quoted in v. 38; and 6:10, discussed in vv. 39–40). Paul, in Romans 10:16, similarly applies the first of these texts to first-century Judaism, while the synoptic Jesus likewise cites the second text to explain the lack of response to his ministry in Mark 4:10–12 and parallels (cf. also Mark 8:17–18; Acts 28:26–27).[271]

John concludes his remarks about Isaiah by explaining that the prophet 'saw Jesus' glory and spoke about him' (v. 41). This claim resembles Jesus' affirmation that Abraham saw his day and rejoiced (8:56). Despite the generally negative response, verse 42 suggests that 'many even among the leaders believed in him'. But this is immediately explained as a secret kind of faith for fear of reprisal and due to misplaced priorities (v. 43). As throughout his Gospel, this clarification appears to be John's way of describing inadequate faith, no doubt to encourage 'secret believers' in his day to go public with their professions of faith. But it will not do to interpret these verses as referring *merely* to affairs at the end of the first century. By that time the Pharisees' counterparts (the sages of formative rabbinic Judaism) were in charge and did not need to fear incurring the wrath of other Jewish leaders, while in John they must still cooperate with

271] Menken (1988a) finds John's translation of Is. 6:10 to be largely his own, fresh rendering of the Hebrew, with slight influence from the Septuagint. Literary dependence on the Synoptics need not be postulated.

the chief priests, especially in Jerusalem (7:32). 'But how could they do that at any time other than when the second temple still existed? And where, then, is the anachronism?' (Ridderbos 1997: 446, n. 220). For further discussion, recall my comments on 9:22; how one interprets that passage will largely determine what one makes of John's remarks here.

If there is one cluster of sayings attributed to Jesus in the entire Fourth Gospel that could plausibly be attributed more to John than to Jesus, it would be verses 44–50. Jesus has finished speaking in public, presumably in the temple. Chapter 13 will move us to the last night of his life and present his private teaching for his disciples. The statements that comprise verses 44–50 read like a summary of numerous major Johannine themes, and they are not introduced or concluded with any indication of a specific place or time that would provide a context for Jesus' teaching. Instead, we read merely that 'Jesus cried out' (v. 44).[272] Indeed, in the light of the ancient convention of creating composite speeches as epitomes of a teacher's sayings, this may be John's way of signalling to his readers that he is providing a summary in his own words of the heart of what Jesus taught on numerous occasions, consistent with the major emphases of John's Gospel (cf. Michaels 1983: 220; Pryor 1992a: 54; Morris 1995: 539).[273]

Verses 44–45 pose little problem, summarizing claims Jesus has made earlier in this Gospel, but also closely paralleling Matthew 10:40–42. Verse 46 echoes Jesus' claim to be the light of the world (8:12; 9:5), contrasted with the darkness that people are urged to shun. Verses 47–48 clarify the senses in which Jesus came both to judge and not to judge (recall above, p. 142). Here Barrett (1978: 434) explains:

> In different passages in John it is said that Jesus acts as judge (5.22, 27; 8.16, 26), and that he does not judge (3.17; 8.15). It is hardly credible that John should have been unaware of this apparent contradiction, or that it should have been undesigned ... The meaning in both Paul and John is that justification and condemnation are opposite sides of the same process; to refuse the justifying love of God in Christ is to incur judgment.

272] Even the NIV's 'then' could mislead. The Greek has merely the weak adversative connective *de* (but). Cf. Whitacre 1999: 324.

273] Witherington (1995: 227) thinks it is worth pondering again the possibility that Jesus is being portrayed as divine Wisdom personified, who calls to people to hear her instruction in order to be wise and to find life (Prov. 8), who is rejected and must return to the One who sent her (*1 Enoch* 42), and who demonstrates that 'in the end one can only learn God's counsel if God gives wisdom and sends the spirit from on high' (Wis. Sol. 9:17–18).

Those who hear Jesus' words 'but do not keep them' (v. 47) remind the reader of the symbolism of the man who built his house on sand in the synoptic parable of the two builders (Matt. 7:26 par.; cf. also Luke 10:16). Verses 49–50 reintroduce the subordinationist strand of Jesus' teaching that he does nothing but what the Father commands him. There may again be an allusion here to the prophet like Moses of Deuteronomy 18:18 (Michaels 1983: 220–221).

What one makes of these two summaries (responses to Jesus in vv. 37–43; key themes of Jesus' teaching in vv. 44–50) will largely depend on what one concludes for each individual motif when it is introduced earlier in the Fourth Gospel. Peder Borgen (1979: 33–34) itemizes a list of the building blocks of traditional influence in verses 44–50, isolating possible source material for almost every clause in this section. Kiyoshi Tsuchido (1984: 613–616) notes a number of these and other parallels to all of 12:20–50 but finds Johannine redaction so pervasive as to make traditional elements inextricable. Against almost everyone, Michael Goulder (1983) finds so many echoes of synoptic tradition in this 'unparalleled' section of John that he postulates literary dependence, especially on Luke, but the resulting corollary is massive Johannine redactional invention. Roman Kühschelm (1990: 131, 138–139) concludes that verses 35–50 are entirely the work of the Fourth Evangelist. All four scholars are working from the same data; their radically divergent conclusions follow because each is applying to John 12 a hypothesis about the nature of the Fourth Gospel built up from his study of the rest of John and the Synoptics more generally, rather than proceeding merely by induction from the text itself.

My conclusions similarly follow from my impression of John's Gospel overall, but I have been able to lay out the evidence passage by passage and even verse by verse. Even in these most Johannine of all the words attributed to Jesus thus far (vv. 44–50), while we may well have a composite collection of key themes and motifs of greatest interest to John and reworded in distinctive Johannine idiom, I see no reason for denying that they reflect concerns of the historical Jesus uttered repeatedly throughout his earthly ministry (similarly E. E. Ellis 1999: 172).

THE FOOTWASHING (13:1–20)

The Passover that will prove fateful for Jesus looms ever nearer (John 13:1a). John introduces the events he is about to narrate by explaining that they will display the full extent of God's love in Christ (v. 1b). The seemingly innocuous beginning of verse 2 has generated a storm of controversy. John writes merely that 'the evening *meal* was being served' (Gk. *deipnon*, i.e., 'supper'), by which time the devil had already put the idea into Judas' heart to betray Jesus (v. 2b). Are we to understand this as the main Passover meal that began the week-long festivities, during which Jesus spoke about the bread and cup as his body and blood, as in the Synoptics? These 'words of institution' never appear in John, but the rest of chapters 13 – 17 make it clear that this is the last night of Jesus' life. And we have already seen that John omits traditions that might be misused to promote an institutionalized sacramentalism (see above, pp. 43 and 79).[274] Nevertheless, a sizable majority of scholars alleges that John has reshaped his traditions in order to have Jesus' last meal with his disciples take place before the start of Passover, so that he can make the crucifixion appear to occur on the afternoon during which the Passover lambs would be slaughtered for the celebratory meal that evening. This then becomes one more way to stress, theologically, that Jesus is the true Lamb of God who died for the sins of the world (recall 1:29, 36) (e.g. Lindars 1972: 442–446; Barrett 1978: 437; Casey 1996: 18–25).

A significant portion of this debate depends on the interpretation of 18:28; 19:14, 31, and 42, all of which I shall address in due course. But let us attempt to read (or better, hear) John 13 as John might have expected his initial Ephesian audience to have understood it. They would already have known, in broad strokes at least, about the story of Jesus' passion, so that it is more likely that they would have thought of the whole cluster of events that culminated in Christ's death rather than just the Last Supper as Jesus showing his followers the full extent of his love (or, even more clearly, with NIV mg., loving them 'to the last'). Verse 1 thus stands as a headline over the entire passion narrative (cf. Ridderbos 1997: 452).[275] Because Passover began with a supper-time meal as its most central ritual (and 1 Cor. 11:20 speaks of the Last Supper explicitly as a *deipnon*), to hear then that the supper was being served (v. 2)[276] would naturally suggest that the Passover had begun (Ridderbos 1997: 455; cf. Michaels 1983: 230; Kleinknecht 1985: 370–371; Burge 2000: 365–367), *not* that this was some separate supper prior to the Passover (as for Casey 1996: 20–21). If

---

274] D. M. Smith (1999: 255) thinks rather that John 'does not wish to portray Jesus' giving himself for his disciples in a way that does not implicate them in an analogous self-giving'.

275] So also Ball (1985), who nevertheless goes too far in dissociating v. 1 from the rest of the narrative by suggesting that it is not referring to the footwashing at all.

276] The Gk. *deipnon* is anarthrous, suggesting a possible translation of 'an evening meal was being served'. More probably, the noun lacks the article because the verb *genomenou* paired with it in the genitive absolute construction also lacks the article, not because the meal itself is simply an ordinary unidentified meal.

there is still any doubt, as Cullen Story (1989: 317) explains, 'The presence of Judas, Jesus' prediction of his betrayal, Judas' departure from the table (implicit in the Synoptics, explicit in John), the affirmation by Peter of unswerving loyalty to Jesus, and Jesus' prediction of his denial – all of these circumstances together form solid lines of connection between the meal in John 13 and the Synoptic account of the holy supper.' Almost certainly, then, John intended his audience to understand that he was beginning to describe events that took place on 'Maundy Thursday' night, as part of the Passover meal, just as they would already have learned in the oral kerygma.

Verse 2 shows specific affinity with Luke 22:3, the one synoptic reference to the coming role of Judas in a context immediately preceding the Last Supper narrative. The role of the devil here makes one think of his similar influence over Ananias and Sapphira in Acts 5:3. The knowledge and authority ascribed to Christ in verse 3 forms another of John's many conceptual parallels to Matthew 11:27.[277] Verses 4–5 depict Jesus washing the feet of his disciples, an incident narrated only in the Fourth Gospel. Barrett (1978: 440) sums up key historical background to this practice:

> The washing of the master's feet was a menial task which was not required of the Jewish slave (in distinction from slaves of other nationalities; *Mekhilta* Exod. 21.2). The degrading character of the task should not however be exaggerated. Wives washed the feet of their husbands, and children of their parents. Disciples were expected to perform acts of personal service for their rabbis (e.g. *Berakoth* 7b: R. Johanan [† AD 279] said in the name of R. Simeon b. Yochai [c. AD 150]: The service of the Law [that is, of teachers of it] is more important than learning it. See 2 Kings 3.11).[278]

But here the master was trying to wash the feet of his disciples! The criterion of double similarity and dissimilarity is well satisfied. The practice

---

277] Verses 1–3 are somewhat 'overloaded' syntactically, leading many scholars to assume that John is adding his own comments to traditional material here. Grossouw (1966), however, accounts for the style of these verses by seeing them as a 'minor prologue' to the Johannine passion narrative, introducing numerous key themes that will subsequently be unpacked.

278] For further historical background and theological interpretation, see esp. Weiss 1979; Thomas 1991a; Pesce and Destro 1999. Bruce (1983: 281) suggests that, in the reference in 1 Pet. 5:5 to an 'apron of humility', 'one may detect the vivid reminiscence of an unforgettable occasion' such as the footwashing being described. The theology of the early creedal text in Phil. 2:5–11 also closely matches that symbolized here by Jesus' behaviour.

emerges out of a Jewish background but takes a radical turn. A few Christians imitate Jesus later but mostly by turning the practice into the very kind of sacramental ritual against which John was protesting. The footwashing also resembles the synoptic parable of Jesus in which the master comes, girds himself, and serves the watchful servants with him at table (Luke 12:37).

As Jesus approaches Peter to wash his feet, this frequent spokesman for the Twelve protests (v. 6). The objection closely resembles his outburst on the road to Caesarea Philippi when he rejected the prophecy of Christ's coming suffering and death (Mark 8:32 pars.; Schneiders 1981). Jesus explains that Peter cannot fully understand what is happening now; only afterwards, that is, after Christ's death and resurrection, will he catch on (v. 7). Again we see that John is careful to distinguish what Jesus' disciples understood before the cross from fuller, post-Easter insights. When Peter still objects, Jesus explains that he must wash Peter's feet; otherwise, 'you have no part with me' (v. 8). Did this language inspire Peter's later rebuke of Simon Magus in almost identical words (Acts 8:21)? Never one to be accused of moderation in all things, Peter now insists that he receive a complete bath (v. 9)! Jesus' reply in verse 10a contains both textual and exegetical difficulties. The external evidence strongly favours one version of the longer reading (as in the NIV, containing the exception clause, i.e., literally 'the one who has washed has no need to wash except the feet'). In an ordinary Passover setting this would mean that one who is purified and prepared for the festival does not need to wash again except for feet that have become dirty (Kieffer 1998). On this specific occasion Jesus is claiming that those who have already become his disciples do not need to repeat their commitments of initiation over and over again; they must merely be cleansed (forgiven) of subsequent sin (cf. Thomas 1991a: 125). But one among the Twelve has never even been initially cleansed, namely Judas (vv. 10b–11).[279]

The entire scene so far exhibits clear parallels to Jesus' teaching on servanthood in Mark 10:35–45 and Matthew 20:20–28, teaching that in Luke's Gospel is inserted explicitly into the Last Supper account (Luke 22:24–28).[280] Verses 12–20 now spell out these implications even more directly. Verse 12 follows somewhat oddly after verse 7, but the disciples'

279] Barrett (1978: 442) further observes that 'Judas has been washed with the other disciples; all possibility therefore of a merely mechanical operation of salvation, whether by baptism or otherwise, is excluded.'

280] For further synoptic parallels, see Talbert (1992: 194), based on the interpretation that 'if the washing in vv. 6–11 symbolizes the forgiveness of disciples' daily sin by Jesus, then ignorance cannot be taken to be absolute. As regularly in the Synoptics, by the very fact that the disciples remain with Jesus, initial misunderstanding yields to at least *partial* understanding after Jesus explains the meaning of his symbolic words and actions. In verse 13 Jesus alludes to two common titles used of him throughout all four Gospels – 'Teacher' and 'Lord' – titles regularly ascribed to rabbis by their disciples (cf. the Aramaic *rab* and *mar*; R. E. Brown 1970: 553). But one of the implications of following a rabbi was to imitate him. So the disciples, metaphorically speaking, must wash each other's feet, following Christ's example (vv. 14–15). The word for 'example' (Gk. *hypodeigma*) occurs only here in the Gospels but fits the Jewish models of exemplary death found in 2 Maccabees 6:28, 4 Maccabees 17:22–23 and Sirach 44:16 (Moloney 1998: 376). Both language and concept reappear in the early creedal material of 1 Peter 2:21–25 as well. The proverb of John 13:16 is found in Matthew 10:24 and Luke 6:40, both times in contexts of persecution, and it will reappear in John 15:20 in precisely such a context. Its application here to humble, menial service is not far removed from the more explicit endurance of the hostility of other people (cf. Lindars 1972: 452–453). Verse 17 forms a short beatitude, like those with which the Sermon on the Mount/Plain begins (esp. in the Lukan form; Luke 6:20–23), enjoining obedience to Christ's commands, just as the parable does with which that Sermon ends (Luke 6:46–49 par.).

The interpretations of Jesus' footwashing described successively in verses 6–11 and 12–17 are often said to contradict each other, thus leading to various theories about stages of tradition and redaction. After surveying these discussions Fernando Segovia (1982: 36–37) concludes that no less than eight reasons make it impossible for a 'harmonizing interpretation' to 'reconcile and resolve all or even most of these difficulties successfully'. These problems are (1) the grammatically overloaded nature of verses 1–4; (2) the contradiction between verses 2b and 27; (3) the unnecessary doublet in verses 1 and 3; (4) the fact that verses 4–5 can be followed smoothly by either verses 6–11 or 12–20; (5) the contradiction between verses 7 and 12; (6) the point of verses 6–11 as explaining Jesus' death versus the point of 12–20 as a model for humble service; (7) the unnecessary doublet of verses 10b–11 and 18–19; and (8) a similar doublet in verses 18 and 26.

On the other hand, literary criticism is increasingly demonstrating that

---

for the disciples to wash one another's feet (i.e., act *as* he did toward disciples) means for them to forgive one another those daily trespasses that characterize one human being's infringement upon another'.

'doublets' – the issue behind objections (3), (7) and (8) – may be intentional devices for theological emphasis. We have already noted an alternate explanation for the tortuous syntax of verses 1–4 – objection (1) – in note 277 above. Verse 27 is better understood as the decisive moment Judas began to carry out his treachery, even though he had plotted it earlier, contra objection (2). Item (4) is hardly an objection against the unity of the passage; if verses 6–11 can follow verses 4–5 smoothly then there is no problem! The 'contradiction' alleged in (5) has been dealt with above (p. 190). And item (6) – the real heart of the matter – is resolved once we realize that the two interpretations are complementary and not contra-dictory (cf. Dunn 1970b). Indeed, both are already implied in verses 6–11 alone, once the longer version of verse 10 is accepted as original (Thomas 1991a: 125). 'In any case we already have in the synoptic tradition another example of the blending of the soteriological and paraenetic value of Christ's death, Mark 10:42–45. There is no reason why the two elements should not always have been held together in John 13:1–20' (Pryor 1992a: 60). In addition, Michal Wojciechowski (1988) finds a chiasm spanning verses 4–12 as part of a traditional core of this passage, which makes a neat division after verse 11 implausible.[281]

Verses 18–20 belong conceptually with verses 21–30 as they narrate Jesus' prediction of Judas' betrayal. But grammatically they are tied more closely with verses 12–17 and may be taken as the transitional conclusion to the footwashing scene. Jesus again stresses that his promises do not apply to every one of the Twelve. He knows whom he has truly chosen spiritually, even if all twelve responded to an outward call (v. 18). The treachery about to be undertaken against him will typologically fulfil Psalm 41:9. Just as David was opposed by an unnamed arch-enemy, so the messianic Son of David will be betrayed by one particularly diabolical foe.[282] Verse 18b perhaps reads more naturally as John's own narrative comment than as a word of Jesus. Verse 19 explains why Jesus is stressing his knowledge of the betrayal in advance: like the rest of his words and works in the Fourth Gospel, this prediction when it is fulfilled should lead to (deeper) belief. The ambiguous absolute *egō eimi* reappears at the end of this verse. Verse 20 concludes this segment of teaching ascribed to Jesus with another close

---

281] Cf. further R. B. Edwards (1994), who stresses that both exemplary service (the moral interpretation) and atoning death (the Christological or soteriological interpretation) are intended by the author of the final form of John 13, and that the two themes are not incompatible. Jesus is both Servant and Saviour. Although we do not atone for anyone's sins, some of us may have to love by laying down our lives, and all of us are called to serve.

282] On the typology, cf. further Carson 1991: 470; on the text form, see Menken 1990.

parallel to Matthew 10:40. 'The identification of sender and agent is firmly fixed' in Jewish thought (*Ber.* 5.5; cf. Acts 9:4–5; 22:7–8; 26:14–15; Matt. 25:40; Talbert 1992: 195).

As with the various pericopae in John 12, there are enough synoptic parallels to every part of 13:1–20 to suggest to a few scholars that the Fourth Gospel was literarily dependent on the Synoptics (see esp. Sabbe 1982). Substantive verbal parallels, however, especially to the synoptic passion narrative *per se*, are so few and far between that this scenario seems unlikely. But it does serve as a caution against those who would so stress the differences between John and the Synoptics that they feel forced to opt for the historicity of one version at the expense of the other. Arland Hultgren (1982) discusses the historical background and Johannine meaning of this passage, persuasively concluding that a symbolic event from the last night of Jesus lies behind John's text, especially given the equally symbolic acts narrated by the Synoptics in their Last Supper accounts.

BETRAYAL AND DENIAL PREDICTED (13:21–38)

John has foreshadowed Judas' betrayal of Jesus in 13:2. Jesus has alluded to the event in verses 18–20. Now he unambiguously declares, 'I tell you the truth, one of you is going to betray me' (v. 21). John describes Jesus' soul as 'troubled', the identical expression Jesus himself used in 11:27. Here is a very human Jesus, not unmoved by developing events (Morris 1995: 554), a good sign of historicity. Except for the extra 'Amen', Jesus' words here parallel Mark 14:8b verbatim. This is the only place in this account where there is enough verbal parallelism with one of the Synoptics to suggest literary dependence. At the same time, this is a sufficiently brief and memorable saying for it easily to have been preserved intact in the oral tradition, even in Greek.

Characteristically, the disciples remain baffled, unable to believe they could be capable of such treachery (v. 22). Verse 23 introduces the first of the Fourth Gospel's five 'beloved disciple' passages (see above, p. 29). Witherington (1995: 238) believes that 'this sentence then is making a claim about the authenticity of the witness of the Beloved Disciple – he understood the mind and meaning of the Word/Wisdom of God'. The reference to 'reclining' fits the description of requirements for the Passover meal (Jeremias 1966: 22–26; Barrett 1978: 446). Jesus and the Twelve would probably have gathered around a 'triclinium', three low rectangular tables forming a square-cornered 'U'. Jesus as the host would have sat in the middle of the 'bottom' of the 'U' and would have placed his two most honoured associates on either side of him (*b. Ber.* 46b). In the light of the ensuing conversation it would appear that these were the beloved disciple and Judas.[283] Simon Peter may have been across the table from Jesus.

Peter, ever impulsive and often the spokesman for the Twelve, motions to John to ask Jesus who will betray him (v. 24). A creator of fiction would probably have just had John or Peter ask the question on his own (R. E. Brown 1970: 574). That Peter gives some kind of signal to John suggests a fairly secretive conversation. This links with the observation that in the Synoptics the disciples all in turn ask publicly, 'Is it I?' (Mark 14:19 par.), whereas Jesus replies simply by telling them that it is someone who is dipping his bread into the dish with him, that is, one of the Twelve (Mark 14:20 pars.). Jesus' reply in John is more specific (v. 26a), enabling those who heard him to know that he was referring to Judas (v. 26b).[284] But even reading John apart from the Synoptics, we would have to assume that this was a 'whispered exchange', since the rest of the gathering does not understand why Judas almost immediately leaves (v. 30; Ridderbos 1997: 471; cf. Michaels 1983: 235; contra Schnackenburg 1982: 30). In verse 27 Jesus may have spoken to Judas loudly enough for all to hear, but he returns to his cryptic style of speech leaving the others bewildered (v. 28). That the disciples might muse that Judas was going out to give something to the poor 'would be particularly appropriate on Passover night', when such almsgiving seems to have been explicitly commanded (Jeremias 1966: 54, 82; Barrett 1978: 448). That others thought he was buying something 'for the Feast' does not contradict this supposition, since the Passover meal initiated the week-long Feast of Unleavened Bread, during which time additional meals every day, including lunches as well as dinners, would require special provisions. Indeed, on the common view that for John this was a meal one day before the Passover, it is hard to see 'why Jesus should send Judas out for purchases for a feast still twenty-four hours away. The next day would have left ample time.' Likewise, 'on any night other than Passover it is hard to imagine why the disciples might have thought Jesus was sending Judas out *to give something to the poor*: the next day would have

---

283] The evidence is mixed as to whether the right or left hand was the more honoured of the two, although the right hand seems more likely. Thus, e.g. R. E. Brown 1970: 574; Witherington 1995: 239; Ridderbos 1997: 469. That Judas would be so honoured could reflect his role as treasurer, but there may be more implied here. 'In the social custom of that day, it was a mark of special favour for the host to dip bread in sauce and personally serve a guest. This act represented love's last appeal to one on the verge of perdition' (Talbert 1992: 195–196).

284] We are probably also meant to recall the citation in v. 18 from Psalm 41:9 about the one who was eating bread with David as the one who lifted up his heel against him (Beasley-Murray 1987: 238).

done just as well' (Carson 1991: 475). For all the scorn Casey (1996: 18–25) pours on Carson and other conservative commentators in the former's confidence that a harmonizing approach to the Gospels is impossible, it is astonishing that he never interacts with observations such as these.

Verses 31–38 turn from Judas to Peter. Many scholars begin at this point the farewell discourse that includes chapters 14 – 16; certainly these verses introduce key themes in a dialogue format, which these later chapters will continue. But, because of the larger blocks of uninterrupted teaching of Jesus in chapters 14 – 16, combined together in a broadly chiastic structure, it is better to treat them separately, as we shall see below (p. 197). Verses 31–35 are not paralleled in the Synoptics and are loaded with Johannine language. Verses 31–32 repeat the theme of the mutual glorification of the Father and the Son in the context of the arrival of Jesus' hour (12:23). But the reference to the 'Son of Man' suggests that Jesus did in fact say something corresponding to these words, however John may have translated them into his own idiom. Verse 33 reiterates the theme of Jesus' departure to a place where no-one can immediately follow him, as enunciated already in 7:33–34 and 8:21–22. The diminutive vocative *teknia* ('children') occurs nowhere else in the Gospels and only seven times in the rest of the New Testament, all in 1 John. But in Mark 10:24 Jesus addresses his followers with what is rendered in the Greek by the cognate *tekna*, and in Matthew 18:3 and 19:4 he admonishes the disciples to become like little children (R. E. Brown 1970: 607). Is this another case of John as author picking up and stressing a genuine expression he learned from the historical Jesus? At the Last Supper Jesus would have played the part of the father of an extended family, 'the disciples being the "children" whose function it was to ask him questions designed to bring out the significance of the occasion' (Bruce 1983: 293), precisely what we see from here to the end of chapter 16. Verses 34–35 similarly employ language that will recur throughout John's epistles (see esp. 1 John 2:7–8), but the concepts cohere well with Jesus' dialogue with the lawyer in Mark 12:28–34 and parallel. The heart of Jesus' ethic is love, grounded in the double love-command of the Torah (Deut. 6:4–5; Lev. 19:18), but Jesus' followers are enabled to love in a significantly new way thanks to Christ's ministry, and especially his death and resurrection (cf. esp. Lindars 1972: 463; Ridderbos 1997: 476).

Verses 36–38 now focus directly on Peter, who, as more than once in the Synoptics, asks for clarification (e.g. Matt. 15:15; Luke 12:1). As in his earlier dialogues with various Jewish leaders, Jesus does not directly answer the question about where he is going (v. 36). He recognizes that the real issue is Peter's premature optimism in his ability to follow him even to martyrdom (v. 37), a theme matched in the synoptic parallels (Mark 14:29, 31 pars.).[285] Verse 38 closes the chapter with Jesus assuring Peter that, far from laying down his life, he will deny him three times before the early morning cockcrow. This assertion matches Mark 14:30 and parallels, partly verbatim. But, as with Jesus' prediction of his betrayal, this pronouncement creates the memorable climax of the passage and forms the one part that would probably have been preserved the most carefully by oral tradition.[286]

'DO NOT LET YOUR HEARTS BE TROUBLED' (14:1–14)

By the time we reach John 14 all commentators agree that Jesus' farewell discourse has begun. To some extent fluid in form, the farewell discourse or 'last testament' was sufficiently common and identifiable among Jewish writings for us to recognize an example of it in chapters 14 – 16 here. Jacob blesses and admonishes his sons just before his death (Gen. 49); Moses does the same for the twelve tribes about to enter the Promised Land (Deut. 33).[287] In intertestamental literature we find entire Testaments ascribed to Adam, Isaac, each of the twelve sons of Jacob, Moses, Job and Solomon. Shorter examples appear scattered throughout the book of *Jubilees.* Although Jesus does not deal with his twelve disciples, one by one, as in the *Testaments of the Twelve Patriarchs,* similar themes of announcing one's approaching death, predicting other future events, reflecting on one's past ministry, 'passing the torch' to one's followers, commissioning their ministry, and promising God's future presence, all mark these chapters off as a discrete testamentary discourse, thoroughly at home in the world of early first-century Judaism (Segovia 1991: 308–316). Still, there are sufficient distinctives, especially in the realm of apocalyptic elements, to

---

285] 'Peter uses precisely the same words as Jesus has used of himself as the Good Shepherd (10.11–18). The same expression will be used in a more general application in 15.13.' 'Peter's protestation is closer to Lk. 22.33 than to Mt. 26.33 (= Mk 14.29), though there are no verbal links' (Lindars 1972: 465). The one exception is the vocative *kyrie.*

286] Only Mark refers to Peter denying Jesus three times before the cock would crow *twice.* Matthew, Luke and John do not include this addition. Thus this is not a problem for a study of the historicity of John, though it may be worth stating the obvious (overlooked by a remarkable number of scholars who immediately charge Mark with contradiction) that, if Peter denied Jesus three times before the cock crowed once, then he denied him those same three times before the cock crowed again!

287] Köstenberger (1999: 144) notes the extensive 'covenant language' in John 13 – 16 and illustrates via the preponderance of the five major verb themes of Exod. 33 – 34 and Deut. in John 14:15–24: 'love', 'obey', 'live', 'know' and 'see'.

suggest a hybrid form and an authentic core of material attributable to Jesus' creativity (Bammel 1993; for further studies of the genre of these chapters cf. esp. Lacomara 1974; M. Winter 1994).[288] In the rest of the New Testament 'Luke comes closest to constructing such a farewell,' both by Jesus (Luke 22:14–38) and by Paul (Acts 20:17–38) (D. M. Smith 1999: 265).

It is still common to find elaborate theories about the formation of John 14 – 16 that parcel this material up into various stages of tradition or redaction. Fernando Segovia (1991: esp. 319–328) modifies his earlier proposals and sees three stages of composition each involving discrete blocks of material: (1) an initial discourse of 13:31 – 14:31; (2) 15:18–16:4a and 16:4b–33 already composed individually, added to the previous material at the same time; and (3) 15:1–17. Each stage is then correlated with developments in the Johannine community. John Painter (1981) likewise identifies three stages of the development of the discourse and of the community's history but reads them from the text in a straightforward consecutive sequence: 13:31 – 14:31, 15:1 – 16:4a, and 16:4b–33. Christian Dietzfelbinger (1997) thinks that 13:31 – 14:31, 15:1 – 16:15 and 16:16–33 are the three blocks that were progressively added together in successive stages. Following more conventional tradition criticism, Udo Schnelle (1989) analyses the language of each major section, dividing each into tradition and redaction rather than imagining growth by the progressive addition of large self-contained blocks of material. More creatively, Andreas Dettwiler (1995) isolates 15:1–17 as a later 're-reading' of 13:1–17, 34–35, and 16:4–33 as a similar 're-reading' of 13:31 – 14:31. Most radically of all, Christina Hoegen-Rohls (1996) believes she can see sufficient signs of post-Easter influence in every portion of the discourse to attribute it all to early Christian invention. The sheer diversity of these approaches, with no hint of a scholarly consensus, suggests that perhaps we should look in an entirely different direction.

Unquestionably there are numerous repetitions and seemingly awkward literary seams throughout John 14 – 16, the most important of which I shall address *en route*. These chapters are also filled with characteristic and distinctive Johannine language and theology. But a fair number of recent studies has concentrated on the potential for reading this discourse as a literary unity. Some of these, of course, do not preclude one or more of the

---

288] There has been a large volume of recent studies, including numerous book-length works, on John 14 – 16. Many of these are purely synchronic and do not deal with questions of historicity. I shall cite or interact only with those that do in some way impinge on historical questions. For a broader survey of recent scholarship, see Klauck 1996.

theories of tradition-critical development surveyed above (e.g. Reese 1972; Boyle 1975). A considerable number of them, however, involve reading this 'testament' as an extended chiasm, which might more naturally suggest a unified composition from the outset. Wayne Brouwer (1999) has surveyed these in the greatest detail and offers his own chiastic outline, which may be more detailed and precise than the data permit. Still, I offer the following observations: (1) John 14:1 begins with the command not to be 'troubled', because of the provisions Christ is making for his followers. John 16:33 concludes the discourse with the promise of peace that Christ can provide despite the 'trouble' the disciples will have in the world. (2) John 14:1–31 introduces numerous themes that 16:5–33 recapitulates: in 14:5 the disciples ask where Jesus is going, while in 16:5 they no longer ask the question; 14:14 and 16:23–24 both deal with petitioning the Father in Jesus' name; 14:16–18 and 16:8–11 both describe the ministry of the Paraclete *vis-à-vis* the world; while 14:19–20 and 16:16–19 both discuss Jesus' prediction that 'in a little while you will not see me and then in a little while you will see me again'. (3) In between these two main sections, 15:1–17 and 15:18 – 16:4 contrast with each other by focusing on the love of Jesus for his disciples versus the hatred of the world for the disciples. (4) The explicit teaching on love appears in 15:9–17, so one could also break 15:1 – 16:4 into 15:1–8 (those who remain in Jesus), 15:9–17 (love as the climactic centre of the chiasm), and 15:18 – 16:4 (those who do not remain in, but oppose, Jesus). (5) Mark Stibbe (1993: 164) finds a seven-part chiasm by including chapters 13 – 17. His verse divisions are thus 13:1–38, 14:1–31, 15:1–11, 15:12–17, 15:8 – 16:4a, 16:4b–33 and 17:1–26. There are enough indications, therefore, of thoughtful construction and unity to this discourse that we need not a priori assume that the material was built up in multiple stages over time.

John 14:1 affords a striking contrast with 12:27. There Jesus declared that his soul was troubled, but he recognizes the need to remain resolute along the road to the cross. Now he calls on the disciples not to be troubled despite the alarming predictions of chapter 13. The NIV margin seems preferable to the NIV text: as good Jews, the Twelve are already believing or trusting in God. Jesus, distinctively, wants them to trust in him just as much. Encouragement not to be afraid is standard in farewell discourses (cf. *1 En.* 92.2; *Test. Zeb.* 10.1–2; *Jub.* 22.23). Commands from the Lord not to fear are in fact far more common in the Synoptics than in John (e.g. Matt. 1:20; 10:26, 31; 28:5; Luke 1:13, 30; 2:10; 5:10; 8:50; etc.). The links between believing in Jesus and believing in God resemble Jesus' claims in the Synoptics concerning his followers 'confessing' him as the key to Jesus' confessing them before the Father on Judgment Day (Matt. 10:32; Luke 12:8).

John 14:2–3 probably draws on temple imagery. The temple was by far the most prominent multiroom house in Jewish thought (see esp. McCaffrey 1988).[289] One probable interpretation of Jesus' words in Luke 2:49 understands him as referring to the temple as 'my Father's house', exactly as here. Jesus' promise to come back and take his disciples to the place he has prepared for them seems to draw on the same kind of tradition as that reflected in 1 Thessalonians 4:16–17, with its explicit reference to a word from the Lord, that is, the historical Jesus (D. Wenham 1995: 308–310, 331–333). The future, eschatological orientation of Jesus' words in John 14:2–3 makes one think of a similar eschatological focus in the synoptic accounts of the Last Supper, most notably with Mark 14:25 and parallels, in which Jesus looks forward to drinking the cup anew with his followers in his coming kingdom (cf. also Luke 22:29–30). For the concept of future places Christ has prepared for his disciples, compare Mark 10:40 and Matthew 25:34.

In John 14:4 Jesus almost 'baits' his disciples by declaring that they know the place to which he is going. Given their frequent misunderstandings, especially in Mark, we should not be surprised to read of Thomas protesting that he does not know (v. 5). 'Thomas (see on 11.16 and cf. 20.24) appears in John as a loyal but dull disciple, whose misapprehension serves to bring out the truth' (Barrett 1978: 458). The word for 'way' (Gk. *hodos*) occurs in John only here (vv. 4, 5 and 6) and in 1:23 on the lips of the Baptist, while it is quite common in the Synoptics. One thinks especially of Matthew 7:13–14 with Jesus' command to follow the narrow rather than the broad way. It is a small step from this kind of saying to Jesus' 'I am' claim in John 14:6 that he is the way, the truth and the life (or perhaps 'the true and living way').[290] Indeed, if the Baptist's ministry involved preparing the way of the Lord (Mark 1:2–3 pars.), for the Messiah to come and claim to be that way proves merely to be the natural fulfilment of the prediction. Is this where the early church got the idea for its self-designation as 'the Way' (e.g. Acts 9:2)? Verse 7 furthers the recurring Johannine theme of Jesus imitating his Father but also recalls

---

289] Alternately, Barrett (1978: 457) notes Jewish parallels to a belief in compartments or multiple dwelling places within heaven. Cf. esp. *1 En.* 39.4 and *2 En.* 61.2. For dwelling places of rest more generally, particularly in Jewish apocalyptic, see the numerous references in Schnackenburg 1982: 50.

290] 'Truth' and 'life' are more distinctively Johannine qualifiers. Witherington (1995: 249–250) notes that 'it is interesting that while "life" may be said to be the key term in the first half of the Gospel (thirty-one times in John 1 – 12, only four thereafter), "truth" is the characteristic theme in John 13 – 21 (twelve instances).'

Matthew 11:27 and parallel. Raymond Brown (1970: 631) finds additional parallels in the ancient Near Eastern covenantal language behind Hosea 13 – 14 and Jeremiah 24:7 and 31:34.

Philip is the next to interrupt Jesus' discourse by asking to be shown the Father (v. 8). As a Jew he would have known of the essential invisibility of God, but also of periodic Old Testament theophanies. Perhaps that is what Philip wants, imagining that it would be an incontrovertible sign (cf. Beasley-Murray 1987: 253; Morris 1995: 571). Somewhat exasperated, Jesus replies by once again encouraging simple trust in him and, if this is not possible, belief on the basis of his words and works (vv. 9–10). The appeal to the testimony of his 'works' (vv. 10–11) coheres with his previous statements to that effect already found to be authentic (above, p. 103; cf. Ensor 1996: 238–241). The greater things that he promises his disciples will do (v. 12) have often been taken to refer to the greater effects of their mission, but perhaps the more pertinent comparison is between old and new ages. Carson (1991: 496) concurs: 'In short, the works that the disciples perform after the resurrection are greater than those done by Jesus before his death insofar as the former belong to an age of clarity and power introduced by Jesus' sacrifice and exaltation.' Again, 'the contrast between the greatness of John the Baptist and the greatness of the least in the kingdom is not entirely dissimilar' (cf. Matt. 11:11–12, 23–24). In any event, it is not likely that the later church would invent a saying ascribed to Jesus susceptible to the interpretation that the disciples were greater than their master. The double-'Amen' formula also points towards authenticity.

With verses 13–14 we return to affirmations with even closer synoptic parallels. The promise of Christ to do whatever the disciples ask the Father in his name immediately calls to mind the threefold 'Ask, seek, knock' command of Matthew 7:7–11 and parallel, and only slightly less quickly the promise of Matthew 18:19–20 to two or three gathered in Jesus' name. The Synoptics do not have an exact parallel to 'asking in my name' but this is what we find pervasively in early Christian behaviour in Acts (2:21, 38; 3:6, 16; 4:7, 10; etc.). A dominical origin for the language is thus most probable. One thinks also of the synoptic Jesus' promise in the context of cursing the fig tree (Mark 11:25 par.).

THE PROMISE OF THE PARACLETE (14:15–31)

How will the disciples be able to cope and continue ministry in the absence of their master? The second half of John 14 answers the question: Jesus will send the Holy Spirit to empower them. A number of distinctive Johannine themes and expressions continue to appear, but several topics and terms are introduced that either occur in John *only* in the farewell discourse or appear here in a concentration disproportionate to the rest of the Gospel. The verb *agapaō* (to love) dominates a large portion of the narrative of this last night of Jesus' life (twenty-five times in chs. 13 – 17) while remaining relatively rare elsewhere (five times in chs. 1 – 12; five times in chs. 18 – 21). 'Keeping' (as in 'keeping the commandments', from Gk. *tēreō*) occurs twelve times in chapters 13 – 17 but only six times in 1 – 12 and not at all in 18 – 21. *Entolē* (commandment) and *entellomai* (to command) appear nine times in 13 – 17 versus four times in 1 – 12 and not at all later on. The unique term for the Spirit ('paraclete' – Gk. *paraklētos*) occurs in the Gospels only in five key passages within the farewell discourse (see below, p. 201). The doctrine of the coinherence or interpenetration of Father and Son, on which is modelled the relationship between God/Christ and believers, occurs nowhere in the New Testament outside this discourse. Jesus' recapitulative expression, 'These things I have spoken' (*tauta lelalēka*) is used five times in chapters 14 – 16 and nowhere else in the Gospels. Two key verbs for 'remember' (*mnēmoneuō* and *hypomimnēskō*) occur four times in chapters 14 – 16 and elsewhere in the Gospels only in Luke 2:61. 'Peace' (*eirēnē*), a common concept in the Synoptics, appears in John only six times, three times in chapters 14 – 16, and three times in chapter 20. 'Heart' (*kardia*) is mentioned twice in John 1 – 12, eight times in chapters 13 – 16, and never again in this Gospel. 'Ask' (*aiteō*) is a verb found in chapters 1 – 12 only three times, but eight times in chapters 13 – 16, and never afterwards in John.

An older generation of more conservative commentators regularly appealed to these kinds of data to suggest that one of the main reasons that John's thought and idiom are so different from the Synoptics is that Jesus spoke in a different way and on different themes when he was privately instructing his disciples rather than publicly teaching the crowds or having a dialogue with opponents (cf. Morris 1969: 134; even as recently as Cullmann 1976: 24). Today this approach is largely discounted because of the common Johannine expressions and motifs that appear throughout the Fourth Gospel irrespective of the location or audience of Jesus' teaching (e.g. Casey 1996: 80–96; cf. esp. his chart on 85). Data like those surveyed above, however, suggest that neither of these polarized positions is sufficiently nuanced. We cannot account for a majority of the distinctives in John by this kind of argument, but it probably does explain a significant minority of the differences. When we reflect on the list of items just surveyed, we can see that each is particularly relevant for Jesus in conversation with his followers on the last night of his life; such concerns were less urgent in other contexts. Thus if, in stretches of the farewell discourse from this point onwards, we at times find fewer linguistic or thematic parallels to the Synoptics, we should not be entirely surprised. Once John had determined to supply considerably more detail concerning Jesus' teaching on this night, certain distinctives were bound to emerge. When these distinctives reappear in John's epistles, in principle he is at least as likely to have reused them because he learned them from Jesus as to have invented them and retrojected them on to Christ's lips.

John 14:15 defines love in a highly Johannine fashion as keeping Christ's commandments (cf. esp. the epistles of John). But as we have just noted, 'love', 'keep' and 'command' all occur especially frequently in the farewell discourse. Apart from the specific language, the concept of verse 15 ably satisfies the double similarity and dissimilarity criterion. Love as obedience to God's commands is an epitome of the Mosaic Law, but Christ here revolutionizes that concept by insisting that the obedience be directed towards *him*. The Synoptics promote both the traditional and this more revolutionary obedience in Mark 12:28–34 and parallel and Matthew 7:24–27 and parallel, respectively, but subsequent Christianity has rarely implemented Jesus' radical teaching on love at all well (cf. further Michaels 1983: 240).

Verse 16 introduces the first of the five Paraclete passages (NIV 'Counsellor'), which present the Holy Spirit in turn as helper (14:16–17), interpreter (14:26), witness (15:26–27), prosecutor (16:7–11) and revealer (16:12–15) (Bruce 1983: 302). In later Jewish literature the term was transliterated into Hebrew and paired with terms for both 'advocate' and 'accuser' (Carson 1991: 509 with references). Again, empowerment by the Spirit is well known throughout the Old Testament, but it is here tied to Jesus in a distinctive way ('another' Paraclete – i.e. substituting for Jesus' physical presence), even as he promises a coming age in which the Spirit will distinctively indwell his followers (v. 17). Jesus' words cohere well with Luke's emphases throughout his Gospel on Jesus' empowerment by the Spirit, and throughout Acts on the new role of the Spirit as baptizing *all* of God's people and indwelling them permanently.[291] But none of that is spelled out at all explicitly here, as one would expect if a later Christian writer were freely inventing central doctrinal material.[292]

In verse 18 Jesus promises that despite his departure he will not leave his

---

291] The textual variant that reads both verbs in this clause as present tenses (see NIV mg.), while clearly the more difficult reading, is probably too difficult to be accepted. The external evidence seems also marginally to favour the future tense. Cf. further Burge 2000: 396, n. 15.

292] 'Spirit of truth' as opposed to the later standard 'Holy Spirit' is also thoroughly Jewish in both concept and syntax (cf. Morris 1995: 577, n. 46). On the Qumran parallels, see esp. Leaney 1972.

followers as 'orphans'.[293] Children without parents were in a particularly helpless situation in antiquity; throughout the Old Testament God's people were commanded to give them special care. Commentators have long debated whether 'I will come to you' refers to Jesus' resurrection or his parousia; given John's predilection for double meanings he may have understood Jesus to imply both (e.g. Barrett 1978: 454). At the same time, verse 19 suggests that a reference to at least the resurrection must be present. Only between his first and second comings would Jesus be invisible to the world but present, through the Spirit, with his followers. And Jesus' prediction of his own resurrection is securely established in the three synoptic sayings of Mark 8:31, 9:31, 10:34 and parallels (on which, see esp. Bayer 1986). 'On that day' – a frequent Old Testament expression for coming eschatological judgment and deliverance (cf. also Matt. 7:22; Mark 13:32; Luke 17:31) – the disciples will better understand Jesus' relationship with his Father (v. 20). Against those who find these predictions relevant solely or largely to the church at the end of the first century, Talbert (1992: 210) observes:

> There is no indication that eschatology is the issue in this thought unit (i.e., revising the traditional futurist eschatology of the church into a realized eschatology). There is no evidence that the struggle with the Jews is uppermost in the Evangelist's mind (i.e., exclusion from the synagogue). What is of concern here is the status of disciples after Jesus' departure, i.e., in relation to Jesus and in relation to the world. (Cf. also Woll 1981.)

Verse 21 elaborates on the theme of verse 15, creating a small inclusio around this paragraph. That God in Jesus will manifest himself only to those who love him matches the point of Acts 10:40–41 – that Christ's resurrection was witnessed only by those whom God had chosen – who were either already disciples or who became disciples by virtue of this revelation.

The apostle Judas (not Iscariot) now interposes a further question: why should Jesus' appearances be so exclusive (v. 22)? Concerning this little-known disciple, Raymond Brown (1970: 641) comments, 'Obviously there is some editorial artificiality; yet if pure invention were involved, why would such an obscure disciple as this Judas be introduced?' As has become

---

293] Lindars (1972: 480) notes that 'Jesus' departure might leave the disciples feeling as if they have lost their father, like pupils after the death of their rabbi (*Mekilta* Exod. 13.1) or like the followers of Socrates (Plato, *Phaedo*, 116a).'

frequent, Jesus does not directly answer the question put to him but simply reaffirms the policy of election. Presumably the implicit answer to Judas's question involves the wilful disobedience of unbelievers as disqualifying them for a divine audience (vv. 22–23). The notion of God dwelling with his people, which is the reward for those who do love and obey Christ, like the idea of a uniquely chosen people, is thoroughly rooted in the Jewish religion but is being redefined with reference to Jesus (cf. further Ridderbos 1997: 508).

In the second Paraclete passage of this discourse, Jesus explicitly equates the *paraklētos* with the 'Holy Spirit', the only place in John's Gospel where this exact expression (*to pneuma to hagion*) occurs (vv. 25–26a). The ministry of the Spirit described in verse 26b proves crucial for understanding the process by which John wrote this Gospel. On the one hand, the freedom he felt to select, interpret, abridge and elaborate on the works and words of the historical Jesus doubtless stemmed from his sense of the Spirit's inspiration depicted here (which 'will teach you all things'). On the other hand, that inspiration is explicitly designed to 'remind you of everything I have said to you'. In other words, John is not freely inventing pious, edifying fiction, but is bringing out the significance of the things Jesus really did and said (cf. Carson 1991: 505; Pryor 1992a: 62; Ridderbos 1997: 509). Because so many scholars have missed either one side or the other of this two-pronged teaching, it is worth restating it, this time in Witherington's words (1995: 253):

> Thus the Spirit is seen as a source of continuing revelation for the disciples, but that revelation is seen as ultimately going back to the exalted Jesus and is not confused with the role of reminding the disciples what Jesus has said during his earthly ministry. The words of the exalted Jesus are basically *not* conveyed in the farewell discourses, they are only promised as something the Spirit *will* bring when the Spirit comes to the disciples.[294]

Verse 27 harks back to John 14:1, creating a small inclusio around this chapter. Jesus promises his disciples his peace, to be distinguished from the

---

294] Cf. also Burge 1987: 210–221. He concludes, 'in the end, the revelatory, witnessing work of the Paraclete remained conservative: preserving the tradition and inhibiting development. But this conservatism did not daunt the spiritual vitality of the community for which the ultimate evolution of office and tradition could reside in harmony with enthusiasm and spiritual vigor' (221). For a different synthesis that nevertheless respects both strands of this function of the Paraclete, see Rahner 2000.

absence of hostility in the world (cf. the similar contrast between Luke 2:14 and Matt. 10:34).[295] Carson (1991: 505) notes that peace 'is one of the fundamental characteristics of the messianic kingdom anticipated in the Old Testament', citing Numbers 6:26, Psalm 29:11, Isaiah 9:6–7, 52:7, 54:23, 57:19, Ezekiel 37:26 and Haggai 2:9. One thinks also of Jesus' promise in the Synoptics that the Spirit will provide the words for believers to use in witnessing even under persecution (e.g. Mark 13:11 pars.). Verse 28 encourages Jesus' disciples to rejoice at his departure rather than to grieve, 'for the Father is greater than I'. This causal clause has generated an enormous amount of controversy throughout church history;[296] all that is important for our discussion is that the subordination of Jesus to the Father clearly expressed here would not have been invented in a community increasingly concerned to exalt Jesus as fully equal to the Father. In verse 29 John's Jesus is again distinguishing between pre- and post-Easter periods. For the time being Jesus' hours are numbered because of the power and plan of Satan, but the devil's apparent victory will prove quite short-lived (vv. 30–31a). 'The prince of this world' is a thoroughly Jewish expression for Satan; the cluster of comments in this verse-and-a-half recalls both Mark 14:41–42 and parallels and Luke 22:53 (Schnackenburg 1982: 30).

The last sentence in John 14:31 creates the single biggest problem for supporters of the unity and authenticity of this discourse. Literally it reads, 'Rise, let us depart from here.' But Jesus keeps talking for another three chapters and seemingly does not leave the upper room until 18:1. Thus even scholars who reject the more elaborate developmental hypotheses surveyed above (p. 196) will often speak of at least two discourses (or two forms of one discourse) that have been joined together at this point (e.g. Woll 1980). There is nothing inherently improbable about such a composition history; even a commentator as conservative as Witherington (1995: 231) suggests that the material in chapters 13 – 17 was perhaps 'offered on two successive nights of the Passover feast leading up to Good Friday, and the Fourth Evangelist has put the material into his own idiom and combined it to convey the gist of these occasions'.[297]

At the same time, one wonders if most scholars have not summarily

---

295] Beutler (1984: 97–98) provides a good catalogue of synoptic parallels to the themes of peace, joy, and the work of the Spirit in this context.

296] On which see esp. Barrett (1982), who includes a reasonable exegesis.

297] Similarly, Whitacre (1999: 338–339), who finds teaching from several occasions combined to form one composite whole. For the whole range of proposed solutions to this problem, see the succinct summary in Carson 1991: 476–482.

rejected a different option simply because it smacks of 'harmonizing'. In John 15:1 Jesus is speaking metaphorically of the vine, an image naturally inspired by the vineyards in the vicinity of the temple, which the little troupe would have passed *en route* to Gethsemane. The temple gates also had a golden vine carved on them (Josephus, *Ant.* 15.395; *War* 5.210; *Midd.* 3.8). Interestingly, John 18:1 does not say that Jesus and his disciples left the house in which they had been staying but rather, literally, that 'they went out beyond the Kidron ravine'. This could suggest that 18:1 refers to the point at which they crossed the valley, after already having been walking through the city and then down from Jerusalem, while Jesus taught and prayed what chapters 15 – 17 summarize (cf. Westcott 1908: 187; Carson 1981b: 123; Haenchen 1984b: 128 [but cf. 131]; Kösten-berger 1999: 158; apparently Burge 2000: 416). Given John's precedent of identifying the location of an episode only after recording words that Jesus spoke there (6:59; 8:20), the absence of a 'proper' introduction to 15:1 proves less surprising. Kenneth Grayston (1990: 126) objects, comment-ing, 'Nobody can easily suggest that, having said, "*Let us go*," Jesus actually went on talking where he was; or perhaps left the supper room and discoursed as he walked along, ending up with an elaborate prayer in public – with someone busily memorizing what he said or even making notes.' I agree; I do not '*easily* suggest it'! The problem is a vexing one. But the picture Grayston rejects closely comports with three pertinent observations: (1) Peripatetic rabbis and philosophers regularly taught and discoursed with their followers as they walked. (2) Making notes or memorizing is precisely what happened at least part of the time in those settings (see above, p. 41). (3) The synoptic Jesus prayed fervently and repeatedly in Gethsemane and wanted his most intimate followers to hear; why should he not have paused somewhere *en route* to pray the gist of chapter 17? Thus it is inappropriately pejorative for Grayston to allege that this kind of suggestion 'trivialises the placing of these chapters' – they may well reflect some composite origin and collection of more private teachings of Jesus for his disciples, as Grayston argues. I am merely suggesting that the alternate scenario sketched out here deserves more serious consideration than it is usually given.

THE VINE AND THE BRANCHES (15:1–17)

John 15 begins with the last of the Fourth Gospel's seven major 'I am' sayings (v. 1). Again Jesus draws on imagery common to both Jewish and synoptic traditions. In the Old Testament and apocrypha Israel was frequently likened to a vine (Ps. 80:8–16; Is. 5:1–7; Jer. 2:21; Ezek. 15; Hos. 10:1; Sir. 24:17–23). In intertestamental Judaism, wisdom and Messiah both appear in vineyard imagery (Sir. 24:27; *2 Bar.* 39.7). Jesus' parable of the wicked vinedressers contains a farmer who stands for God (Mark 12:1–12 pars.), just as here in John. In the parable of the barren fig tree there is explicitly a 'gardener' (*ampelourgos*, Luke 13:7), as also here. Matthew 20:1–16 and 21:28–32 likewise contain parables about workers in vineyards. The synoptic accounts of the Lord's Supper, of course, describe Jesus speaking symbolically about the 'fruit of the vine' (Mark 14:25 pars.). To hear Jesus, who claimed to embody the hopes of Israel in so many ways, speak of himself as the 'true vine' should therefore cause no surprise (Morris 1995: 593).

But if Christ is the vine, then logically his followers are the vine's branches. While Jesus does not say this in so many words until verse 5, verses 2–4 presuppose that identification. Fruitless branches are cut off and thrown into the fire (vv. 2a, 6). Again, the imagery parallels the parable of the wicked vinedressers who are replaced by tenants who will give the master the fruit due to him (Matt. 21:41). 'A branch that does not bear fruit' is therefore 'not simply a living, unproductive branch, but a dead branch' (R. E. Brown 1970: 675). Such branches represent people who are disciples only in their own eyes and not in reality (cf. Carson 1991: 515). The branches that wither remind us of the withered fig tree (Mark 11:12–14, 20–25 par.) and the seed that grew up in rocky soil (Mark 4:6 pars.). Being thrown out and burned mirrors the fate of the weeds in the parable of the wheat and tares (Matt.13:24–30).

True disciples, however, like fruitful vine branches, will be pruned so that they can bear even more fruit (v. 2b). These branches represent people who are already 'clean' (v. 3). The English loses the play on words among the Greek *airei* (cuts off – v. 2a), *kathairei* (prunes – v. 2b) and *katharoi* (clean – v. 3). That these similarities appear only in Greek and not in the Aramaic equivalents to these three words does not count against the authenticity of the concepts ascribed to Jesus, but demonstrates merely that John has translated and/or paraphrased them in a memorable fashion. After all, the constructions following the Greek uses of *pas* (every) in this verse seem to be examples of 'nominative pendens', which is often a Semitism (R. E. Brown 1970: 666; contra Barrett 1978: 473).

The point of Jesus' parabolic speech comes to the fore in verses 4 and 7–8.[298] Would-be disciples must 'remain' in Christ, just like branches must stay attached to the vine. Only then can they bear fruit and glorify God. While *menō* (remain) is one of John's favourite verbs, it is also new covenant language for the internalization of God's Law. 'We are not far

---

[298] On the interplay between the literal and metaphorical levels of vv. 1–8, see esp. van der Watt 1994.

from the Old Testament new covenant texts, all of which promise a renewed heart or a right mind or the presence of the Spirit in the new covenant people, such that they will obey what God says' (Carson 1991: 516). Verse 7b echoes John 14:14 and the synoptic parallels cited there. Bearing fruit to the Father's glory (v. 8) harks back to people seeing the disciples' good works and glorifying their heavenly Father in Matthew 5:16. The combination of metaphor and explanation in verses 1–8 thus differs only a little from numerous synoptic parables, and the imagery is all quite familiar. We may ascribe the essence of this passage to the historical Jesus with some confidence (E. E. Ellis 1999: 177–179; more cautiously, R. E. Brown 1970: 669).

In verses 9–17 Jesus resumes talking about love, including the epitome of sacrificial love that he will demonstrate on the cross and that he calls his followers to imitate. This love, like remaining attached to Jesus, proves equally crucial for Christian fruit-bearing. The *Odes of Solomon* (8.20–21) similarly joins both of these themes: 'Pray and abide continually in the love of the Lord; you beloved ones, in the Beloved.' Verse 9 provides the thesis statement for this section with Jesus' command to 'remain in my love'. Verse 10 affirms what John's epistles will develop at length – the mutual interchangeability of love and obeying Christ's commands. But there is synoptic precedent for this combination in Jesus' replies both to the rich young ruler (Mark 10:17–21 pars.) and to the lawyer who asked about the greatest commandment (Mark 12:28–34 par.). Verse 11 combines the refrain 'I have told you this', unique to the farewell discourse among the Gospels but recurring three times in John's epistles, with the purpose clause 'that your joy may be complete' (cf. 1 John 1:4; 2 John 12). The theme of joy appears frequently in the Synoptics, especially in Luke, but occurs in John prior to this verse only in 3:29 (ascribed to the Baptist). But in the upper room discourse we find it seven times, all on the lips of Jesus. It would thus seem that John has again picked up a concept genuinely rooted in the teaching of both the Baptist and Jesus and incorporated it into his distinctive terminology and emphasis.

With verse 12 Jesus ups the ante. It is demanding enough to love as the Father has loved Jesus (v. 9), but now we must love as Christ has loved the disciples. Spelling this out explicitly, Jesus observes that giving one's life for one's friends is the ultimate expression of love (v. 13), which act he will shortly perform. Lest his disciples have any doubt, he goes on immediately to specify that they are his friends if they do what he commands, namely, to remain in his love (v. 14). 'The notion of a friend of God has deep Jewish roots'; one may compare Isaiah 41:8 on Abraham, Exodus 33:11 on Moses, *Jubilees* 20:21 on the Israelites, *Pirke Aboth* 6:1 on those concerned with Torah, Wisdom of Solomon 7:27 on holy souls, and Philo (*Who Is the*

Heir? 21) on all wise persons (Talbert 1992: 214). In the Sermon on the Mount the essence of righteous living is love for one's enemies (Matt. 5:43–47 par.). Morris (1995: 599) observes:

> Some have raised the question whether the love that dies for enemies is not greater than that which is concerned for friends, but that is not before us here. In this passage Jesus is not comparing the love that sacrifices for enemies with that which sacrifices for friends. He is in the midst of friends and is speaking only of friends. With respect to them he is saying that one cannot have greater love than to die for them.

If the disciples are Jesus' friends, then they are more than 'servants' (v. 15). Clearly, even the most honoured believer will always stay a slave of God in certain respects; Jesus will even reuse the term of his followers within a few verses (cf. v. 20). His point here, however, is that he will no longer treat them *merely* as hired help (cf. Schnackenburg 1982: 111). Interestingly in John, Jesus has not previously used the word *doulos* (slave/servant) with respect to the Twelve, but the word appears frequently in the Synoptics, including in a large number of parables in which servants represent faithful or faithless followers of Christ. Is this another example of John presupposing on the part of his audience knowledge from the early Christian kerygma?[299] Verse 16a restates what we have seen before – that rabbi Jesus took the initiative to call and commission his followers rather than sifting through applicants, as more conventional Jewish teachers of his day would have proceeded. Even the verb for 'choose' in this verse (*eklegomai*) reappears in both Luke 6:13 and Acts 1:2 for the initial selection of the Twelve. A further repetition of the synoptic 'ask, seek and knock' commands rounds out verse 16, even as verse 17 closes the paragraph by ending where it began – with the command to love one another. 'In sum, just as 1 Corinthians 13 has been called the New Testament's "ode to love," so also Jn. 15:1–17 is the magna carta of the Christian love commandment' (Ridderbos 1997: 522).[300] Again, even if

---

299] Grundmann (1959) thinks that he detects in chs. 13 – 17 the main lines of an early Christian eucharistic liturgy and that vv. 13–16 receive their contents and meaning from the Lord's Supper. If this proved true, we would have yet another example of 'interlocking' between John and the Synoptics.

300] O'Grady (1978) helpfully analyses the numerous similarities and differences between this passage and John 10:1–18, in which the Good Shepherd is likewise prepared to lay down his life in sacrificial love for his sheep.

Johannine idiom clearly colours this text, the Jewishness of the general concepts, numerous similarities to the Synoptics, and distinctive theological twists all combine to support the authenticity of the sayings attributed to Jesus (in the sense of *ipsissima vox*).

FUTURE HATRED FOR THE DISCIPLES (15:18 – 16:4)

Jesus now shifts abruptly from commanding the disciples to love each other to predicting that 'the world' will hate them. This, too, follows from the principle that the disciples must experience what Christ has experienced (v. 18). The Synoptics likewise portray Jesus depicting that his disciples will be hated and persecuted (Matt. 10:29; Mark 13:13 par.; Luke 6:22; 19:14). Verses 19–20 explain why. Here is John's characteristic dualism: one is either of the world or of the elect (v. 19). The beatitudes and woes in Luke's Sermon on the Plain reflect similar, polarized contrasts between the persecutors and the oppressed (Luke 6:20–26). Verse 20 reapplies the maxim of John 13:16 in a context almost identical to its two synoptic uses (Matt. 10:24; Luke 6:40).[301] In verse 21 we read again of all this happening 'because of my name'. 'John frequently has "in my name", but the phrase with the preposition *dia* (on account of) occurs nowhere else in the Fourth Gospel. It is thus reasonable to suppose that he has taken over the whole phrase from his source; in fact, it occurs in Mt. 10.22 ("you will be hated by all for my name's sake"), just before the saying quoted in the last verse' (Lindars 1972: 494). Similarly, Dodd (1963: 409) observes that all the synoptic parallels to these initial verses in this section in John 'more naturally suggest that they belong to a nucleus of tradition common to all, worked up by each according to his particular tendency'.

Verse 22 reiterates the logic of varying degrees of accountability, exhibited already in 9:41. The most important synoptic parallels are Jesus' teaching on degrees of punishment in Luke 12:47–48 and the contrary-to-fact conditions in Matthew 11:20–24 about the wicked cities in Old

---

301] Lindars (1972: 493–494) believes that the verbatim reappearance of the proverb of 13:16 'is yet further proof that the second discourse [chs. 15 – 16] has been composed as a commentary on chapter 13'. He means to distinguish two stages of redaction by this remark, but there is no reason Jesus himself could not similarly have commented on his earlier words.

302] Cf. Bruce (1983: 314): 'It is emphasized repeatedly in the Synoptic Gospels that the generation to which Jesus came bore greater responsibility than any previous generation, because men and women of earlier days had not heard his teaching or seen his mighty works, as his own contemporaries did.'

Testament times repenting if they would have seen Jesus' miracles.[302] Verse 23 repeats the frequent theme of Jesus in John that behaviour towards him matches and implies behaviour towards the Father. Verse 24 repeats the two key ideas of verses 21–22, thus creating a little chiasmus with verse 23 as its climactic centre: (1) hostility against the disciples, Jesus and the Father (vv. 21, 24b); (2) contrary-to-fact conditions describing the world's guilt (vv. 22, 24a); (3) hatred for Jesus and the Father (v. 23). Verse 24 also refers explicitly to Jesus' 'works' in a fashion consistent with John's earlier authentic references (Ensor 1996: 241–244). All of this typologically fulfils a psalm in which the king was irrationally hated (v. 25; Ps. 69:4, cf. also 35:19). Psalm 69 is applied to Jesus in John 2:17, Matthew 27:34 and Romans 15:3 as well. A dominical origin for this application would adequately explain these three otherwise independent references. Labelling the Hebrew Scriptures as 'their Law' matches Jesus' words to his opponents when he speaks of 'your Law' (recall on 10:34). Ridderbos (1997: 525) explains:

> The appeal to what is 'written' occurs frequently in rabbinic literature and is no less characteristic for the Fourth Gospel than for the other Gospels (cf. 6:31, 45; 10:34; 12:14, 16), further proof of the extent to which its entire presentation of Jesus' self-revelation has its roots in the Old Testament to the same degree. Therefore the reference here to 'their' law is clearly intended not to distance the reader from the law as belonging exclusively to 'Judaism' but to place the Jews' hatred in the perspective of a law that they themselves regarded as holy and inviolable (cf. 5:39).

John 15:26 returns to discussing the Paraclete. As in 14:16 he is called the 'Spirit of truth', a Semitic turn of phrase. As throughout the Old Testament, he is God's Spirit and therefore proceeds from the Father. In keeping with John's overall emphasis on testimony, the Spirit bears witness, enabling the disciples to do the same (v. 27). But this function proves equally central to the Synoptics, in which the Spirit empowers the disciples 'to stand firm under hostile questioning and to testify faithfully about Jesus to their prosecutors (vv. 26–27; cf. Mark 13:11; Matt. 10:19; Luke 12:11–12)' (Michaels 1983: 262). Throughout the Gospel of Luke, Jesus is presented as the consummately Spirit-empowered person; throughout both Luke and Acts the 'filling of the Spirit' leads God's people to witness in bold proclamation (see esp. Acts 5:32). That the disciples have been with Christ 'from the beginning' strikingly echoes one of the criteria for replacing Judas in Acts 1:22 (cf. also Luke 1:2). Carson (1991: 529–530) comments:

This is one of the small touches that locate the setting in the closing hours of the ministry of Jesus. By the end of the first century, it could not be said of many that they had been with Jesus 'from the beginning'. Doubtless the first witnesses set something of a model for later ones. Even so, to cast the discourse this way means John is not simply telling his readers what to do and how to live, blithely ignoring anachronisms. Rather, his help for his readers is indirect, by explaining in some detail *what happened back there* – even if the details he selects are of particular relevance to his readers.

Despite the chapter break, 16:1–4 continues the thought of 15:18–27. As noted above (p. 200), Jesus employs the *tauta lelalēka* formula, distinctive in the Gospels to the farewell discourse, to summarize his purposes in this section. As in Matthew 18:6–9 and Mark 9:42–48, Jesus is concerned that his disciples in no way go astray (v. 1; from Gk. *skandalizō*).[303] The issues surrounding 9:22 and 12:42 emerge once more in 16:2, except that here the reference to excommunication from the synagogues is explicitly future. If even just one of these three references, therefore, were authentic, it would be this one. The pages of Acts are filled with precisely the kind of rejection predicted here. 'If the language seems extreme when it argues that those who kill the disciples will see it as an act of worship, remember that Paul himself before his conversion seems to have seen such actions as a religious duty and a way of showing zeal for God and God's law (cf. Gal. 1:13–14)' (Witherington 1995: 262).[304] As for verses 3–4, 'similar judgment on individual synagogues in Roman Asia is implied in Rev 2:9 and 3:9, which should not be universalized as though it were applicable to all synagogues of that time and place' (Beasley-Murray 1987: 278). Verse 4 continues the concern to distinguish what was true

---

303] Barrett (1978: 484) notes the similar warning in Mark 14:27–31. 'This, like the present warning, is set in the context of the last supper, and John is probably developing traditional last supper material in the light of actual persecution.'

304] In addition, the phrase 'the hour is coming' 'is reminiscent of the prophetic-apocalyptic expression "the days are coming," which frequently relates to the onset of the judgments of the Lord (as e.g. in Jer 7:32; 9:25, and often in Luke, 17:22; 19:43; 21:6; 23:29) but also to God's deliverance and kingdom (e.g. Jer 16:14–15; 31:31–40)'. 'Examples of action on the basis of this conviction may be seen in the martyrdom of Stephen, recounted in Acts 7; the death of James the brother of Jesus, who according to Josephus was stoned at the instigation of the high priest Ananus II (*Ant.* 20.200); and the execution of Polycarp by the Romans' (Beasley-Murray 1987: 278). Talbert (1992: 217) adds references to Justin, *Dial.* 1.33; 95.4; *Sanh.* 9.6; and *Num. R.* 21.

before the crucifixion from post-Easter events. Jesus did not need to warn his disciples about this persecution at the outset of his ministry, because they would not experience it while he was alive. This comports exactly with the teaching of the rest of the New Testament, even as persecution begins in Jerusalem quickly after Pentecost.

Raymond Brown (1970: 694) helpfully lays out all of the conceptual parallels between 15:18 – 16:4 and the Synoptics in chart form. Once again we are struck by their frequency, even though few are verbally similar enough to postulate literary dependence. Readers of a synopsis proceeding through the farewell discourse miss almost all of these parallels for this reason, making it easy to overemphasize John's uniqueness. Obviously John has put his stamp on this material, but is scarcely creating *de novo*.[305] Schnackenburg (1982: 94–95) itemizes six features of 15:1 – 16:4 that suggest it is 'a suitable continuation of Jesus' farewell discourse' and that it was composed on the basis of chapter 14: (1) the inner community between Jesus and the disciples; (2) obeying Christ's commandments; (3) the promises of answered prayer; (4) keeping Jesus' word; (5) the 'world' as a hostile force; and (6) the role of the Paraclete as helper. Schnackenburg, of course, attributes this 'continuation' to the compositional work of one or more editors. But if an adequate explanation of the 'seam' of 14:31 has been found (see above, p. 205), it would appear at least as appropriate to attribute the continuation to Jesus himself.

FURTHER ENCOURAGEMENT (16:5–33)
The rest of Jesus' farewell discourse repeats and elaborates themes already raised in earlier sections. John 16:5–15 provides more teaching about the Paraclete. Verses 16–24 promise that the disciples' grief will turn into joy. Verses 25–33 demonstrate that Jesus has been speaking cryptically and, even when the disciples think they understand better than they have in the past, they are still missing the point.

John 16:5 begins this segment with one of the odder apparent contradictions in the Gospel. Here Jesus complains that no-one is asking (present tense) where he is going. Yet in 13:36 Simon Peter asked that very

---

305] Cf. Pryor (1992a: 65–66): 'We need to note that the section has several points of contact with the synoptic tradition. Three themes are present: the world's hatred of Christians because of Christ; Christians will be brought to trial; and Christians will bear witness through the indwelling Spirit. All of these elements are brought together in Mk 13:9–13; Matt 10:17–22, 24f; and Luke 12:2–9. This is evidence of a body of gospel tradition relating to persecution and which John is aware of, and which he shapes in his own distinctive way.'

question! Also in 14:5 Thomas lamented that the disciples did not know where Jesus was going and proceeded to ask, 'so how can we know the way?' But before we jump to theories of historical contradiction or editorial ineptitude, we ought to consider the merits of past attempts to solve this problem (cf. Carson 1991: 533 for a listing). The most convincing of these is the one that understands Jesus to be ruing that the disciples *at that very moment* are not asking the question. Barrett (1978: 485) puts it this way:

> It seems both necessary and justifiable to emphasize the present tense (*erōta*); John does not write (*erōtēse*), which would involve a flagrant contradiction with 13.36; 14.5. Here he is dealing simply with the disciples' immediate reaction to the words of Jesus. The thought of his departure fills them with grief; but if only they had asked where he was going, and grasped that it was to the Father, they would not have grieved but recognized that his departure was for their advantage. (Cf. also Burge 2000: 436.)

A literary observation lends particular credence to Barrett's explanation. In 14:1–31 the disciples three times interrupt Jesus' discourse to ask questions. But, beginning with 15:1, Jesus speaks without interruption. It makes sense, therefore, for 16:5 to be suggesting that they ought to be asking questions again. In fact, that is precisely what the rest of this chapter demonstrates, as 16:5–33 contains two further interruptions by the disciples. They seem to have understood Jesus' statement in 16:5 exactly as I have interpreted it. While they do not again repeat the exact words of this verse, the questions they do ask get at the identical issue (vv. 17–19).

Meanwhile, the disciples have begun to grieve (v. 6). Whatever they fail to understand about Jesus' departure, the very fact that he claims to be leaving them triggers entirely credible human emotions. The identical word for grief (Gk. *lypē*) appears in Luke 22:45 to explain the disciples' fatigue in Gethsemane. Jesus stresses again that his departure is for their good, so that the Paraclete can come (v. 7). Numerous Old Testament texts promise the gift of the Spirit in the messianic age (e.g. Is. 11:1–10; 42:1–4; 44:1–5; Ezek. 36:24–27; Joel 2:28–32; etc.). The Synoptists' narratives likewise testify to a dramatic change between the flight of the disciples later this same evening (Mark 14:50 pars.) and their bold preaching before the same opposition less than two months later, attributed to the power of the Spirit (Acts 2 – 5).[306]

306] Even Haenchen (1984b: 143), who rarely makes comments supportive of John's historicity, here observes that 'John is nevertheless not so far removed from the Synoptics as

Verses 8–11 form the distinctively new portion of verses 5–15. Here Jesus explains that part of the Paraclete's ministry will be to convict the world, literally, 'concerning sin and righteousness and judgment' (v. 8). The parallelism in this verse and in verses 9–11 that unpack these three thoughts suggests that all refer to negative traits of the fallen world order. This is understandable enough with reference to the world's sin and coming judgment, but it means that 'righteousness' probably refers to the world's sham righteousness – good deeds apart from commitment to Christ that cannot merit salvation (cf. esp. Carson 1979).[307] The forensic context recalls the 'lawsuit' character of many Old Testament prophetic indictments of Israel (see above, p. 57), while the specific role of the Spirit is not unlike that found in *1 Enoch* 14.1 and 89.62–63, 70 and in *Testament of Judah* 20.5 (Schnackenburg 1982: 129–130).[308] Interestingly, righteousness and judgment recur together in a similar judicial context in Acts 24:25 as Paul testifies before Felix. Luke 3:19 employs the identical verb for 'convict' (Gk. *elenchō*) for John the Baptist's denunciation of Herod Antipas. The judgment of the 'prince of this world' (v. 11) recalls Jesus' teaching in Luke 10:18 and 11:20 that in his ministry he is dealing the decisive deathblow to Satan.

That Jesus has much to tell the Twelve that they cannot now bear (v. 12) makes good sense in the contexts both of their grief at this juncture and of their frequent misunderstandings more generally. Thus, while the Paraclete's ministry to unbelievers will be largely one of convicting them, he will 'guide' believers 'into all truth' (v. 13a). The verb *hodēgeō* appears frequently in the Old Testament, apocrypha and Synoptics for the guidance provided by a teacher; it is especially prominent in the Wisdom of Solomon for a key role played by personified Wisdom (Barrett 1978: 489, with references). While Jesus' promise encompasses more than simply inspiring his disciples to write further Scripture, it surely includes what John understood himself to be doing in producing this Gospel (cf. Bruce 1983: 320). Thus, with Morris (1995: 621), we should stress that 'the attempt of some scholars to "go back to the original Jesus" and bypass the

---

these references might make it appear. In their own way, the synoptic words of institution (of the Lord's Supper) make it clear that Jesus' death makes God newly accessible, and John says precisely that more emphatically and expressly: prior to Jesus there was no access to God.'

307] D. M. Smith (1999: 294–295) arrives at comparable conclusions by defending the translation 'prove wrong' for *elenchō*. Burge (2000: 439–440) suggests 'expose'.

308] Derrett (1999) thinks Susanna's 'histrionic Daniel' (45–59) offers important background to vv. 8–11 with its illustration of the Jewish maxim that bringing a crucial plea before the king requires an intercessor.

teaching of the apostles is shown by Jesus himself to be misguided. The same source lies behind both.' Verses 13b–15 again unpack the ministry of the Paraclete, repeating concepts already presented earlier in the farewell discourse.[309] Against those who think that John here, especially in verse 15, articulates a theology that blurs historical distinctions, so that anything from God can appropriately be predicated of Jesus, Witherington (1995: 398, n. 59) emphasizes that the logic is rather that 'everything from the spirit is from Jesus, for all things have been given to Jesus by the Father and the Spirit is Jesus' agent'. The last verb in verse 15 (lit. 'announce'; from Gk. *anangellō*; NIV 'make known') understandably never occurs in the Synoptics but rather, as here, appears five times in Acts for Jesus' post-resurrection ministry through the Spirit.

In John 16:16 Jesus again cryptically affirms his imminent departure, to be followed by an equally quick reappearance. Verses 17–19 describe the confusion this causes the disciples, followed by Jesus' awareness of their questions. Modern commentators reflect confusion, too, as they debate whether Jesus was referring to coming again after his resurrection, at his parousia, or both (cf., e.g. R. E. Brown 1970: 729–730; Michaels 1983: 271). J. D. M. Derrett (1998b: 208–209) even thinks the second 'seeing' will be the spiritual apprehension of life though the Spirit and paraphrases Jesus' claim as 'A little while and you will observe me no more; and again, after a little while you shall inwardly apprehend me.' In any event, the fact that John leaves the statement undeciphered and stresses the disciples' ignorance prior to Jesus' death and resurrection once again demonstrates that he is not intentionally blurring pre- and post-Easter perspectives.

As we have become accustomed to observing, we next see the Johannine Jesus refusing to respond directly to the disciples' questions. Instead, he promises that their current grief, based on whatever they are imagining him to mean by his coming departure, will later be transformed into joy (vv. 20–24). This paragraph tips the scales in favour of interpreting Jesus' reappearance 'in a little while', discussed in verses 16–19, as primarily a reference to the resurrection, inasmuch as Jesus describes the continuance of a period of normal life on earth, including the need to make requests of God in prayer. The description of weeping and mourning (v. 20) reflects standard Jewish behaviour at funerals (recall above, p. 167). The transformation from sorrow to happiness Jesus now likens to the experience of

---

309] On v. 14 Barrett (1978: 490) germanely comments, 'Glory is the natural accompaniment of the Messiah in his coming at the last day; cf. Mark 13.26, and many other passages in Jewish and Christian literature. The Spirit, by realizing the eschatological functions of Christ, gives him this glory by anticipation.'

a woman after her labour pains have ended and she has given birth to a child (v. 21). The metaphor is thoroughly Jewish, both in language and in concepts, drawing especially on the notion of a period of suffering (or birth pangs) prior to the arrival of the messianic age in all its fullness.[310] Lindars (1972: 509) finds a striking parallel to this little parable among the hymns of the Dead Sea Scrolls (1QH 11:9–10) and concludes that 'there is no reason to doubt that [Jesus] could have used this imagery in a similar way to express the arrival of the New Age. The verse may, then, be a genuine parable about the coming Age, which John has taken over as the central item of teaching in this paragraph' (cf. further Dodd 1963: 369–373, 419–420). While there is no direct synoptic parallel, Acts 2:34–36 depicts Peter at Pentecost declaring 'that the resurrection-ascension brought forth a Messiah' (R. E. Brown 1970: 732); perhaps this kind of dominical teaching inspired Peter's preaching.

Verse 22 relates Jesus' 'parable' to the teaching he had just previously given. While not explaining the metaphor *per se*, Jesus offers a more prosaic application that exactly matches in form the standard two-part rabbinic parable: first the *māšāl* (the symbolic story or picture) and then the *nimšāl* (explanation).[311] Verses 23–24 return to Christ's theme of asking 'in his name' after the resurrection. Instead of asking Jesus directly, as the disciples can do while he is physically present with them, they will ask the Father by means of his power or authority. Again, we see the very Hebraic connotations of prayer in someone's name coming to the fore. Verse 24b concludes the paragraph with another close parallel to the 'Ask, seek, knock' saying of the Sermon on the Mount (Matt. 7:7–11 par.) (cf. further Lindars 1972: 510; Ridderbos 1997: 539–540). The combination of 'in that day' with the future-tense verbs in these two verses shows again that John is careful to distinguish between what happened before the cross and what was possible only afterwards.

310] Beasley-Murray (1987: 285–286) elaborates: 'The parable of v 21, despite its simplicity and naturalness, is replete with echoes of OT prophecy, and it has the important function of emphasizing the eschatological nature of the event in view, namely the death and resurrection of Jesus. The figure of the pangs of childbirth is frequent in the OT for the swift coming of God's judgment upon wrongdoers (cf. e.g. Isa 21:2–3; Jer 13:21; Mic 4:9–10). Isa 66:7–14 is an example of the same image applied to bringing to birth the new age of salvation … In this connection Isa 26:16–21 is particularly important, since it combines the "little while" of God's coming for judgment with the figure of a woman writhing in her labor pains and a startling promise of resurrection.'

311] For samples of over a hundred of the oldest rabbinic parables, in English translation with a brief commentary, see McArthur and Johnston 1990.

John 16:25–33 brings Jesus' farewell discourse to its close. In verse 25a Jesus insists that there has been a sense in which his entire earthly ministry has involved figurative speech (Gk. *paroimiai*), that is, speaking parabolically or cryptically. One thinks of the equally generalizing comment in Mark 4:34, that 'He did not say anything to them without using a parable.' Ridderbos (1997: 542) remarks that 'it is nowhere more clear than in this veiled language that the Evangelist, though he stands in the full light of fulfillment, is nevertheless, as a transmitter of Jesus' words and works, fully conscious of the pre-Easter redemption-historical situation in which they were spoken and done'. In the near future, Jesus will speak more plainly (v. 25b), but verse 26a makes it clear that he is referring to the period of time after the resurrection ('in that day' when the disciples will petition the Father in Jesus' name, as in v. 23). Verses 26b–27 elaborate on the direct access disciples will have to God through Jesus' power and authority, made possible by the Father's love. 'It has been rightly said that this does not contradict the idea of the heavenly intercession of the Son (Ro. 8:34; Hb. 7:25) because that intercession is not concerned with the ongoing answering of prayer but with the Christian's status before God, which is grounded on the priestly work of Christ' (Ridderbos 1997: 543; citing R. E. Brown 1970: 735). But Jesus will have to return to the Father to inaugurate this new era of salvation-history; so verse 28 completes the paragraph by returning to the thought of Jesus' departure. The entire contrast between present and future in verses 25–28 closely resembles the theme of the 'messianic secret' in Mark (and to a lesser degree in the other Synoptics). Mark's Jesus similarly explains that this period of ambiguity and silence will last only until he has been raised from the dead (Mark 9:9).

Nevertheless, when the disciples assert that Jesus is speaking unambiguously at that very moment (v. 29), their claim proves premature. Verse 30 contains several verbal reminiscences of Peter's confession in 6:68–69. But that declaration, whether a Johannine equivalent to the synoptic confession on the road to Caesarea Philippi or a precursor to it, proved equally inadequate because of the serious misunderstandings Peter subsequently disclosed in Mark 8:31–33 and parallels. Thus John 16:31 should not be taken as a straightforward declarative sentence implicitly praising the disciples. It is either an ironic, almost sarcastic exclamation (so the NIV) or it is a question (so Moloney 1998: 457). Either way, Jesus' point is to retort, 'You think you finally believe? This very night you will all abandon me' (cf. v. 32).[312] By speaking of the disciples all being 'scattered',

---

312] Carson (1991: 548–549) observes the constant pattern not only in the Fourth Gospel but also in the Synoptics of 'damping down' enthusiastic confessions of faith (e.g. John 6:

John echoes the explicit quotation by the synoptic Jesus of Zechariah 13:7 (see Mark 14:27; Matt. 26:31). Unlike the Synoptics, however, John never narrates the flight of the Twelve from the garden of Gethsemane. An inventor of fiction would presumably have had to narrate the fulfilment of Jesus' prophecy for his readers to know the event to which it referred; John, on the other hand, can presuppose that knowledge from the core kerygma.[313]

For the last time in the Fourth Gospel, Jesus rounds out his words with the *tauta lelalēka* ('I have told you these things') formula (John 16:33a). He creates an inclusio with both 14:1 and 27 by referring again to the peace available to the disciples. He immediately qualifies his promise by stressing that this 'peace' does not imply the absence of hostility from the world. Thus Jesus in Luke 12:51–52 can declare, 'Do you think I came to bring peace on earth? No, I tell you, but division. From now on there will be five in one family divided against each other ... ' Spiritually, however, the disciples can have peace because after the resurrection they will clearly understand that Christ has overcome the world (John 16:33b) and that the complete victory in body and soul, still awaiting the consummation of all things, is nevertheless guaranteed.

JESUS' 'HIGH-PRIESTLY' PRAYER (17:1–26)

The fifth and final chapter describing Jesus' time with his disciples before his arrest in Gethsemane appends to his more formal farewell discourse what has often been called his high-priestly prayer. Ending such a discourse with a prayer is entirely in keeping with the genre and finds numerous Jewish parallels. Most noteworthy are *Jubilees* 22.28–30 and Sirach 51:1–12, 29 (cf. also *Jub.* 1.19–21; *4 Ezra* 8.19b–36). Enric Cortès (1976) treats chapter 17 as part of a larger study of all of chapters 13 – 17 and

---

68–78; Mark 8:29–33 pars.; 10:28–31, 38–40; and 14:29–31), because it will be only after the cross and resurrection that the disciples will gain true understanding and can proceed with complete accuracy to proclaim the good news from God.

313] Carson (1991: 549) helpfully comments on the apparent contradictions of the beloved disciple reappearing at the cross and of Jesus' cry of dereliction in Mark 15:34 par. Nothing in any of the four Gospels states that the disciples' flight on Thursday night kept all of them away from Golgotha the next afternoon. Indeed, all four Gospels agree that Peter trailed Jesus to the high priest's courtyard almost immediately after his initial flight from the garden. So, too, Jesus' words here in John 16:32 affirming the presence of the Father appear in the context of the disciples' flight. They should not be generalized to form a timeless, abstract statement of the relationship of Father and Son that precludes the necessary but very temporary divine abandonment of Jesus on the cross.

identifies significant parallels to Genesis 49 and its targums, the *Testaments of the Twelve Patriarchs* and Deuteronomy 33. Still, the Johannine Jesus adds his unique style to this genre, especially in the amount of intercession for others contained in John 17, reminiscent more of various apocalyptic genres (Schnackenburg 1982: 199–200). This chapter repeats and summarizes several key themes of the larger farewell discourse (see esp. Black 1988) and forms a tightly knit literary unity that renders tradition-critical dissection unnecessary (see Sprecher 1993: esp. 281–282).[314] One of the most intriguing observations, which I shall develop below, is how all the petitions in Matthew's account of the Lord's Prayer (Matt. 6:9–13) find linguistic or conceptual parallels in this chapter, and with only one exception occur in the identical sequence (see esp. Walker 1982). This could suggest some kind of 'midrashic' expansion of an original prayer of Jesus, but it could equally argue for authenticity via the criteria of multiple attestation and coherence.

Looking 'towards heaven' (John 17:1a) was a standard Jewish posture for prayer. The first of the three main segments of Jesus' prayer finds him praying largely for himself (vv. 1b–5). As in Matthew 6:9, Jesus addresses God as 'Father' (presumably with an underlying Aramaic *Abba*, a key hallmark of authenticity – recall above, p. 114), and his posture demonstrates he is looking to his Father 'in heaven'. Clear Johannine emphases pervade the rest of this paragraph: Jesus' 'hour' (NIV 'time') has come, Jesus has authority to bestow eternal life, and he and his Father mutually glorify each other. At the same time, the glorification of the Father by the Son in verse 1b resembles the petition 'hallowed be thy name', in the Lord's Prayer. Verse 2 contains numerous Semitisms, suggesting an Aramaic original (most notably the construction *pasa sarx* – lit. 'all flesh' – cf. further Lindars 1972: 518–519), and thematically parallels Jesus' Great Commission (Matt. 28:18–20). Given the way in which 'eternal life' substitutes for 'kingdom of God' in John (see above, p. 50), verse 2 becomes an equivalent of sorts to the petition 'Thy kingdom come' from the Lord's Prayer, (cf. Matt. 6:10).

Verse 3 is perhaps best seen as John's own 'targumic' commentary on Jesus' prayer, interrupting the flow of verses 1–2 and 4–5 with a specific definition of eternal life. Otherwise this would be the only place in the Gospels where Jesus was said to speak of himself by name ('Jesus' [+ 'Christ' in the later sense of more a name than a title]).[315] Verses 4–5, then, resume

---

314] Burge (2000: 459) turns the material of R. E. Brown (1970: 750) into a helpful chart of five major components shared by each of the three main sections of this chapter, further supporting its unity.

315] Cf. Barrett (1978: 503): 'This verse must be regarded as parenthetical, but this does

Jesus' words with a parallel to 'Thy will be done on earth as it is in heaven.' 'Completing the work you gave me to do' (v. 4) is the same as performing God's will, while the contrast between Jesus' time 'on earth' (v. 4) and his return to God's presence (in heaven; v. 5) completes the conceptual parallel with this petition from the Lord's prayer. 'The idea that in the ministry Jesus already possessed glory appears in the Synoptic Gospels in the account of the Transfiguration (especially Luke ix 32)', even if 'the full recognition of Jesus as the Son of God stems from his death (Mark xv 39), resurrection and ascension (Acts ii 36, v 31) (R. E. Brown 1970: 751–752).[316] The pre-existence implied in verse 5 is no stronger than that implied by the accounts of the virginal conception in Matthew and Luke (Blomberg 1987: 163–164).

In verses 6–19 Jesus turns to praying for his current disciples. This material in turn subdivides into five discrete segments: (1) verses 6–8 speak of Christ's revelation of God's name and the disciples' resulting belief; (2) verses 9–11a explicate the affirmation that Jesus prays for them and not the world; (3) verses 11b–15 comprise the petition for God to keep the disciples just as Jesus has kept them; (4) verse 16 reaffirms that the disciples, like Jesus, are not of the world; and (5) verses 17–19 form Jesus' prayer for his followers' sanctification.[317]

Old Testament background for the sort of revelation described in verses 6–8 may be found in Deuteronomy 12:5, 21, Psalms 9:10, 22:22, Isaiah 55:13, 62:2, 65:15–16 and elsewhere (R. E. Brown 1970: 754). As before, 'your name' (v. 6a; see NIV mg.) reflects the Semitic metaphor of 'name' used for 'power' or 'authority'. Against the common conviction that verse 6b cannot describe the highly erratic faith of the disciples prior to the crucifixion, Carson (1991: 559) explains:

> In this context, the proper comparison is not between the faith-status of the disciples *before* the resurrection and the faith-status of the disciples *after* the resurrection, but between the belief and

---

not mean that it is a gloss. John felt the necessity of a definition of eternal life, and being unable to use a footnote incorporated it into the prayer, to which it is grammatically attached.' Even from a consistently evangelical perspective, Witherington (1995: 269) agrees.

316] On the temporal perspective of these verses, Beasley-Murray (1987: 297) comments, 'Admittedly the entire Last Discourses and the prayer have been written from the Evangelist's position of the post-Pentecostal period; but the distinctive stance of the prayer is that Jesus stands not *after* the hour, but *in* the hour wherein his final work for God and man takes place, as v 19 makes plain.'

317] For an almost identical outline and elaboration, see Malatesta 1971.

obedience of the *disciples before* the resurrection and the unbelief and disobedience of the *world before* the resurrection. Judged by those standards – i.e. placing them at their proper location in the stream of redemptive history – the first disciples stand out ... At the fundamental level, Jesus' assessment of his closest followers is entirely realistic, and in no way a contradiction of 16:31–32. After all, despite the generous assessment in 17:6, Jesus goes on to ask the Father to keep them safe (17:11).

Verses 7–8 continue Jesus' praise for the Twelve and again resemble the 'Johannine thunderbolt' in the Synoptics (Matt. 11:27 par.). 'With certainty' in verse 8 is perhaps an overtranslation of the Greek *alēthōs*, which means simply 'truly'. The subordinationist strand of Jesus acting merely as his Father's agent continues in these verses as well and, as I have repeatedly noted, was unlikely to have been invented in a church increasingly concerned to stress Jesus' equality with the Father and his outright deity.

Verse 9 at first appears jarring and seems to conflict with the Synoptics' emphasis on Jesus mission to the 'lost'. But John, too, has been concerned throughout his Gospel for 'outreach', and verses 20–26 of this very prayer will reintroduce that concern. So Jesus' restriction to praying for the disciples rather than for the world must be limited to this very specific context. Jesus is not *at this very moment* praying for anyone other than his followers, because they are the only ones present and the ones about to undergo the greatest challenge to their faith to date – observing the arrest and execution of their master. As God answers Jesus' prayer and strengthens the disciples' faith after the resurrection, these same men will become God's agents for evangelizing the lost (cf. the identical sequence of thoughts in Luke 22:31–32, also in the context of the Lord's Supper).[318] Verse 10 finds a striking parallel in the words of the father to the prodigal son in Luke 15:31. That the disciples have all they could ever want amply fulfils the request from Matthew 6:11 to 'give us today our daily bread'. John 17:11a completes this segment with Jesus' rationale for his request: he

---

318] Cf. Barrett (1978: 506): 'It must be emphasized once more that John, having stated (3.16) the love of God for the *kosmos*, does not withdraw from that position in favour of a narrow affection for the pious. It is clear (see especially v. 18) that in this chapter also there is in mind a mission of the apostolic church to the world in which men will be converted and attached to the community of Jesus. But to pray for the *kosmos* would be almost an absurdity, since the only hope for the *kosmos* is precisely that it should cease to be the *kosmos* (see on 1.10).' See also Bruce 1983: 331.

will no longer be bodily present with them.

The next subunit of verses 6–19 begins with Jesus' only appeal to God as 'Holy Father' (v. 11b). But 2 Maccabees 14:36 and 3 Maccabees 2:2 contain addresses to God as 'holy Lord of all holiness' and 'Holy One among the holy', respectively. The prayer for protection, paralleling Jesus' ministry thus far (v. 12) matches what Lady Wisdom did for Abraham according to Wisdom of Solomon 10:5, using the same two Greek verbs as here (*tēreō* and *phylassō*). And the protective power of God's name is already well attested in the Hebrew Scriptures themselves (see esp. Prov. 18:10; cf. R. E. Brown 1970: 759, 764). Still, Jesus recognizes that Judas has never truly been a follower, but rather 'the one doomed to destruction' (lit. 'son of perdition'). Here appears the identical Greek expression predicated of Antichrist in 2 Thessalonians 2:3; did Paul get the phrase from early Christian tradition of Jesus' teaching (so D. Wenham 1995: 318–319)? That Jesus specifies no one Scripture that is fulfilled supports historicity; a later redactor would no doubt have clarified the reference (suggestions focus primarily on Pss. 41:9 and 109:4–13), as in the vast majority of Old Testament fulfilment quotations.

Verse 13 is thoroughly Johannine in content and structure. But the combination of joy amid the hostility of the world was a common early Christian motif found in both the Synoptics (Matt. 5:11) and Paul (1 Thess. 1:6) (R. E. Brown 1970: 765). Verse 14 employs Semitic style by using past tenses for future, prophesied events. We find similar Greek aorists translating probable underlying Hebrew perfects in Mary's Magnificat (esp. Luke 1:51–54). Thus, 'it would be wrong to conclude from this use of the aorist that Jesus was already speaking as the exalted Christ' (Schnackenburg 1982: 183). Verse 15 creates an inclusio with verse 11b, as Jesus returns to praying for the disciples' protection. It contains the clearest verbal allusion to the Lord's Prayer with the petition that God keep his followers 'from the evil one' (cf. Matt. 6:13). Conceptually, this subunit clearly corresponds to the larger request, 'lead us not into temptation but deliver us from evil'.

If it were not for the inclusio of verses 11b–15, verse 16 would seem to belong with this immediately preceding material. As it stands, it is perhaps better to see it as a transitional summary, grammatically unattached to its immediate context, that stresses the difference between Jesus and his followers on the one hand and the world on the other, thus preparing the way for the prayer of sanctification in verses 17–19. The language of not being 'of the world' recurs in 18:36 and fits John's customary use of 'world'. But it is also an apt summary of much of Jesus' teaching. The double similarity and dissimilarity criterion again comes into play: Jesus has not promoted monasticism or communalism (contra the Essenes) nor even the more standard Jewish combination of legalism, nomism and ethno-centrism; yet like the faithful Jew he stresses that his disciples follow a higher moral standard than the rest of humanity. But Christianity has no better captured the balance between 'in the world but not of it', while frequently using this slogan to sum up verses 13–16 here.

Jesus' prayer turns directly to the theme of sanctification in verses 17–19. The petition is for growth in moral living – separation from sin. These verses imply more than, but surely include, the only missing petition from the Lord's Prayer thus far: 'forgive us our debts, as we also have forgiven our debtors' (Matt. 6:12). The link with Jesus' own sanctification calls to mind the command at the climax of the antitheses in the Sermon on the Mount – 'Be perfect, therefore, as your heavenly Father is perfect' (Matt. 5:48 – especially when 'perfect' is understood as 'mature'; cf. Blomberg 1992: 115). Verse 17 resembles Psalm 119:142, but with God's word now including Christ's teaching as well as the Torah. Verse 18 again calls to mind the sending of the Twelve and the Seventy in the Synoptics (Matt. 10:14; Luke 10:3). The verb for 'sanctify' (Gk. *hagiazō*) in both verses 17 and 19 'accords with the OT meaning of "consecrate" in sacrificial contexts, whereby "consecrate" can be synonymous with "sacrifice" (cf. Deut 15:19, 21)' (Beasley-Murray 1987: 301). Throughout this little section, the pattern of Jesus exactly mirroring the Father so that his followers might imitate him continues. Given the theological problems that Christianity would later wrestle with, in the light of its conviction of the relationship between Father and Son not always being transferrable to the relationship between Jesus and the disciples, one wonders if verses like these could have been created without foundation in the utterances of the historical Jesus.

The same is true of the unity requested in the final section of Jesus' prayer (vv. 20–26). Here Jesus envisions people coming to faith through the ministry of the disciples and prays for them as well as for the Twelve (v. 20). He petitions the Father that they might experience the same kind of unity among themselves and the same kind of relationship with God (both Father and Son) as he has with God (v. 21). Safeguarding the ontological distinctions between God and humanity is not a concern of this verse, which observation itself supports authenticity. Jesus may well have the emphasis on 'unity' at Qumran in mind as part of the background to his prayer; that Essene sect often referred to itself as 'the unity' (Heb. *yaḥad*) (Beasley-Murray 1987: 302). Unity in the church was no doubt an important concern for John at the end of the first century, but that concern did not arise for the first time then. Divisions among Jewish groups and between Jews and Gentiles existed already in Jesus' lifetime, divisions that would have been exacerbated by Jesus' choice of disciples from diverse backgrounds. Verse 21 again employs the vocative 'Father', once more reminiscent of the Synoptic *Abba*. A *Sitz im Leben Jesu* for this petition is entirely imaginable.[319]

Verses 22–23 repeat the thoughts of verses 20–21 and incorporate Jesus' earlier references to glory into them. The prayed-for unity is not an end in itself but displays massive evangelistic potential. This observation proves relatively unique among ancient Jewish and Christian writers and even more so in the light of the actual splintering of both religions into numerous competing factions. Would an early Christian writer of fiction have invented a petition ascribed to the praying Jesus when it had so obviously been unfulfilled?

Verses 24–26 close chapter 17 and conclude Jesus' prayer by summarizing key themes. Verse 24a again echoes the 'Johannine thunderbolt', with Jesus once more addressing God as 'Father'. This is the last of no less than fifty-one verses in John where Adelbert Denaux (1992: 193–199) finds some verbal parallelism to Matthew 11:25–27 or Luke 10:21–22, verses otherwise usually couched in such 'Johannine' language that their authenticity is suspect (but unnecessarily so). Verse 24b resembles Wisdom of Solomon 7:25 and 9:10, in which Wisdom is said to be a pure emanation of God's glory and one who comes forth from God's glorious throne in heaven. Likewise 'the Son partakes of the very qualities of the Father and derives them from the Father' (Witherington 1995: 271).[320] Verse 25 addresses God again as Father, this time qualifying the invocation with the adjective 'righteous', a unique expression of direct address to God within the New Testament. Verse 26 creates a partial *inclusio* with verse 6, with its theme of revealing God's 'name', thus uniting

---

319] Cf. further Agourides (1968: 145), who notes that there are no parallels here with what 1 John says about unity, that Jesus is not concerned with general church unity so much as with that of the apostles and Jews and Gentiles within the church to promote missionary work, and that 'Jesus's petition for unity does not necessarily imply a period of long duration; it is not in conflict with His own and the Apostles' belief, recorded in the Synoptic tradition, that the "end" was a matter of the Apostolic generation'. Schnackenburg (1982: 189) lists six reasons why many exegetes have concluded that vv. 20–21 were an addition to John's text by a later hand. After responding to these arguments, he concludes that these verses are 'not alien to the passage as a whole and they have to be explained in the light of Jn 17'. It is also interesting to raise the question of whether this prayer could have been at least part of the inspiration for Paul's programmatic affirmation of the equality of all persons, despite human diversity, in Christ (Gal. 3:28).

320] Lindars (1972: 531) notes that 'I desire' translates the Greek *thelō*, matching Mark 14:36, and that 'whom thou hast given me' is another case of the Semitic use of the neuter

the two sections of Jesus' prayer that focus on his followers. And it concludes with a final reference to God's marvellous *agapē* (love), which permeated the climactic centre of the farewell discourse (15:9–17) even as it proved central to the ethic of the synoptic Jesus, too.

A survey of scholarship on the issue of the authenticity of John 17 reveals almost every conceivable position. Ernst Käsemann (1968: esp. 72–77) typifies the most radical scepticism, in which John's Christ seems quasi-docetic and virtually none of the prayer can be ascribed to the historical Jesus. This view, however, does not appear today nearly as often as it did a generation ago. Most critics continue to attempt to parcel the chapter up into competing units of tradition and redaction (the reconstruction in Stanley 1980: 246–266 is representative). Lindars (1972: 517) reflects a cautious middle ground, noting the Johannine characteristics on the one hand and the consistency with the synoptic Jesus on the other. Even as conservative a commentator as Pryor (1992a: 71) makes three observations that he thinks support the view that John 17 was composed only at the time of the writing of the entire Gospel: (1) verses 1–5 take up the thought of 13:31–32, creating an inclusio around the entire farewell discourse; (2) the prayer replaces the synoptic prayer of Jesus in Gethsemane (cf. also 12:27–28); and (3) themes found already in the farewell discourse are summarized in this prayer. But if Jesus spoke anything at all like the words attributed to him in 13:31 – 16:33, observations (1) and (3) make as much sense on the supposition of authenticity as on theories of later composition. As for (2), if John did freely invent material as a kind of equivalent to Christ's Gethsemane prayer, John 12:27–33 contains the far more obvious parallel. But we have frequently seen John's Jesus anticipating in cryptic form material that appears in the Synoptics only later and more explicitly, a sequence that is historically quite plausible.

It seems better, therefore, to side with a different group of commentators who find genuine historical reminiscences pervading all of Jesus' high-priestly prayer, even while readily conceding that the styles and themes of the chapter are equally Johannine. Carson (1991: 552), for example, convincingly concludes:

> A more sympathetic reading both of the Synoptics and of John suggests several compelling points of connection. If the prayers of

---

singular for the relative pronoun and of the *casus pendens* construction as in v. 2. R. E. Brown (1970: 772) believes that 'we may have here the Johannine equivalent of the words that Jesus speaks in Luke's account of the Last Supper: "You shall eat and drink at my table in my kingdom" (Luke xxii 30)'.

John 12:27–28 and John 17 are put together, Jesus' obedience and his suffering coalesce. Psychologically it is altogether convincing that as he approached the cross Jesus should betray both resolution and horror, both filial obedience and personal agony. Both strands are found in John and in the Synoptics. For instance, if Luke records the anguish of Gethsemane (Lk. 22:41–45), he also insists, 'As the time approached for him to be taken up to heaven, Jesus resolutely set out for Jerusalem' (Lk. 9:51). The Synoptists, after all, are the ones who report Jesus' determined 'not as I will, but as you will' (Mt. 26:39; Mk. 14:36; Lk. 22:42).

Nor is there good reason to think that John 17 is the Evangelist's theological expansion of the last element of the petition 'Glorify your name!' (12:28), or a creative re-creation of the 'Gethsemane' prayers placed in a different location. However much the different Evangelists chose to emphasize distinct aspects of our Lord's prayers, and reported those prayers in their own idiom, it is surely too much to be asked to believe that Jesus prayed only once on his way to the cross.

Damiano Marzotto (1977) points out five major themes in the Targums to Exodus 19 – 20 that reappear, often with verbal parallels, in John 17: the observance of the Word of God, God's transmission of the Word at his invitation to his people by means of a messenger, the unity of the people of God, the investiture of authority in his messenger because people believe in him, and the sanctification of his people by the Word of God. While it is not impossible that a Jewish John steeped in the traditional exposition of the Scriptures of his day should create a prayer for Jesus with all these parallels, it is not at all clear that a predominantly Gentile Christian community in Graeco-Roman Asia would have appreciated a majority of them. It seems far more likely that this prayer goes back at least to an early Aramaic-speaking Jewish-Christian community (thus almost certainly in Palestine), if not to the historical Jesus himself.[321] S. Agourides (1968) concurs; we may perhaps be permitted one more lengthy citation, since our perspective stands so contrary to the critical consensus. In the light of Qumran's eschatology, he asks (139):

Why, then, must it be considered historically improbable that Jesus should have believed Himself to be the one sent by God in the Last

---

321] Similarly, Dowd (1993) points out numerous parallels between the theology of prayer of the Johannine Jesus more generally and Exod. 33 – 34. She does not address questions about the historical Jesus *per se*, but the same kind of logic could be applied.

Days, that He should have expressed this consciousness by joining the figures of the Davidic Messiah and the Suffering Servant or the Son of Man, and even more the figure of his pre-existence in God? And, on the other hand, is it historically likely that the early Church would have taught things about Jesus which, in the opinion of the people of the period, He could not have believed about Himself? But if the men of this age were able to believe in such possibilities, why could not Jesus believe in these possibilities with respect to Himself? And is it not historically more likely that the early Church believed in such consciousness in Jesus, despite His tragic end, for the very reasons that He believed Himself to be the Son of God, that He interpreted His coming death as the central part of His mission, and that He believed in His return and imparted this faith to His disciples, than that the primitive Church interpreted Jesus in the light of ideas derived not from the great dimensions of His historic and unique personality, but from the needs of a new religious community?

Agourides' rhetorical questions arise out of his study on John 17 but can in fact be applied to numerous portions of the Fourth Gospel.

JESUS' ARREST (18:1–14)

We come now to what scholars have regularly called the passion narrative. Here John more closely follows the specific developments and sequence of events that the Synoptics also depict for a longer period of time than anywhere else in his Gospel. Still, he regularly inserts details and entire episodes that the Synoptics lack.[322] Where he does describe the same incidents, the verbal parallelism is so meager that theories of literary dependence on the Synoptics (e.g. Lang 1999) seem improbable.[323] More commonly, theories of dependence on some combination of written and oral pre-Markan sources have been postulated.[324] More significantly for our

---

322] Burge (2000: 485–486) offers three helpful, concise summaries of twelve major elements John and the Synoptics have in common, seven significant Johannine omissions, and nine additional Johannine episodes.

323] Even more idiosyncratic and unlikely is the thesis of Crossan (1988) that the 'Cross Gospel' portion of the *Gospel of Peter* is the sole source for the Gospel Passion narratives and that everything else in the canonical accounts is redactional invention, often inspired by Old Testament texts applied to Jesus.

324] For representative theories, with considerably divergent details, cf. Borgen 1959; Buse 1960; Haenchen 1970; and Fortna 1978.

purposes, John can again be viewed as presupposing important pieces of information that his audience already knows from the common Christian kerygma, even as he supplements that kerygma with primarily unparalleled information.

John 18:1 provides an immediate example of this phenomenon. The garden called Gethsemane is never mentioned by name. But the combination of geographical and horticultural details makes the location clear for those who already know the broad contours of the story: Jesus and the disciples crossed the Kidron valley and went where there was an olive grove. In fact, the very name Gethsemane means 'oil-press' and thus 'denotes an olive orchard on the slopes of the Mount of Olives' (Lindars 1972: 539).[325]

John also seems to presuppose knowledge of Christ's agonizing prayers in the garden. Verse 11b betrays a recollection of that struggle ('Shall I not drink the cup the Father has given me?'), but John throughout his passion narrative is more interested in the events that show Jesus 'in control' up to the very end (see esp. Ford 1995; cf. Senior 1991: 52–53).[326]

Only John tells us that Jesus and the Twelve had often gathered in Gethsemane (v. 2), but this fits Luke 21:37: 'Each day Jesus was teaching at the temple, and each evening he went out to spend the night on the hill called the Mount of Olives.' Likewise, only John makes reference to a 'detachment of soldiers' accompanying the Jewish officials in the arresting party (v. 3). The Greek *speira* (cohort) in this context has generated two huge controversies: first, does it refer here to Roman rather than Jewish soldiers, as in its most common uses elsewhere in Hellenistic Greek? Second, if it does, is it historically plausible to imagine Romans and Jews together in this specific setting?

Josef Blinzler (1959: 64–69; cf. esp. Bammel 1984a: 39–40) has set forth the most detailed case for viewing the company in the garden as

---

325] Cf. Ridderbos (1997: 573): 'The narrative in John is extremely concise. The focus is on a few high points in a story with which his readers were undoubtedly familiar. There is no attempt to give a comprehensive account of the course of events.' Dodd (1963: 67, 68) notes the difference with the beginning of the synoptic passion narratives and comments, 'If we regard the description as the result of "editing" or "correcting" Mark, it would seem a singularly pointless proceeding, with no possible interest for readers at Ephesus in the late first century. The whole matter is trivial, and for that reason it appears to me one of the strongest pieces of evidence we have yet found that John was here writing in independence of Mark, and yet on the basis of good information, probably handed down in a separate strain of tradition.'

326] Cf. Morris (1995: 655) on how both elements are present in the Synoptics, too, and thus complementary and not contradictory.

exclusively Jewish, making nine major allegations: (1) The Synoptics know nothing of Romans present in Gethsemane. (2) A cohort (600 men) is far too large to be in the garden for this occasion. (3) There is no evidence that Pilate had any previous knowledge of this arrest. (4) If Roman soldiers had been involved, Jesus would have been held in a Roman prison, not taken to the home of the high priest. (5) In the Septuagint, *speira* is used only of non-Roman troops, while John, in speaking of the 'commander' of these troops in verse 12, employs a Greek word (*chiliarchos*) that is never used of Roman officers in the Septuagint. (6) In secular Greek *chiliarchos* can denote civilian as well as military officials. (7) The use of *speira* in verse 3, as distinct from the Jewish attendants, does not necessarily make the officials Romans. (8) The use of the definite article with *speira* need not mean 'the well-known' (Roman) cohort. (9) That the Jewish temple guard was inadequate for the job is hardly credible.

A majority of scholars have not been convinced by these allegations, however. Items (6), (7), (8) and (9) are not arguments against identifying the cohort as Roman, nor do they support equating the soldiers with the Jewish temple guard. They merely allow for either Roman or Jewish identification. Observations (1) and (3) are arguments from silence, which may not prove much. In fact, there may be hints in the Synoptics of counter-evidence. Mark 14:48 and parallels refer to the arresting party coming with 'swords and clubs', swords being more naturally associated with Roman soldiers and clubs with the Jewish guard (although one does find exceptions to both generalizations). And the ease with which the Jewish officials and Pilate cooperated after the crucifixion (Matt. 27:62–66; 28:11–15) could suggest some prior knowledge on Pilate's part of Jesus' arrest. As for point (2), the nomenclature for divisions of the Roman army was frequently used even when the number of participating soldiers was far less than that suggested by their label. On the other hand, given Jesus' fame, the potential for a riot, and the precaution exhibited by a Roman centurion with another famous Jewish prisoner a generation later (Paul, guarded by 270 men; Acts 23:23), it is perhaps not unreasonable to imagine the authorities bringing a similar number to Gethsemane.[327] Argument (4) is not at all self-evident, especially if the Jewish leaders had

---

327] Cf. Beasley-Murray (1987: 322): 'Apart from the fact that a cohort could denote a "maniple" of 200 soldiers, there is no need to understand that the entire company of soldiers in the Antonia garrison was dispatched. The troops were stationed in the Antonia during festivals precisely to prevent riots; it is comprehensible that the Jewish leaders asked for their presence in case of violent resistance when their own police attempted to arrest Jesus.'

taken the initiative to approach the Romans.[328] Observation (5), finally, seems of limited value, since the contexts in the Septuagint of these two terms describe events that took place (or purportedly took place) before Rome was ever an occupying force in Palestine (e.g. 1 Esdr. 1:9; Jud. 14:12; 1 Macc. 3:35; 16:19). No-one could thus mistake the officials in question for Romans. But in the first century the words *were* most commonly used for Romans, including *every other use* within the New Testament (Matt. 27:27; Mark 15:16; Acts 10:1; 21:31; 27:1 for *speira*; Mark 6:21; Rev. 6:15; 19:18; and eighteen times in Acts 21 – 25 for *chiliarchos*).

Several scholars recognize that John was depicting a Roman presence in the garden but deny that this was historically plausible (e.g. Schnackenburg 1982: 222; Casey 1996: 180–181). But, in addition to the arguments embedded in the above response to Blinzler, we may add that all the Synoptics agree that the arresting party thought they were confronting a dangerous person with a large following. The term *lēstēs* (Mark 14:48 pars.) is often translated as 'thief' or 'robber' but more properly means an 'insurrectionist'. Some scholars have understandably thus referred to John's account here as even more credible than the more abbreviated synoptic portraits (e.g. Dodd 1963: 86; J. A. T. Robinson 1985: 241–242).

John 18:4–9 presents the major addition to the account of Jesus' arrest in the Fourth Gospel, demonstrating his knowledge of and authority over even the events that would lead to his execution. Instead of waiting for Judas to step forward, Jesus takes the initiative and addresses the authorities, asking them whom they are seeking (v. 4). When they answer, 'Jesus of Nazareth' (a standard way for a Jew to be identified – by a single name plus place of origin), he replies 'I am he' (v. 5; Gk. *egō eimi*). It is hard to know if we are to hear overtones of the divine name again here or not. In favour of that interpretation is the response of at least some in the arresting party – 'they drew back and fell to the ground' (v. 6) – as if John were depicting some quasi-magical response to Jesus' supernatural power! If so, one could understand why many categorically reject the historicity of the scene.[329] On the other hand, the language is sufficiently vague and restrained to enable us to imagine nothing more than a small group of

---

328] Morris (1995: 657) concurs, noting the constant Roman anxiety about outbreaks of violence at the great festivals. He adds, 'It is likely that the Jewish authorities would have brought in the Romans as soon as possible in view of their ultimate aim (and, we might add, in view of the fact that on a previous occasion the Temple guards had failed to arrest Jesus, 7:44ff.).'

329] D. M. Smith (1999: 330) adds, 'That such a thing actually happened and the synoptic accounts ignored it is scarcely conceivable historically.'

leaders, stunned that the man they came to arrest would step forward so forthrightly, who stepped backward on the hillside in surprise and stumbled over each other causing several to fall down. The Fourth Evangelist could easily have viewed this as another example of a deeper, divine meaning in events that also had a more ordinary explanation.[330] Dodd (1963: 75–77) recognizes that the recoil of the arresting party affords the biggest challenge to defenders of historicity in this pericope but adds that 'it is just here that the apparent reminiscences of passages in the Old Testament suggest that the evangelist is working on traditional materials' (76). Dodd refers specifically to Psalms 35:4 and 27:2; Douglas Moo (1983: 246–247) adds 56:9 into the mix as well.

The dialogue between Jesus and his antagonists repeats itself (vv. 7–8a), and then Jesus asks them to let his disciples go (v. 8b). In the Synoptics they flee on their own (see esp. Mark 14:50–52); John is continuing to recast his narrative to show Jesus in charge. But nothing is written of the authorities granting permission, nor is it likely they would have done so. The same historical events are simply being viewed from two different theological perspectives. John makes his perspective even more explicit by stressing that this fulfilled one of Jesus' own statements (v. 9; recall esp. 6:39).[331] Mark, too, goes out of his way to stress the predictions of Jesus, especially with respect to his death and resurrection, as reliable prophecy (on which see esp. Gundry 1993).

With verse 10 John resumes narrating events that readers of the Synoptics would have known (Mark 14:46–49 pars.). Again, John assumes

---

330] Cf. Carson (1991: 578–579): 'The Evangelist has already testified to the effect of Jesus' words on temple officials sent to arrest him (7:45–46); indeed, it is not at all unlikely that some of the same personnel are again involved. If they have been awed by Jesus before, if they have been dumbfounded by his teaching, his authority, his directness in the full light of day in the precincts of the temple where they most feel at home, it is not hard to believe that they are staggered by his open self-disclosure on a sloping mountainside in the middle of the night – the more so if some of them hear the overtones of God's self-disclosure in the prophecy of Isaiah. It may take them a few seconds to pull themselves together and regroup; in the Evangelist's eyes, their physical ineptitude was another instance of people responding better than they knew.'

331] Pryor (1992a: 75) notes that this is the first of two places in John where Jesus' words are said to be fulfilled (cf. 21:19). John 10:28–29 and 17:12 reinforce 6:39 on this theme. Pryor asks if v. 8 should be seen 'as symbolic of something even more profound taking place and which the evangelist himself referred to in 11:50. Jesus is arrested and the disciples set free – and this is a symbol of the deeper truth to which the gospel of the early Christians bear [sic] witness: Jesus dies for the spiritual relief and benefit of his people.'

a basic understanding of the story. He does not mention Judas's kiss or the authorities' move to arrest Jesus (Mark 14:46), but it would make sense at that moment for Simon Peter to attack the high priest's servant (John 18:10). That he has a sword at all makes sense only in the light of Luke 22:35–38 and his misinterpretation of Jesus' metaphor there.[332] That he cut off the servant's *right* ear agrees, uniquely, with Luke 22:50. Only John supplies the man's name – Malchus – completely without theological motivation and therefore probably reflecting historical accuracy (cf. Dodd 1963: 77–80). As in the Synoptics, Jesus rebukes Peter (v. 11a), though John tells nothing of Jesus' subsequent healing of Malchus's ear. Verse 11b is unique to John, but expresses sentiments deeply rooted both in Old Testament language (for the 'cup' of God's wrath, cf. Ps. 75:8; Is. 51:17, 22; Jer. 25:15; Ezek. 23:31–33; etc.) and in synoptic passion narrative theology (Mark 14:36 pars.; cf. Mark 10:38 par.).

The arresting officers thus proceed with their task (v. 12) and deliver Jesus to the former Jewish high priest Annas (v. 13). Verses 13–14 introduce the next major Johannine addition to the passion narrative, continued in verses 19–23 – a separate informal hearing before Annas (cf. J. A. T. Robinson 1985: 248) prior to Jesus being delivered to the high priest, Caiaphas (vv. 13b–14, 24). Here John clearly relies on good, historical tradition. All who had held the office of high priest continued to be designated by that term (cf. Josephus, *War* 4.151, 160). After all, in the Torah the appointment was for life (Num. 35:25), even though the Romans were preventing the Jews from obeying this Law. Barrett (1978: 524) elaborates:

> Annas had been high priest from A.D. 6–15 (Josephus, *Ant.* xviii 26–35) and was succeeded not only by his son-in-law Caiaphas but also by five sons (*Ant.* xx 198), so that Luke and John are doubtless correct in seeing that he retained great influence, especially since his deposition by the Roman procurator Gratus could have no validity in Jewish opinion. Accordingly there is no historical difficulty in the statement that Jesus first appeared before him. (Cf. further Blinzler 1959: 86–89; Dodd 1963: 88–96; R. E. Brown 1970: 833–835; Senior 1991: 59.)

It is unclear what the full function of verses 13b–14 are, but they at least

---

332] In addition, Barrett (1978: 521) observes, 'It is often said that to carry such a weapon on Passover was forbidden … In any case regulations would be dispensed with by men who foresaw real and imminent danger.'

make the reader think back to Caiaphas's plotting in 11:45–53 and set the stage for further ominous developments.[333]

INITIAL INTERROGATIONS OF PETER AND JESUS (18:15–27)

John 18:15–27 intentionally breaks up the story of Peter's three denials into two parts, creating a sandwich effect around the account of Jesus' hearing before Annas. John will later narrate Jesus' trial by Pilate (18:28 – 19:16) and Peter's reinstatement by Jesus (21:15–19), both of which also take the form of questions and answers, so we may speak of the passage here as the 'initial interrogations' of these two men. All four Gospels narrate the episode of Peter's threefold denial of Christ. Raymond Brown (1970: 838–839) lays out the salient similarities and differences in a helpful chart.[334] The introductory information in verses 15–16a and the account of Jesus' hearing before Annas are unique to John.

Thus it is only from the Fourth Gospel that we learn of 'another disciple' who accompanies Peter to the high priest's courtyard where Jesus is being taken (v. 15). This other disciple 'was known to the high priest'; hence the two are able to gain access to the palace grounds (v. 16). We commented in our introduction on the various theories surrounding this disciple, including the common supposition that he is the same figure as the 'beloved disciple', introduced first by that designation in 13:23 (above, p. 31).[335] That John the apostle and Galilean fisherman should have links with the high-priestly family is not as surprising or unrealistic as many think, not only because of the priestly lineage among his relatives but also because of the thriving fish industry that would have served landlocked Jerusalem

---

333] For conflicting approaches to the source criticism of 18:1–14 as a whole, cf. Dormeyer (1995), who argues for a blend of redaction and a pre-Markan source, with Matera (1990), who believes that similarities with the Synoptics can be accounted for completely by John's direct use of Mark, combined with other independent traditions and his own redaction.

334] Sabbe (1995) argues for John's direct dependence on the Synoptics, but the detailed charts he sets out with verbal parallelism demonstrate how slight the potentially literary connections turn out to be.

335] On the plausibility of the equation, see esp. Neirynck 1975. Talbert (1992: 235) points out that Vaticanus and Sinaiticus, the Byzantine textual tradition, and other later witnesses read, 'the other disciple', modifying the more original p[66] and attesting to an early interpretative tradition that equated this individual with the beloved disciple. The apocryphal *Gospel of the Hebrews* made the same equation, linking the anonymous disciple with the apostle John and adding that he used to supply fish to the high priest's court when he worked for Zebedee.

(see above, p. 35; cf. also Morris 1995: 666, n. 37). If the anonymous disciple is not John, then the possible connections with the high priests are almost endless. Raymond Brown (1970: 841) adds that 'to invent a disciple of Jesus who inexplicably was acceptable at the palace of the high priest is to create a difficulty where there was none'. Thus, with Dodd (1963: 86), 'This vivid narrative ... is either the product of a remarkable dramatic flair, or it rests on superior information' (cf. also D. M. Smith 1999: 334–335).

The minor discrepancies among the Gospel parallels with respect to Peter's denials became notorious after Harold Lindsell's well-publicized harmonization (1976: 174–176) that claimed that Peter actually denied Jesus six times! This kind of hypothesis brings more sober harmonization into disrepute, since each Gospel emphasizes Jesus' prediction that Peter would make three denials and then goes on to narrate exactly that number. Nevertheless, it is completely historically credible to imagine a crowd of people huddled around a fire, seeing Peter come and go from their midst, shooting questions and accusations at him in a number of ways, so that more than three people may have accosted Peter. Once that is accepted, and we recall the freedom ancient writers felt to paraphrase a speaker's words, there is nothing in the Gospels' accounts of Peter's denials that would have qualified as a 'contradiction' by the historiographical standards of the first-century Mediterranean world (cf. esp. Morris 1995: 671–672). Peter would still have replied to his accusers only three times. Rodney Whitacre (1999: 434–435) thinks that John creates a problem by narrating Peter's denials in Annas's, not Caiaphas's (as in the Synoptics), courtyard. But even this goes beyond anything John's text states.[336] Moreover, the two men's residences may have been adjacent and have shared the same courtyard (Burge 2000: 497); archaeology, may indeed have uncovered the very neighbourhood of these homes in the wealthy 'upper city' of Jerusalem (Burge 2000: 493).

With respect to the details of John's version we may add the following observations. Only John identifies the first female servant who addresses Peter as a doorkeeper (v. 16; Gk. *thurōros*), but women appear in this role in both 2 Samuel 4:6 LXX and Acts 12:13. John narrates Peter's first denial in the briefest form of all the accounts as simply *ouk eimi* ('I am not he'), perhaps to contrast directly with Jesus' repeated use of *egō eimi* (with at times overtones of the divine 'I am'; cf. Witherington 1995: 288). John alone refers to a 'charcoal fire' (Gk. *anthrakian*; NIV translates merely 'fire'), but Mark 14:54 agrees there was a *phōs* (light; NIV 'fire') around which the people were warming themselves.

336] The same is true for alleged contradictions regarding the timing of the denials.

To heighten the contrast between Peter's cowardice and Jesus' courage, John now interrupts his narration of the denials and turns to the events unfolding within the high priest's chambers (vv. 19–23).[337] That Annas should ask Jesus about 'his disciples' and 'his teaching' (v. 19) makes good historical sense: these were two elements likely to incite a crowd to riot and get the Jews into trouble with Rome (recall 11:47–48). Jesus replies by stressing that he has 'spoken openly to the world' (v. 20). One recalls similar words spoken in the garden according to Mark 14:49 and parallels. Jesus' declaration 'cannot mean that Jesus never spoke to his disciples in private; all four Gospels controvert the suggestion. But what he said to them in private was of a piece with what he said in public. He did not maintain one message for public consumption and another, more dangerous one for a secret group of initiates' (Carson 1991: 584). Jesus then specifies both synagogue and temple as primary venues for this teaching, a statement with which all four Gospels again concur.[338] If one assumes that John's readers knew Mark or a pre-Markan kerygma, they may well have thought first of all of Jesus' very recent teaching in the temple earlier that very week (Mark 11:27 – 12:44 pars.). Verse 21 may suggest that 'the high priest is not proceeding in the correct legal form. It was his duty to produce his witnesses (and in Jewish law witnesses for the defense should be called first). Jesus is saying that that should not be at all difficult' (Morris 1995: 669).

One of Annas's officials now slaps Jesus for what he perceives to be an impudent retort (v. 22), perhaps perceiving a violation of Exodus 22:28. Jesus denies that he has broken any law and challenges his captors to specify where he has not told the truth (v. 23). 'Such self-assurance before authority was probably startling; for Josephus, *Ant.* XIV. ix. 4; #172, tells us that the normal attitude before a judge was one of humility, timidity, and mercy-seeking' (R. E. Brown 1970: 826). The entire incident makes one think of a very similar episode involving Paul a generation later (cf. Acts

---

337] Against the views that see this literary 'seam' as a sign of the editing of sources or the clumsy combination of separate traditions, see esp. Evans 1982. Mark has a similar kind of intercalation of episodes, which Evans finds smoother than those of John, suggesting that John's Gospel may be following even more primitive tradition here.

338] Lieu (1999) discusses the role of the temple in John as the place for the manifestation of the divine presence, where Jesus must be both revealed and rejected. Thus the reference to synagogue and temple here has nothing to do with the subsequent separation of the Johannine community from Judaism. The comparative reticence of the Fourth Gospel about the synagogue *vis-à-vis* the temple fits more the historical realities of pre-70 Israel than the Judaism of John's day.

23:1–5). The Synoptics will record a subsequent incident in which Christ was similarly slapped (Mark 14:65 pars.). That Jesus does not literally 'turn the other cheek' (Matt. 5:39) is not a contradiction of that command from the Sermon on the Mount but confirmation that Jesus was there speaking metaphorically (cf. further Blomberg 1992: 113).[339] Verse 24 rounds out this pericope by mentioning, almost in passing, the more elaborate and possibly more formal trial before Caiaphas and the Sanhedrin, on which the Synoptics focus so much attention (Mark 14:53–65 pars.). Once again John is skipping over an event he can assume his audience already knows well, while still making enough mention of it so that his readers can relate to their additional background knowledge what he does narrate (cf. Bauckham 1998c: 158).

John 18:25–27 shifts back outside and completes the account of Peter's denials.[340] For a second time Peter is questioned about being one of Jesus' disciples. John simply uses the third-person plural, 'they asked' (Gk. *eipon*, turned into a passive in the NIV: 'was asked'), without specifying who the questioners are. Again Peter replies with a simple 'I am not [he]' (*ouk eimi*; v. 25). The last person to accost Peter is described in more detail than any of the other questioners in any of the Gospel accounts – 'a relative of the man whose ear Peter had cut off'. His question is also phrased more specifically, appropriate for one who had accompanied the arresting officers in the garden (v. 26). John does not attribute any specific words to Peter for his final reply, commenting merely that he 'denied it'. As in all the accounts, a rooster crows, fulfilling Jesus' prediction (v. 27; recall 13:38). While Jesus has remained in control of himself with his life on the line, fulfilling his own prophecy, Peter has failed utterly in keeping his rash promises (recall 13:37).[341]

339] Carson (1991: 585) adds, 'Jesus did not call anyone names; he had nothing for which to apologize. Nor was he refusing to "turn the other cheek": that ought to be clear from the cross itself. But turning the other cheek without bearing witness to the truth is not the fruit of moral resolution but the terrorized cowardice of the wimp.'

340] 'The scene may still be the courtyard of Annas's house, or Annas and Caiaphas may have shared the same residence, in which case there would have been one courtyard. It is not impossible, as some commentators have thought, that Jesus was taken through the courtyard on the way to the wing where Caiaphas lived, and that this was the occasion for Jesus to turn and look at Peter just after the third denial (Luke 22:61). But we have no certain knowledge on these points' (Morris 1995: 671).

341] On John's intentions in depicting the various comparisons and contrasts between Jesus and his Father and between Jesus and his disciples, esp. Peter, throughout 18:1–27, see Giblin 1984.

JESUS AND PILATE (18:28 – 19:16)

Whereas Jesus' trial before the Sanhedrin is abbreviated almost to the point of non-existence, the Fourth Gospel expands the Synoptics' account of Jesus' trial before Pilate. John 18:28 – 19:16 offers an artfully crafted narrative in seven scenes, as Pilate moves back and forth inside and outside his Praetorium (for the overall structure, see Baum-Bodenbender 1984: esp. 96). The structure is arguably chiastic, with a climactic central focus on Jesus as king in 19:1–3 (Burge 2000: 488). Once again, while there are numerous points of contact with the synoptic tradition, verbal parallelism is limited to a handful of details, including short memorable quotations,[342] so that literary dependence appears unlikely (cf. esp. Dodd [1963: 96–120], who also argues for 'a high degree of [historical] verisimilitude' [120]).

Verse 28 picks up the narrative of Jesus under arrest where it left off in verse 24. It confirms that John knows of a separate hearing before Caiaphas that did not result in Jesus' acquittal, but it tells us nothing more. That it was 'early morning' (Gk. *prōï–* lit. 'early') agrees with what Mark 15:1 spells out. Only John refers to Pilate's 'palace' (Gk. *praitōrion,* from the Latin, *praetorium*), but the Synoptics will introduce the same term later (Mark 15:16 par.). The expression referred to the official residence of a governor of a Roman province. 'The governor of Judaea normally lived at Caesarea (where there was another praetorium, Acts 23:35), but came to Jerusalem for the great feasts, to quell disturbances' (Barrett 1978: 531, n. 28).[343]

Considerable controversy surrounds John's statement that the Jews remained outside Pilate's residence so as not to defile themselves and be unable to 'eat the Passover' (Gk. *phagōsin to pascha*). A sizeable majority of commentators takes this expression in its most common sense of referring

---

342] 'Are you the king of the Jews?' (18:33); 'You say [so]' (18:37; NIV 'You are right in saying'); 'I find no basis for a charge' (18:38); 'release "the king of the Jews"?' (18:39); 'crown of thorns', 'put it on his head', and 'Hail, king of the Jews' (19:2); and 'handed him over … to be crucified' (19:16). Even with all these convergences, in most cases different inflectional forms of the Greek words appear, so that the parallelism is by no means verbatim.

343] Two sites compete with each other as scholars try to identify the Jerusalem praetorium: the Antonia Fortress overlooking the temple grounds, and Herod's palace on the west side of the city. The discovery of the possible site of the 'Lithostrotos' – the paving stones outside the praetorium (see below, p. 246) – tips the scales in favour of the former (e.g. Lindars 1972: 564–565). For a detailed examination of Pilate's practice of coming to Jerusalem at feast time, see Kinman 1991.

to the initial evening meal of the week-long feast, in which the Passover lamb was served and the haggadah or liturgy recited. This then forces the meal of John 13 to be something other than the normal, festive meal with which Passover began, and Jesus is thus crucified on the afternoon of the day during which the lambs would be slaughtered for the upcoming Passover meal (in this case on Friday evening). Because the Baptist twice called Jesus the 'Lamb of God' early on in this Gospel (recall John 1:29, 36), it is assumed that John has changed the chronology here in service of his theology – Jesus is the Passover Lamb.[344] On this view, John flatly contradicts the Synoptics (recall Casey 1996: 18–25). While most scholars adopting this reconstruction then find the Synoptic dating more correct, J. A. T. Robinson (1985: 252–254) represents a minority that has preferred John to the Synoptics.

It is not at all clear, however, that this is an accurate description of the state of affairs in the Fourth Gospel. We have already seen that, *apart from the problems caused by 18:28 and later texts*, the most natural way to take chapter 13 is as a description of the normal Passover meal (above, pp. 187–188). When we read 18:28 in its narrative sequence, after the accounts of chapters 13 – 17, we would naturally assume that by 'eating the Passover' John is referring to upcoming meals in the week-long feast of the Unleavened Bread (cf. esp. B. D. Smith 1991). The Mishnah demonstrates later rabbinic concern for purity throughout the seasonal festivals and devotes an entire tractate to 'Mid-Festival Days' (*Moed Katan*) and another to the festal offerings (*Hagigah*), including offerings brought in between the first and last days of feasts (e.g. *Hag.* 1:3). The tractate *Oholoth* (18:7, 10) demonstrates that the dwelling places of Gentiles, but not their open courtyards, were considered unclean.

Against the objection that 'eating the Passover' cannot refer to these later festival meals, Strack and Billerbeck (1924: 837–838) noted how 2 Chronicles 35:7–9 referred to the various sacrificial animals offered throughout Passover week – not just to the lamb of the first evening's meal, as *pesah* – the Hebrew for 'Passover'. Thus the word came to refer not just

---

344] Even as conservative a commentator as Morris (1995: 684–695) accepts this theological reconstruction but, at the historical level, argues for Jesus following a different calendar than the Jewish leaders in his celebration of Passover. We know from Qumran that such calendrical disparity existed, but it is impossible to imagine two widespread, competing schemes within Jerusalem at the same time, given the chaos that would have resulted. It is, of course, possible that Jesus alone followed a unique timetable, knowing that he would not live to celebrate the Passover on the proper evening, but such a reconstruction of events does not require this otherwise unsubstantiated hypothesis.

to the festival but to the various animals offered in sacrifice during the festival. Strack and Billerbeck cite numerous later rabbinic sources that continue this linguistic development. It is true that all this legislation refers to the entire week and its sacrifices and not to one specific meal, all by itself, after the opening Passover supper. But when one moves from generalized, legal material to historical narrative and reads of a subsequent 'eating of the Passover' after the initial meal of the feast, the natural assumption is that one or more of the remaining festival meals is in view (see esp. Carson 1991: 589–590; for a detailed treatment, cf. Geldenhuys 1950: 649–670). After all, the ceremonial uncleanness that the Jewish leaders would have incurred in entering Pilate's Praetorium would have lasted only until sundown, so that they would not have been defiled in eating an evening meal on Friday. Only if it were the lunchtime *ḥᵃgîgâ*, would uncleanness have been an issue (Strack-Billerbeck 1924: 838–839; Köstenberger 1999: 146).[345]

Verse 29 introduces Pontius Pilate without any narrative explanation of his identity. John can assume his readers are familiar with a name that even appears in one of the New Testament 'creeds' (1 Tim. 6:13). If Pilate had in fact agreed to help the Jewish leaders in arresting Jesus, his accommodating their scruples in coming outside to meet them is scarcely improbable. Despite the overall ruthlessness with which extrabiblical sources, especially Josephus, portray Pilate,[346] he was in an impossible situation in governing Judea. If he gave in too much to Jewish sensitivities, he risked being perceived as disloyal to Caesar. If he paid them no attention, he risked public protest on such a scale that Rome would again become irate.[347]

'Pilate first asked the representatives of the Sanhedrin the nature of the charge. This is also supplied in the special material of Luke (Lk. 23.2),

---

345] Unfortunately, Strack and Billerbeck ultimately accept the critical consensus that John and the Synoptics conradict each other, despite these observations. Somewhat differently, Story (1989: 318–323) argues that the Jewish leaders were so busy with the events of the previous evening that they had not yet had time to eat the initial Passover meal as they should have. But it is unclear that their dealings with Jesus would have started early enough on Thursday night to get in the way of eating a meal that began shortly after sundown. Hamilton (1992: 333) defends a position similar to Story's.

346] The fullest analysis of Pilate in the ancient sources, inside and outside the canon, appears in Bond 1998, with historical conclusions on 194–202. More briefly, cf. McGing (1991), who concludes there are no significant discrepancies between the Pilate of the Gospels and the information we glean from extracanonical sources.

347] For the portrayal of Pilate in this passage, see esp. Giblin 1986.

where the "many things" of Mk. 15.3 are specified. Although this must be regarded as an authentic item, omitted by Matthew and Mark, John's version of it is entirely independent of Luke' (Lindars 1972: 552). Characteristically, John elaborates with information not found in the Synoptics (vv. 30–32). The nature of the Jewish leaders' response in verse 30 further supports initial collaboration between Pilate and the Sanhedrin. As Carson (1991: 590) expounds, this agreement

> explains the truculence of their reply; otherwise their words appear impossibly insolent. The fact that Pilate had sufficiently agreed with their legal briefs to sanction sending in a detachment of troops had doubtless encouraged them to think that he would ratify the proceedings of the Sanhedrin and get on to other business. To find him opening up what was in fact a new trial made them sullen.[348]

John 18:31 brings us to another huge historical controversy. Particularly in the light of major studies like those of Hans Lietzmann (1934) and Paul Winter (1974), it has been alleged that the Sanhedrin did indeed have the right to inflict capital punishment on individuals who broke Jewish laws to which the death penalty was attached. Witness, for example, the stoning of Stephen (Acts 7:54 – 8:1), the inscription in the temple threatening death to Gentiles who entered areas reserved for Jews (Josephus, *War* 6.124–126), and the Sanhedrin's execution of James the Lord's brother in the early 60s (Josephus, *Ant.* 20.197–203). On the other hand, Coponius, the first procurator of Judea in AD 6, was endowed by the emperor with the 'highest power', defined as 'the power unto killing' (Josephus, *War* 2.117), which is most naturally interpreted as arrogating the right to inflict capital punishment to himself. Josephus' discussion in *War* 6.124–126 seems to suggest that permission to execute transgressors of the temple ban was an exception, made as a special concession to the Jews. The stoning of Stephen reads like mob action begun with the barest of legal pretences;[349] and the martyrdom of James came when Judea was awaiting a new Roman governor (cf. esp. Blinzler 1959: 157–163). The rabbinic literature supplies apparent confirmation of these conclusions, especially in its tradition that

---

348] Cf. Michaels (1983: 300): 'The question had to be asked as a matter of procedure. The answer of the Jewish authorities (v. 30) probably reflects their impatience at this formality, as if to say, "You know very well what the charges are. Let's get on with it."'

349] Haenchen (1984b: 179), only rarely favourable to the historicity of John, remarks here that Stephen's stoning 'was vigilante justice pure and simple. Verse 31 has thus not been historically contradicted up to the present time'.

capital punishment had been taken from the Jews forty years before the destruction of the temple in AD 70 (*j. Sanh.* 1.1; 7.2) (cf. further Bruce 1980: 11–12; Legasse 1997: 54–56).[350] The detailed studies of the Johannine account of Jesus' Roman trial by August Strobel (1980: esp. 43–45) and A. N. Sherwin-White (1965) refute additional charges of Lietzmann, Winter and similar studies, while strongly supporting the historicity of John 18:31. Indeed, the Synoptics leave it unclear as to why the Sanhedrin passed Jesus on to the Roman authorities. Only John offers a reasonable explanation (R. E. Brown 1970: 849). At the theological level, John sees a second example here of Jesus' own prophecy being fulfilled (v. 32; recall 12:32).

Pilate next poses the question to Jesus that would most have concerned Rome: does he claim to be some kind of king, for which he would be guilty of treason or sedition (v. 33)? All four Gospels agree that the charge against Jesus in Rome's eyes was claiming to be the king of the Jews (cf. 19:19 pars.). But how would John have learned of the specifics of Pilate's interrogation of Jesus behind closed doors? For those who allow for the possibility of a resurrection, he could have told his disciples the story himself. Even apart from this possibility, Carson (1991: 587) continues:

> Perhaps some of the court attendants became Christians in the early years of rapid growth in the Christian church, and passed on their recollections to the apostolic leadership. Some court records were public, and therefore available to those willing to do some research (such as Luke: cf. Lk. 1:1–4). We do not know where John obtained his information, but our ignorance is not threatening unless some startling reason is advanced as to why John should have told us how he found out, or unless there is overwhelming reason to think that John *could not* have known. And neither condition applies.

Jesus' seemingly evasive answer (v. 34) may in fact reflect faithfulness to Jewish tradition. 'If Pilate says he heard this from Jewish authorities, which he does (v. 35), then Jesus as a loyal Jew is expected to say nothing against his fellow Jews in a Gentile court (cf. 1 Cor. 6:1ff.). Even at the brink of death, Jesus shows more concern for others than for himself, even for the Jewish authorities as well as for his own followers' (Witherington 1995: 291).

In verse 35 Pilate appears to adopt the rhetorical ploy, already illustrated

---

350] The number of years may simply be a round one. But, if taken literally, it would bring us to AD 30, the very year that seems most likely for Jesus' crucifixion!

several times in the Fourth Gospel, of a 'superior' refusing directly to address the topic of conversation initiated by a 'subordinate'. That the proceedings were initiated largely by the chief priests fits their leadership role in Jerusalem. But Pilate still needs to know what Jesus is claiming for himself, so repeats his request for information. Like Pilate, Jesus does not directly address the question put to him. But he does elaborate on the nature of his kingship, thus conceding that he does claim to be one kind of king (v. 36). But it is not one that poses any legal or military threat to Rome. Here is the only other place, after 3:3 and 5, that 'kingdom' teaching, so central to the synoptic Jesus, appears in John. That Jesus' kingdom is 'not of this world' employs Johannine language, but the overall concept coheres perfectly with the core of synoptic teaching accepted as authentic via the dissimilarity criterion by even many of the most sceptical of scholars.[351]

Pilate presses the question of Jesus' kingship (v. 37a). Jesus' reply is literally translated, 'You say that I am a king' (v. 37b). 'You say' renders the Greek *sy legeis*, which is exactly what appears in the three synoptic parallels to this verse, without the subsequent content clause. The NIV reads, 'You are right in saying I am a king,' because this two-word Greek expression could be used as a veiled affirmative (see esp. Catchpole 1971). But the original utterance (and this may be one place where Jesus had to speak in Greek; cf. Porter 2000: 158) was considerably more ambiguous, more akin to 'That's your way of putting it, not mine,' and thus quite likely to be authentic. The rest of verse 37 expresses more Johannine thoughts; that Jesus did speak about truth, however, has been defended above (p. 198).

Pilate's dismissive, 'What is truth?' (v. 38) is in keeping with his 'rough' character attested to in all the ancient sources that describe this prefect. While it seems that John's Jesus is not silent as early in his interrogation as in the Synoptics (cf. Mark 15:5 pars.), John 19:9 knows the tradition of Jesus' silence and the Synoptics have probably just compressed the account. 1 Timothy 6:13 speaks of the 'good confession' Christ Jesus made 'while testifying before Pontius Pilate' (cf. John's use of 'testify' in 18:37), a reference that fits John's more 'talkative' Jesus better than the Synoptics' portrait (R. E. Brown 1970: 861). Pilate's attempt to dismiss the charges against Jesus matches what we read in Luke 23:4 and 14.

Verses 39 and 40 introduce yet another incident that has proved historically suspect. No extracanonical source unambiguously attests to a regular Roman custom of releasing one Jewish prisoner each year at

---

351] On the overall theology reflected both in this verse and on the interrogation by Pilate more generally, see esp. Söding 1996.

Passover. On the other hand, Josephus (*Ant.* 20.209), Livy (5.13), and especially the Talmud (*b. Pes.* 91a; cf. Blinzler 1959: 218–221) may attest to the custom or, more likely, to partially analogous Roman practices, so that the account, narrated in all four Gospels, is not inherently improbable (see esp. Chavel 1941; Merritt [1985] adduces parallel Babylonian, Assyrian and Greek customs). Mariano Marco (1971) thoroughly surveys the discussion and concludes by citing the early form critic Martin Dibelius approvingly: 'Although we know nothing, he says, of a similar amnesty as a custom, *there are no motives for doubting this episode*; to suppose that one should seriously treat it as an invention is to attribute to the first narrators a creative will and ability that they do not show on any other occasion' (160; trans. and emphasis mine). That Barabbas is called an insurrectionist (Gk. *lēstēs*; NIV 'had taken part in a rebellion') matches Luke's special information that he had been thrown in prison for an uprising and a murder in the city (Luke 23:19).

Thus far the events in Jesus' trial before Pilate in John closely follow the synoptic sequence. Luke adds a brief hearing before Herod Antipas (Luke 23:6–12), which could be inserted somewhere in John 18:29–38, but the Galilean tetrarch refuses to pass judgment and returns Jesus to Pilate. John 19:1 moves the trial to a new stage: Pilate orders Jesus to be scourged. The Synoptics, too, describe this incident, but later in their narrative of events (Mark 15:15 pars.). Mark, however, describes the flogging merely with the aorist participle *phragellōsas*, syntactically subordinate to the statement that, literally, 'he delivered Jesus … in order that he might be crucified'. Mark's wording thus allows for the flogging to have happened at any time prior to the conclusion of Jesus' trial (similarly Blinzler 1959: 234–235; Beasley-Murray 1987: 335; Kiehl 1990: 114). It is thus unnecessary to assume that Jesus was flogged twice within the same hearing, a supposition for which there is no obvious historical precedent. While Sherwin-White (1963: 27–28) argues that this scourging, parallel to Luke 23:14–22, was the comparatively light *fustigatio*, designed by Pilate as an attempt to be rid of Jesus, Christ's subsequently weakened condition and quick death on the cross suggest that he received the horrid *verberatio* (Blinzler 1959: 223–226). Flogging in conjunction with Roman legal proceedings appears in Acts 22:24 (and possibly 16:22), as well as Josephus (*War* 2.306).

Along with the scourging, Matthew, Mark and John all agree that the Roman soldiers mock Jesus by dressing him in a royal robe, giving him a crown of thorns and hailing him as if he were a king (John 19:2–3 pars.). They are mimicking the 'Hail Caesar' cry of their era (R. E. Brown 1970: 875); for similar mockery, compare Philo, *Flaccus* 6.36–39. Pilate then parades Jesus outside his headquarters in this macabre dress (v. 4), declaring to the onlookers, 'Here is the man' (v. 5).

The dramatic scenario of the presentation of Jesus to 'the Jews' is typically Johannine, but we may wonder whether the evangelist's creative sense has not been controlled by some details that he found in his tradition. If he were inventing with complete freedom, this would have been the perfect moment to have had Pilate say, 'behold the king!' (as in vs. 14). Instead we find the enigmatic 'behold the man!' (R. E. Brown 1970: 890)[352]

The Jewish leaders now for the first time in John's account call explicitly for Christ's crucifixion (v. 6). John again proves historically credible in referring exclusively to the 'chief priests and their officials' (recall above, p. 136). That the Fourth Gospel describes the specific leaders in charge in Jerusalem and not the Pharisees, who played a larger role earlier in the Gospel and later in the first century, demonstrates that John is not creating theological fiction, despite his stylized use of the 'Jews' in verse 7 and elsewhere (Ritt 1989: 183–190; cf. Ridderbos 1997: 601). 'In saying, "Take him and crucify him yourselves," Pilate was teasing them again. He knew very well that they could execute no capital sentence against him, and, even if they could, crucifixion was not a form of execution normally authorized by Jewish law' (Bruce 1983: 360). One thinks, too, of the unique reference in Matthew 27:24 to Pilate declaring himself innocent of Jesus' blood.

In verse 7 the authorities shift gears and complain that Christ has violated *Jewish* law by claiming to be God's Son. The Synoptics demonstrate this in detail with their far fuller account of Jesus' trial before the Sanhedrin; John seems to be assuming knowledge of that story here (cf. esp. Luke 22:67–71; cf. Beasley-Murray 1987: 338). 'Even if the procurator was not obliged to take note of purely religious offenses, he was nevertheless obliged to consider as far as possible the religious sentiments and the wishes of the populace' (Blinzler 1959: 230). Claiming to be the

---

352] Böhler (1995) thinks 19:5 *is* a proclamation of kingship, as in v. 14, based on the language of 1 Sam. 9:17 LXX in which Samuel acclaims Saul. But it seems unlikely that the Roman Pilate would have made such an allusion, and even at the level of Johannine redaction the association seems overly subtle. Suggit (1983) thinks v. 5 is Messianic, at least for John, since *anthrōpos* is used thirteen times in the Fourth Gospel of Jesus and parallels the title 'Son of Man'. John likes to repeat statements of importance, thus v. 14 can be seen as duplicating the thought of v. 5. This is somewhat more plausible at the level of Johannine redaction but still probably not what any early Christian would have believed Pilate himself thought. Houlden (1981) discusses the merits of, but ultimately rejects, the interpretation and textual variant that make v. 5 describe a statement by Jesus of Pilate.

Messiah in the specific way that the Synoptics depict Jesus doing (i.e. also claiming to be the heavenly Son of man; cf. Mark 14:62–63 pars.) unites the charges of claiming to be king and Son of God under one heading (cf. J. A. T. Robinson 1985: 263).[353] He had offended both Israel and Rome; contra many, we need not try to excise one or the other in our historical reconstruction (rightly Dodd 1963: 115).

When Pilate hears the additional charges against Jesus, 'he was even more afraid' (v. 8). He probably thought of a 'son of God' as a Graeco-Roman 'divine man'. He would have known of stories of gods appearing to people in human form (cf. Acts 14:11). His wife's warning him about Jesus based on her nightmare (Matt. 27:19) would have heightened his superstitious fright. 'Doubtless this fear would be increased by the thought of the vengeance that could be taken by a divine being on one who had maltreated him' (Beasley-Murray 1987: 339). So he asks Jesus whence he comes (v. 9a). At one level, this need mean nothing more than what Luke 23:6 explains, that Pilate here discovers that Jesus is a Galilean, under Herodian jurisdiction. But in context Pilate's question probably resounds with spiritual overtones as well (Dewailly 1985). At this juncture, Jesus falls silent (v. 9b; recall my comments above, p. 242).[354] Pilate tries to threaten Jesus into replying by describing the life-and-death authority that he wields (v. 10), but Jesus retorts as any good Jew might have that even imperial authority is God-given (v. 11a; see Talbert [1992: 240] for numerous parallels throughout both testaments and the apocrypha). Verse 11b proves more enigmatic as Jesus adds that the one who handed him over to Pilate 'is guilty of a greater sin'. Commentators debate whether Caiaphas, a larger body of Jewish people, Judas, or the devil behind all of them is in view here. Whichever suggestion be accepted, the idea coheres perfectly with Luke 12:47–48 – Jesus' teaching about degrees of punishment and the greater responsibility resting on the shoulders of those to whom much has been entrusted.

As in the Synoptics Pilate remains unconvinced of Jesus' guilt but must deal with the increasing clamour from the growing crowds outside. Unique to John is their charge that if Pilate releases Jesus he is 'no friend of Caesar' (v. 12). 'John's picture of a Pilate worried about what might be said at Rome has a very good chance of being historical,' comments Raymond Brown (1970: 890). He goes on to cite Philo, *To Gaius* 38.301–302, who

---

353] On the kind of blasphemy involved, cf. Wead 1969 with Bock 1998.

354] Because John emphasizes Jesus' silence *less* than the Synoptics do, Zeller's view (1993) that vv. 8–11 are redactional, influenced by Hellenistic portraits of philosophers remaining silent before their judges, proves unconvincing.

describes Pilate's inflexibility after dedicating Roman shields in Herod's palace until certain Jews 'mentioned that the Emperor Tiberius would not approve his violating their customs', at which point he acceded to their demands to remove the shields. In fact, 'friend of Caesar' (*amicus Caesari*) at times functioned as a technical term for Roman leaders who were particularly loyal to and favoured by the emperor (Tacitus, *Ann.* 6.8). That the Jewish leaders should threaten Pilate in this way is thus entirely credible.

So Pilate brings Jesus outside the Praetorium and sits down on the *bēma* or judgment seat (v. 13a).[355] Josephus describes similar arrangements during the procuratorship of Gessius Florus in the mid-60s (*War* 2.301). The outdoor paving stones are referred to in Aramaic as *Gabbatha* (v. 13b). Excavations have revealed precisely such stones near the Antonia Fortress in what could be the very site described here, though they come from a slightly later date and there is no way to be sure. But they do contain markings suggesting that the Roman soldiers may have played games here (like the gambling described in v. 23).[356] J. A. T. Robinson (1985: 267–268) perhaps captures the best balance by suggesting that while *Gabbatha* may not be identical to the Pavement shown to tourists today, these stones nevertheless give a vivid impression of what this area would have looked like in first-century Jerusalem.

With verse 14 we come to the third passage in John that leads many scholars to think he contradicts the Synoptics concerning the day of Christ's death (e.g. Casey 1996: 22–25; recall my discussion at 13:1 and 18:28). The NIV reads, 'It was the day of Preparation of Passover Week,

---

355] This is the only place in the New Testament where *bēma* is used of the judgment seat without having the article prefix, that is, it is 'a' judgment seat, not 'the' judgment seat. It may signify that a temporary judgment seat was set up on the Pavement. One would have expected that the normal *bēma* would have been inside the Praetorium. For a discussion of the possibility that John's text should be understood as claiming that Pilate sat Jesus on the *bēma*, furthering the mockery, see Barrera 1991. Blinzler (1959: 240–241) observes that sitting on the judgment seat was precisely how death sentences had to be pronounced. The procedure also fits Matt. 27:19, which finds Pilate sitting on the *bēma* earlier in the trial as well.

356] Cf. Bruce (1983: 358–359): 'If the praetorium where this took place was the Antonia fortress, it is at least a coincidence to recall that part of the Roman pavement or courtyard on that site can still be seen as marked out for the 'king game' (Gk. *basilinda*); it has been conjectured (but precariously) that this was an appropriate spot for the mock coronation ceremony.' Lindars (1972: 571) thinks that 'the details given here certainly give the impression that John knows the place he is describing', while R. E. Brown (1970: 893) suggests that 'since the place name has no obvious symbolism, it may be historical'.

about the sixth hour.' The Greek of the first part of this verse reads merely, *ōn de paraskeuē tou pascha* ('now it was the preparation of the Passover'). Out of context, this clause could be understood to mean that it was the day before Passover; hence, the claim of John's contradictory chronology. Ridderbos (1997: 456), however, observes that this sense of the expression is not elsewhere attested. Moreover, because 'the Passover' could just as easily mean the week-long festival and because 'the day of Preparation' could mean Friday (the day of preparation for the Sabbath; cf. *Did.* 8.1 and *Mart. Polyc.* 7.1),[357] in a context in which we have reason to believe that the initial Passover meal has already been eaten, it is completely appropriate to understand John to mean that 'it was Friday of Passover week' (Story 1989: 318; Ridderbos 1997: 606; Burge 2000: 508; cf. further Blomberg 1987: 177–178). This assessment is bolstered by the fact that, in every other occurrence of *paraskeuē* in the New Testament including its other two uses in John, the term unambiguously means the day before the Sabbath (Matt. 27:62; Mark 15:42; Luke 23:54; John 19:31, 42).

That Pilate passed his verdict at about the sixth hour (noon) creates another chronological difficulty. Mark 15:25 states that the crucifixion began at the third hour (9.00 am). But in a world with no more sophisticated a time-keeping device than a sundial, writers did not refer to the hours of the day with nearly the precision that we do. Just as the twelve-hour night from six in the evening to six in the morning was divided into four watches, people often thought of the daylight hours in four three-hour increments. If Pilate's verdict and the start of Jesus' crucifixion occurred somewhere roughly equidistant between 9.00 am and noon, one writer could very easily have 'rounded up' and the other 'rounded down', especially when John explicitly uses the qualifying word 'about' (Gk. *hōs* or 'as') (cf. further Blomberg 1987: 180; and the literature there cited; see also Burge 2000: 507–508).[358]

Pilate tries one last time to free Jesus, but the growing crowds simply clamour all the more loudly for his crucifixion. Hypocritically, the chief priests once again swear loyalty to Caesar alone (v. 15; cf. Talbert 1992: 241). J. A. T. Robinson (1985: 266) remarks that 'it is also to be observed that the final cynical thrust that won Pilate's acquiescence, "We have no king but Caesar" (19.15f), reveals a Jewish obsequiousness to Rome that is

---

357] To this day the name in Modern Greek for Friday remains the same: *Paraskeuē*.

358] Karavidopoulos (1992) surveys all the major solutions to this problem suggested throughout church history. His own suggestion, that Mark's terminology comes from the later liturgical labels for times of the day based on the various Christian worship services, seems far-fetched. For a solution, cf. also Morris 1995: 708.

scarcely credible in a document written after the Jewish revolt of 66–70.'
More precisely, it is scarcely credible that it could have been *invented* in the
light of Jewish attitudes after the war with Rome. True to the form of mob
hysteria, we have degenerated from logical discourse to verdict by volume.
Pilate concedes and hands Jesus over to be executed (v. 16).[359] This expression does not mean a literal delivering of Jesus to the Jewish authorities but
is a description of the death sentence (Blinzler 1959: 242).[360]

Despite the fact that Johannine scholars in general are more optimistic
about recovering historical facts from John's Passion narrative than they are
with almost any other major section of the Fourth Gospel (e.g. Blank
1989), Casey (1996:186–187) enumerates various reasons for rejecting
John's historicity here, too. The three that involve John 18:28 – 19:16 are
(1) The scourging is improbable since Pilate publicly declared he found no
fault in Jesus. It was therefore invented as part of John's anti-Semitic
portrait of the Jewish leaders and a damning influence on Pilate's interrogation of Jesus. (2) John 19:7 is anachronistic, reading later Johannine
theology into the charge against Jesus. (3) The rest of the trial account
stresses Jesus as king, a major Johannine redactional motif. In reply to (1),
we may observe that Jewish influence in the scourging is indirect at best.
Ironically, John is *less* anti-Semitic if we accept his text as it stands: it is
Rome, via Pilate, that is portrayed as ruthless and harsh. Roman rulers were
scarcely above punishing people who were legally innocent.[361] As for (2), we
have already seen that this verse is substantiated by the Markan portrait of
Christ's trial before the Sanhedrin (above, p. 244), and it is Mark that
Casey otherwise follows as historical especially when seemingly differing
from John. Concerning objection (3), the theme of Jesus' kingship proves
at least as prominent in the Synoptics and passes numerous tests of
authenticity – multiple attestation, dissimilarity, and coherence with Jesus'
'kingdom' teaching (cf. also Ridderbos 1997: 593–594). 'It is thus with
excellent historical justification that John brings out the theme of kingship
in his passion narrative' (Barrett 1978: 540).[362]

359] On the historical plausibility of this conclusion to the trial, see esp. Sherwin-White
1963: 47.

360] Bammel (1984a: 437–438, 443) discusses examples in Josephus of similar
collaboration of Roman and Jewish officials in the executions of various criminals.

361] For a relatively balanced portrait of Pilate with respect to the events of the trial, see
Legasse 1997: 61–69.

362] For a more positive and credible assessment of the distinctives of the trial narrative in
John, see Blinzler (1959: 184–186), who recapitulates and develops many of the points
surveyed here.

THE CRUCIFIXION (19:17–30)

The crucifixion of Christ is one of those rare details in the Gospels confirmed by non-Christian sources from antiquity. Josephus (*Ant.* 18.63–64) declares that 'Pilate ... condemned him to the cross'; Tacitus (*Ann.* 44.3), that Jesus was 'executed in the reign of Tiberius by the procurator Pontius Pilate'. Lucian (*Peregr.* 11, 13) twice makes reference to the Jews' crucifixion of their 'wise king'. Not surprisingly, the actual death of Jesus finds numerous synoptic parallels as well. The road to the cross at Golgotha, crucifixion between two criminals, the titulus, gambling for Jesus' clothes, the presence of the women, and the offer of a drink are repeated in both John and the Synoptics. But again John omits certain material: the role of Simon of Cyrene, the offer of an initial sedative, various sayings from the cross, the reactions of the bystanders, and the cosmic signs at the moment of Jesus' death. Conversely, he significantly expands on the Synoptics with the dialogue about the titulus, the seamless robe, Jesus' words to Mary and John, and his final sayings just before his death. Once again, precise verbal parallelism with the Synoptics proves minimal; it is limited to vocabulary not likely to have varied much in oral tradition: 'skull', 'Golgotha', 'the king of the Jews', 'garments', 'vinegar' and 'sponge'. As consistently throughout the Fourth Gospel, it is not impossible that John has thoroughly reworked the Synoptics (see esp. Sabbe 1994), but if he has we shall never be able to demonstrate it. Theories of his use of independent tradition are simpler and more natural (see esp. Dodd 1963: 121–136; cf. R. E. Brown 1970: 916).

Only John mentions that Jesus carries his own cross (v. 17). It was, however, standard procedure, for convicted criminals to carry the horizontal crossbeam as they were led to the site of their crucifixion (cf. Plutarch, *Div. Veng.* 554a-b), so Mark 15:20b and parallels are most naturally interpreted as implying the same. Only the Synoptics then go on to describe how one Simon of Cyrene, coming in from the fields, was compelled to assist Jesus (Mark 15:21 pars.). Their wording suggests that Simon encountered the procession already at the edge of town. The natural harmonization remains the most plausible explanation: in his overly weakened state from the flogging, Jesus could not continue on his own (Dodd 1963: 125; R. E. Brown 1970: 899; Bruce 1983: 366; J. A. T. Robinson 1985: 276).[363] It is possible that John's omission of this detail stems from the later Gnostic claim that Simon was crucified in Jesus' place;

363] Casey's claim (1996: 188) that by adding 'himself' (NIV 'his own'; Gk. *heautō*, lit. just 'with him') John 'was deliberately contradicting true tradition' merely shows how eager Casey is to discredit John, however slim the support for his views.

John does not want to offer any suggestions that Jesus did not suffer everything God required of him (cf. Talbert 1992: 242).

Despite the skull-like appearance of the rocks in the hillside at 'Gordon's Calvary', a popular tourist site in modern-day Jerusalem, the actual site of Golgotha is far more likely to be near the Church of the Holy Sepulchre (Legasse 1997: 86).[364] But the landscape at Gordon's Calvary enables one to visualize better how the area around the crucifixion may have appeared in Jesus' day. The use of Aramaic (*Golgotha*) again points to very early tradition (v. 17). That Romans (and corrupt Jews!) employed crucifixion is well attested in ancient sources (see esp. Josephus, *War* 1.97 and 7.203).[365] The Synoptics confirm that Jesus was crucified between two other convicts (v. 18), adding that they too were charged with insurrection (Mark 15:27 pars.).

In keeping with one customary practice, Pilate had a placard prepared to nail atop the cross with the charge against Jesus (v. 19a).[366] The variety in the description of the wording of the titulus among the four Gospels fits the natural freedom of paraphrase found throughout the New Testament, and the ancient Mediterranean world more generally, though it is just possible that a more strict, additive harmonization works here (see G. M. Lee 1968). Multilingual notices abounded in Jesus' day; one finds them in imperial decrees (e.g. Josephus, *Ant.* 14:191), in the Jewish temple inscription (Josephus, *War* 5.194; 6.125), and on Roman tombstones still visible today (Blinzler 1959: 254–255). Public executions usually took place where large numbers of travellers could see them, as deterrents to further crime, so Rome would want as many as possible to understand the nature of each crime (v. 20). By calling Jesus 'the king of the Jews', Pilate does not for one minute believe the claim. The chief priests protest but Pilate remains firm (vv. 21–22). Ridderbos (1997: 609) may be correct in surmising that 'Pilate had given the matter careful thought and thus paid back the Jews for forcing him to act against his will.' For parallel language, Raymond Brown (1970: 902) cites the expression of the Seleucid king, Demetrius, in 1 Maccabees 13:38 ('All the grants that we have made to you remain valid').

364] Visitors should not be confused by the fact that the church is located within the walled-in portion of Old Jerusalem. These above-ground walls date only to the late Middle Ages; excavations of the ancient walls below today's street level have demonstrated that the present site of the church would have been outside the city in Jesus' day. This in fact 'was the usual site for public executions, especially important in a Jewish setting so that the sacred city would not be profaned by the presence of a dead body' (Senior 1991: 103).

365] The most helpful and detailed study of the practice remains Hengel 1977.

366] For the fullest and most accurate discussion of the titulus, see Bammel (1984b).

All four Gospels agree that the soldiers cast lots for Jesus' clothing (Mark 15:24 pars.). Nothing in the chronological indicators of any of the accounts enables us to locate this event at one precise moment during the crucifixion, so one can scarcely speak of contradiction here. Only John sees a fulfilment of Scripture (vv. 23–24), suggesting that it was not the Old Testament that inspired the Gospel writers to invent details of Christ's passion narrative but rather the Gospel writers in different ways looking back on the events of the passion and finding Old Testament parallels in various places. Here Psalm 22:18 is interpreted typologically; this psalm appears repeatedly in the passion narratives, suggesting it may have formed part of an early Christian testimonium (a chain of key Old Testament fulfilment quotations; cf. Bruce 1983: 369). 'The clothes of an executed criminal were a recognized perquisite of the executioners' (Barrrett 1978: 550). The outer garments may have included a belt, sandals, robe and head covering (Carson 1991: 612). Despite centuries of allegorical inter-pretation of the seamless robe as a symbol for the unity of the church, John makes nothing of this detail and neither should we (Moo 1983: 255–256).[367] Specifically, John introduces two separate garments where the Old Testament speaks only of clothing in general and says nothing about a seamless robe. An inventor of fiction would probably have made the 'prophecy' and its fulfilment correspond more exactly (Bruce 1983: 370).

All four Gospels agree that several women watched the crucifixion from a certain distance (Mark 15:40–41 pars.). John's women are 'near the cross' (v. 25a), at least near enough for Jesus to speak to them. One can readily imagine them approaching cautiously at first and coming closer only after a time (Blinzler 1959: 256–257), or standing nearby at first and then moving away as death approached (R. E. Brown 1970: 904). That we are not given enough information to choose between these equally plausible alternatives means that we have no right to speak of John contradicting the Synoptics at this point. The names of the women vary from Gospel to Gospel (in John, see 19:25b), but it is quite possible that Mary (the mother of Jesus), another Mary (wife of Clopas and mother of James the younger and Joseph), Salome (wife of Zebedee, mother of James and John, and sister to Mary the mother of Jesus), and Mary Magdalene were all present (cf. Bruce 1983: 371).[368] Nothing compels us to adopt this harmonization, but neither does any part of it seem improbable.

367] Cf. Ridderbos (1997: 610, n. 136): 'This detail seems to have no other significance than to explain what was done with one specific garment, which was clearly distinguished from the "division" of the rest of Jesus' clothes.'

368] Morris (1995: 717) plausibly suggests that the reason Salome is not named is because

Verses 26–27 are unique to John's Gospel. Ethelbert Stauffer (1960b: 136–138) finds precedent for this 'testamentary disposition' from the cross. At the very least, 'the language is that of binding agreements' (Talbert 1992: 244), as in Tobit 7:11–12, in which Tobias is given Sara as his wife with the words 'You are her relative and she is yours.'[369] If Joseph, Jesus' adoptive father, has passed away by this time, as the silence about him in all the Gospels during Jesus' adult ministry suggests, Jesus would surely need to see that his mother Mary would be adequately cared for by a male head of household in the patriarchal culture of first-century Israel. If his biological siblings had not yet come to faith,[370] it would be only natural for him to choose his most beloved disciple, himself a nephew of Mary, to care for his mother. Later church tradition believed that John and Mary did remain together, even during his much later ministry in Ephesus, but whether this is simply surmised from this passage or derived from independent evidence is impossible to determine (R. E. Brown et al. 1978: 266). Barrett (1978: 551) thinks any conversation between Jesus and his friends from the cross is improbable because Josephus (*Life* 420–421) 'shows both that there was a real danger of continued rebellious action, and that permission would be needed to approach the crosses'. Actually, the text of Jospehus makes neither claim, describing merely how Josephus later saw many captives crucified, including three former acquaintances and told the Roman general, Titus, about them. Titus then ordered the three removed from the cross and attempted to save their lives but two nevertheless died. Carson (1991: 615–616) comments that,

> apart from the fact that four Roman auxiliaries were unlikely to be terrified by a few women in deep mourning, the Roman authorities, if we are to judge by Pilate, were well aware that neither Jesus nor his disciples posed much of a threat. More important, the 'notice' (v. 19) was meant to be read. If people could be close enough to the cross to read a sign, close enough (according to all four Gospels) to hear some of Jesus' utterances, it is difficult to see why vv. 25–27 should be assessed so negatively.

John never names himself or his brother or any of his family. 'It would be quite in keeping that he should not name his mother.'

369] On possible additional Johannine symbolism in the interchange, see Zumstein 1997.

370] The scepticism described in John 7:3–5 has dissipated in Acts 1:14, but it may have taken a special resurrection appearance from Jesus (1 Cor. 15:7) to bring about the change of heart.

Verse 28 presents the typological fulfilment of a second Hebrew Scripture (either Ps. 22:15 or 69:21). Again neither passage is specific enough to have generated John's narrative; instead, once the event is firmly planted in the early Christian tradition, the Evangelist can comb the Scriptures looking for a conceptual parallel (Moo 1983: 278). The Synoptics, too, record a final offer of vinegar to Jesus (Mark 15:36 pars.), though without recording Jesus' words 'I am thirsty.' Obviously, he would have thirsted, and this time the offer of a drink, 'far from dulling the senses, may be intended to preserve or revive full consciousness' (Bruce 1983: 373).[371] John clarifies the reason for the offer of a drink, while in Mark and Matthew Jesus has most recently just been misinterpreted as calling for Elijah (Mark 15:35 par.). Much ink has been spilled debating whether anything legitimately called 'hyssop' (v. 29) could have been long and strong enough to hold a drink that could be extended to Jesus on the cross.[372] The short answer is that there was such a plant, though reconstructions vary somewhat (see esp. Beetham and Beetham 1993; cf. Kiehl 1990: 137; Carson 1991: 621; Morris 1995: 719–720, n. 75).

Verse 30 states that Jesus 'received the drink', but this language is sufficiently vague (as are the synoptic parallels) either to allow for Jesus merely to have put his lips to the sponge or for him actually to have swallowed a little.[373] Only in John does Jesus then say, 'It is finished.' Like his cry of thirst, the statement is patently true at a literal level, though John, like later Christian readers, doubtless saw theological significance as well. Interestingly, 'I am thirsty' comes at roughly the same juncture as the synoptic cry of divine abandonment; Jesus would obviously have been spiritually thirsty at this awful moment. 'It is finished' can then just as easily be taken to have a double meaning as well – as a statement of the completion of Christ's atoning work, just prior to his expiry (and his final word from the cross; Luke 23:46).[374]

371] Commentators, however, are divided over this issue. Bampfylde (1969: 248–249) reflects the opposite conviction that the drink would have helped to put Jesus out of his misery by bringing on a loss of consciousness.

372] The debate raged in antiquity, too, even affecting one late textual variant that substituted for 'hyssop' the quite similar Greek word for 'javelin'!

373] It is the earlier offer of wine mixed with myrrh (or gall) that the Synoptics more clearly state Jesus did not accept (Mark 15:23 par.).

374] On the theology of this passage, see esp. Witkamp 1996; on John's literary artistry, esp. with respect to irony, see Brawley 1993. Regarding the famous *tetelestai*, Bergmeier (1988: 289) translates, 'es ist verwirklicht' ('it is realized' or, in Elizabethan English, 'it has come to pass').

CONFIRMATION OF DEATH AND BURIAL (19:31–42)

This segment contains two parts, the first stressing that Jesus really did die (vv. 31–37); the second, that he was buried in an identifiable tomb (vv. 38–42). The first pericope is largely unparalleled, while the second contains new information with respect to Nicodemus not found in the synoptic accounts (which refer only to Joseph of Arimathea). Apart from names, the only significant verbatim parallelism comes with the expression 'the body of Jesus' (John 19:38 pars.), scarcely sufficient to demonstrate literary dependence (cf. further Dodd 1963: 137–139). As for historicity, even Casey (1996: 190–192) can object to these two accounts solely on the grounds that significant portions do not appear in the Synoptics.[375] In fact, there is considerable evidence for their historical reliability.

John again explains that it was 'the day of Preparation' (Gk. *paraskeuē*; v. 31a) and then specifies that the next day was to be 'a special Sabbath', that is, the Sabbath during Passover week, which was thus doubly sacred. This reference should put beyond reasonable doubt that *paraskeuē* in 19:14 was referring to the day before the Sabbath and not the day before the start of the Passover festival. The parallel in Mark 15:42 further reinforces this conclusion (cf. esp. Carson 1991: 622; Morris 1995: 684–695; Ridderbos 1997: 618).[376] It is astonishing how many Johannine scholars brush aside these data, having already decided that John must contradict the Synoptics concerning the day of Christ's death. Those who do recognize this tension often then merely conclude that John contradicts himself (e.g. Schnackenburg 1982: 288). But this hypothesis is surely a counsel of despair, requiring us to believe that the final author or redactor could not even remember what he wrote a scant seventeen verses earlier!

Because of the law of Deuteronomy 21:23, the Jewish leaders could not leave Jesus' corpse hanging on the cross overnight (cf. also Josephus, *War* 4.317). Breaking the bones of crucifixion victims (v. 31b) seems to have been in part an act of mercy to speed their deaths (cf. *Gosp. Pet.* 4.14). 'It

---

375] He also complains that more would surely have been made of the *empty tomb* later on if a literal bodily resurrection had occurred (191). But it was precisely the belief in resurrection that made emphasis on the tomb unnecessary. The lack of any repeated visitation or veneration of any tomb in the first decades of Christianity stands out strikingly against the universal practice of ancient Mediterranean cultures and is an argument in favour of Jesus' bodily resurrection.

376] In n. 3, Carson adds that there was nothing to prohibit the execution from taking place on one of the days of the Passover festival. In fact, *Sanh.* 11.4, citing Deut. 17:13, insists that the execution of a rebellious teacher should take place during one of the three major annual Jewish festivals, as a lesson to the people.

is of interest that the bones of a man crucified in this period, discovered in the area north of Jerusalem, had been broken; one leg was simply fractured, the other was smashed to pieces' (Beasley-Murray 1987: 354; cf. J. A. T. Robinson 1985: 279–280). So the legs of the men crucified with Christ are broken (v. 32), but when the soldiers come to Jesus they find that he is already dead (v. 33), as Mark 15:44 confirms. The unusual speed of his death is almost certainly related to the severe flogging he had previously received (19:1). So, instead of breaking his legs, one of the soldiers thrusts a spear into his side (v. 34).[377] In a world without modern medical techniques for determining the exact moment of death, this may have been the easiest way to ensure Jesus had no spark of life left in him as the authorities prepared to take his body off the cross (Bruce 1983: 375; Beasley-Murray 1987: 354). Commentators and physicians alike have debated the medical significance of the outflow of water and blood.[378] What first-century readers would have recognized was John's emphasis on the complete and genuine death of Jesus. Whatever anti-docetic strains John's Gospel contains overall, here appears a climactic presentation of Jesus' full humanity (Talbert 1992: 245, with references; cf. Bruce 1983: 376).

We should not be surprised, therefore, that John takes this occasion to insert another of his 'anonymous disciple' references, attesting that this account is based on eyewitness testimony that is utterly factual (v. 35). That an author could refer to himself with the demonstrative pronoun *ekeinos* (lit. 'that one'; NIV 'he') is demonstrated by Josephus in *War* 3.202. Despite the obvious theology of this episode, it is difficult to square this asseveration of truth with theories that find John inventing incidents that never happened (so also R. E. Brown 1970: 948; Legasse 1997: 97). In the words of Byrskog (2000: 236), 'This is an event presented at a historical distance and open for everyone who attended the event to observe. The episode is part of the history of the past. Hence, faith and truth are not swallowed up entirely by the present dimension of the story; rather, truth finds its basis in the concrete observation of a past event, and faith is

---

377] Michaels (1967) speculates that this soldier may have been the centurion of Mark 15:39 pars., whose confession of Jesus' divine sonship could have had this additional foundation. But we have no way of knowing this.

378] For a survey of the options, see Beasley-Murray 1987: 355–358. One of the best appears in the study by the doctor-turned-theologian, John Wilkinson (1975), who concludes that the blood is from Jesus' heart, the water from the surrounding pericardial sac, and that this combination is exactly what one should expect from a victim who had expired only minutes earlier.

aroused in relation to that truth.' Whitacre (1999: 467) adds that, unlike other narrative asides in John, 19:35 'reads very much like the testimony of the later disciples at the end of the Gospel' and may have been added 'by John's disciples to underscore his witness to the death of Jesus'.

To be sure, verses 36–37 proceed to find typological fulfilment of Scripture in the fact that Jesus' bones were not broken and in the piercing of his side. But it is difficult to find one passage that matches the 'quotation' in verse 36; suggestions commonly focus on Exodus 12:46, Numbers 9:12 and Psalm 34:20. If John were inventing 'history' to correspond to a specific Hebrew Scripture, he could have done so far more clearly (cf. Moo 1983: 278). Verse 37 finds a much closer counterpart in Zechariah 12:10, but its use in a completely different context in Matthew (Matt. 24:30) also suggests a traditional origin.[379] And the theological heart of this 'fulfilment' is the outflow of water and blood, which has nothing corresponding to it in the Zechariah quotation (cf. Moo 1983: 214).[380]

With verses 38–42 we resume contact with events also narrated in the Synoptics (cf. Mark 15:42–47 pars.). The account of Jesus' burial continues John's anti-docetic motif. But the introduction of Joseph of Arimathea and the specifics of Jesus' entombment seem theologically unmotivated. Joseph does not become the object of extensive later Christian hagiography. We are not even sure where Arimathea was located, although the best guess may be the Judean village formerly known as Ramathaim-Zophim (1 Sam 1:1; cf. Bruce 1983: 378). Dominic Crossan (e.g. 1991: 391–394) stands among a small minority of contemporary commentators in disputing the essential authenticity of this account; his arguments have been adequately refuted by O'Collins and Kendall (1994).[381] As so often elsewhere, John introduces this man without the kind

---

379] Scholars have often found evidence for one or both of these verses being part of an early Christian testimonium (see esp. Dodd 1963: 42–45; cf. Menken 1993).

380] For the possible theological significance of Jesus' bones not being broken, see esp. B. W. Longenecker 1995. On the key theological emphases of all of vv. 17–37, cf. Minear 1983a.

381] In Blomberg 1998: 100 and n. 4, I mistakenly attributed Crossan's position to O'Collins and Kendall through an unfortunate misreading of my handwritten notes. Crossan (1998: 153) used the error to illustrate how 'we biblical scholars make mistakes' just as 'ancient inspired authors also made mistakes'. When I contacted the editor of our book to see if I could correct my mistake for the next printing, he consulted the contributors and informed me that Crossan strenuously objected, because he could then no longer exploit my mistake for the point he wished to argue. Clearly, concerns for scholarly accuracy are at this point being subordinated to other motives. Crossan (1998: 148–155) all but accuses me of a kind of duplicity that refuses to admit that presuppositions

of explanation one would expect if his audience had not already heard of the individual. It is Mark and Luke who tell us that Joseph was on the Sanhedrin; and Matthew, that he was rich. That an observer of the events of Jesus' life and death, even on the Jewish high council, should come to some level of faith is entirely in keeping with the impact all four Evangelists describe Jesus had. That he would guard it carefully would be a practical necessity (v. 38), especially in the light of the crucifixion.

'Bodies of criminals condemned and executed by the Romans were commonly left to the vultures' (Barrett 1978: 559). Philo, however, remarks, 'I have known instances before now of men who had been crucified when this festival and holiday was at hand being taken down and given up by their relations' (*Flacc.* 83). The Mishnah makes provisions for the Jewish court to provide tombs for those whom they execute (*Sanh.* 6.5). Joseph's request of Pilate is therefore credible, especially in the light of the disgrace affixed in Jewish thought to an unburied corpse. Joseph may

> have been aware that he had no right to make the request, since he was unrelated to Jesus. But he was equally aware that none of the brothers of Jesus would have taken this step. His position and wealth naturally will have commended him to Pilate; nevertheless he should have been denied what he asked in view of the nature of Jesus' offense against Caesar. That Pilate acceded to it is in line with John's whole account of the trial of Jesus. Pilate knew well that the charge against Jesus was unfounded, and so he released the body to Joseph. (Beasley-Murray 1987: 358)

Carson (1991: 629) concurs and adds that Pilate's granting Joseph's request 'may have been a final snub against the Jewish authorities'.

For the third and final time in John, and only in John, Nicodemus now appears (v. 39a). Accompanying Joseph, he brings an enormous amount of spices, fit for a royal burial (vv. 39b–40a). And that may have been their exact intention. Josephus (*Ant.* 17.199) describes five hundred servants carrying spices to anoint the body of Herod the Great upon his death. The

---

concerning the nature of Scripture prevent me from ever labelling any biblical passage as unhistorical (but see my comments above, pp. 66–67; and cf. Blomberg 1984: 433–434 for precisely the kind of counter-example Crossan requests). Crossan therefore doubts if any dialogue with people like me is useful (255). Contra Crossan's suggestions (1995) that the major contours of all four Gospel passion narratives stem from later stages of redaction altering the earliest account (found in the *Gospel of Peter*) and from the 'historicization' of Old Testament prophecy, see esp. Evans 1996.

wealth of the ben Gurion family (see above, p. 92) would certainly have allowed Nicodemus to buy this 75lb assortment of items. Nicodemus, however, probably still does not understand Jesus' true identity; one expecting a resurrection would not be this concerned about a corpse (see esp. Sylva 1988)! Once again, John is not reading back later Christian faith into his pre-Easter narrative.

John's description of Jesus' burial involves additional cloths besides the shroud (v. 40b) in which the body would be wrapped (which is all that the Synoptics mention – Mark 15:46 pars.). The plural may simply be generalizing (cf. R. E. Brown 1970: 942) but it may have a facecloth in mind as well (recall John 11:44 and cf. 20:7). 'What is stressed is that this tomb had never been used by anyone' (v. 41). 'Thus there was no excuse for mistaking it for someone else's tomb, nor was it likely that anyone would visit this tomb by accident' (Witherington 1995: 313). Verse 42 once again makes it clear that it was Friday (Gk. *paraskeuē*), the day before the Sabbath, so that the burial had to proceed quickly before the new day began at dusk when Jews had to rest from work. That Joseph's tomb was near the site of the crucifixion helped matters considerably. [382]

RESURRECTION AND APPEARANCE TO MARY MAGDALENE (20:1–18)

The resurrection is the greatest and most significant of all of the miracles attributed to Jesus. It also causes acute problems for the historian. All of the scientific, philosophical and history-of-religions issues encountered in the assessment of miracle stories in general come back into play here with renewed intensity. If one follows Gerd Lüdemann's candid starting point (1995), that revivification of a dead corpse to unending new life cannot occur under any circumstance, then one rules out in advance the historic Christian explanation of the resurrection narratives. Many argue that the historian simply cannot pass judgment on a resurrection claim, but this, too, masks ideological commitments, most notably the Humean notion that no amount of evidence for a miracle could ever be greater than the evidence against it, a view that has been frequently debunked in the history of philosophy (see esp. C. Brown 1984: 79–100). It lies beyond the scope of this volume to go into these questions further (but see Blomberg 1987: 100–110; 1997: 351–354; and the literature on the resurrection cited in both).[383] As throughout the book, our task is the narrower one of seeing if

---

382] The location of the tomb will most probably have been in the vicinity of what is today the Church of the Holy Sepulchre. See esp. Taylor 1998.

383] To which should be added esp. Davis, Kendall and O'Collins 1997.

the text of John coheres with an early first-century Palestinian Jewish setting and if it meshes with or contradicts the synoptic narratives.

Without question, the four Gospel accounts of the resurrection pose problems for would-be harmonizers. Yet it is by no means as self-evident as many critics suggest that a plausible reconciliation of the Gospel parallels is impossible to achieve. John Wenham devotes his entire book *Easter Enigma: Are the Resurrection Accounts in Conflict?* (1984) to the question and lays out a credible synthesis of the data. A listing of a possible sequence of events that harmoniously takes into account all of the information in the Gospels appears in books by George Ladd (1975: 91–93) and Murray Harris (1983: 69–71); compare already Westcott 1908: 335–336. The fullest defence of the historicity of all four resurrection narratives together is found in the work of William Craig (see esp. 1989). One could, in fact, argue that later fabrications would have tried to avoid the appearance of minor inconsistency further. Even John's Gospel reflects sober restraint in comparison with a later apocryphal work like the *Gospel of Peter*. And the earliest Jewish and pagan critics of the resurrection understood the Gospel writers to be making historical claims, not writing myth or legend. They merely disputed the plausibility of those claims (cf. esp. Dudrey 2000). I shall comment here only on those items that affect the account in the Gospel of John.

Once again, we find John roughly paralleling the synoptic sequence of events but with very few signs of literary dependence and with unique features outweighing duplicated ones (see esp. Dodd 1963: 142, 147–148; contra Neirynck 1984). John 20:1–18 has spawned numerous compositional hypotheses, most of which envision more disunity than is present (see the survey in G. R. Osborne 1984: 207–208; cf. Michaels 1983: 326–327 for a probable chiasmus in vv. 1–8). There is one place where John and Luke prove strikingly parallel (John 20:3, 5 and Luke 24:12), suggesting to some scholars the use of a common tradition unique to these two evangelists (e.g. Lindars 1961). But a handful of important textual witnesses omits Luke 24:12, so it is not entirely clear that this verse would have been in Luke's autograph (cf. Curtis 1971; Mahoney 1974: 41–69).

All four Evangelists agree that a group of women set out for Jesus' tomb early on the Sunday morning after the Friday on which he was crucified. John mentions only Mary Magdalene by name (20:1), but her first-person plural language in verse 2 is best taken as her speaking for more than one person: 'we don't know where they have put him'. For safety reasons alone, it is historically improbable that a single woman would have gone out by herself at this time of day to a graveyard in the environs of Jerusalem (Morris 1995: 734; cf. Bruce 1983: 384). An inventor of fiction, trying to commend belief in Jesus' resurrection, would be unlikely to have created women as the first witnesses, much less have focused almost exclusively on one who was formerly demon-possessed (Luke 8:2) and who could therefore be considered out of her mind when she first reported such news (see esp. Byrskog 2000: 75–81). A patriarchal culture would not have given her words nearly as much credence as if they had first come from the male apostles; in some Jewish legal contexts, women's testimony was considered inadmissible (*Rosh Ha-Shan.* 1.8).[384] Even developing Christianity muted, though never entirely effaced, the important role Mary is said to have played early on (Setzer 1997).

Where John has Mary setting out 'while it was still dark', Mark 16:2 states that the women were on their way to the tomb 'just after sunrise'. In the first century, this would scarcely have seemed to be the contradiction we moderns make it in our obsession with scientific precision (cf. J. A. T. Robinson 1985: 288). Light dawned slowly every morning, and Mark agrees with John that it was 'early' (Gk. *prōi*). Mark, Luke and John all use the Greek expression *tē mia tōn sabbatōn* (lit. 'on the first of the Sabbaths'), an idiom that the NIV correctly translates as 'on the first day of the week'. The expression may have become fixed in the early Aramaic oral tradition and may have had 'the appearance of a Greek neuter plural' (Morris 1995: 733, n. 7). 'Perhaps the reason for the first day emphasis is that the evangelists all wrote for or as part of communities that worshiped on the first day of the week (Sunday)' (Witherington 1995: 324).

Mary Magdalene appeared first in 19:25 without any introduction; the stone that had sealed the tomb entrance is likewise first mentioned here without further explanation. John may again be assuming his readers' knowledge of the core account of Jesus' resurrection (cf. R. E. Brown 1970: 982; Michaels 1983: 323). Ancient tombs have been discovered in Israel that are comprised of caves, closed off by large boulders rolled down a sloping incline to their entrance. John may be assuming also his readers' knowledge of why Mary and her unnamed companions were coming to the tomb (Mark 16:1 pars.), although John's account is coherent on its own inasmuch as it would have been appropriate for them to go simply to mourn (cf. *Gosp. Pet.* 12.50, 52–54). If she did bring spices to anoint Jesus' body as well, it is probably because she had no knowledge of Nicodemus' earlier provision (recall John 19:30–31).

384] So also Witherington (1995: 329), who adds, 'Christianity already labored under the burden of trying to explain the idea of a crucified Messiah. It is implausible that they made things doubly difficult by conjuring up appearance stories to witnesses that outsiders would be disposed to doubt from the outset.' For the theological significance of Mary Magdalene as a major witness to the resurrection, see esp. O'Collins and Kendall 1987.

It is impossible to be sure whether Mary stayed with her companions on the entire trip to the tomb; it would seem that she may have run ahead, seen the empty tomb, and then run off to tell the apostles (v. 2) before the angels appeared to the other women (Mark 16:3–7 pars.) (for detail, see J. Wenham 1984: 82–83, 86, 90–95). That Mary did return and report to at least some of the disciples coheres with Luke 24:9, in which the larger group tells the men what they encountered. However one solves the problem of the ending of Mark (see Blomberg 1997: 74–75; 355–356), the silence depicted in Mark 16:8 is obviously not the state in which the women remained or they would never have been described as witnesses to the resurrection at all! That they would have assumed at first that the body had been placed somewhere else fits the frequency of grave-robbing in the ancient world (Talbert 1992: 249, with references) and coheres with the oldest known alternate explanation for the resurrection among early sceptics and opponents of Christianity (Matt. 27:62–66; 28:11–15).

Only John includes the episode of Peter and the beloved disciple running off to the tomb (vv. 3–9). Ridderbos (1997: 629–630) remarks that 'this interlude is characteristically graphic (vss. 3–6) and realistically precise (vss. 6–7), as is the case whenever "the disciple whom Jesus loved" is present as a witness',[385] and that 'all this clearly indicates the independent knowledge – knowledge closely associated with the disciple whom Jesus loved (cf. 19:35) – of the author and the presentation and the structure of his narrative'.[386] Luke 24:24 provides independent corroboration of John's account here, citing Cleopas and his unnamed companion on the road to Emmaus explaining to Jesus, still incognito, that 'some of our companions went to the tomb and found it just as the women had said, but him they did not see'. Speculations about 'competition' between Peter and John in early Christianity have run rampant in the light of this passage. Clearly some contrast is implied, but how much 'mirror-reading' we are permitted – inferring circumstances in the Ephesian church at the end of the first

---

385] Whether Luke 24:12 is original or an early scribal tradition, it remains testimony to the fact that Christians early on saw no conflict between referring to Jesus' burial 'cloths' in the plural and to a shroud or 'cloth' in the singular (Luke 23:53). J. A. T. Robinson (1985: 291) describes Luke's and John's *othonia* (linen cloths) as a generic term for everything used to wrap up the corpse.

386] Cf. Dodd's frequently cited remark (1963: 148): 'I cannot for long rid myself of the feeling (it can be no more than a feeling) that this *pericopé* has something indefinably first-hand about it. It stands in any case alone. There is nothing quite like it in the gospels. Is there anything quite like it in all ancient literature?'

century from the details of this narrative – is not entirely clear.[387] Pryor's
conclusions (1992a: 87) seem least exaggerated and therefore most secure.
The beloved disciple 'is a model for all disciples of what the fact must
mean: Jesus is glorified, risen from the dead, and the empty tomb demands
this response of faith'. Again, 'if the BD is the founding father of the
community, then the point becomes obvious: not a denigration of Peter,
for the tradition has Peter as the first disciple to see the risen Lord, but an
elevation of the BD as a man of true spiritual insight and therefore to be
heard, trusted and revered, as well as being a model for all' (cf. also Byrne
1985).

More striking perhaps than the comparison between Peter and John in
verses 3–9 are two other features. First, the two apostles both see the burial
cloths lying neatly with the facecloth 'folded' (NIV) or 'rolled up' (NRSV).
The Greek of verse 7 has suggested to some commentators that somehow
the form of the missing corpse was preserved, which could then readily
account for at least one of the apostles immediately suspecting a
resurrection (see esp. Balagué 1966). But this may be over-interpretation.[388]
Second, whatever one makes of the beloved disciple's belief (v. 8), as
contrasted with Peter's apparent lack of further belief at this stage, verse 9
closes the paragraph with the Fourth Evangelist's aside that neither man yet
understood 'from Scripture that Jesus had to rise from the dead'.
Obviously, if Jesus really did predict his resurrection, as both the Synoptics
and John claim (see above, p. 202), and if John saw the empty tomb and
cared-for graveclothes and 'believed', then the key part of verse 9 will be
that *the scriptural basis* for the resurrection was still unclear (Burge 2000:
554). This fits well with the facts that no Old Testament passage literally
predicts the resurrection of a Messiah, and that the synoptic Jesus during
his resurrection appearances stressed the Christological reinterpretation of

---

387] Kevin Quast's reasonably convincing study (1989) is a detailed, book-length work that
concludes that the Fourth Evangelist is trying to point to both Peter and the beloved
disciple as different but valued paradigms of discipleship in a community more inclined to
denigrate Peter in favour of the beloved disciple.

388] The origin of the mysterious Shroud of Turin, with an image of a crucified man on it,
has still not been satisfactorily explained. But the battery of tests that fragments from the
Shroud were subjected to in 1988 at three different laboratories around the world all
concluded that it was an eleventh- or twelfth-century piece of cloth, much too late to have
had anything to do with the time of Christ. Earlier tests that seemed to point in the
opposite direction (see Blomberg 1987: 107) were apparently flawed; unless new evidence
comes forth, appeal to the Shroud in discussions of the historicity of the resurrection seems
pointless and even counter-productive.

the Hebrew Scriptures (Luke 24:25–27, 44–49). Once again, John is not trying to read later full-orbed Christian faith back into his narrative at a time when it did not yet exist.[389] One recalls the identical phenomenon in 2:22 (cf. esp. Delebecque 1989).

Later that 'Easter' Sunday, Mary makes her way back to the tomb and continues to mourn. Maybe she returned with Peter and John and remained after they left (vv. 10–11). Peering into the dark cave entrance she sees two angels in white (v. 12). It is especially interesting, if John is independent of the Synoptics, that his description should match exactly the most natural harmonization of the accounts in Matthew (one angel – 28:2), Mark (one young man dressed in white – 16:5) and Luke (two men dressed in dazzling apparel – 24:4). Strict, additive harmonization can at times yield a plausible historical solution to apparently discrepant narratives![390]

The angels ask why Mary is crying, to which she replies by restating her fear that the body has been taken away (v. 13). In John's Gospel no-one has yet been described as having seen the resurrected Jesus.[391] As Mary turns around, she sees another person, who repeats and unpacks the angels' question (v. 14). Presumably he looks *less* angelic than the other two individuals, so that she mistakes him for a gardener (recall 19:41).[392] This

---

389] Texts that Christians have seen as typologically foreshadowing resurrection 'on the third day', as in 1 Cor. 15:4, include Hos. 6:2 and Jon. 1:7. For the resurrection of the Messiah, cf. Is. 53:10–12 and Ps. 16:10. But none of these texts means this much in its original context. From this Morris (1995: 737) correctly deduces that 'it was belief in the resurrection that came first. Believers did not manufacture a resurrection to agree with their interpretation of prophecy. They were first convinced that Jesus was risen and in the light of that came to see a fuller meaning in some Old Testament passages.' Cf. also Ridderbos (1997: 631): 'This disciple does not represent true post-Easter discipleship *over against* Peter (the "race" with Peter) but rather acts in conjunction with Peter as a fellow witness of the empty tomb before Jesus has appeared to anyone and before even these two disciples have come to understand that Jesus must arise from the dead.' Again, 'the real resurrection narrative is still to come. In it the first post-Easter testimony is accorded not to the beloved ("ideal") disciple but to Mary Magdalene, while the beloved disciple and Peter were still "at home" (vs. 10).'

390] Taken on its own, John's account finds conceptual parallels in the two angels described in 2 Macc. 3:26 and Acts 1:10. The former are said to be splendidly dressed; the latter, clothed in white.

391] In fact, in *none* of the canonical Gospels is the resurrection itself ever witnessed or described. This contrasts markedly with the fantastic elements of later apocryphal accounts, esp. in the *Gospel of Peter*. Cf. also Witherington 1995: 328.

392] Wyatt (1990) thinks that the theme of the garden is meant to recall the original paradise in Eden, which Jesus' resurrection begins to recreate.

element is not likely to have been invented by later Christians trying to *exalt* Jesus.[393] Jesus addresses her with the same vocative that he used with his mother in 2:4. Perhaps she has not yet looked closely at the speaker, but the Synoptics likewise attest that the resurrected Jesus differed sufficiently in appearance from his pre-Easter state so as not always to be recognizable immediately (see esp. Luke 24:13–35; cf. v. 37 and Matt. 28:17). Still assuming the body has been taken and placed somewhere else, Mary asks where she can find it (v. 15). John's purpose in making so much of Mary's mistaken assumptions may have to do with the same counter-charge Matthew had to refute of the disciples' stealing the body (Matt. 28:13–14; cf. later in Tertullian, *Spect.* 30).

At this point Jesus calls Mary by her name, probably in the original Aramaic equivalent to our 'Miriam'. Something in the form or contents of the address apparently facilitates Mary's recognition of her 'Teacher', which is what she calls Jesus in reply (v. 16). This time John preserves in Greek transliteration the Aramaic, which suggests that it was an important element of the story and a very ancient, probably authentic, detail (cf. R. E. Brown 1970: 990–991). Even here, Mary does not use an exalted Christological title for Jesus, which again supports historicity.

Verse 17 has puzzled readers over the centuries. The literal 'Do not touch me' (Gk. *mē mou haptou*) might better be rendered in this context 'Stop clinging to me' (NASB; cf. Barrett 1978: 565–566). Mary does not recognize that Jesus cannot remain with her permanently in his resurrected body and that he must soon ascend to heaven and return to his Father.[394] The Greek *anabainō*, which the NIV renders 'return', more literally means to 'go up'. Luke is the only Evangelist to narrate the actual ascension tradition (Luke 24:51; Acts 1:9), but John may presuppose knowledge of it here.[395] To describe this intermediate stage between resurrection and ascension cuts against the grain of John's redactional tendency to collapse all of the events from crucifixion to exaltation into the single concepts of 'glorification' and 'lifting up' and suggests that the account reflects a

---

393] Talbert (1992: 251) notes three anti–docetic elements here: (1) the person Mary encounters is the same she saw crucified; (2) he is still corporeal; and (3) the ascension takes place after the resurrection, not before the crucifixion as certain Gnostics asserted.

394] For a punctuation of the verse different from the standard translations, see McGehee 1986.

395] There are also conceptual parallels with Matt. 28:9–10 (cf. Pryor 1992a: 88). D'Angelo (1990) suggests that we are in the thought world of *Apoc. Moses* 31.3–4 here with Jesus wanting to avoid ritual pollution during the period between his resurrection and ascension, but this alleged parallel seems more remote.

genuine historical conversation (cf. Bruce 1983: 383). So, too, Jesus' words 'my Father and your Father' and 'my God and your God' diverge from John's more exalted Christology that probably would not have put Mary and Jesus on this apparently equal footing. Mary therefore leaves (or did Jesus disappear from Mary?) and reports back to the disciples (v. 18), just as the larger group of women does in the Synoptics (Matt. 28:8; Luke 24:9).

JESUS APPEARS TO THE ELEVEN (20:19–29)

Verses 19–23 bring us to 'Easter' Sunday evening, presumably back in Jerusalem. This appearance of the risen Jesus matches the event described in Luke 24:36–43, although again John diverges in many of the details he narrates. There are only two places where verbal parallelism is close enough to suggest literary dependence – in verse 19b in which Jesus stands in the midst of the disciples and says to them, 'Peace be with you!' and in verse 20a when, 'after he said this, he showed them his hands and side'. Curiously, just as in John 20:3, the parallels appear only in Luke and are absent from the Western manuscript tradition of that Gospel. These Western 'non-interpolations', while not on their own garnering enough internal or external support to be labelled original, do suggest some relationship between John and Luke as the early textual tradition developed, bringing the two Gospels closer in line with each other than they may originally have been. Put together, however, the Lukan and Johannine material form a coherent whole (see esp. G. R. Osborne 1984: 246–251).

Only John describes the disciples (presumably the original Twelve minus Judas and Thomas) gathering 'with the doors locked for fear of the Jews' (v. 19a). But this links well with Mark's emphasis on their fright and flight the previous Thursday evening (Mark 14:50–52 pars.). That Jesus' closest followers could be in real danger from the same authorities who had just crucified their leader can scarcely be doubted. The *Gospel of Peter* 7.26 reports a search for the disciples on the grounds that they were evildoers and had tried to burn the temple. The story may be apocryphal, but its author similarly recognized the precarious situation in which the disciples found themselves.

Suddenly, 'Jesus came and stood among them' (v. 19b). The language and context suggest that he simply appeared in their midst rather than coming through an unlocked door. 'John offers no explanation of this power, nor is it possible to supply one; though it is legitimate to compare Paul's doctrine of the spiritual body (1 Cor. 15.44)' (Barrett 1978: 568). Jesus shows the ten his hands and side, in part to prove that it is really he (v. 20). 'Hands' include the wrists in both Greek and Hebrew usage, which is what would have been nailed to the cross (Lindars 1972: 610; cf. v. 25).

Luke 24:40 refers also to nail marks in Jesus' feet, a statement that gained historical support for the first time when an ossuary (bone-box) of a first-century crucified Jew named Johanan was discovered in Palestine in 1968, with a nail still intact that had been driven through his ankle-bones (R. E. Brown 1970: 1022). The account in John 19:31–36 explains the scar in Jesus' side. But we might have expected a glorified body to be free from scars altogether (and indeed after Christ's ascension, it may be), so one could argue that this detail is a pointer to historicity here. Casey (1996: 195–196) objects that the imagery closely parallels that of 2 Baruch 50.2 and 51.1: 'We must infer that Luke 24.39 and John 20.20 are separate attempts to assert that the risen Jesus was identical to the historical Jesus, and that they are not more literally accurate than 2 Baruch.' But most students of ancient Jewish views on resurrection find the perspectives of 2 Baruch even *more* literal (or better put, more akin to resuscitation than resurrection) than the Gospel accounts (most recently, cf. Bauckham 1998d: esp. 91–92)! And given John's anti-docetic emphases, it is unlikely that his description here involves a body that is less than fully human, even if resurrection indicates a radically transformed humanity.

Twice Jesus uses the standard Jewish greeting of *šâlôm* to pronounce 'peace' on the disciples (vv. 19, 21). Then he proceeds to commission the ten: 'As the Father has sent me, I am sending you.' This formula is thoroughly Johannine, summarizing the relationships between Father and Son, and between Jesus and his disciples, stressed throughout the Gospel. But we have also seen that this *šālîah* (sending) motif is traditional in origin and likely authentic (Witherington 1995). Verses 22–23a have generated enormous amounts of commentary as Jesus breathes on the disciples and charges them to 'Receive the Holy Spirit.' Many critical scholars find this a radically transformed Johannine equivalent of Pentecost (Acts 2). At the opposite end of the spectrum are those who believe Jesus' behaviour to be exclusively symbolic and foreshadowing the later bestowal of the Spirit (see esp. Carson 1991: 649–655). An intermediate option seems best. On the one hand, this passage forms the climax of John's recurring motif of the Holy Spirit; no other passage within his Gospel so qualifies as the fulfilment of all of Jesus' prior predictions about the Paraclete's coming ministry (chs. 14 – 16). On the other hand, Thomas is not present on this occasion, yet John would surely agree that he, too, was subsequently endowed with the Spirit. And chapter 21, even if a later addition (on which see below, pp. 272–273), shows that the final editor of the Gospel did not see the disciples as yet ready for the mission they would soon undertake. John undoubtedly knows the traditions of Christ's ascension and outpouring of the Spirit fifty days after the resurrection (Acts 1 – 2) and can assume his audience knows the basic storyline, too.

It seems, therefore, that John and Luke are describing separate events, both equally real and significant. As I have phrased it elsewhere,

> The resurrection of Jesus was the climactic vindication of his sinless life and unjust death, yet his ascension to the right hand of the Father was needed to complete the process and to make public to the universe his triumph and sovereignty. So also Jesus' breathing out the Spirit gave the disciples the authority to lead the company of his followers, even though the full, public and permanent manifestation of this gift would arrive only at Pentecost. To put it almost simplistically, in John 20 the disciples receive the Spirit; in Acts 2 they are filled with the Spirit, who empowers them to preach the gospel boldly. (Blomberg 1987: 168)[396]

Once again, evidence of Johannine redaction (Swetnam 1993) combines with distinctive features that suggest a traditional origin (Wojciechowski 1987). John can put into his own words concepts that Jesus genuinely articulated and descriptions of activities that he truly undertook.

Verse 23b draws on Isaiah 22:22 and closely resembles the structure and content of Jesus' promises to Peter in Matthew 16:19b and to the Twelve in Matthew 18:18. Indeed, this text in John helps make sense of at least part of what Jesus had in mind with his promises about binding and loosing in the Matthean passages.[397] Jesus' breathing on the disciples is probably meant to call to mind the creation narratives (the identical verb is used in Gen. 2:7 LXX) and later Jewish commentary on them. 'That John intended to depict an event of significance parallel to that of the first creation of man cannot be doubted; this was the beginning of the new creation' (Barrett 1978: 570). The role of the apostles in the early chapters of Acts, preaching and keeping an eye on the spread of the gospel to new cultural areas, probably comprises a large part of the fulfilment of Jesus' words here.

Verse 24 sets the stage for the next resurrection appearance. John explains that Thomas was not present with this initial gathering on the Sunday evening of the resurrection. As in 11:16 and 21:2 he is also called by his 'nickname', Didymus, meaning the 'twin'. As with Judas earlier

---

396] Cf. Bruce 1983: 397, n. 18; Michaels 1983: 335; Hatina (1993), responding to Carson; and van Rossum (1991), showing significant patristic support for this interpretation.

397] In fact, the emphases of John and Matthew belong together as two parts of a larger whole, as stressed by Hansen 1997.

(6:71), John specifies that Thomas was 'one of the Twelve', perhaps again to heighten the ignominy of his reaction. His scepticism in verse 25 fits what little we can deduce from his previous comments in this Gospel: 'a man who is not afraid to bluntly contradict Jesus (Jn. 14:5) and who has a touch of cynicism (Jn. 11:16)' (Craig 1989: 279). Against those who think John has created verse 25 on the basis of Psalm 22:16, Moo (1983: 283–284) observes that Thomas speaks only of Jesus' wounded hands and not also of his feet.

A week later the eight-day festival of the Unleavened Bread would just have concluded and the disciples would be preparing to return to Galilee (v. 26; cf. Moule 1957; Bruce 1983: 393). Once again, John (unwittingly?) harmonizes an oft-cited tension within the Synoptics: Matthew and Mark refer only to appearances in Galilee; Luke, only to those in and around Jerusalem. John recognizes both (see ch. 21) and arranges them in a plausible sequence. At this juncture Jesus appears as before and offers the identical greeting. But since Thomas is now present, Jesus invites him to reach out and touch him and confirm for himself that Jesus is truly raised from the dead (v. 27).

Thomas' reply forms the Christological climax of the entire Gospel of John as he exclaims, 'My Lord and my God!'(v. 28).[398] By the end of the first century, Christians may be hearing ontological overtones in this confession. Not surprisingly, Casey (1996: 197) finds here the final clinching sign that John flatly contradicts on a large scale the Jewish identity of Jesus of Nazareth. But, in fact, while the combination of titles mirrors Graeco-Roman parallels, most notably the way Domitian wanted people to refer to him in the 90s (Barrett 1978: 572), it is equally conceivable as a Jewish equivalent to Israel's confession, 'O Yahweh our God' (Pryor 1992a: 90). The ascription of these two titles to Jesus clearly expands on classic Jewish monotheism, but we have already noted that the works of Hurtado have demonstrated partial precedents for this expansion, while Bauckham has highlighted the evidence for this development in the earliest stages of Jewish Christianity (see above, p. 73).[399] Schnackenburg

---

398] Bruce (1983: 393) sees here the climactic corroboration of John 1:1, 'The Word was God', analogous to the role played by the centurion's confession in Mark's Gospel, 'Surely this man was the Son of God' (Mark 15:39).

399] Cf. also Witherington (1995: 344): 'The context shows that this confession does not mean Jesus is the Father, and so we are witnessing here an example of the early Christian expansion of what the concept of monotheism amounted to, namely, that it involved more than one person in the Godhead. That this confession is made without strain in this Gospel is partly due to the fact that throughout Jesus is portrayed as God's divine Wisdom.'

(1982: 333) captures the correct balance: 'It is necessary, in this confession of Jesus' divinity on the lips of Thomas, to guard against both a watering down and a dogmatic fixation.' This text clearly corresponds for the evangelist to 1:1. Yet Thomas does not say, 'You are God', but only calls out to Jesus in the confession 'My God'. Schnackenburg continues:

> The evangelist is not yet thinking from the point of view of the teaching of the two natures, he combines the Godhead of Jesus with the revelatory and saving function of the Son: he is the *Messiah*, the Son of God, that is, he is the Messiah to the extent that he is the Son of God, and the Son of God in his messianic ministry. This functional understanding can be found expressed likewise in the personal confession formula: '*My* Lord and *my* God'.

What is more, if ever there is a time in the Gospels for a relatively clear ascription of deity to Jesus, surely it is precisely in this kind of context, *after* the resurrection.

That John is not inventing out of whole cloth seems confirmed by the response attributed to Jesus in verse 29, by no means unilaterally praising Thomas. Instead, in the beatitude form well known from the Sermon on the Mount/Plain,[400] Jesus blesses the greater faith of those who believe without having the kind of proof Thomas required. Thomas has proved exemplary for John's major emphasis with respect to miracles: they should provoke belief. Verses 30–31 will restate precisely this. But another side to John's presentation can be more readily rooted in the teaching of the historical Jesus: signs do not convince everyone and they shouldn't be necessary (recall above, p. 87). On the episode with Thomas overall, Carson (1991: 657–658) correctly queries:

> Are we to think that the church made up a story that pictures one of the Twelve as incredulous to the point of unreasonable obstinacy (v. 25), and that reports the Lord's public reproof of that apostle (vv. 27, 29)? Even if the narrative has an apologetic purpose, that is scant reason for assessing it as unhistorical: it is surely as justifiable to conclude that the account was chosen precisely because it was so suitable. At least one part of the story (v. 25) finds parallel elsewhere (Lk. 24:39); and the portrait of Thomas is in thorough agreement with what we learn of him from 11:16 and 14:5. The speed with which Thomas' pessimistic unbelief was transformed into joyful

---

400] Even closer parallels of form *and content* appear in Luke 10:23 and Matt. 13:16.

faith is surely consistent with the experience of the other witnesses (*e.g.* vv. 16, 20).[401]

It is important to stress at this juncture, too, that belief in Christ's bodily resurrection is attested at an extraordinarily early date in Christian history. It is one of the items Paul declares was passed on to him by Christian tradition, probably at the very outset of his Christian experience in about AD 32 (see 1 Cor. 15:1–8, complete with an itemization of various appearances). Even Lüdemann (1995: 15) admits this much. Morris (1995: 751) pushes the logic further:

> Some writers almost give the impression that at first there was no thought of a resurrection, but that bit by bit the apostles became familiar with this thought. Eventually they built up more and more circumstantial tales until the whole church was convinced. The church at first had no idea of a resurrection. That is plain enough. But there was no gradual acceptance of the idea with more and more 'appearances' being manufactured. The plain fact is that all told we read of five appearances on the one day (to Mary Magdalene, to the women, to the two on the way to Emmaus, to Peter, and to the ten). Then there are five more spread out over forty days, and after that no more with the exception of the appearance to Saul of Tarsus. This is no gradual building up of 'appearances' but rather the reverse. They were progressively restricted, not built up. Moreover, as Thomas makes abundantly clear, the appearances were not at first welcomed. They were resisted as idle talk, and those who had not actually seen Jesus for themselves refused point blank to accept the stories. Only the plainest of evidence could have convinced a skeptic like Thomas. But convinced he was, which shows us that the evidence was incontrovertible.

Morris's language may be overstated in places; certain people do believe incredible things. And the sequence in which the resurrection accounts arose need not correspond to the sequence in which they are narrated (though this kind of mirror-reading is precisely what drives a large percentage of the hypotheses of those who find the Gospel more reflective of end-of-the-first-century realities than of the historical Jesus). But Morris's basic argument seems persuasive.

401] One of the best discussions of the theology of this chapter and the rise of Easter faith is de la Potterie 1984. For the unified structure of the chapter, see D. A. Lee 1995.

Equally important in this context is the study by Ladd (1975: 93), who itemizes seven points on which the Gospels show no disagreement, all of which support the historical credibility of the resurrection: (1) Jesus is truly dead and buried. (2) The disciples were not prepared for his death and are overcome with confusion. (3) The tomb is found on Easter morning to be empty. (4) The empty tomb itself is not a proof of the resurrection, for it can be argued that the body has been stolen or placed elsewhere. (5) The disciples had certain experiences that they took to be appearances of Jesus bodily risen from the dead. (6) Contemporary Judaism had no concept of a dying and rising Messiah. Finally, (7) the disciples proclaimed the resurrection of Jesus in Jerusalem near where he had been buried.

THE PURPOSE OF THE GOSPEL (20:30-31)

Verses 30–31 bring John 20 to a close, and most readers have sensed they could form an appropriate ending to the Gospel overall. Here is Johannine theology pure and simple, in an unequivocal statement of a central purpose of the book: to foster faith in Jesus as the Messiah and divine Son, which leads to eternal life. These verses also explain that John's purpose served as a criterion for the selection out of a larger body of material of what he chose to include. It is possible to take the reference to 'miraculous signs' in verse 30 as referring only to the resurrection appearances just narrated (Michaels 1983: 333) but, given John's use of this expression throughout his Gospel, it is more natural to see the signs as referring to all of Jesus' words and works previously narrated (Roberts 1987). At the same time, we shall note below (p. 271) reasons for taking chapter 21 as an integral part of the original Gospel. In that light, parallels elsewhere in the Johannine literature, which demonstrate that purpose statements could be placed prior to the complete end of a particular document or section (John 12:36b–37; 1 John 5:13; Rev. 22:5), suggest that 20:30–31 need not represent where John had initially planned to stop (Talbert 1992: 258).

These verses raise the further, fairly pointed question of whether the Fourth Evangelist could have believed that substantially mythical or legendary accounts of Jesus' life could create or nurture Christian faith.[402] This is a different question from a broader one often raised: can unhistorical accounts narrated in a historical form communicate theological truths? Of course they can, as Jesus' parables demonstrate, and there is nothing *in principle* that would prevent us from saying the same thing about an entire Gospel. Rather, the narrower question here is whether

---

402] On the translation and interpretation of 'believe', affected also by the textual variants for v. 31, see above (p. 62).

unhistorical stories about a figure that both author and audience knew was a real man from the not-too-distant past could be invented and function to bring to Christian faith persons who did not previously have it (or to increase confidence in Christ among those who already demonstrated some faith). Certainly, if readers did not know the events were unhistorical, they might unwittingly believe, but this conclusion would make the Gospel deceptive. It is not nearly as obvious that the conscious creation (and reception) of myth or legend attributed to the historical Jesus would cause anyone at the end of the first century to grow in Christian conviction, especially as the hostility, ostracism, and even martyrdom facing Christians was at that time substantially increasing as well (cf. esp. Bruce 1980: 18).

FISHING IN GALILEE (21:1–14)

It has become common among modern scholars to speak of John 21 as an appendix added by a different author or editor than the person responsible for the bulk of the rest of the Gospel (e.g. Barrett 1978: 576; cf. even Witherington 1995: 352). Some would go so far as to pit the message of this chapter against the rest of the volume (e.g. W. Braun 1990). John Breck (1992) identifies and responds to seven major arguments supporting this hypothesis: (1) John 20:30–31 reads like the true ending to the Gospel. (2) Chapter 21 does not demonstrate the disciples undertaking the mission for which Jesus' actions in John 20 prepared them. (3) The emphasis in chapter 21 is on seeing and believing, whereas in chapter 20 it was on not seeing but still believing. (4) The 'we' of 21:24 demonstrates redaction by the larger Johannine community. (5) John 21 is ecclesiological whereas chapters 1 – 20 are Christological. (6) John 21 develops themes found only in earlier interpolations into the Gospel, especially in chapters 5 – 6. (7) The vocabulary and style of this final chapter differ significantly from that of the rest of the Gospel.

On the other hand, regarding (1), we have already observed a Johannine tendency to include purpose statements followed by epilogues (above, p. 271; cf. further Schenk 1992). Argument (2) is not nearly as much of a problem on the view that chapter 20 is intentionally narrating something only preliminary to Pentecost. Points (3) and (5) are probably false disjunctions. Item (4) indeed demonstrates editorial work, but it may involve either more or less redaction than simply chapter 21 as a discrete unit (recall above, pp. 38–39). Argument (6) depends on acknowledging earlier interpolations, a trend that is quickly and rightly dying off in Johannine research. Finally, de Solages and Vacherot (1979) have intensely scrutinized the style and vocabulary of chapter 21 – item (7), some of which are dictated by the unique contents of the chapter – and find no statistically significant variation from the language of the previous twenty chapters.

Seven arguments, admittedly of varying strengths, can also be advanced for taking the bulk of chapter 21 as a theological and literary unity with the rest of the Gospel (or at least with 1:19 – 20:31). More specifically, these are elements of the chapter without which one could argue that the Gospel is less complete: (1) Peter's reconciliation with Jesus and recommission; (2) the prediction of the coming fates of Peter and the beloved disciple; (3) a further balancing of the Gospel's dominant realized eschatology with futurist emphases; (4) the reaffirmation of Jesus going ahead of the disciples and providing for them; (5) further clarification of the coming mission of the church; (6) a fully triumphant Jesus; and (7) further clues concerning the identity of the beloved disciple (cf. Carson 1991: 667). In addition, the use of a prologue in 1:1–18 makes the presence of an epilogue (ch. 21) less surprising (see esp. P. F. Ellis 1992). And numerous themes in chapter 21 specifically go back to the start of Jesus' ministry: commissioning the disciples, both named and anonymous; special reference to Nathanael and Cana; ministry in Galilee more generally; and the role of signs (see esp. Franzmann and Klinger 1992). Other features tie in with important themes scattered throughout the Gospel, particularly in the provision of bread and fish in the feeding of the five thousand and in the allusions to Jesus' death in the subsequent bread-of-life discourse (ch. 6; for fuller lists, cf. Minear 1983b with Gaventa 1996). Thus it is not nearly as unusual today as it was a half-century ago to find scholarly support for John 21 as an integral part of the overall Gospel, composed by the same hand that was responsible for the majority of chapters 1 – 20 (cf. further G. R. Osborne 1981).[403]

John 21:1 begins with a narrative introduction to prepare the reader for an additional appearance of Jesus to the disciples in Galilee. Matthew and Mark refer only to appearances by Jesus in Galilee; Luke, only to appearances in and around Jerusalem. John knows accounts of both and puts them in a plausible historical sequence. Indeed, the Markan tradition has the young man in the tomb command the women to tell the disciples that Jesus is going ahead of them to Galilee and will meet them there (Mark 16:7 par.). So we should not be surprised to find them doing precisely that, after the festival of Unleavened Bread has concluded in Jerusalem (cf. Lindars 1972: 619).

In verse 2 John specifies several of the disciples involved. All have appeared by name before in this Gospel, except for 'the sons of Zebedee'.

403] A sizeable majority still dissents, however. Largely presupposing the correctness of the consensus, Spencer (1999) goes on to point our numerous ways ch. 21 nevertheless connects back with and elucidates chs. 1 – 20.

This expression for James and John would have become quickly known in the early church (cf. Mark 1:19 pars.). Particularly if the author of the Fourth Gospel *is* John, he can expect his audience to recognize who these two sons are. Somewhat more puzzling is the reference to two additional unnamed disciples (but recall 1:35).[404] Perhaps they are not named because they are less prominent; in any event they do provide further corroborating testimony to the coming resurrection appearance.

No blame should be laid on Peter for announcing that he was returning to his fishing boats (v. 3a). What else were the disciples to do while they waited for Jesus, who had already demonstrated the ability to 'disappear' for a full week? 'It was better for [Peter] to employ his time usefully than to remain idle' (Bruce 1983: 399). Again we have an example of inter-locking with the Synoptics. John has nowhere previously told us that many of the disciples were former fishermen, but this fact, too, would quickly have circulated within the early church (cf. R. E. Brown 1970: 1069).

The rest of verses 3b–6 closely parallels the miraculous fish catch narrated only in Luke 5:1–11 at the outset of Jesus' ministry. Many scholars believe that the two passages comprise a doublet – alternate accounts of only one, original tradition. Interestingly, even though the account in John is couched as a resurrection appearance, many of these same scholars believe John's version is more original, largely because the disciples do not at first recognize Jesus (v. 4; cf. Sabourin 1977: 136–137; Latourelle 1988: 161–165; Twelftree 1999: 324–335). This overlooks the repeated pattern of Jesus not being immediately recognized in his resurrection appearances, a feature absent from the earlier call narratives. To those who find it unlikely that the disciples should more than once fail to recognize their Lord, Grant Osborne (1984: 258) replies that this 'ignores human fallibility. Peter, who was frustrated after a night of unsuc-cessful fishing, might easily have been so tired and discouraged that he failed to recognize Jesus who had helped the fishermen before.' There are enough differences as well as similarities to suggest that Luke 5 and John 21 narrate completely separate events (cf. also Craig 1989: 286–290).[405] At

---

404] Boismard (1998) thinks that one of these anonymous disciples must be the eyewitness source behind the Fourth Gospel, since the sons of Zebedee are not mentioned in ch. 1. But this assumes that John 1 intends to give a comprehensive list of all disciples present and that only an eyewitness source can account for this material. Neither of these assumptions is at all probable in the light of what we know about the composition of the Gospel more generally.

405] As for the literary question, arguments for John's independence from Luke (see esp. Dodd 1963: 144–145) prove more persuasive than those for dependence (see esp. Neirynck

the same time, we may also assume that John could expect his audience to have heard of the story of the miraculous fish catch early in the disciples' career with Christ. At both the historical and literary levels, then, this account makes good sense as a deliberate 'replay' of the earlier event. The one miracle accompanied the disciples' (and especially Peter's) call; the second will confirm their recall (cf. esp. Wiarda 1992: 71).

Fishermen ancient and modern attest that often the best time to catch fish is at night, but this time the disciples are not so fortunate (v. 3b). Part of the problem in not recognizing Jesus 'early in the morning' (v. 4) could simply have been their distance from shore ('about a hundred yards' – v. 8) and the lack of full daylight. The question Jesus asked could have been posed by any onlooker (v. 5). The vocative plural address, *paidia* (NIV 'friends'), comes from the cognate *pais* ('child' or 'servant'), more common in the Synoptics than in John, but this specific form appears in the New Testament only here and in 1 John 2:14 and 18. That Jesus should ask the disciples if they have anything to eat more closely parallels his question in the resurrection appearance narrated in Luke 24:41 than anything in Luke 5:1–11. That the disciples should obey the command from one they do not yet recognize (v. 6) could be due to the thought 'that a man standing on the shore might detect some indication of fish that was not apparent to them' (Morris 1995: 762).

The huge number of fish suddenly filling their nets would immediately have called to mind Jesus' earlier miraculous provision. Not surprisingly, this is the moment that the beloved disciple exclaims to Peter, 'It is the Lord' (v. 7a). Ever impulsive, Peter immediately jumps into the water and hurries towards the shore (v. 7b). Both disciples' responses – recognition versus action – are in keeping with their characters as depicted throughout the Gospels.[406] The other disciples remain in the boat to guide it to land (v. 8).[407] The charcoal fire they discover Jesus has prepared (v. 9) will remind

---

1990). Significant verbatim parallelism is limited to the words 'fish' and 'nothing'. Significant words in different lexical forms include only 'night', 'nets' and 'a great amount'.

406] The best way to understand Peter's behaviour in v. 7 is to translate, 'he tied something around his robe for he was lightly clad' – i.e. this robe was all he was wearing. *Gymnos* often means 'wearing only an undergarment', not always literally 'naked'. Peter's action was the appropriate way to free up his body for swimming without inappropriately exposing himself. See further Soards 1983: 283–284; and cf. Michaels 1983: 340.

407] Morris (1995: 763) thinks 'we have another example of John's love of precision in the statement that they were about two hundred cubits (i.e., a hundred yards) from the shore'. Burge (2000: 583 and n. 14) notes that the Greek words for 'boat' in vv. 6 and 8 differ from each other and could be taken to refer to two different sizes of boats. 'Recently members of

at least Peter and John of the identical kind of fire in the high priest's courtyard in which Peter three times denied knowing Jesus (18:18). Even more explicit reminders of his denial are soon to come (vv. 15–19). The bread and fish already prepared will call to mind the feeding of the five thousand (6:1–15).[408] Jesus commands his followers to bring him some of their fish, presumably to add to those cooking over the fire (v. 10). Had Jesus initially been preparing only enough for himself to eat? John reports that the catch amounted to 153 fish (v. 11b). Despite numerous attempts to find allegorical significance in the number (all of them relatively far-fetched; see the succinct survey in Carson 1991: 672–673), the best explanation is that the disciples counted them (van der Loos 1965: 677; Ridderbos 1997: 663; Moloney 1998: 550)! Fishermen 'have always loved to preserve the details of unusual catches' (Morris 1995: 764; cf. R. E. Brown 1970: 1076). Likewise, the untorn net (v. 11b) probably does not symbolize the unity of the church. It certainly contrasts with the tearing of the nets in Luke 5:6; perhaps the disciples are meant to recognize a greater empowerment after the resurrection than before. If there is any additional symbolism it may be that 'Jesus can enable the disciple to bring in even a large catch of disciples without losing any' (Witherington 1995: 355; recall 6:39; 10:29).[409]

In verse 12 Jesus simply invites the disciples to eat breakfast with him. The latter half of this verse somewhat enigmatically adds that none of them dared to ask him who he was. There is still something different enough about his resurrected state that confuses them, even though they could not deny that it was Jesus. This kind of touch is not likely to have been added by an author solely intent on inventing details that would convince the unwitting. One thinks again of Matthew 28:17 – 'When they saw him, they worshipped him; but some doubted.' Verse 13 concludes the storyline with the group eating the bread and fish. We may be meant to continue recalling the feeding of the five thousand, but if we are to see specific

---

Kibbutz Ginosar in Galilee found such a first-century fishing boat (now on display at the Beit Yigal Allon Museum, Ginosar), and its size gives some insight. Its length is 26.5 feet and its width 7.5 feet. If this bears any resemblance to Peter's boat, seven men would have filled it – which lends further support to the notion that these men use two vessels.'

408] Derrett (1997) finds significant Old Testament background in the miraculous bread God provided for Elijah, in the provisions for crossing the Jordan in Joshua's day, and in the blessing of Asher (Gen. 49:20). The first of these seems plausible; the second, just possible; and the third, highly improbable.

409] van der Loos (1965: 678) thinks that the only spiritual significance is to be found in the 'superabundant fertility of the disciples' preaching'.

eucharistic significance here, John does not spell it out (and fish as a substitute for wine was a post-first-century development in the early church). John rounds out the narrative by identifying this as the third time Jesus appeared in resurrected form to his disciples (v. 14). He is presumably not counting the appearance to Mary by herself but only the appearances to a group of 'the disciples' (Ridderbos 1997: 664). 'That there was in the Evangelist's mind some evidential value in this episode in support of Jesus' resurrection is confirmed by this verse, which forms a literary *inclusio* with v. 1' (Carson 1991: 674–675). Christology has by no means given way to ecclesiology, although the subordinate point that the disciples 'can do no successful mission work without Jesus' may be present (recall 15:5; cf. Witherington 1995: 355).

THE FUTURE FOR PETER AND JOHN (21:15–23)

Peter three times denied Jesus during the last night of his life (John 18:15–18, 25–27 pars.). Now Jesus will three times repeat a commissioning to reinstate him as the leader of the disciples. Addressing him as 'Simon son of John' (v. 15) echoes the language of his initial call in 1:42. Commentators debate whether Jesus' question 'do you truly love me more than these?' means 'do you love me more than you love the other disciples?' 'do you love me more than you love other things?' or 'do you love me more than the other disciples love me? (cf. G. R. Osborne 1981: 308; Carson 1991: 675–676; Witherington 1995: 356). The last of these options is probably the best (likewise D. M. Smith 1999: 395–396). But the point need not be settled in a study of authenticity. All of the interpretations agree that Jesus is calling on Peter to declare where his ultimate loyalty lies, precisely what was needed from one who had so vehemently denied his Lord. Peter affirms that he does now love Jesus in this way. Jesus responds by charging him to feed his lambs, drawing on the well-known Old Testament metaphor of shepherding a flock for leading God's people (recall under 10:1–18).[410] 1 Peter 5:2 uses this identical metaphor in its charge to Christian elders; is it based on a reminiscence of this exchange between Jesus and Peter? The dialogue continues with two repetitions of the original question and answer, at which point Peter is grieved (vv. 16–17).[411] But

---

410] Talbert (1992: 261) notes an interesting parallel in the later rabbinic compilation *Aboth de Rabbi Nathan* 17: Moses, about to leave the world, appoints Joshua as shepherd of the people of Israel and charges him to feed the flock, quoting Song of Songs 1:8.

411] No material difference exists in this context between the various terms for 'love'; see esp. Carson 1996: 51–53). McKay (1985) thinks he can discern a slightly stronger sense for *agapaō* over against *phileō* in the light of slight distinctions between synonyms elsewhere in

Peter's offence was serious, especially in that he had protested that he was willing to die for Christ (13:37). That is precisely what a good shepherd must be prepared to do for his sheep (10:11, 15), and Jesus must ensure that Peter is serious about his recommitment. One recalls the command by Jesus to Peter on the night of his arrest, unique to Luke's Gospel: 'And when you have turned back, strengthen your brothers' (Luke 22:32b). It is arguable that only a recommissioning of the kind described in John 21 could have strengthened Peter for the fearless preaching and testimony before the Sanhedrin that Acts 2 – 5 narrates.

Moreover, near the end of Peter's life circumstances will take a distinctively unpleasant turn. Jesus continues in verse 18 by predicting that when Peter is old he will stretch out his hands and someone else will dress him and lead him where he does not want to go. The double-'Amen' intro-duction to this solemn announcement supports its authenticity. This formula has not appeared since 16:23; John is clearly not just scattering it about randomly. More importantly, the cryptic nature of the verse makes it probable that no one has tampered with Jesus' words here. Later Christian tradition would teach that Peter was martyred, being crucified upside down during Nero's persecution of Christians in Rome in the mid-60s (*Acts Pet.* 37–39; Eusebius, *Eccl. Hist.* 3.1; cf. also *1 Clem.* 5.4). But, while 'stretching out one's hands' could refer here to the posture of a victim of crucifixion (see esp. Barrett 1978: 585 with parallel extracanonical references),[412] it need mean nothing more than what the rest of the verse specifies – that someone else will grab hold of Peter and pull him against his will to undesirable places (cf. R. E. Brown 1970: 1107). Bultmann (1971: 713) plausibly suggested that this may have been a popular proverb that implied, 'In youth a man is free to go where he will; in old age a man must let himself be taken where he does not will.' If this is the case, Jesus has made its application at least specific enough to refer to some kind of martyrdom (v. 19). But a prophecy *ex eventu* would probably have been even clearer.

In one last example of interlocking with the Synoptics, Jesus ends his words to Peter with the identical charge with which he first called him by the Sea of Galilee: 'Follow me!' (cf. Mark 1:17 pars.). This command

---

John, but not to the extent that popular preachers have often alleged. Certainly it does not appear that there are any differences in the varying Greek words for 'tend' and 'sheep' in this interchange between Peter and Jesus.

412] Derrett (1995) thinks the verse foretells Peter's crucifixion but also finds various allusions to the Old Testament accounts of Samson. Most of these seem fairly vague, however.

appears elsewhere in John only in 1:43, with respect to Philip, but it is common in the Synoptics (cf. also Matt. 8:22; 9:9; 19:21; Mark 2:14; 10:21; Luke 5:27; 9:59; 18:22).

Peter now enquires about the destiny of the beloved disciple (vv. 20–21). The two have been compared and contrasted in both chapters 20 and 21; the early chapters of Acts likewise refer to them in several places as close companions (Acts 3:1, 3, 11; 4:13, 19; 8:14). It seems odd that the Evangelist would insert the parenthetical material here about the beloved disciple being the one who had leaned against Jesus and asked him at the Last Supper who would betray him. If this information was needed to clarify who the beloved disciple was, we would have expected it earlier.[413] Perhaps it is supplied here because it is this intimate relationship that in part explains why John escapes Peter's fate, while Peter's previous behaviour may in part explain the need for his martyrdom (cf. a similar logic in the risen Christ's words to Paul in Acts 9:16).

Jesus answers Peter with the memorable response 'If I want him to remain alive until I return, what is that to you? You must follow me' (v. 22). Beasley-Murray (1987: 410) inquires if it 'is reasonable to suggest that this presentation of the relations of Peter and the Beloved Disciple, to the Lord and to each other, was made for the benefit of churches which were inclined to exalt one over against the other', as in 1 Corinthians 1 – 4. It probably is, but one should stress, with Barrett (1978: 586), that 'it is not the intention of this passage to belittle either Peter or the beloved disciple'. Quoting Bultmann (1971: 716), Barrett continues, 'The really characteristic feature of the passage is that both men are represented as on the same level; the Lord decreed one thing for the one man and another for the other.' Again the cryptic nature of Jesus' words would seem to vouchsafe their authenticity. Verse 22 is included to dispel a rumour circulating in the later church that the beloved disciple would not die before Christ returned. If the Fourth Evangelist felt free to create words of Jesus, he would surely have created a prediction that explicitly denied this rumour (cf. R. E. Brown 1970: 1118; G. R. Osborne 1984: 264). Instead we read a more opaque saying that clearly could have given rise to such a later misunderstanding. Hence, the need for clarification (v. 23) proves historically probable as well.

413] On the hypothesis that ch. 21 was added by a later hand, one would all the more have expected that this clarification would appear the first time the beloved disciple was mentioned – i.e., in v. 7.

FINAL TESTIMONY (21:24–25)

It also seems likely that the beloved disciple has just died, thus necessitating this clarification (e.g. Beasley-Murray 1987: 412; Talbert 1992: 262; Pryor 1992a: 93). Somewhat less probable but still possible is the hypothesis that he has become quite old and near death, creating a similar crisis of confidence in Jesus' miscommunicated prophecy (e.g. Bruce 1983: 408; Carson 1991: 682; Morris 1995: 775). Verses 24 and 25, then, make good sense as the 'imprimatur' on the Gospel from its final editor or editors (Lindars 1972: 641; Schnackenburg 1982: 372).[414] But the link between verse 24 and 21:1–23, combined with the links between all of John 21 and the rest of the Gospel, suggest that this final editor is responsible for the relatively uniform style of the whole work (recall above, p. 38). At the same time, 'the natural reading' of verse 24

> must lead us to conclude that the BD [beloved disciple] had a direct hand in the composition of all that precedes 21:24. He is more than just the authority figure at the back of the Johannine theology. That theology and the gospel's narratives must reflect quite accurately his own perception of Jesus. It is difficult to see why 'wrote' would have been used if the BD had not been involved in the initiative to write the gospel, even though the pupil/amanuensis was also active in a more than scribal capacity. (Pryor 1992a: 94)[415]

John 21:25 brings the Gospel to a close with the hyperbolic observation that Jesus did many other things not written in this volume, all of which put together could not be contained by a whole world full of books.[416] 'The

---

414] Burge (2000: 591) would limit this redaction to v. 24, with the 'I' of v. 25 referring again to John the apostle.

415] Cf. Bruce 1983: 409; Carson 1991: 685; Tovey 1997: 270; Byrskog 2000: 237–238. Balancing this observation is the equally important reminder from R. E. Brown (1970: 1129): 'Even if the claim of v. 24 is taken seriously, we should not let modern historical preoccupations distract us from the Johannine theological understanding of true witness. The witness is *true* not only because it ultimately stems from an eyewitness but also because it concerns Jesus who is the truth (xiv 6) and whose own witness was true (v 31–32). It is *witness* not only because it comes from one who was there but also because the Paraclete has expressed himself in the memories and in the theological reflections that are found in the Gospel (xv 26).' It is unclear whether Brown's subsequent work always retained this balance, however, as theology at times seemed to be stressed at the expense of history.

416] Birdsall (1994) has adequately refuted those who argue that v. 25 was not part of the text of John's Gospel at some stage in the scribal transmission of the document. The rhetorical flourish is conventional' (Talbert 1992: 264; comparing Philo's *Post. Cain* 43.144).[417] Ignace de la Potterie (1986) thinks that 21:24–25 forms an inclusio with 20:30–31 and frames a larger chiasmus within John 21. But not all of the parallels in the proposed chiasmus are clear, while 21:24–25 could have been composed by a final editor in deliberate imitation of 20:30–31 (Schnackenburg 1982: 374). At the same time, Grant Osborne (1984: 266) seems correct when he stresses that either verses 24–25 'are the work of a first-rate storyteller who knew how to weave in authentic-sounding details, or they are the written-down version of an eyewitness account'. In view of the cumulative evidence that the commentary section of this book has amassed, the latter seems overwhelmingly more likely. And, I would add, that eyewitness account repeatedly appears reliable.

---

suggestion of Delebecque (1986a) that v. 25 implies an infinite number of possible ways to redact the Gospel, given the inexhaustible significance of Jesus, seems to go well beyond the demonstrable meaning of the verse.

417] Lindars (1972: 642) similarly cites this text and in addition notes 1 Macc. 9:22 and *Exod. Rab.* 30.22. R. E. Brown (1970: 1130) compares Eccles. 12:9–12 and the Talmudic tractate *Soph.* 16a.

CONCLUSIONS

SUMMARY OF FINDINGS

The extreme hostility in Britain of Maurice Casey to the Fourth Gospel, matched by the almost wholesale rejection of its historicity by the Jesus Seminar in America, is not representative even of the current critical consensus, nor is it justified. Johannine scholars have come a long way in the past generation, finding the Gospel considerably more Jewish and historical than was the norm in the 1950s. Still, more of it proves suspect than not in the eyes of most. Yet one looks long and hard to find careful, convincing documentation of what in many circles has become more a presupposition than the conclusion of a sustained argument. In fact, a surprisingly powerful case for overall historicity and the general trustworthiness of the document can be mounted.

Most scholars simply assume that it has been proved that John, the apostle, the son of Zebedee, did not write the Fourth Gospel. The classic arguments in favour of apostolic authorship have been more ignored than refuted. While each requires some nuancing, a strong case can still be made for John as author. It is likely, however, that a final editor or editors added 21:24–25 at some point after John's death and that they stylistically re-worked the document to generate the overall uniformity it now presents, perhaps adding certain other small narrative portions, most notably the passages that speak of the beloved disciple in the third person and perhaps part or all of 21:20–23 and other material that leads up to this episode. The point is not so much to rehabilitate Johannine authorship as to stress the foundation of the Gospel on apostolic, eyewitness testimony at most points.

The early church traditions, that John wrote to the Christian community in and around Ephesus near the end of the first century, still provide the best suggestions with respect to date and provenance. The combination

283

of Jewish and Hellenistic, even anti-Gnostic, elements in the Fourth Gospel is adequately explained by the two-pronged nature of the opposition that the Johannine community faced in this setting. Revelation 2 – 3 corroborates the fact that Christians in Asia Minor in the 90s found certain local synagogues intensely hostile to them and had to contend also with Gnostic-like false teachers from within. One need not resort to theories of successive stages either of redaction or of the life and location of the Johannine Christians to explain the combination of material in the Gospel that responds to each prong of opposition. Such stages are not impossible in theory, just virtually impossible to demonstrate given the nature of the data, and probably unnecessary.

Likewise, John may have used written sources, but if he did he has so reworked them that they are not at present recoverable. What stands out, rather, is the literary and stylistic unity of the document, notwithstanding a few puzzling 'seams'. We may speak more confidently, however, with respect to John's relationship to the Synoptics. The lack of all but a tiny handful of words repeated verbatim in passages where John parallels the Synoptics makes literary dependence unlikely or, again, if present, irrecoverable. Still, John seems to know a fair cross-section of the material found in the Synoptics, including uniquely Matthean and Lukan traditions, and he assumes a fair amount of knowledge of that 'core kerygma' on the part of his audience. This alone can account for the number of people, places and events John describes in ways that presuppose information otherwise attested only in one or more of the first three Gospels. It also provides one of the major explanations for why he did or did not include various material in his own Gospel.

No doubt John felt it important to omit, add, select, abbreviate, paraphrase, interpret, rearrange, and put into his own words the traditions and memories he recorded. But there are no passages that have emerged from our consecutive study of the Gospel pericopae that can be said to have been created or invented without any historical foundation whatsoever. To use the colour-coding of the Jesus Seminar, a little is red, much is pink, some is grey (if the changes have to do more with editing and style than substance – putting synoptic-like concepts into Johannine vocabulary and language),[418]

418] Funk and Hoover (1993: 36) define grey alternately as 'I would not include the item in the database, but I might make use of some of the content in determining who Jesus was' and 'Jesus did not say this, but the ideas contained in it are close to his own.' Grey can be an acceptable label when it is taken to mean that, while the words of a saying reflect a mixture of Jesus' wording and the later Gospel writer's favourite vocabulary, the essence of the teaching is faithful to Jesus' original intent.

but nothing is demonstrably black.[419]

Scholars have in most instances suggested plausible explanations for Johannine redactional activity. Much of it revolves around John's distinctive theological emphases, which in turn are frequently tied in with the unique chronological and geographical sequence of the events he chooses to narrate. Once one recognizes similar principles of selection at work in the redaction of each of the Synoptics, John does not appear particularly more or less historical than they, especially when we recognize that the overall outline that the Synoptics share counts as only one independent witness and not three. Further distinctives emerge because of John's desire to contextualize the Gospel for the Christians in his specific audience and the concerns they face, as well as from his more dramatic form of the larger literary genre of theological biography.

Numerous other features of the Fourth Gospel support a global verdict of historicity. These include the many points of 'interlocking' with the Synoptics – places where either the Johannine or the synoptic tradition contains puzzling material that is explained only by information in the other tradition. Archaeological and topographical studies have confirmed John's consistent accuracy concerning the geography of Palestine overall as well as specific sites. Traces of pre-70 Jewish culture dot John's landscape, while the Pauline epistles contain various echoes of otherwise uniquely Johannine tradition. Narrative asides scattered about the Gospel show that John was concerned to distinguish what the disciples understood before Christ's death and resurrection from insights obtained only after Easter. The recurring motif of 'testimony', presented in almost a forensic fashion, designed to convince people of the truth of Christianity (or bolster fledgling faith) and supported particularly by the contents and placement of the 'beloved disciple' passages, further reinforces John's historical intent.

419] I.e. that which bears no relationship to the historical Jesus at all. Cf. already the findings of Hoskyns and Davey 1947: esp. 126. In taking notes for this book, I meticulously copied information from the Jesus Seminar's two major works (Funk and Hoover 1993; Funk 1998) on the sayings and deeds of Jesus, respectively, pericope-by-pericope, assuming I would interact with them in the commentary section of this volume. But when it was time to write up that material, I had precious few Jesus Seminar arguments against authenticity or historicity, just a lot of assumptions and presuppositions. What arguments I had found appeared better articulated elsewhere, and I *have* interacted with those sources; so I simply decided there was no point in citing either of the two books of the Jesus Seminar as I proceeded. Conversely, those works interact with only a handful of the hundreds of sources I have cited; indeed, they seem entirely unaware even of the perspectives of those sources!

Still, none of these overall considerations substitutes for a careful passage-by-passage analysis of the entire Gospel. This is what the second major portion of this book presents. The commentary is intentionally highly selective, focusing almost exclusively on issues that help us answer questions such as the following: Is this material credible in an early first-century Palestinian-Jewish milieu? Does it reflect the appropriate combination of consistency with both Judaism and early Christianity and the distinctive touches of the historical Jesus as reflected in the Synoptics? Are there any necessary contradictions with synoptic information? Are there correlations? It is impossible to summarize the verse-by-verse study of the bulk of this book; reviewers should not imagine that reading this 'conclusion' can adequately inform them of the contents of these 210 pages! But I enumerate a few highlights.

The prologue (1:1–18) is primarily not a recounting of historical information but sets the stage theologically for the rest of John's work. The exalted Christology it presents is relatively unique among the Gospels but must be assessed in the light of recent study of the broader forms of Jewish monotheism current in Jesus' day and the earliness of the rise of high Christology in Christianity more generally. The historical narrative proper begins with 1:19. The distinctive information about Jesus in conjunction with John the Baptist in 1:19–51 and 3:22–30 is increasingly being accepted as historical, especially in that it exalts John early on and shows Jesus emerging initially out of the Baptist's circle of followers.

The first miracle (2:1–11) closely parallels Jesus' parable of the wineskins in the Synoptics in both imagery and meaning. The clearing of the temple (2:12–25) is a notorious crux; it is almost impossible to choose between taking this account as a reworked and relocated version of the synoptic parallels or as a similar but separate incident. In either case, the crucial core of the passage coheres with synoptic material widely accepted as authentic. The unparalleled account of Jesus and Nicodemus (3:1–21) is plausible to the extent that we can assess it, once we compile the Jewish traditions about the wealth and power of the ben Gurion family, and once we recognize that verses 16–21, like 31–36 later in this chapter, are probably to be taken as John's own commentary and not further teachings of Jesus (or the Baptist).

The powerful story of Jesus and the Samaritan woman (4:1–42) coheres well with the recurring synoptic emphasis on Jesus' compassion for and ministry to the outcasts of his world. The healing of the official's son (4:43–54) can be taken as a variant of a Q-passage and demonstrates fundamental coherence with that narrative. John 5:1–18 contains the identical combination of pronouncement story plus miracle as the synoptic healing of the paralytic and even has a verbatim parallel in its command from Jesus to the lame man (v. 8). The subsequent discourse (vv. 19–47) is the first of the seven so-called discourses of John in chapters 1 – 11; in fact, it is the only one that is completely uninterrupted. It begins with a short proverbial saying (v. 19) and can be viewed as a homiletical development of that small 'metaphor'. It is the first extended passage attributed to Jesus with a large concentration of major, Johannine language and themes, including sustained, lofty Christology. But it balances this emphasis with a subordinationist strand unlikely to be an early Christian invention of Jesus doing only what the Father commands. The same may be said of Jesus' concession that his own self-witness proves inadequate.

The first two sections of John 6 (feeding the five thousand – vv. 1–15; walking on the water – vv. 16–21) run closely parallel to the Synoptics. The appended material, culminating in the bread of life discourse (vv. 22–59), flows naturally from the first of the two miracles in the chapter and forms a tightly knit unity in a midrashic style of Old Testament interpretation demonstrable in shorter form in several synoptic parables. The concluding teaching about eating Christ's flesh and drinking his blood and the confession from Peter that it elicits (vv. 60–71) anticipate the establishment of the eucharist and Peter's confession on the road to Caesarea Philippi, both as presented only in the Synoptics, without demonstrating anachronism in their current context.

John 7:1 – 10:21 comprises material related to the feast of the Tabernacles, probably in AD 29. The unbelief (7:1–13) by Jesus' brothers is unlikely to have been invented. The polarization of the audiences throughout these chapters tells against the suggestion that John is unrelenting in his negative portrait of the Jewish people, and even of the religious leaders. Jesus' primary claims all dovetail with key symbolism of the Tabernacles ceremonies: Jesus as living water (7:37–52), the light of the world (8:12–30), illustrated by his curing the blind man (9:1–12), and the messianic shepherd (10:1–21). The climactic debate with certain individuals who seemingly professed belief (8:31–59) culminates in one of the strongest Christological claims attributed to Jesus anywhere (8:58), but in its Jewish context it would still have been heard more as a claim to be God's agent than as an exact equation with the Father. Charges of John's portrait of Jesus and the Jews here (and elsewhere) as anti-Semitic are thoroughly unjustified.

The healing of the blind man (ch. 9) also coheres with several synoptic healing accounts, especially involving Jesus' use of saliva. The fears of synagogue excommunication, first introduced in this chapter (v. 22), fit better the limited context of growing hostility in Jerusalem prior to Jesus' crucifixion than they do an end-of-the first century setting, where empire-wide curses, often postulated, seem non-existent. His claims to be the good shepherd (10:1–21) closely mirror the synoptic parable of the lost sheep. They continue during the feast of Dedication (or Hanukkah – 10:22–42) where they are equally appropriate in the light of the Maccabean deliverance commemorated. Further infringement of the broader, early Jewish definitions of blasphemy, by too close association with God, compare and contrast appropriately with Antiochus' unwarranted belief that he was *Epiphanes*, God manifest.

The resurrection (or better, resuscitation) of Lazarus (11:1–44) forms Jesus' most dramatic miracle to date but is no different in kind, only in magnitude from two synoptic miracles. The characterizations of Mary and Martha closely resemble what we learn from Luke's Gospel, and Jesus' emotions disclose the depth of his humanity at several key points. That this miracle formed a catalyst for the Jewish authorities to plot to arrest Jesus (11:45–57) does not contradict the synoptic emphasis on the temple-clearing incident playing this role, since both the Fourth Gospel and the Synoptics acknowledge multiple events that provoked the authorities to do away with Christ.

Beginning in chapter 12, points of contact with the Synoptics appear more regularly, especially in the passion narrative proper (chs. 18 – 19). The anointing at Bethany is narrated in a chronologically more precise location in John (12:1–11), with added information about Mary and Judas that fits what little we can piece together about them from the Synoptics. John's version of the so–called triumphal entry (12:12–19) closely resembles the synoptic accounts; added information, most notably about the palm branches, proves historically plausible. John 12:20–36 contains largely unparalleled information, based on the request by some Greeks to see Jesus, which triggers a little parable and its expansion. But the themes throughout find numerous synoptic parallels, even if literary dependence is precluded. Verses 37–50 present two summaries of Jesus' ministry and teaching thus far, one by John as narrator (vv. 37–43) and the other attributed to Jesus in no specific setting (vv. 44–50), a tip-off that John may be collecting here and putting in his own words central themes of Jesus pervasive in this Gospel.

The footwashing (13:1–20) introduces two major themes, one Christological and the other ecclesiological, that find close parallels in the synoptic accounts of the Last Supper, especially in Luke. Nevertheless John does not narrate the actual partaking of bread and wine and the 'words of institution' found in the Synoptics and Paul, just as they do not recount the footwashing. The predictions of Jesus' betrayal and denial run more closely parallel to the Synoptics (13:21–38). The farewell discourse (chaps. 14 – 16) is unique to John. Characteristic and distinctive Johannine themes permeate it, yet virtually every one finds conceptual parallels in the

Synoptics: Jesus' predicting his death and resurrection, future hostility for the disciples, the coming role of the Holy Spirit, the invitation to ask more (and more directly) from God, sorrow turning to happiness, God's people as a vineyard and the centrality of the double love-command. Despite a few puzzling literary seams, John 14 – 16 is best treated as a unity, especially because of a probable chiastic structure that encompasses it all. John 17 proves equally distinctive, but this 'high-priestly' prayer contains allusions to every petition of the so-called Lord's Prayer of Matthew and Luke, in all but one instance in the identical sequence.

In chapters 18 – 19 John follows the synoptic order and choice of events more closely but still manages to present more unparalleled than paralleled material in virtually every pericope. As with the material about John the Baptist, a growing number of scholars sees John as even more consistently historical in his presentation than the Synoptics, answering a variety of questions that the Synoptics leave unresolved and presenting additional information that closely squares with other historical data. Examples include the presence of Romans as well as Jews in the arresting party in the garden, the hearing before Annas, and several additional items in the trial with Pilate that explain why the Jews had to involve the Romans and how they were able to persuade them to become involved. The emphasis on Jesus crucified as a 'king of the Jews' duplicates a theme otherwise more prominent in the Synoptics. The description of Jesus' behaviour and words from the cross combines with the role of the beloved disciple as a witness to the manner of his death to demonstrate clearly an anti-docetic motive concerned to vouchsafe the historicity of the material recalled. The burial by Joseph of Arimathea is paralleled in the Synoptics and seems particularly historically secure. The frequent charge that John presents the crucifixion of Christ a day earlier than the Synoptics do simply cannot withstand careful scrutiny of each of the relevant texts, interpreted *in their narrative sequence*.

How one assesses the resurrection narratives (chs. 20 – 21) will depend largely on broader scientific, philosophical and historiographical presuppositions. But if the questions are more limited, answers do emerge with some clarity. Again, while giving largely different information, John in no way contradicts the Synoptics. Plausible harmonizations of the specific details surrounding any given appearance and of an overall sequence of all the canonical Gospels' resurrection appearances have regularly been presented, though largely ignored (and sometimes mocked) by the critical establishment. John 20:28 contains the Christological climax of the Fourth Gospel with Thomas's confession. It fits flawlessly the purpose statement articulated a scant two verses later (vv. 30–31). But it is hard to see how that purpose could be fulfilled if Thomas's words were not based on an underlying, genuine change of heart.

Chapter 21 shifts from the primarily Christological concerns of chapter 20 to primarily ecclesiological matters, but neither is absent altogether from either chapter. Increasing numbers of scholars are recognizing thematic and stylistic features that link chapter 21 with chapter 20 on the one hand and with the entire Gospel on the other. Theories that relegate chapter 21 to an 'appendix' tacked on by a later writer are thus appropriately and increasingly being discarded, though probably still held by a majority of scholars.

IMPLICATIONS OF THESE RESULTS

It is important to stress that my analysis, like the Fourth Gospel itself, is highly selective. We could go back through John again, this time focusing primarily on the stylistic redaction of the Gospel, but this would prove of limited value in answering historical questions. As stated in my intro-duction, no-one disputes that John has written up his material in his preferred vocabulary and style. But the presence of these elements teaches us nothing about the historicity or authenticity of the underlying material (see above, p. 65). Or again, we could reread the Gospel, but this time highlighting the distinctive theology that John stresses at each point. Doubtless, John differs more from the Synoptics than any of them do from each other, not least in particular theological emphases (for a brief overview, see Blomberg 1997: 162–167). But the only way this kind of survey would shed further light on historical questions is if one still holds to the tired, old, and frequently debunked, false dichotomy between history and theology (which a surprising number of scholars unfortunately still maintains).[420] That a passage promotes a writer's theological agenda teaches us nothing about the historicity of its concepts. Only the kinds of questions raised and the criteria applied in this work can help us make progress on that front. Fervently ideological writings can sometimes narrate accurate history, just as dispassionately 'objective' chronicles can make all kinds of factual mistakes (cf. esp. Tovey 1997; Byrskog 2000).

Yet another way to produce a separate manuscript at least as long as this one would be to proceed through the Gospel of John assessing in detail the debates over literary dependence on or independence from the Synoptics. We have seen, however, that there is not a single instance in John, when one compares the parallel accounts in a Greek synopsis, where there is enough verbal parallelism (the identical words in the identical grammatical forms or changed in morphologically insignificant ways) to make theories

---

420] For the debunking, see already Marshall 1970; cf. now Hengel 2000.

of direct, literary dependence at all probable. What little does appear usually involves words without which the particular story could scarcely have been told or which would quickly have taken fixed form in oral tradition. Once again, this does not disprove Johannine dependence on the Synoptics; it just means that the data in their current form will probably never be able to make such a theory probable. But if John is largely or exclusively independent, in a literary sense, from the Synoptics, then the numerous points at which criteria like multiple attestation and coherence apply help us to authenticate large portions of this Gospel.

Finally, we could have proceeded through the Fourth Gospel looking for different kinds of history-of-religions parallels.[421] There are fascinating ways in which John's material resembles that found in various Hellenistic sources, particularly in early Gnosticism. A sufficient catalogue of data could be compiled to suggest that John frequently uses Gnostic-like language to counter Gnostic (or simply docetic) tendencies increasingly inflicting his community (see esp. Schnelle 1992, without endorsing his specific tradition criticism). But it is now generally admitted that all such instances do not add up to anything nearly as impressive as the catalogue of Old Testament and other early Jewish parallels, which are what I have focused on here. Given those parallels, the next question that is not asked nearly often enough is whether it is likely that an anonymous Christian, having ministered perhaps a majority of his adult life in largely Hellenistic circles and clearly capable of drawing on Hellenistic terminology to further his purposes, would have been able to invent, or even have been interested in inventing, material with so many consistent echoes of the contents and forms of Hebrew Scripture and Palestinian Judaism in the context of early first-century Israel as we find in John's Gospel. It may be that it is both simpler and more plausible to ascribe this consistent tendency to the historical Jesus, with matching Johannine narrative emphases having a very early origin in the transmission of the tradition and, indeed, inspired by the practices of Jesus himself. On theories of apostolic authorship, after all, John is involved with the tradition at virtually every step of the way.

To what, then, does all of this evidence add up? I underline once more that we are not assessing the Gospel by modern standards of historio-graphical precision, which would be both anachronistic and unfair, but by the literary conventions of the first-century Mediterranean world. At every stage we must take into account authorial intention, literary genre and

---

421] The most voluminous catalogue of ancient cross–references in both Jewish and Graeco-Roman sources appears throughout the forthcoming commentary on John from Hendrickson by Craig S. Keener.

form, and the circumstances of the Johannine community. The very inspiration that John apparently felt coming from the promised Paraclete's ministry at one and the same time gave him the freedom to write up his material as distinctively as he did while also constraining him to limit himself to what Jesus really did and taught (see above, p. 203).

At the end of this investigation there remains a striking amount of evidence for the overall historical trustworthiness and credibility of John's Gospel that one simply would not imagine was present unless one had worked through the material as we have. One certainly does not gain this impression from the liberal consensus, but then, with a handful of exceptions, those scholars do not interact in detail (and often not at all) with the majority of the secondary literature on which I have relied most heavily.

Conservatives, too, seem to be part of this consensus at times, at least by their silence – that is, in relying almost wholly on the Synoptics and leaving John to one side in doing their own historical Jesus research. And a few opt out of the process altogether, by decrying all historical Jesus research as anathema to the gospel, severely criticizing their colleagues who enter into the foray, and falling back on an unfalsifiable (and therefore unverifiable) fideism that simply *presupposes* the historicity of the Gospels as a necessary first move in authentic Christian faith.[422]

Even as this position consistently but inaccurately accuses almost all of the guild of Gospel scholars of 'playing the same game', however diverse their historical conclusions turn out to be, they unwittingly adopt one of the fundamental premises of Crossan, Funk and various others in or sympathetic to the Jesus Seminar, namely that there are only two possible 'camps' one can be in. Either one *presupposes* that Scripture must be historical (a view for which no historical arguments can be offered) or one engages in true historical research, in which case one must be committed a priori to finding numerous non-historical portions of the Gospels (see above, pp. 66–67; cf. the particularly candid methodological observations in Funk 1996: 64–65, esp. in describing the 'pretend questers'). Framed this way, each camp is correct in identifying the opposite one as historically biased, theologically unfalsifiable, and thus to be rejected! Fortunately, there is a third option, contrary to the claims of representatives of both of the previous two positions, and that is to engage in genuine historical inquiry, as a large number of moderately conservative to moderately liberal

---

422] The most consistent advocate of this approach over the past generation has been Robert Thomas, whose perspective can be gleaned most recently from the collection of essays, and particularly his, in Thomas and Farnell 1998.

scholars are doing, to try to bracket one's presuppositions as much as possible, and not to conclude in advance that any document must be either errant or inerrant. At the same time, historians of antiquity regularly build up a general impression of the trustworthiness or lack thereof of any given document that they are studying, which impression if more often corroborated than challenged can become almost a 'functional non-negotiable', but that is a quite different matter. In theory (and hopefully, therefore, in practice), in such instances, enough counter-evidence can always lead to a changed perspective.

This *via media* also stresses that historical research, by its very nature, especially in investigating ancient documents, cannot adjudicate on any document in its entirety. This investigation is not claiming to have demonstrated historically that all of John's Gospel would have been considered accurate by the conventions of its day. It is simply pointing out a surprisingly large amount of evidence that points in the direction of historicity. Theoretically, other material *could* be unhistorical, but I have not encountered any arguments that tip the scales in that direction. For individuals, Christians or otherwise, who wish to make a theological statement about the inspiration or inerrancy of the Gospels, other considerations will have to come into play. Kierkegaard's famous 'leap of faith' cannot be avoided. But it must be stressed that such a leap moves in the direction in which the historical evidence is already pointing, even with respect to John's Gospel. It is not a leap simply in the dark, or, worse still, a leap in spite of a majority of the evidence pointing in a contrary direction. Conversely, those who choose to dispute the cumulative effect of the arguments presented here will have to do so by means of an equally thorough analysis of John's Gospel and by presenting consistent, adequate refutations of these arguments. Continuing to affirm that John is more unhistorical than not without this kind of painstaking research will have to be declared an approach that is a leap of otherwise unfounded faith.

I began this book by quoting Casey (1996), Hanson (1991), Barrett (1978) and Lindars (2000), and it is appropriate to conclude by referring again to these studies. Barrett and Lindars have in fact regularly provided arguments in their detailed exegesis that support a significant amount of historicity in John, more than their introductory generalizations might suggest. Extremely consistently, Hanson finds Old Testament and later Jewish parallels to the form and concepts of passages in John that should support historicity, rather than challenging it as he alleges. All three writers, however, do find significant contradictions and unhistorical material in John, whereas several other recent commentators have in each case proposed plausible, less sceptical explanations of the apparent discrepancies.

Much more radically, Casey mounts a full-scale assault on John's Gospel, declaring it massively unhistorical, theologically dangerous, and unworthy of inclusion in the canon. At the outset of his work it appeared as if he would provide the pleasant exception to the trend of the most liberal commentators largely ignoring conservative scholarship. But in fact he interacted with it in detail only at the outset of his volume, with respect to two very controversial issues, and then declared its case baseless and moved on with only occasional asides to conservative alternatives. In most cases in which he dealt in any detail with conservative discussion, I have responded in the course of the commentary to his or to others' similar arguments. One can conclude only that his sweeping charges are far from proven. Rather, in answering the question raised by the title of his book, one may affirm with considerable confidence that John's Gospel is true – not merely theologically (as, e.g. for Barrett and Lindars) but also historically.[423]

423] As for the Jesus Seminar's opinions concerning the Fourth Gospel, also cited in my introduction, they epitomize the worst of what passes for Gospels scholarship today. As we have just noted (above, p. 258, n. 419), their findings consistently fail to present what even a sizeable majority of contemporary Johannine scholarship concludes, and they ignore evangelical scholarship altogether.

BIBLIOGRAPHY

Ackerman, James S. (1966), 'The Rabbinic Interpretation of Psalm 82 and the Gospel of John (John 10:34)', *HTR* 59: 186–191

Agourides, Savas (1968), '"High Priestly Prayer" of Jesus', *TU* 102: 137–145

Albright, William F. (1956), 'Recent Discoveries in Palestine and the Gospel of St. John', in William D. Davies and David Daube (eds.), *The Background of the New Testament and Its Eschatology*, 153–171, Cambridge: Cambridge University Press

Anderson, Paul N. (1996), *The Christology of the Fourth Gospel: Its Unity and Disunity in the Light of John 6*, Tübingen: Mohr

Ashton, John (1986), 'The Transformation of Wisdom: A Study of the Prologue of John's Gospel', *NTS* 32: 161–186

—— (1991), *Understanding the Fourth Gospel*, Oxford: Clarendon

—— (1994), *Studying John: Approaches to the Fourth Gospel*, Oxford: Clarendon

Askwith, Edward H. (1910), *The Historical Value of the Fourth Gospel*, London: Hodder & Stoughton

Attridge, Harold W. (1980), 'Thematic Development and Source Elaboration in John 7:1–36', *CBQ* 42: 160–170

Augenstein, Jörg (1997), '"Euer Gesetz" – Ein Pronomen und die johanneische Haltung zum Gesetz', *ZNW* 88: 311–313

Aus, Roger (1988), *Water into Wine and the Beheading of John the Baptist*, Atlanta: Scholars

Backhaus, Knut (1991), *Die 'Jüngerkreis' des Täufers Johannes*, Paderborn: Schöningh

Badke, William B. (1990), 'Was Jesus a Disciple of John?' *EQ* 62: 195–204

Bailey, Kenneth E. (1991), 'Informal Controlled Oral Tradition and the

Synoptic Gospels', *AJT* 5: 34–54

—— (1993), 'The Shepherd Poems of John 10: Their Culture and Style', *NESTTR* 14: 3–21

Balagué, M. (1966), 'La prueba de la Resurrección (Jn 20, 6–7)', *EstBíb* 25: 169–192

Balfour, Glenn (1995), 'The Jewishness of John's Use of the Scriptures in John 6:31 and 7:37–38', *TynB* 46: 357–380

Ball, R. M. (1985), 'S. John and the Institution of the Eucharist', *JSNT* 23: 59–68

Baltz, Frederick W. (1996), *Lazarus and the Fourth Gospel Community*, Lewiston: Mellen

Bammel, Ernst (1970), '"Ex illa itaque die consilium fecerunt ..."', in Ernst Bammel (ed.), *The Trial of Jesus*, 11–40, London: SCM; Naperville: Allenson

—— (1984a), 'The *Titulus*', in Ernst Bammel and Charles F. D. Moule (eds.), *Jesus and the Politics of His Day*, 353–364, Cambridge: Cambridge University Press

—— (1984b), 'The Trial before Pilate', in Ernst Bammel and Charles F. D. Moule (eds.), *Jesus and the Politics of His Day*, 415–451, Cambridge: Cambridge University Press

—— (1993), 'The Farewell Discourse of the Evangelist John and Its Jewish Heritage', *TynB* 44: 103–116

Bampfylde, G. (1969), 'John xix 28: A Case for a Different Translation', *NovT* 11: 247–260

Barker, Margaret (1970), 'John 11.50', in Ernst Bammel (ed.), *The Trial of Jesus*, 41–46, London: SCM; Naperville: Allenson

Barnett, Paul W. (1986), 'The Feeding of the Multitude in Mark 6/John 6', in David Wenham and Craig Blomberg (eds.), *Gospel Perspectives*, vol. 6, 273–293, Sheffield: JSOT

Barrera, J. Trebolle (1991), 'Posible substrato semítico . . . en Jn 19,13', *FN* 4: 51–54

Barrett, C. K. (1978), *The Gospel According to St. John*, 2nd ed., London: SPCK; Philadelphia: Westminster

—— (1982), '"The Father Is Greater Than I" (John 14:28): Subordinationist Christology in the New Testament', in C. K. Barrett, *Essays on John*, 19–36, London: SPCK

Barton, Stephen (1993), 'The Believer, the Historian and the Fourth Gospel', *Theol* 96: 289–302

Bauckham, Richard (1993a), 'The Beloved Disciple as Ideal Author', *JSNT* 49: 21–44

—— (1993b), 'Papias and Polycrates on the Origin of the Fourth Gospel', *JTS* 44: 24–69

—— (1996), 'Nicodemus and the Gurion Family', *JTS* 47: 1–37

—— (1997), 'Qumran and the Fourth Gospel: Is There a Connection?' in Stanley E. Porter and Craig A. Evans (eds.), *The Scrolls and the Scriptures: Qumran Fifty Years After*, 267–279, Sheffield: Sheffield Academic Press

—— (1998a), *God Crucified: Monotheism and Christology in the New Testament*, Grand Rapids: Eerdmans

—— (ed.), (1998b), *The Gospels for all Christians: Rethinking the Gospel Audiences*, Grand Rapids: Eerdmans

—— (1998c), 'John for Readers of Mark', in Richard Bauckham (ed.), *The Gospels for all Christians: Rethinking the Gospel Audiences*, 147–171, Grand Rapids: Eerdmans

—— (1998d), 'Life, Death, and the Afterlife in Second Temple Judaism', in Richard N. Longenecker (ed.), *Life in the Face of Death: The Resurrection Message of the New Testament*, 80–95, Grand Rapids: Eerdmans

Baum-Bodenbender, Rosel (1984), *Hoheit im Niedrigkeit: Johanneische Christologie im Prozess Jesu vor Pilatus (Joh 18,28–19,16a)*, Würzburg: Echter

Bayer, Hans (1986), *Jesus' Predictions of Vindication and Resurrection*, Tübingen: Mohr

Beasley-Murray, George R. (1987), *John*, Waco: Word

Beckwith, Roger (1985), *The Old Testament Canon of the New Testament Church and Its Background in Early Judaism*, London: SPCK, 1985; Grand Rapids: Eerdmans, 1986

Beetham, F. G. and P. A. Beetham (1993), 'A Note on John 19:29', *JTS* 44: 163–169

Belleville, Linda L. (1980), '"Born of Water and Spirit": John 3:5', *TrinJ* 1: 125–141

Berger, Klaus (1997), *Im Anfang war Johannes: Datierung und Theologie des vierten Evangeliums*, Stuttgart: Quell

Bergmeier, Roland (1988), 'ΤΕΤΕΛΕΣΤΑΙ Joh 19³⁰', *ZNW* 79: 282–290

—— (1995), 'Gottesherrschaft, Taufe und Geist: Zur Tauftradition in Joh 3', *ZNW* 86: 53–73

Beutler, Johannes (1984), *Habt keine Angst: Die erste johanneische Abschiedsrede (Joh 14)*, Stuttgart: Katholisches Bibelwerk

—— (1990), 'Greeks Come to See Jesus (John 12,20f)', *Bib* 71: 333–347

—— (1991), 'Der alttestamentlich-jüdische Hintergrund der Hirtenrede in Johannes 10', in Johannes Beutler and Robert T. Fortna (eds.), *The Shepherd Discourse of John 10 and Its Context*, 18–32, Cambridge: Cambridge University Press

—— (1994), 'Two Ways of Gathering: The Plot to Kill Jesus in John

11.47–53', *NTS* 40: 399–406

Beutler, Johannes and Robert T. Fortna (eds.) (1991), *The Shepherd Discourse of John 10 and Its Context*, Cambridge: Cambridge University Press

Birdsall, J. Neville (1994), 'The Source of Catena Comments on John 21:25', *NovT* 36: 271–279

Bishop, Eric F. F. (1960), 'The Door of the Sheep – John x.7–9', *ExpT* 71: 307–309.

Bjerkelund, Carl J. (1987), Tauta Egeneto: *Die Präzisierungssätze im Johannesevangelium*, Tübingen: Mohr

Black, David A. (1988), 'On the Style and Significance of John 17', *CTR* 3: 141–159

Blank, Josef (1989), 'Die Johannespassion: Intention und Hintergründe', in Karl Kertelge (ed.), *Der Prozess gegen Jesus: Historische Rückfrage und theologische Deutung*, 148–182, Freiburg: Herder

Blinzler, Josef (1959), *The Trial of Jesus*, Cork: Mercier

Blomberg, Craig L. (1983), 'Midrash, Chiasmus, and the Outline of Luke's Central Section', in R. T. France and David Wenham (eds.), *Gospel Perspectives*, vol. 3, 217–261, Sheffield: JSOT

—— (1984), 'New Testament Miracles and Higher Criticism: Climbing Up the Slippery Slope?' *JETS* 27: 425–438

—— (1985), 'Tradition and Redaction in the Parables of the Gospel of Thomas', in David Wenham (ed.), *Gospel Perspectives*, vol. 5, 177–205, Sheffield: JSOT

—— (1986a), 'The Legitimacy and Limits of Harmonization', in D. A. Carson and John D. Woodbridge (eds.), *Hermeneutics, Authority, and Canon*, 135–174, repr. Grand Rapids: Baker, 1995

—— (1986b), 'The Miracles as Parables', in David Wenham and Craig Blomberg (eds.), *Gospel Perspectives*, vol. 6, 327–359, Sheffield: JSOT

—— (1987), *The Historical Reliability of the Gospels*, Leicester: Inter-Varsity Press

—— (1990), *Interpreting the Parables*, Leicester: Inter-Varsity Press.

—— (1992), *Matthew*, Nashville: Broadman

—— (1993), 'To What Extent Is John Historically Reliable?' in Robert B. Sloan and Mikeal C. Parsons (eds.), *Perspectives on John: Method and Interpretation in the Fourth Gospel*, 27–56, Lewiston: Mellen

—— (1994), '"Your Faith Has Made You Whole": The Evangelical Liberation Theology of Jesus', in Joel B. Green and Max Turner (eds.), *Jesus of Nazareth: Lord and Christ*, 75–93, Grand Rapids: Eerdmans; Carlisle: Paternoster

—— (1995), 'The Globalization of Biblical Interpretation: A Test Case – John 3–4', *BBR* 5: 1–15

—— (1997), *Jesus and the Gospels: An Introduction and Survey*, Nashville: Broadman & Holman; Leicester: Inter-Varsity Press, 1997

—— (1998), 'The Jesus of History and the Christ of Faith: Harmony or Conflict?' in Paul Copan (ed.), *Will the Real Jesus Please Stand Up?*, 99–116, Grand Rapids: Baker

—— (1999), *Neither Poverty Nor Riches: A Biblical Theology of Material Possessions*, repr. Downers Grove: InterVarsity Press, 2001

—— (2001), 'The Diversity of Literary Genres in the New Testament', in David A. Black and David S. Dockery, eds., *Interpreting the New Testament*, 2nd ed., 272–295, Nashville: Broadman & Holman

Bock, Darrell L. (1995), 'The Words of Jesus in the Gospels: Live, Jive, or Memorex?' in Michael J. Wilkins and J. P. Moreland (eds.), *Jesus Under Fire: Modern Scholarship Reinvents the Historical Jesus*, 73–99, Grand Rapids: Zondervan

—— (1998), *Blasphemy and Exaltation in Judaism and the Final Examination of Jesus*, Tübingen: Mohr, 1998; Grand Rapids: Eerdmans, 2000

Böhler, Dieter (1995), '"Ecce Homo!" (Joh 19, 5) ein Zitat aus dem Alten Testament', *BZ* 39: 104–108

Boismard, Marie-Émile (1998), 'Le disciple que Jésus aimait d'après Jn 21,1ss et 1,35ss', *RB* 105: 76–80

—— (1999), 'Bethzatha ou Siloé', *RB* 106: 206–218

Bond, Helen K. (1998), *Pontius Pilate in History and Interpretation*, Cambridge: Cambridge University Press

Booser, Kimberly D. (1998), 'The Literary Structure of John 1:1–18: An Examination of Its Theological Implications concerning God's Saving Plan through Jesus Christ', *EJ* 16: 13–29

Borchert, Gerald L. (1996), *John*, vol. 1, Nashville: Broadman & Holman

Borgen, Peder (1959), 'John and the Synoptics in the Passion Narrative', *NTS* 5: 246–259

—— (1965), *Bread from Heaven*, Leiden: Brill

—— (1977), 'Some Jewish Exegetical Traditions as Background for Son of Man Sayings in John's Gospel (Jn 3,13–14 and Context)', in Marinus de Jonge (ed.), *L'Évangile de Jean: Sources, rédaction, théologie*, 243–258, Gembloux: Duculot; Leuven: Louvain University Press and Peeters

—— (1979), 'The Use of Tradition in John 12.44–50', *NTS* 26: 18–35

—— (1987), 'John and the Synoptics: Can Paul Offer Help?' in Gerald F. Hawthorne and Otto Betz (eds.), *Tradition and Interpretation in the New Testament*, 80–94, Grand Rapids: Eerdmans

—— (1993), 'John 6: Tradition, Interpretation and Composition', in Martinus C. de Boer (ed.), *From Jesus to John: Essays on Jesus and New Testament Christology*, 268–291, Sheffield: JSOT

Bowen, Clayton R. (1930), 'The Fourth Gospel as Dramatic Material', *JBL* 49: 292–305

Bowker, John (1967), 'Speeches in Acts: A Study in Proem and Yelammedenu Form', *NTS* 14: 96–111

Boyle, John L. (1975), 'The Last Discourse (Jn 13,31–16,33) and Prayer (Jn 17): Some Observations on Their Unity and Development', *Bib* 56: 210–222

Braun, François-Marie (1929), 'L'expulsion des vendeurs du temple', *RB* 38: 178–200

Braun, Willi (1990), 'Resisting John: Ambivalent Redactor and Defensive Reader of the Fourth Gospel', *SR* 19: 59–71

Brawley, Robert L. (1993), 'An Absent Complement and Intertextuality in John 19:28–29', *JBL* 112: 427–443

Breck, John (1992), 'John 21: Appendix, Epilogue or Conclusion?' *StVTQ* 36: 27–49

Broadhead, Edwin K. (1995), 'Echoes of an Exorcism in the Fourth Gospel?' *ZNW* 86: 111–119

Brodie, Thomas L. (1993), *The Quest for the Origin of John's Gospel: A Source-Oriented Approach*, New York: Oxford University Press

Brouwer, Wayne (1999), 'The Literary Development of John 13–17: A Chiastic Reading', McMaster University: PhD dissertation

Brown, Colin (1984), *Miracles and the Critical Mind*, Exeter: Paternoster; Grand Rapids: Eerdmans

Brown, Raymond E. (1966, 1970), *The Gospel according to John*, 2 vols., Garden City: Doubleday

—— (1979), *The Community of the Beloved Disciple*, New York: Paulist

—— (1997), *An Introduction to the New Testament*, New York: Doubleday

Brown, Raymond E., Karl P. Donfried, Joseph A. Fitzmyer and John Reumann (eds.) (1978), *Mary in the New Testament*, Philadelphia: Fortress; New York: Paulist

Brownson, James V. (1995), 'John 20:31 and the Purpose of the Fourth Gospel', *RefRev* 48: 212–216

Bruce, F. F. (1980), 'The Trial of Jesus in the Fourth Gospel', in R. T. France and David Wenham (eds.), *Gospel Perspectives*, vol. 1, 7–20, Sheffield: JSOT

—— (1983), *The Gospel of John*, Basingstoke: Pickering & Inglis; Grand Rapids: Eerdmans

Bull, Robert J. (1975), 'An Archaeological Context for Understanding John 4:20', *BA* 38: 54–59

Bultmann, Rudolf (1971), *The Gospel of John*, Oxford: Blackwell; Philadelphia: Westminster

Burge, Gary M. (1984), 'A Specific Problem in the New Testament Text and Canon: The Woman Caught in Adultery (John 7:53 – 8:11)', *JETS* 27: 141–148

—— (1987), *The Anointed Community: The Holy Spirit in the Johannine Tradition*, Grand Rapids: Eerdmans

—— (1992), *Interpreting the Fourth Gospel*, Grand Rapids: Baker

—— (2000), *John*, Grand Rapids: Zondervan

Burkett, Delbert (1991), *The Son of Man in the Gospel of John*, Sheffield: JSOT

—— (1994), 'Two Accounts of Lazarus' Resurrection in John 11', *NovT* 36: 209–232

Burridge, Richard A. (1992), *What Are the Gospels? A Comparison with Graeco-Roman Biography*, Cambridge: Cambridge University Press

Burrows, E. W. (1974), 'Did John the Baptist Call Jesus "The Lamb of God?" ' *ExpT* 85: 245–249

Buse, Ivor (1960), 'St. John and the Passion Narratives of St. Matthew and St. Luke', *NTS* 7: 65–76

Byrne, Brendan (1985), 'The Faith of the Beloved Disciple and the Community in John 20', *JSNT* 23: 83–97

Byrskog, Samuel (2000), *Story as History – History as Story*, Tübingen: Mohr

Calvin, John (1555), *A Harmony of the Gospels: Matthew, Mark and Luke* (trans. A. W. Morrison, 1972), Edinburgh: St. Andrew; Grand Rapids: Eerdmans

Camarero María, Lorenzo (1997), *Revelaciones solemnas de Jesús: Derás cristológico en Jn 7–8 (Fiesta de las Tiendas)*, Madrid: Publicaciones Claretianas

Campbell, R. J. (1982), 'Evidence for the Historicity of the Fourth Gospel in John 2:13–22', in Elizabeth A. Livingstone (ed.), *Studia Evangelica*, vol. 7, 101–120, Berlin: Akademie

Capper, Brian J. (1998), '"With the Oldest Monks ...": Light from Essene History on the Career of the Beloved Disciple?' *JTS* 49: 1–55

Caragounis, Chrys C. (1986), *The Son of Man*, Tübingen: Mohr

—— (1998), 'Jesus, His Brothers and the Journey to the Feast (John 7:8–10)', *SEÅ* 63: 177–187

Carson, Donald A. (1978), 'Current Source Criticism of the Fourth Gospel: Some Methodological Questions', *JBL* 97: 411–429

—— (1979), 'The Function of the Paraclete in John 16:7–11', *JBL* 98: 547–566

—— (1981a), *Divine Sovereignty and Human Responsibility*, London: Marshall, Morgan & Scott; Atlanta: John Knox

—— (1981b), 'Historical Tradition in the Fourth Gospel: After Dodd, What?' in R. T. France and David Wenham (eds.), *Gospel Perspectives*, vol. 2, 83–145, Sheffield: JSOT

—— (1982), 'Understanding Misunderstandings in the Fourth Gospel', *TynB* 33: 59–91

—— (1987), 'The Purpose of the Fourth Gospel: John 20:31 Reconsidered', *JBL* 106: 639–651

—— (1991), *The Gospel According to John*, Grand Rapids: Eerdmans; Leicester: Inter-Varsity Press

—— (1996), *Exegetical Fallacies*, 2nd ed., Grand Rapids: Baker; Carlisle: Paternoster

Casey, Maurice (1996), *Is John's Gospel True?* London: Routledge

Cassidy, Richard J. (1992), *John's Gospel in New Perspective*, Maryknoll: Orbis

Catchpole, David R. (1971), 'The Answer of Jesus to Caiaphas (Matt. XXVI.64)', *NTS* 17: 213–226

Charles, J. Daryl (1989), ' "Will the Court Please Call in the Prime Witness?": John 1:29–34 and the "Witness"-Motif', *TrinJ* 10: 71–83

Charlesworth, James H. (1995), *The Beloved Disciple: Whose Witness Validates the Gospel of John?* Valley Forge: Trinity

—— (1996), 'The Dead Sea Scrolls and the Gospel according to John', in R. Alan Culpepper and C. Clifton Black (eds.), *Exploring the Gospel of John*, 65–97, Louisville: Westminster John Knox

—— (ed.) (1972), *John and Qumran*, London: Geoffrey Chapman

—— (ed.) (1992), *The Messiah: Developments in Earliest Judaism and Christianity*, Minneapolis: Fortress

Chavel, Charles B. (1941), 'The Releasing of a Prisoner on the Eve of Passover in Ancient Jerusalem', *JBL* 60: 273–278

Chilton, Bruce (1980), 'John XII 34 and Targum Isaiah LII 13', *NovT* 22: 176–178

Cipriani, Settimio (1967), 'La confessione di Pietro in Giov. 6, 69–71 e suo rapporti con quella dei Sinottici (Mc. 8, 27–33 e paralleli)', in P. Giovanni Canfora (ed.), *Atti della XIX Settimana Biblica*, 93–111, Brescia: Paideia

Cleary, Michael (1988), 'The Baptist of History and Kerygma', *ITQ* 54: 211–227

Coakley, James F. (1988), 'The Anointing at Bethany and the Priority of John', *JBL* 107: 241–256

—— (1995), 'Jesus' Messianic Entry Into Jerusalem (John 12:12–19 par.)', *JTS* 46: 461–482

Collins, C. John (1995), 'John 4:23–24, "In Spirit and Truth": An Idiomatic Proposal', *Presbyterion* 21: 118–121

Collins, Raymond F. (1986), 'John's Gospel: A Passion Narrative?' *BibTod* 24: 181–186

Coloe, Mary (1997), 'The Structure of the Johannine Prologue and Genesis 1', *ABR* 45: 40–55

Connick, C. Milo (1948), 'The Dramatic Character of the Fourth Gospel', *JBL* 67: 159–169

Cortès, Enric (1976), *Los discursos de Adiós de Gn 49 a Jn 13–17*, Barcelona: Herder

Cory, Catherine (1997), 'Wisdom's Rescue: A New Reading of the Tabernacles Discourse (John 7:1–8:59)', *JBL* 116: 95–116

Cotterell, F. Peter (1985), 'The Nicodemus Conversation: A Fresh Appraisal', *ExpT* 96: 237–242

Craig, William L. (1989), *Assessing the New Testament Evidence for the Historicity of the Resurrection of Jesus*, Lewiston: Mellen

Cribbs, F. Lamar (1970), 'A Reassessment of the Date of Origin and the Destination of the Gospel of John', *JBL* 89: 38–55

Crossan, John Dominic (1988), *The Cross That Spoke: The Origins of the Passion Narrative*, San Francisco: Harper & Row

—— (1991), *The Historical Jesus*, San Francisco: HarperSanFrancisco

—— (1995), *Who Killed Jesus?* London: HarperCollins

—— (1998), 'Concluding Reflections: Reflections on a Debate', in Paul Copan (ed.), *Will the Real Jesus Please Stand Up?* 147–155, Grand Rapids: Baker

Cullmann, Oscar (1976), *The Johannine Circle*, London: SCM; Philadelphia: Westminster

Culpepper, R. Alan (1975), *The Johannine School*, Missoula: Scholars

—— (1980), 'The Pivot of John's Prologue', *NTS* 27: 1–31

—— (1983), *Anatomy of the Fourth Gospel*, Philadelphia: Fortress

—— (1993), 'The AMHN, AMHN Sayings in the Gospel of John', in Robert B. Sloan and Mikeal C. Parsons (eds.), *Perspectives on John: Method and Interpretation in the Fourth Gospel*, 57–101, Lewiston: Mellen

—— (1994), *John, the Son of Zebedee*, Columbia: University of South Carolina Press

Curtis, K. Peter G. (1971), 'Luke xxiv.12 and John xx. 3–10', *JTS* 22: 512–515

Cuvillier, Élian (1996), 'La figure des disciples en Jean 4', *NTS* 42: 245–259

D'Angelo, Mary R. (1990), 'A Critical Note: John 20:17 and Apocalypse of Moses 31', *JTS* 41: 529–536

Dahl, Nils A. (1990), ' "Do Not Wonder!": John 5:28–29 and Johannine Eschatology Once More', in Robert T. Fortna and Beverly R. Gaventa (eds.), *The Conversation Continues: Studies in Paul and John*, 322–336, Nashville: Abingdon

Danna, Elizabeth (1999), 'A Note on John 4:29', *RB* 106: 219–223

Daube, David (1956), *The New Testament and Rabbinic Judaism*, London: Athlone

Davies, Margaret (1992), *Rhetoric and Reference in the Fourth Gospel*, Sheffield: Sheffield Academic Press

Davis, Stephen T., Daniel Kendall and Gerald O'Collins (eds.) (1997), *The Resurrection: An Interdisciplinary Symposium on the Resurrection of Jesus*, Oxford: Oxford University Press

de Jonge, Marinus (1973), 'Jewish Expectations about the "Messiah" according to the Fourth Gospel', *NTS* 19: 246–270

de la Fuente, Alfonso (1998), 'Trasfondo cultural del cuarto evangelio', *EstBíb* 56: 491–501

de la Potterie, Ignace (1984), 'Genèse de la foi pascale d'après Jn. 20', *NTS* 30: 26–49

—— (1986), 'Le témoin qui demeure: le disciple que Jésus aimait', *Bib* 67: 343–359

de Solages, Bruno (1979), *Jean et les Synoptiques*, Leiden: Brill

de Solages, Bruno with J.-M. Vacherot (1979), 'Le chapitre XXI de Jean: est-il de la même plume que le reste de l'Évangile?' *Bulletin de littérature ecclésiastique* 80: 96–101

Deeley, Mary K. (1997), 'Ezekiel's Shepherd and John's Jesus: A Case Study in the Appropriation of Biblical Texts', in Craig A. Evans and James A. Sanders (eds.), *Early Christian Interpretation of the Scriptures of Israel*, 252–264, Sheffield: Sheffield Academic Press

Delebecque, Éduard (1986a), 'La mission de Pierre et celle de Jean: note philologique sur Jean 21', *Bib* 67: 335–342

—— (1986b), '"Lazare est mort" (note sur Jean 11,14–15)', *Bib* 67: 89–97

—— (1989), 'Retour sur Jean XX, 9', *RB* 96: 81–94

Denaux, Adelbert (1992), 'The Q-Logion: Mt 11,27/Lk 10,22 and the Gospel of John', in Adelbert Denaux, (ed.), *John and the Synoptics*, 163–99, Leuven: Louvain University Press and Peeters

Derrett, J. Duncan M. (1963), 'Water Into Wine', *BZ* 7: 80–97

—— (1991), 'Circumcision and Perfection: A Johannine Equation', *EQ* 63: 211–224

—— (1995), 'ἐξώννυμι, φέρω, ἄλλος: The Fate of Peter (Jn 21:18–19)', *FN* 8: 79–84

—— (1997), '"Αρτος and the Comma (Jn 21:9)', *FN* 10: 117–128

—— (1998a), '"Dost Thou Teach Us?" (John 9:34c)', *DR* 116: 183–194

—— (1998b), 'Not Seeing and Later Seeing (John 16:16)', *ExpT* 109: 208–209

—— (1999), 'Advocacy at John 16:8–11', *ExpT* 110: 181–182

Dettwiler, Andreas (1995), *Die Gegenwart des Erhöten*, Göttingen: Vandenhoeck & Ruprecht

Devillers, Luc (1999), 'Une piscine peut en cacher une autre: À propos de Jean 5,1–9a', *RB* 106: 175–205

Dewailly, Louis-Marie (1985), 'D'où es-tu? (Jean 19, 9)', *RB* 92: 481–496

Dewey, Kim E. (1980), '*Paroimiai* in the Gospel of John', *Semeia* 17: 81–99

Dietzfelbinger, Christian (1997), *Der Abschied des Kommenden: Eine Auslegung der johanneischen Abschiedsreden*, Tübingen: Mohr

Dodd, Charles H. (1954), *The Interpretation of the Fourth Gospel*, Cambridge: Cambridge University Press

—— (1963), *Historical Tradition in the Fourth Gospel*, Cambridge: Cambridge University Press

Domeris, William R. (1983), 'The Johannine Drama', *JTSA* 2: 29–35

—— (1993), 'The Confession of Peter according to John 6:69', *TynB* 44: 155–167

Dormeyer, Detlev (1995), 'Joh 18.1–14 Par. Mk 14.43–53: Methodologische Überlegungen zur Rekonstruktion einer vorsynoptischen Passionsgeschichte', *NTS* 41: 218–239

Dowd, Sharyn E. (1993), 'Toward a Johannine Theology of Prayer', in Robert B. Sloan and Mikeal C. Parsons (eds.), *Perspectives on John: Method and Interpretation in the Fourth Gospel*, 317–335, Lewiston: Mellen

Dowell, Thomas M. (1990), 'Jews and Christians in Conflict: Why the Fourth Gospel Changed the Synoptic Tradition', *LouvStud* 15: 19–37

Draper, James A. (1997), 'Temple, Tabernacle and Mystical Experience in John', *Neot* 31: 263–288

Dudrey, Russ (2000), 'What Writers Should Have Done Better: A Case for the Resurrection of Jesus Based on Ancient Criticisms of the Resurrection Reports', *Stone-Campbell Journal* 3: 55–78

Dungan, David L. (1999), *A History of the Synoptic Problem*, New York: Doubleday

Dunkerley, Roderic (1959), 'Lazarus', *NTS* 5: 321–327

Dunn, James D. G. (1970a), 'The Messianic Secret in Mark', *TynB* 21: 92–117.

—— (1970b), 'The Washing of the Disciples' Feet in John 13:1–20', *ZNW* 61: 247–252

—— (1983), 'Let John Be John', in Peter Stuhlmacher (ed.), *Das Evangelium und die Evangelien*, 309–339, Tübingen: Mohr

—— (1991), 'John and the Oral Gospel Tradition', in Henry Wansbrough (ed.), *Jesus and the Oral Gospel Tradition*, 351–379, Sheffield: JSOT

Dvorak, James D. (1998), 'The Relationship Between John and the Synoptic Gospels', *JETS* 41: 201–213

Edwards, M. J. (1994), '"Not Yet Fifty Years Old": John 8.57', *NTS* 40: 449–454

Edwards, Ruth B. (1988), 'χάριν ἀντὶ χάριτος (John 1.16): Grace and the Law in the Johannine Prologue', *JSNT* 32: 3–15

—— (1994), 'The Christological Basis of the Johannine Footwashing', in Joel B. Green and Max Turner (eds.), *Jesus of Nazareth: Lord and Christ*, 367–383, Carlisle: Paternoster; Grand Rapids: Eerdmans

Ehrman, Bart D. (1988), 'Jesus and the Adulteress', *NTS* 34: 24–44

Eller, Vernard. (1987), *The Beloved Disciple: His Name, His Story, His Thought*, Grand Rapids: Eerdmans

Ellis, E. Earle (1977), 'How the New Testament Uses the Old', in I. Howard Marshall (ed.), *New Testament Interpretation*, 199–219, Exeter: Paternoster; Grand Rapids: Eerdmans

—— (1988), 'Background and Christology of John's Gospel: Selected Motifs', *SWJT* 31: 24–31

—— (1993), 'Background and Christology of John's Gospel', in Robert B. Sloan and Mikeal C. Parsons (eds.), *Perspectives on John: Method and Interpretation in the Fourth Gospel*, 1–25, Lewiston: Mellen

—— (1999), *The Making of the New Testament Documents*, Leiden: Brill

Ellis, Peter F. (1992), 'The Authenticity of John 21', *StVTQ* 36: 17–25

Emerton, John A. (1966), 'Melchizedek and the Gods: Fresh Evidence for the Jewish Background of John x.34–36', *JTS* 17: 399–401

Ensor, Peter W. (1996), *Jesus and His Works: The Johannine Sayings in Historical Perspective*, Tübingen: Mohr

—— (2000), 'The Authenticity of John 4.35', *EQ* 72: 13–21

Eppstein, Victor (1964), 'The Historicity of the Gospel Account of the Cleansing of the Temple', *ZNW* 55: 42–58

Ernst, Josef (1994), *Johannes der Täufer – der Lehrer Jesu?* Freiburg: Herder

Evans, Craig A. (1981), 'The Voice From Heaven: A Note on John 12:28', *CBQ* 43: 405–408

—— (1982), '"Peter Warming Himself": The Problem of an Editorial "Seam"', *JBL* 101: 245–249

—— (1989), 'Jesus' Action in the Temple: Cleansing or Portent of Destruction?' *CBQ* 51: 237–270

—— (1993), *Word and Glory: On the Exegetical and Theological Background of John's Prologue*, Sheffield: JSOT

—— (1996), 'The Passion of Jesus: History Remembered or Prophecy Historicized?' *BBR* 6: 159–165

Farmer, William R. (1952), 'The Palm Branches in John 12,13', *JTS* 3: 62–66

Flanagan, N. (1981), 'The Gospel of John as Drama', *BibTod* 19: 264–270

Ford, Josephine M. (1995), 'Jesus as Sovereign in the Passion according to

John', *BTB* 25: 110–117

Fortna, Robert T. (1970), *The Gospel of Signs*, Cambridge: Cambridge University Press

—— (1978), 'Jesus and Peter at the High Priest's House: A Test Case for the Question of the Relation Between Mark's and John's Gospels', *NTS* 24: 371–383

—— (1988), *The Fourth Gospel and its Predecessor*, Philadelphia: Fortress

France, R. T. (1985), *The Gospel According to Matthew*, Leicester: Inter-Varsity Press; Grand Rapids: Eerdmans

Franzmann, Majella and Michael Klinger (1992), 'The Call Stories of John 1 and 21', *StVTQ* 36: 7–15

Fredriksen, Paula (1999), *Jesus of Nazareth, King of the Jews*, New York: Knopf

Freed, Edwin D. (1961), 'The Entry Into Jerusalem in the Gospel of John', *JBL* 80: 329–338

—— (1983), 'Who or What Was before Abraham in John 8:58?' *JSNT* 17: 52–59

Funk, Robert W. (1996), *Honest to Jesus: Jesus for a New Millennium*, San Francisco: HarperSanFrancisco

—— (ed.) (1998), *The Acts of Jesus: The Search for the Authentic Deeds of Jesus*, San Francisco: HarperSanFrancisco

Funk, Robert W. and Roy W. Hoover, and the Jesus Seminar (1993), *The Five Gospels: The Search for the Authentic Words of Jesus*, New York: Macmillan

García-Moreno, Antonio (1991), 'Autenticidad e historicidad del IV Evangelio', *ScriptTheol* 23: 13–67

Gardner-Smith, Percival (1938), *Saint John and the Synoptic Gospels*, Cambridge: Cambridge University Press

Gaventa, Beverly R. (1996), 'The Archive of Excess: John 21 and the Problem of Narrative Closure', in R. Alan Culpepper and C. Clifton Black (eds.), *Exploring the Gospel of John*, 240–252, Louisville: Westminster John Knox

Geiger, Georg (1992), 'Die *Egō Eimi*-Worte bei Johannes und den Synoptikern', in Adelbert Denaux (ed.), *John and the Synoptics*, 466–472, Leuven: Louvain University Press and Peeters

Geivett, Douglas and Gary R. Habermas (eds.) (1997), *In Defense of Miracles: A Comprehensive Case for God's Action in History*, Downers Grove: InterVarsity Press

Geldenhuys, Norval (1950), *The Gospel of Luke*, London: Marshall, Morgan & Scott, 1950; Grand Rapids: Eerdmans, 1951

Gerhardsson, Birger (1961), *Memory and Manuscript*, Lund: Gleerup

Giblin, Charles H. (1980), 'Suggestion, Negative Response and Positive

Action in St John's Portrayal of Jesus (John 2.1–11; 4.46–54; 7.2–14; 11.1–44)', *NTS* 26: 197–211

—— (1984), 'Confrontations in John 18,1–27', *Bib* 65: 210–232

—— (1986), 'John's Narration of the Hearing Before Pilate (John 18,28–19,16a)', *Bib* 67: 221–239

—— (1992), 'Mary's Anointing for Jesus' Burial-Resurrection (John 12,1–8)', *Bib* 73: 560–564

Goetz, Stewart C. and Craig L. Blomberg (1981), 'The Burden of Proof', *JSNT* 11: 39–63

Goulder, Michael D. (1983), 'From Ministry to Passion in John and Luke', *NTS* 29: 561–568

Grappe, Christian (2000), 'Jean 1,14 (–18) dans son contexte et à la lumière de la literature intertestamentaire, *RHPR* 80: 153–169

Grayston, Kenneth K. (1990), *The Gospel of John*, London: Epworth; Philadelphia: Trinity

Grigsby, Bruce (1985), 'Washing in the Pool of Siloam – A Thematic Anticipation of the Johannine Cross', *NovT* 27: 227–235

—— (1986), ' "If Any Man Thirsts …": Observations on the Rabbinic Background of John 7,37–39', *Bib* 67: 101–108

Grossouw, William K. (1966), 'A Note on John XIII 1–3', *NovT* 8: 124–131

Grundmann, Walter (1959), 'Das Wort von Jesu Freunden (Joh. XV,13–16) und das Herrenmahl', *NovT* 3: 62–69

—— (1984), 'The Decision of the Supreme Court to Put Jesus to Death (John 11:47–57) in Its Context: Tradition and Redaction in the Gospel of John', in Ernst Bammel and Charles F. D. Moule (eds.), *Jesus and the Politics of His Day*, 295–318, Cambridge: Cambridge University Press

Guilding, Aileen (1960), *The Fourth Gospel and Jewish Worship*, Oxford: Clarendon

Gundry, Robert H. (1993), *Mark: A Commentary on His Apology for the Cross*, Grand Rapids: Eerdmans

Haenchen, Ernst (1970), 'History and Interpretation in the Johannine Passion Narrative', *Int* 24: 198–219

—— (1984a, 1984b), *John*, 2 vols., Philadelphia: Fortress

Ham, Clay (1998), 'The Title "Son of Man" in the Gospel of John', *Stone-Campbell Journal* 1: 67–84

Hamilton, John (1992), 'The Chronology of the Crucifixion and the Passover', *Churchman* 106: 323–338

Hansen, Steven E. (1997), 'Forgiving and Retaining Sin: A Study of the Text and Context of John 20:23', *HBT* 19: 24–32

Hanson, Anthony T. (1973), 'The Old Testament Background to the

Raising of Lazarus', *TU* 112: 252–255

—— (1991), *The Prophetic Gospel: A Study of John and the Old Testament*, Edinburgh: T. & T. Clark

Harner, Philip B. (1970), *The 'I Am' of the Fourth Gospel*, Philadelphia: Fortress

Harris, Elizabeth (1994), *Prologue and Gospel: The Theology of the Fourth Evangelist*, Sheffield: Sheffield Academic Press

Harris, Murray J. (1983), *Raised Immortal*, London: Marshall, Morgan and Scott, 1983; Grand Rapids: Eerdmans, 1985

—— (1986), ' "The Dead Are Restored to Life": Miracles of Revivification in the Gospels', in David Wenham and Craig Blomberg (eds.), *Gospel Perspectives*, vol. 6, 295–326, Sheffield: JSOT

Harvey, Anthony E. (1977), *Jesus on Trial: A Study in the Fourth Gospel*, London: SPCK; Atlanta: John Knox

Hatina, Thomas R. (1993), 'John 20,22 in Its Eschatological Context: Promise or Fulfillment?' *Bib* 74: 196–219

Hayward, C. T. R. (1978), 'The Holy Name of the God of Moses and the Prologue of St John's Gospel', *NTS* 25: 16–32

Headlam, Arthur C. (1948), *The Fourth Gospel as History*, Oxford: Blackwell

Heil, John P. (1991), 'The Story of Jesus and the Adulteress (John 7,53–8,11) Reconsidered', *Bib* 72: 182–191

Hemer, Colin J. (1989), *The Book of Acts in the Setting of Hellenistic History*, ed. Conrad H. Gempf, Tübingen: Mohr

Hengel, Martin (1977), *Crucifixion in the Ancient World and the Folly of the Message of the Cross*, London: SCM; Philadelphia: Fortress

—— (1989), *The Johannine Question*, London: SCM; Philadelphia: Trinity

—— (1996), 'Zur Wirkungsgeschichte von Jes 53 in vorchristlicher Zeit', in Bernd Janowski and Peter Stuhlmacher (eds.), *Der leidende Gottesknecht: Jesaja und seine Wirkungsgeschichte*, 49–91, Tübingen: Mohr

—— (2000), *The Four Gospels and the One Gospel of Jesus Christ*, London: SCM; Harrisburg: Trinity

Higgins, Angus J. B. (1960), *The Historicity of the Fourth Gospel*, London: Lutterworth

Hill, Charles E. (1997), 'The Identity of John's Nathanael', *JSNT* 67: 45–61

—— (1998), 'What Papias Said About John (and Luke): A "New" Papian Fragment', *JTS* 49: 582–629

Hoegen-Rohls, Christina (1996), *Der nachösterliche Johannes: Die Abschiedsreden als hermeneutischer Schlüssel zum vierten Evangelium*, Tübingen: Mohr

Holland, H. Scott (1923), *The Fourth Gospel*, London: John Murray

Holst, Robert (1976), 'The One Anointing of Jesus: Another Application of the Form-Critical Method', *JBL* 95: 435–446

Horsley, Richard A. and John Hanson (1985), *Bandits, Prophets, and Messiahs*, Minneapolis: Winston

Hoskyns, Edwyn C. and Francis N. Davey (ed.) (1947), *The Fourth Gospel*, London: Faber & Faber

Houlden, J. Leslie (1981), 'John 19⁵: "And he said to them, Behold, the man"', *ExpT* 92: 148–149

Hultgren, Arland J. (1982), 'The Johannine Footwashing (13.1–11) as Symbol of Eschatological Hospitality', *NTS* 28: 539–546

Hunter, W. Bingham (1985), 'Contextual and Genre Implications for the Historicity of John 11:41b–42', *JETS* 28: 53–70

Hurtado, Larry W. (1988), *One God, One Lord: Early Christian Devotion and Ancient Jewish Monotheism*, Philadelphia: Fortress

Jackson, Howard M. (1999), 'Ancient Self-Referential Conventions and Their Implications for the Authorship and Integrity of the Gospel of John', *JTS* 50: 1–34

James, Stephen A. (1979), 'The Adulteress and the Death Penalty', *JETS* 22: 45–53

Jeremias, Joachim (1966), *The Eucharistic Words of Jesus*, London: SCM; New York: Scribner's

Johnson, Luke T. (1989), 'The New Testament's Anti-Jewish Slander and the Conventions of Ancient Polemic', *JBL* 108: 419–441.

Johnston, E. D. (1962), 'The Johannine Version of the Feeding of the Five Thousand – An Independent Tradition?' *NTS* 8: 151–154

Joubert, S. J. (1993), 'A Bone of Contention in Recent Scholarship: The "Birkat Ha-Minim" and the Separation of Church and Synagogue in the First Century AD', *Neot* 27: 351–363

Kalantzis, George (1997), 'Ephesus as a Roman, Christian, and Jewish Metropolis in the First and Second Centuries C.E.', *Jian Dao* 8: 103–119

Karavidopoulos, Jean (1992), 'L'heure de la crucifixion de Jésus selon Jean et les Synoptiques: Mc 15,25 par rapport à Jn 19,14–16', in Adelbert Denaux (ed.), *John and the Synoptics*, 608–613, Leuven: Louvain University Press and Peeters

Käsemann, Ernst (1968), *The Testament of Jesus: A Study of the Gospel of John in the Light of Chapter 17*, London: SCM

Katz, Paul (1997), 'Wieso gerade nach Efrajim? (Erwägungen zu Jh 11,54)', *ZNW* 88: 130–134

Keener, Craig S. (1999), 'Is Subordination Within the Trinity Really Heresy? A Study of John 5:18 in Context', *TrinJ* 20: 39–51

Kemper, Friedmar (1987), 'Zur literarischen Gestalt des Johannesevangeliums', *TZ* 43: 247–264

Kennedy, George A. (1984), *New Testament Interpretation Through Rhetorical Criticism*, Chapel Hill: University of North Carolina Press

Kieffer, René (1998), 'L'arrière-fond juif du lavement des pieds', *RB* 105: 546–555

Kiehl, Erich H. (1990), *The Passion of Our Lord*, Grand Rapids: Baker

Kiley, Mark (1995), 'The Geography of Famine: John 6:22–25', *RB* 102: 226–230

Kim, Seyoon (1983), *'The "Son of Man"' as the Son of God*, Tübingen: Mohr; Grand Rapids: Eerdmans, 1985

Kinman, Brent (1991), 'Pilate's Assize and the Timing of Jesus' Trial', *TynB* 42: 282–295

—— (1994), 'Jesus' Triumphal Entry in the Light of Pilate's', *NTS* 40: 442–448

Kippenberg, Hans G. (1971), *Garizim und Synagoge*, Berlin: de Gruyter

Klauck, Hans-Josef (1996), 'Der Weggang Jesu: Neue Arbeiten zu Joh 13–17', *BZ* 40: 236–250

Kleinknecht, Karl T. (1985), 'Johannes 13, die Synoptiker und die "Methode" der johanneischen Evangelienüberlieferung', *ZTK* 82: 361–388

Knapp, Henry M. (1997), 'The Messianic Water Which Gives Life to the World', *HBT* 19: 109–121

Koester, Craig R. (1990), 'Messianic Exegesis and the Call of Nathanael', *JSNT* 39: 23–34

—— (1995), 'Topography and Theology in the Gospel of John', in Astrid Beck, Andrew Bartelt, Paul Raabe and Chris Franke (eds.), *Fortunate the Eyes That See*, 436–448, Grand Rapids: Eerdmans

Kossen, H. B. (1970), 'Who Were the Greeks of John XII 20?' in W. C. van Unnik (ed.), *Studies in John*, 97–110, Leiden: Brill

Köstenberger, Andreas J. (1996), 'Frühe Zweifel an der johanneischen Verfasserschaft des vierten Evangeliums in der modernen Interpretationsgeschichte', *EJT* 5: 37–46

—— (1998), 'Jesus as Rabbi in the Fourth Gospel', *BBR* 8: 97–128

—— (1999), *Encountering John: The Gospel in Historical, Literary and Theological Perspective*, Grand Rapids: Baker

Kovacs, Judith L. (1995), '"Now Shall the Ruler of this World Be Driven Out": Jesus' Death as Cosmic Battle in John 12:20–36', *JBL* 114: 227–247

Kowalski, Beate (1996), *Die Hirtenrede (Joh 10,1–18) im Kontext des Johannes-evangeliums*, Stuttgart: Katholisches Bibelwerk

Kreitzer, Larry J. (1998), 'The Temple Incident of John 2:13–25: A Preview of What Is to Come', in Chrstopher Rowland and Crispin H.

T. Fletcher-Louis (eds.), *Understanding, Studying and Reading*, 93–101, Sheffield: Sheffield Academic Press

Kremer, Jacob (1985), *Lazarus: Die Geschichte einer Auferstehung*, Stuttgart: Katholisches Bibelwerk

Kügler, J. (1998), 'Der König als Brotspender: Religionsgeschichtliche Überlegungen zu JosAs 4,7; 25,5 und Joh 6,15', *ZNW* 89: 118–124

Kühschelm, Roman (1990), *Verstockung, Gericht und Heil: Exegetische und Bibeltheologische Untersuchung zum sogenannten, 'Dualismus' und 'Determinismus', in Joh 12,35–50*, Frankfurt am Main: Anton Hain

Kylie, Mark (1995), 'The Geography of Famine: John 6:22–25', *RB* 102: 226–230

Kysar, Robert (1976), *John, The Maverick Gospel*, Atlanta: John Knox

Labahn, Michael (1998), 'Eine Spurensuche anhand von Joh 5.1–18', *NTS* 44: 159–179

Lacomara, Aelred (1974), 'Deuteronomy and the Farewell Discourse (Jn 13:31 – 16:33)', *CBQ* 36: 65–84

Ladd, George E. (1975), *I Believe in the Resurrection of Jesus*, London: Hodder & Stoughton; Grand Rapids: Eerdmans

—— (1993), *A Theology of the New Testament*, rev. and ed. Donald A. Hagner, Grand Rapids: Eerdmans

Landis, Stephan (1994), *Das Verhältnis des Johannesevangeliums zu den Synoptikern: Am Beispiel von Mt 8,5–13; Lk 7,1–10; Joh 4,46–54*, Berlin: de Gruyter

Lang, Manfred (1999), *Johannes und die Synoptiker: Analyse von Joh 18–20 vor dem markinischen und lukanischen Hintergrund*, Göttingen: Vandenhoeck & Ruprecht

Latourelle, René (1988), *The Miracles of Jesus and the Theology of Miracles*, New York: Paulist

Lea, Thomas D. (1994), 'Who Killed the Lord? A Defense Against the Charge of Anti-Semitism in John's Gospel', *CTR* 7: 103–123

—— (1995), 'The Reliability of History in John's Gospel', *JETS* 38: 387–402

Leaney, A. R. C. (1972), 'The Johannine Paraclete and the Qumran Scrolls', in James H. Charlesworth (ed.), *John and Qumran*, 38–61, London: Geoffrey Chapman

Lee, Dorothy A. (1995), 'Partnership in Easter Faith: The Role of Mary Magdalene and Thomas in John 20', *JSNT* 58: 37–49

Lee, E. Kenneth (1953), 'The Drama of the Fourth Gospel', *ExpT* 65: 173–176

Lee, G. M. (1968), 'The Inscription on the Cross', *PEQ* 100: 144

Legasse, Simon (1997), *The Trial of Jesus*, London: SCM

Leidig, E. (1980), 'Natanael, ein Sohn des Tholomäus', *TZ* 36: 374–

375

Levinskaya, Irina (1996), *The Book of Acts in Its Diaspora Setting*, Carlisle: Paternoster; Grand Rapids: Eerdmans

Lewis, Frank G. (1908), *The Irenaeus Testimony to the Fourth Gospel: Its Extent, Meaning, and Value*, Chicago: University of Chicago Press

Lietzmann, Hans (1934), 'Der Prozess Jesu', *Sitzungsberichte der Preussischen Akademie der Wissenschaftenen* 14: 313–322

Lieu, Judith (1999), 'Temple and Synagogue in John', *NTS* 45: 51–69

Lincoln, Andrew T. (2000), *Truth on Trial: The Lawsuit Motif in the Fourth Gospel*, Peabody: Hendrickson

Lindars, Barnabas (1961), 'The Composition of John XX', *NTS* 7: 142–147

—— (1971), *Behind the Fourth Gospel*, London: SPCK

—— (1972), *The Gospel of John*, London: Marshall, Morgan & Scott, 1972; Grand Rapids: Eerdmans, 1981

—— (1977), 'Traditions Behind the Fourth Gospel', in Marinus de Jonge (ed.), *L'Évangile de Jean: Sources, rédaction, théologie*, 107–124, Leuven: Louvain University Press and Peeters

—— (1981a), 'Discourse and Tradition: The Use of the Sayings of Jesus in the Discourses of the Fourth Gospel', *JSNT* 13: 83–101

—— (1981b), 'John and the Synoptic Gospels: A Test Case', *NTS* 27: 287–294

—— (1992), 'Rebuking the Spirit: A New Analysis of the Lazarus Story of John 11', *NTS* 38: 89–104

—— (2000), 'John', in R. Alan Culpepper (ed.), *The Johannine Literature*, 30–108, Sheffield: Sheffield Academic Press

Lindsell, Harold (1976), *Battle for the Bible*, Grand Rapids: Zondervan

Longenecker, Bruce W. (1995), 'The Unbroken Messiah: A Johannine Feature and Its Social Functions', *NTS* 41: 428–441

Longenecker, Richard N. (1970), *The Christology of Early Jewish Christianity*, London: SCM, Naperville: Allenson

Lüdemann, Gerd (1994), *The Resurrection of Jesus: History, Experience, Theology*, Minneapolis: Fortress

Lüdemann, Gerd with Alf Özen (1995), *What Really Happened to Jesus: A Historical Approach to the Resurrection*, Louisville: Westminster John Knox

Mahoney, Robert (1974), *Two Disciples at the Tomb: The Background and Message of John 20.1–10*, Bern: Herbert Lang; Frankfurt am Main: Peter Lang

Maier, Gerhard (1981), 'Johannes und Matthäus–Zweispalt oder Viergestalt des Evangeliums?' in R. T. France and David Wenham (eds.), *Gospel Perspectives*, vol. 2, 267–291, Sheffield: JSOT

Malatesta, Edward (1971), 'The Literary Structure of John 17', *Bib* 52: 190–214

Malzoni, C. V. (1999), ' "Moi, je suis la résurrection": Jean 11, 25 dans la tradtion syriaque ancienne', *RB* 106: 421–440

Manns, Frédéric (1985), 'Exégèse rabbinique et exégèse johannique', *RB* 92: 525–538

Marchadour, Alain (1988), *Lazare: Histoire d'un Récit, Récits d'une histoire*, Paris: Cerf

Marco, Mariano H. (1971), 'Un problema de crítica histórica en el relato de la Pasión: la liberación de Barrabás', *EstBíb* 30: 137–160

Marcus, Joel (1998), 'Rivers of Living Water from Jesus' Belly (John 7:38)', *JBL* 117: 328–330

Marshall, I. Howard (1970), *Luke: Historian and Theologian*, Exeter: Paternoster; Grand Rapids: Zondervan

Martin, James P. (1964), 'History and Eschatology in the Lazarus Narrative', *SJT* 17: 332–343

Martin, Troy W. (1998), 'Assessing the Johannine Epithet "The Mother of Jesus" ', *CBQ* 60: 63–73

Martyn, J. Louis (1979), *History and Theology in the Fourth Gospel*, 2nd ed., Nashville: Abingdon

Marzotto, Damiano (1977), 'Giovanni 17 e il Targum di Esodo 19–20', *RivBib* 25: 375–388

Matera, Frank J. (1990), 'Jesus Before Annas: John 18,13–14. 19–24', *ETL* 66: 38–55

Mathews, Kenneth A. (1988), 'John, Jesus and the Essenes: Trouble at the Temple', *CTR* 3: 101–126

McArthur, Harvey K. and Robert M. Johnston (1990), *They Also Taught in Parables*, Grand Rapids: Zondervan

McCaffrey, James (1988), *The House With Many Rooms: The Temple Theme of Jn 14,2–3*, Rome: Pontifical Biblical Institute

McDonald, J. Ian H. (1995), 'The So-Called *Pericope de adultera*', *NTS* 41: 415–427

McGehee, Michael (1986), 'A Less Theological Reading of John 20:17', *JBL* 105: 299–302

McGing, Brian C. (1991), 'Pontius Pilate and the Sources', *CBQ* 53: 416–438

McGrath, James F. (1998), 'A Rebellious Son? Hugo Odeberg and the Interpretation of John 5.18', *NTS* 44: 470–473

McKay, K. L. (1985), 'Style and Significance in the Language of John 21:15–17', *NovT* 27: 319–333

—— (1996), ' "I Am" in John's Gospel', *ExpT* 107: 302–303

Mead, A. H. (1985), 'The Βασιλικός in John 4.46-53', *JSNT* 23: 69–72

Meier, John P. (1991, 1994), *A Marginal Jew: Rethinking the Historical Jesus*, 2 vols., New York: Doubleday

Menken, Maarten J. J. (1985), 'The Quotation from Isa 40,3 in John 1,23', *Bib* 66: 190–205

—— (1988a), 'Die Form des Zitates aus Jes 6,10 in Joh 12,40', *BZ* 32: 189–209

—— (1988b), 'The Provenance and Meaning of the Old Testament Quotation in John 6:31', *NovT* 30: 39–56

—— (1989), 'Die Redaktion des Zitates aus Sach 9,9 in Joh 12,15', *ZNW* 80: 193–209

—— (1990), 'The Translation of Psalm 41.10 in John 13.18', *JSNT* 40: 61–79

—— (1993), 'The Textual Form and the Meaning of the Quotation from Zechariah 12:10 in John 19:37', *CBQ* 55: 494–511

—— (1996), 'The Origin of the Old Testament Quotation in John 7:38', *NovT* 38: 160–175

Merritt, Robert L. (1985), 'Jesus Barabbas and the Paschal Pardon', *JBL* 104: 57–68

Michaels, J. Ramsey (1967), 'The Centurion's Confession and the Spear Thrust', *CBQ* 29: 102–109

—— (1983), *John: A Good News Commentary*, San Francisco: Harper & Row

Millard, Alan (2000), *Reading and Writing in the Time of Jesus*, Sheffield: Sheffield Academic Press

Miller, Edward L. (1980), 'The Christology of John 8:25', *TZ* 36: 257–265

—— (1989), *Salvation-History in the Prologue of John*, Leiden: Brill

—— (1993), 'The Johannine Origins of the Johannine Logos', *JBL* 112: 445–457

—— (1999), '"In the Beginning": A Christological Transparency', *NTS* 45: 587–592

Mills, Watson E. (1995), *The Gospel of John*, Lewiston: Mellen

Mimouni, S. C. (1997), 'La "Birkat Ha–minim", une prière juive contre les judéo chrétiens', *RSR* 71: 275–298

Minear, Paul S. (1983a), 'Diversity and Unity: A Johannine Case-Study', in Ulrich Luz and Hans Weder (eds.), *Die Mitte des Neuen Testaments*, 162–175, Göttingen: Vandenhoeck & Ruprecht

—— (1983b), 'The Original Functions of John 21', *JBL* 102: 85–98

Moloney, Francis J. (1998), *The Gospel of John*, Collegeville: Liturgical

—— (2000), 'The Fourth Gospel and the Jesus of History', *NTS* 46: 42–58

Moo, Douglas J. (1983), *The Old Testament in the Gospel Passion Narratives*,

Sheffield: Almond

Morgan-Wynne, J. E. (1980), 'The Cross and the Revelation of Jesus as ἐγώ εἰμι in the Fourth Gospel (John 8.28)', in Elizabeth A. Livingstone (ed.), *Studia Biblica 1978*, vol. 2, 219–226, Sheffield: JSOT

Morris, Leon (1969), *Studies in the Fourth Gospel*, Exeter: Paternoster; Grand Rapids: Eerdmans

—— (1995), *The Gospel According to John*, 2nd ed., Grand Rapids: Eerdmans

Motyer, Stephen (1997), *Your Father the Devil? A New Approach to John and 'The Jews'*, Carlisle: Paternoster

Moule, Charles F. D. (1957), 'The Post-Resurrection Appearances in the Light of Festival Pilgrimages', *NTS* 4: 58–61

—— (1975), 'The Meaning of "Life" in the Gospel and the Epistles of St. John: A Study in the Story of Lazarus, John 11:1–44', *Theol* 78: 114–125

Mounce, William D. (1981), 'The Origin of the New Testament Metaphor of Rebirth', University of Aberdeen: PhD thesis

Mowvley, Henry (1984), 'John 1¹⁴⁻¹⁸ in the Light of Exodus 33⁷–34³⁵', *ExpT* 95: 135–137

Muilenburg, James (1932), 'Literary Form in the Fourth Gospel', *JBL* 51: 40–53

Müller, Karlheinz (1969), 'Joh 9,7 und das jüdische Verständnis des ˘iloh-Spruches', *BZ* 13: 251–256

Müller, Mogens (1991), '"Have You Faith in the Son of Man?" (John 9.35)', *NTS* 37: 291–294

Muñoz-León, Domingo (1977), 'El substrato targúmico del Discurso del Pan de Vida: Nuevas aportaciones', *EstBíb* 36: 217–226

—— (1987), '¿Es el Apóstol Juan el discípulo amado?' *EstBíb* 45: 403–492

Murphy-O'Connor, Jerome (1990), 'John the Baptist and Jesus: History and Hypotheses', *NTS* 36: 359–374

—— (2000), 'Jesus and the Money Changers (Mark 11:15–17; John 2: 13–17)', *RB* 107: 42–55

Mussner, Franz (1967), *The Historical Jesus in the Gospel of St John*, New York: Herder & Herder

Neirynck, Frans N. (1975), 'The "Other Disciple" in Jn 18,15–16', *ETL* 51: 113–141

—— (1979), *Jean et les Synoptiques*, Leuven: Louvain University Press and Peeters

—— (1984), 'John and the Synoptics: The Empty Tomb Stories', *NTS* 30: 161–187

—— (1990), 'John 21', *NTS* 36: 321–336

—— (1995), 'Jean 4,46–54: Une leçon de méthode', *ETL* 71: 176–184

Nereparampil, Lucius (1978), *Destroy This Temple: An Exegetico-Theological Study on the Meaning of Jesus' Temple-Logion in John 2:19*, Bangalore: Dharmaram

Neusner, Jacob (1971), *The Rabbinic Traditions about the Pharisees Before 70*, 3 vols., Leiden: Brill

—— (1989), 'Money-Changers in the Temple: The Mishnah's Explanation', *NTS* 35: 287–290

Neyrey, Jerome H. (1987), 'Jesus the Judge: Forensic Process in John 8,21–59', *Bib* 68: 509–542

—— (1989), '"I Have Said: You are Gods": Psalm 82:6 and John 10', *JBL* 108: 647–663

—— (1994), 'What's Wrong With This Picture? John 4, Cultural Stereotypes of Women, and Public and Private Space', *BTB* 24: 77–91

—— (1996), 'The Trials (Forensic) and Tribulations (Honor Challenges) of Jesus: John 7 in Social Science Perspectives', *BTB* 26: 107–124

Nicklas, Tobias (2000a), 'Die Prophetie des Kaiaphas: Im Netz johanneischer Ironie', *NTS* 46: 589–594

—— (2000b), '"Unter dem Feigenbaum": Die Rolle des Lesers im Dialog zwischen Jesus und Natanael (Joh 1, 45–50)', *NTS* 46: 193–203

Nordsieck, Reinhard (1998), *Johannes: Zur Frage nach Verfasser und Einstehung des vierten Evangeliums*, Neukirchen-Vluyn: Neukirchener

O'Collins, Gerald and Daniel Kendall (1987), 'Mary Magdalene as a Major Witness to Jesus' Resurrection', *TS* 48: 631–646

—— (1994), 'Did Joseph of Arimathea Exist?' *Bib* 75: 235–241

O'Day, Gail R. (1992), 'John 7:53 – 8:11: A Study in Misreading', *JBL* 111: 631–640

O'Grady, John F. (1978), 'The Good Shepherd and the Vine and the Branches', *BTB* 8: 86–89

—— (1982), 'Recent Developments in Johannine Studies', *BTB* 12: 54–58

O'Neill, J. C. (1995), '"Making Himself Equal With God" (John 5.17–18): The Alleged Challenge to Jewish Monotheism in the Fourth Gospel', *IBS* 17: 50–61

Okure, Teresa (1988), *The Johannine Approach to Mission: A Contextual Study of John 4:1–42*, Tübingen: Mohr

Osborne, Basil (1973), 'A Folded Napkin in an Empty Tomb: John 11:44 and 20:7 Again', *HeyJ* 14: 437–440

Osborne, Grant R. (1981), 'John 21: Test Case for History and Redaction in the Resurrection Narratives', in R. T. France and David Wenham (eds.), *Gospel Perspectives*, vol. 2, 293–328, Sheffield: JSOT

—— (1984), *The Resurrection Narratives: A Redactional Study*, Grand

Rapids: Baker

Pagels, Elaine H. (1999), 'Exegesis of Genesis 1 in the Gospels of Thomas and John', *JBL* 118: 477–496

Painter, John (1981), 'The Farewell Discourses and the History of Johannine Christianity', *NTS* 27: 525–543

—— (1986), 'John 9 and the Interpretation of the Fourth Gospel', *JSNT* 28: 31–61

—— (1989), 'Tradition and Interpretation in John 6', *NTS* 35: 421–450

—— (1993), *The Quest for the Messiah: The History, Literature, and Theology of the Johannine Community*, 2nd ed., Edinburgh: T. & T. Clark; Nashville: Abingdon

Parker, Pierson (1956), 'Two Editions of John', *JBL* 75: 303–314

—— (1962), 'John the Son of Zebedee and the Fourth Gospel', *JBL* 81: 35–43

Parsons, Mikeal C. (1993), 'A Neglected ΕΓΩ ΕΙΜΙ Saying in the Fourth Gospel? Another Look at John 9:9', in Robert B. Sloan and Mikeal C. Parsons (eds.), *Perspectives on John: Method and Interpretation in the Fourth Gospel*, 145–180, Lewiston: Mellen

Paschal, R. Wade, Jr. (1981), 'Sacramental Symbolism and Physical Imagery in the Gospel of John', *TynB* 32: 151–176

Payne, Philip B. (1980), 'The Authenticity of the Parable of the Sower and Its Interpretation', in R. T. France and David Wenham (eds.), *Gospel Perspectives*, vol. 1, 163–207, Sheffield: JSOT

—— (1981), 'Jesus' Implicit Claim to Deity in His Parables', *TrinJ* 2:3–23

Pearce, Keith (1985), 'The Lucan Origins of the Raising of Lazarus', *ExpT* 96: 359–361

Pendrick, Gerard (1995), 'Μονογενής', *NTS* 41: 587–600

Perry, John M. (1993), 'The Evolution of the Johannine Eucharist', *NTS* 39: 22–35

Pesce, M. and A. Destro (1999), 'La lavanda dei piedi di Gv 13, 1–20, il *Romanzo di Esopo* e i *Satarnalia* di Macrobio', *Bib* 80: 240–249

Pilgaard, Aage (1987), 'The Gospel of John as Gospel Writing', in Lars Hartman and Birger Olsson (eds.), *Aspects on the Johannine Literature*, 44–55, Stockholm: Almqvist & Wiksell

Plumer, Eric (1997), 'The Absence of Exorcisms in the Fourth Gospel', *Bib* 78: 350–368

Poirier, John C. (1996), '"Day and Night" and the Punctuation of John 9.3', *NTS* 42: 288–294

Pollard, T. E. (1973), 'The Raising of Lazarus (John xi)', *TU* 112: 434–443

Porter, Stanley E. (2000), *The Criteria for Authenticity in Historical-Jesus Research*, Sheffield: Sheffield Academic Press

Potter, R. D. (1959), 'Topography and Archaeology in the Fourth Gospel',

TU 73: 329–337

Pryor, John W. (1990), 'Jesus and Israel in the Fourth Gospel – John 1.11', *NovT* 32: 201–218

—— (1991), 'John 3.3, 5: A Study in the Relation of John's Gospel to the Synoptic Tradition', *JSNT* 41: 71–95

—— (1992a), *John, Evangelist of the Covenant People*, London: Darton, Longman & Todd; Downers Grove: InterVarsity Press

—— (1992b) 'Justin Martyr and the Fourth Gospel', *SecCent* 9: 153–169

—— (1997), 'John the Baptist and Jesus: Tradition and Text in John 3:25', *JSNT* 66: 15–26

Quast, Kevin (1989), *Peter and the Beloved Disciple: Figures for a Community in Crisis*, Sheffield: JSOT

Rahner, Johanna (2000), 'Vergegenwärtigende Errinerung: Die Abschiedsreden, der Geist-Paraklet und die Retrospektive des Johannesevangeliums', *ZNW* 91: 72–90

Reese, James M. (1972), 'Literary Structure of Jn 13:31 – 14:31; 16:5–6, 16–33', *CBQ* 34: 321–331

Reich, Ronny (1995), '6 Stone Water Jars', *Jerusalem Perspective* 48: 30–33

Reim, Günter (1978), 'Joh 9 – Tradition und zeitgenössische messianische Diskussion', *BZ* 22: 245–253

—— (1983), 'Targum und Johannesevangelium', *BZ* 27: 1–13

—— (1984), 'Joh. 8.44 – Gotteskinder/Taufelskinder wie antijudaistisch ist, "die wohl antijudaistischste Äusserung des NT"?' *NTS* 30: 619–624

Rein, Matthias (1995), *Die Heilung des Blindgeborenen (Joh 9): Tradition und Redaktion*, Tübingen: Mohr

Reiser, William E. (1973), 'The Case of the Tidy Tomb: The Place of the Napkins of John 11:44 and 20:7', *HeyJ* 14: 47–57

Rese, Martin (1996), 'Das Selbstzeugnis des Johannesevangeliums über seinen Verfasser', *ETL* 72: 5–111

Reynolds, H. R. (1906), *The Gospel of St. John*, vol. 1, London: Funk & Wagnalls

Ridderbos, Herman N. (1997), *The Gospel According to John: A Theological Commentary*, Grand Rapids: Eerdmans

Riesner, Rainer (1980), 'Jüdische Elementarbildung und Evangelienüberlieferung', in R. T. France and David Wenham (eds.), *Gospel Perspectives*, vol. 1, 209–223, Sheffield: JSOT

—— (1984), *Jesus als Lehrer*, Tübingen: Mohr

—— (1987), 'Bethany Beyond the Jordan (John 1:28): Topography, Theology and History in the Fourth Gospel', *TynB* 38: 29–63

Ritt, Hubert (1989), 'Plädoyer für Methodentreue: Thesen zur Topographie und Chronologie der Johannespassion', in Karl Kertelge (ed.), *Der Prozess gegen Jesus: Historische Rückfrage und theologische*

Deutung, 183–190, Freiburg: Herder

Roberts, Colin (1987), 'John 20:30–31 and 21:24–25', *JTS* 38: 409–410

Robinson, J. Armitage (1908), *The Historical Character of St. John's Gospel,* London: Longmans-Green

Robinson, John A. T. (1955), 'The Parable of the Shepherd', *ZNW* 46: 233–240

—— (1959), 'The New Look on the Fourth Gospel', *TU* 73: 338–350

—— (1976), Redating the New Testament, London: SCM; Philadelphia: Westminster

—— (1985), The Priority of John, ed. J. F. Coakley, London: SCM, 1985; Oak Park: Meyer-Stone, 1987

Rochais, Gerárd (1981), *Les récits de résurrection des morts dans le Nouveau Testament,* Cambridge: Cambridge University Press

—— (1993), 'Jean 7: une construction littéraire dramatique, à la manière d'un scénario', *NTS* 39: 355–378

Rowland, Christopher (1984), 'John 1.51, Jewish Apocalyptic and Targumic Tradition', *NTS* 30: 498–507

Ruckstuhl, Eugen (1987), *Die literarische Einheit des Johannesevangeliums,* Göttingen: Vandenhoeck & Ruprecht

Sabbe, Maurits (1982), 'The Footwashing in Jn 13 and Its Relation to the Synoptic Gospels', *ETL* 58: 279–308

—— (1991), 'John 10 and Its Relationship to the Synoptic Gospels', in Johannes Beutler and Robert T. Fortna (eds.), *The Shepherd Discourse of John 10 and Its Context,* 75–93, Cambridge: Cambridge University Press

—— (1994), 'The Johannine Account of the Death of Jesus and Its Synoptic Parallels (Jn 19,16b–42)', *ETL* 70: 34–64

—— (1995), 'The Denial of Peter in the Gospel of John', *LouvStud* 20: 219–240

Sabourin, Leopold (1977), *The Divine Miracles Discussed and Defended,* Rome: Catholic Book Agency

Sabugal, Santos (1974), '"… Y la Verdad os hará libres" (Jn 8,32a la luz de TPI Gen 15,11)', *Augustinianum* 14: 177–181

—— (1977), *La curación del ciego de nacimiento (Jn 9,1–41): Analisís exegético y teólogico,* Madrid: Escuela Bíblica

Sanday, William (1872), *The Authorship and Historical Character of the Fourth Gospel,* London: Macmillan

—— (1905), *The Criticism of the Fourth Gospel,* Oxford: Clarendon

Sanders, E. P. (1985), *Jesus and Judaism,* London: SCM; Philadelphia: Fortress

Sandy, D. Brent (1991), 'John the Baptist's "Lamb of God": Affirmation in Its Canonical and Apocalyptic Milieu', *JETS* 34: 447–459

Schein, Bruce E. (1980), *Following the Way: The Study of John's Gospel,*

Minneapolis: Augsburg

Schenk, W. (1992), 'Interne Strukturierungen im Schluss-Segment Johannes 21: Συγγραφή and σατυρικόν/ἐπίλογος', *NTS* 38: 507–530

Schenke, Ludger (1989), 'Joh 7–10: Eine dramatische Szene', *ZNW* 80: 172–192

—— (1998), *Johannes Kommentar*, Düsseldorf: Patmos

Schlosser, Jacques (1990), 'La parole de Jésus sur la fin du Temple', *NTS* 36: 398–414

Schnackenburg, Rudolf (1968, 1980, 1982), *The Gospel According to John*, 3 vols., London: Burns & Oates; New York: Herder & Herder/Seabury

Schneemelcher, Wilhelm (ed.) (1991), *New Testament Apocrypha*, vol. 1, Cambridge: James Clarke; Louisville: Westminster John Knox

Schneiders, Sandra M. (1981), 'The Foot Washing (John 13:1–20): An Experiment in Hermeneutics', *CBQ* 43: 76–92

—— (1987), 'Death in the Community of Eternal Life', *Int* 41: 44–56

—— (1998), '"Because of the Woman's Testimony …": Reexamining the Issue of Authorship in the Fourth Gospel', *NTS* 44: 513–535

Schnelle, Udo (1989), 'Die Abschiedsreden im Johannesevangelium', *ZNW* 80: 64–79

—— (1992), *Antidocetic Christology in the Gospel of John*, Minneapolis: Fortress

—— (1996), 'Die Tempelreinigung und die Christologie des Johannes-evangeliums', *NTS* 42: 359–373

—— (1998), *Das Evangelium nach Johannes*, Leipzig: Evangelische

Schulz, Hans-Joachim (1994), *Die apostolische Herkunft der Evangelien*, 2nd ed., Freiburg: Herder

Schweizer, Eduard (1996), 'What About the Johannine "Parables"?' in R. Alan Culpepper and C. Clifton Black (eds.), *Exploring the Gospel of John*, 208–219, Louisville: Westminster John Knox

Scobie, Charles H. H. (1982), 'Johannine Geography', *SR* 11: 77–84

Segal, Alan F. (1977), *Two Powers in Heaven*, Leiden: Brill

Segalla, Giuseppe (1981), 'Un appello alla perseveranza nella fede in Gv 8,31–32?' *Bib* 62: 387–389

Segovia, Fernando F. (1982), 'John 13:1–20, The Footwashing in the Johannine Tradition', *ZNW* 73: 31–51

—— (1991), *The Farewell of the Word: The Johannine Call to Abide*, Minneapolis: Fortress

Senior, Donald P. (1991), *The Passion of Jesus in the Gospel of John*, Collegeville: Liturgical

Setzer, Claudia (1997), 'Excellent Women: Female Witness to the Resurrection', *JBL* 116: 259–272

Shaw, Alan (1974), 'The Breakfast by the Shore and the Mary Magdalene

Encounter as Eucharistic Narratives', *JTS* 25: 12–26

Sherwin-White, Adrian N. (1963), *Roman Society and Roman Law in the New Testament*, Oxford: Oxford University Press

—— (1965), 'The Trial of Christ', in D. E. Nineham et al., *Historicity and Chronology in the New Testament*, 97–116, London: SPCK

Siegman, Edward F. (1968), 'St. John's Use of Synoptic Material', *CBQ* 30: 182–198

Silva, Moisés (1988), 'Approaching the Fourth Gospel', *CTR* 3: 17–29

Simonis, A. J. (1967), *Die Hirtenrede im Johannesevangelium*, Rome: Pontificio Instituto Biblico

Smalley, S. (1978), *John: Evangelist and Interpreter*, Exeter: Paternoster

Smith, Barry D. (1991), 'The Chronology of the Last Supper', *WTJ* 53: 29–45

Smith, D. Moody (1963), 'John 12:12ff. and the Question of John's Use of the Synoptics', *JBL* 82: 58–64

—— (1992), *John Among the Gospels*, Minneapolis: Fortress

—— (1993), 'Historical Issues and the Problem of John and the Synoptics', in Martinus C. de Boer (ed.), *From Jesus to John*, 252–267, Sheffield: JSOT

—— (1999), *John*, Nashville: Abingdon

Soards, Marion L., Jr. (1983), Τόν ἐπενδύτην διεζώσατο, ἦν γὰρ γυμνός, *JBL* 102: 283–284

Söding, Thomas (1996), 'Die Macht der Warheit und das Reich der Freiheit: Zur johanneischen Deutung des Pilatus-Prozesses (Joh 18,28–19,16)', *ZTK* 93: 35–38

—— (2000), '"Was Kann aus Nazareth schon Gutes kommen?" (Joh 1.46): Die Bedeutung des Judeseins Jesu im Johannesevangelium', *NTS* 46: 21–41

Spencer, Patrick E. (1999), 'Narrative Echoes in John 21: Intertextual Interpretation and Intratextual Connection', *JSNT* 75: 49–68

Sprecher, Marie-Therese (1993), *Einheitsdenken aus der Perspektive von Joh 17*, Bern: Lang

Staley, Jeff (1986), 'The Structure of John's Prologue', *CBQ* 48: 241–264

Stanley, David M. (1980), *Jesus in Gethsemane: The Early Church Reflects on the Suffering of Jesus*, New York: Paulist

Stanton, Graham N. (1974), *Jesus of Nazareth in New Testament Preaching*, Cambridge: Cambridge University Press

—— (1994), 'Jesus of Nazareth: A Magician and a False Prophet Who Deceived God's People?' in Joel B. Green and Max Turner (eds.), *Jesus of Nazareth: Lord and Christ*, 164–180, Carlisle: Paternoster; Grand Rapids: Eerdmans

Stauffer, Ethelbert (1960a), 'Historische Elemente im vierten Evangelium', in Ernst-Heinz Amberg and Ulrich Kuhn (eds.), *Bekenntnis zur Kirche*, 33–51, Berlin: Evangelische

—— (1960b), *Jesus and His Story*, London: SCM; New York: Knopf

Stibbe, Mark W. G. (1992), *John as Storyteller: Narrative Criticism and the Fourth Gospel*, Cambridge: Cambridge University Press

—— (1993), *John*, Sheffield: JSOT

Story, Cullen I. K. (1989), 'The Bearing of Old Testament Terminology on the Johannine Chronology of the Final Passover of Jesus', *NovT* 31: 316–324

—— (1991), 'The Mental Attitude of Jesus at Bethany: John 11.33,38', *NTS* 37: 51–66

Strack, Hermann L. and Paul Billerbeck (1922, 1924, 1926, 1928a, 1928b, 1961), *Kommentar zum Neuen Testament aus Talmud und Midrasch*, 5 vols., München: Beck

Strobel, August (1980), *Die Stunde der Wahrheit*, Tübingen: Mohr

Sturch, R. L. (1980), 'The Alleged Eyewitness Material in the Fourth Gospel', in Elizabeth A. Livingstone (ed.), *Studia Biblica 1978*, vol. 2, 313–327, Sheffield: JSOT

Suggit, John (1983), 'John 19⁵: "Behold the Man" ', *ExpT* 94: 333–334

Swetnam, James (1980), 'The Meaning of πεπιστευκότας in John 8, 31', *Bib* 61: 106–109

—— (1993), 'Bestowal of the Spirit in the Fourth Gospel', *Bib* 74: 556–576

Sylva, Dennis (1988), 'Nicodemus and His Spices (John 19.39)', *NTS* 34: 148–151

Talbert, Charles H. (1992), *Reading John*, New York: Crossroad

Tasker, Randolph V. G. (1960), *The Gospel According to John*, London: Tyndale; Grand Rapids: Eerdmans

Taylor, Joan E. (1997), *The Immerser: John the Baptist within Second Temple Judaism*, Grand Rapids: Eerdmans

—— (1998), 'Golgotha: A Reconsideration of the Evidence for the Sites of Jesus' Crucifixion and Burial', *NTS* 44: 180–203

Temple, Sydney (1961), 'A Key to the Composition of the Fourth Gospel', *JBL* 80: 220–232

Thatcher, Thomas (1996), 'The Riddles of Jesus in the Fourth Gospel', Southern Baptist Theological Seminary: PhD dissertation

—— (1999), 'The Sabbath Trick: Unstable Irony in the Fourth Gospel', *JSNT* 76: 53–77

Theissen, Gerd (1983), *The Miracle Stories of the Early Christian Tradition*, Philadelphia: Fortress; Edinburgh: T. & T. Clark

Theissen, Gerd and Annette Merz (1997), *The Historical Jesus: A Comprehensive Guide*, London: SCM; Minneapolis: Fortress, 1998

Theissen, Gerd and Dagmar Winter (1998), *Die Kriterienfrage in der Jesusforschung: Vom Differenzkriterium zum Plausibilitätskriterium*, Freiburg: Universitätsverlag; Göttingen: Vandenhoeck & Ruprecht

Thomas, John C. (1991a), *Footwashing in John 13 and the Johannine Community*, Sheffield: JSOT

—— (1991b), 'The Fourth Gospel and Rabbinic Judaism', *ZNW* 82: 159–182

—— (1995), '"Stop Sinning Lest Something Worse Come Upon You": The Man at the Pool in John 5', *JSNT* 59: 3–20

—— (1998), *The Devil, Disease and Deliverance: Origins of Illness in New Testament Thought*, Sheffield: Sheffield Academic Press

Thomas, Robert L. and F. David Farnell (1998), *The Jesus Crisis*, Grand Rapids: Kregel

Thompson, Marianne M. (1988), *The Humanity of Jesus in the Fourth Gospel*, Philadelphia: Fortress

—— (1996), 'The Historical Jesus and the Johannine Christ', in R. Alan Culpepper and C. Clifton Black (eds.), *Exploring the Gospel of John*, 21–42, Louisville: Westminster John Knox

Tovey, Derek (1997), *Narrative Art and Act in the Fourth Gospel*, Sheffield: Sheffield Academic Press

Tragan, Pius-Ramon (1980), *La parabole du 'Pasteur' et ses explications: Jean 10, 1–18*, Rome: Editrice Anselmiana

Trites, Allison A. (1977), *The New Testament Concept of Witness*, Cambridge: Cambridge University Press

Trocmé, Etienne (1996), 'L'arrière-plan du récit johannique de l'expulsion des marchandes du temple (Jean 2, 13–22)', in H. Cancik (ed.), *Geschichte-Tradition-Reflexion*, vol. 2, 257–264, Tübingen: Mohr

Trudinger, Paul (1997), 'The Cleansing of the Temple: St John's Independent, Subtle Reflections', *ExpT* 108: 329–330

Tsuchido, Kiyoshi (1984), 'Tradition and Redaction in John 12.1–43', *NTS* 30: 609–619

Turner, John D. (1991), 'The History of Religions Background of John 10', in Johannes Beutler and Robert T. Fortna (eds.), *The Shepherd Discourse of John 10 and Its Context*, 33–52, Cambridge: Cambridge University Press

Twelftree, Graham H. (1999), *Jesus the Miracle Worker: A Historical and Theological Study*, Downers Grove: InterVarsity Press

Valentine, Simon R. (1996), 'The Johannine Prologue – A Microcosm of the Gospel', *EQ* 68: 291–304

van Belle, Gilbert (1985), *Les parentheses dans l'Évangile de Jean*, Leuven: Louvain University Press and Peeters

—— (1988), *Johannine Bibliography 1966–1985*, Leuven: Louvain

University Press and Peeters

—— (1994), *The Signs Source in the Fourth Gospel: Historical Survey and Critical Evaluation of the Semeia Hypothesis*, Leuven: Louvain University Press and Peeters

—— (1998), 'The Faith of the Galileans: The Parentheses in Jn 4:44', *ETL* 74: 27–44

van der Horst, Pieter W. (1994), 'The Birkat ha-minim in Recent Research', *ExpT* 105: 363–368

van der Loos, Hendrik (1965), *The Miracles of Jesus*, Leiden: Brill

van der Watt, Jan G. (1994), ' "Metaphorik" in Joh 15,1–8', *BZ* 38: 67–80

—— (1995), 'The Composition of the Prologue of John's Gospel: The Historical Jesus Introducing Divine Grace', *WTJ* 57: 311–332

Vanhoye, Albert (1970), 'La composition de Jean 5,19–30', in Albert Descamps and André de Halleux (eds.), *Mélanges Bibliques en hommage au R. P. Béda Rigaux*, 259–274, Gembloux: Duculot

van Rossum, J. (1991), 'The "Johannine Pentecost": John 20:22 in Modern Exegesis and in Orthodox Theology', *StVTQ* 35: 149–167

van Tilborg, Sjef (1996), *Reading John in Ephesus*, Leiden: Brill

van Unnik, W. C. (1979), 'Luke's Second Book and the Rules of Hellenistic Historiography', in J. Kremer (ed.), *Les Actes des Apôtres*, 37–60, Leuven: Louvain University Press and Peeters

van Voorst, Robert E. (2000), *Jesus Outside the New Testament*, Grand Rapids: Eerdmans

Viviano, Benedict T. (1998), 'The Structure of the Prologue of John (1:1–18): A Note', *RB* 105: 176–184

von Wahlde, Urban C. (1981), 'The Witnesses to Jesus in John 5:31–40 and Belief in the Fourth Gospel', *CBQ* 43: 385–404

Wagner, Josef (1988), *Auferstehung und Leben: Joh 11,1–12,19 als Spiegel johanneischer Redaktions- und Theologiegeschichte*, Regensburg: Pustet

Walker, William O., Jr (1982), 'The Lord's Prayer in Matthew and in John', *NTS* 28: 237–256

—— (1994), 'John 1.43–51 and "The Son of Man" in the Fourth Gospel', *JSNT* 56: 31–42

Wallace, Daniel B. (1990), 'John 5,2 and the Date of the Fourth Gospel', *Bib* 71: 177–205

—— (1993), 'Reconsidering "The Story of Jesus and the Adulteress Reconsidered"', *NTS* 39: 290–296

Wansbrough, Henry (ed.) (1991), *Jesus and the Oral Gospel Tradition*, Sheffield: JSOT

Watson, Wilfred G. E. (1970), 'Antecedents of a New Testament Proverb', *VT* 20: 368–370

Wead, David W. (1969), 'We Have a Law', *NovT* 11: 185–189

Webb, Robert L. (1991), *John the Baptizer and Prophet*, Sheffield: JSOT

Wegner, Uwe (1985), *Der Hauptmann von Kafarnaum*, Tübingen: Mohr

Weiss, Herold (1979), 'Foot Washing in the Johannine Community', *NovT* 21: 298–325

Wenham, David (1984), *Gospel Perspectives*, vol. 4: *The Rediscovery of Jesus' Eschatological Discourse*, Sheffield: JSOT

—— (1995), *Paul: Follower of Jesus or Founder of Christianity?* Grand Rapids: Eerdmans

—— (1997), 'The Enigma of the Fourth Gospel: Another Look', *TynB* 48: 149–178

—— (1998), 'A Historical View of John's Gospel', *Themelios* 23: 5–21

Wenham, John (1984), *Easter Enigma: Are the Resurrection Accounts in Conflict?* Exeter: Paternoster; Grand Rapids: Zondervan

Westcott, B. F. (1908), *The Gospel According to St. John*, repr. Grand Rapids: Baker, 1980

Westerholm, Stephen (1978), *Jesus and Scribal Authority*, Lund: Gleerup

Westermann, Claus (1998), *The Gospel of John in the Light of the Old Testament*, Peabody: Hendrickson

Whitacre, Rodney A. (1999), *John*, Leicester: Inter-Varsity Press

Wiarda, Timothy (1992), 'John 21.1–23: Narrative Unity and Its Implications', *JSNT* 46: 53–71

Wilcox, Max (1977), 'The "Prayer" of Jesus in John XI.41b–42', *NTS* 24: 128–132

Wilkinson, John (1975), 'The Incident of the Blood and Water in John 19.34', *SJT* 28: 149–172

Williams, Catrin H. (2000), *I Am He: The Interpretation of 'Anî Hû' in Jewish and Early Christian Literature*, Tübingen: Mohr

Williams, Francis E. (1967), 'The Fourth Gospel and Synoptic Tradition: Two Johannine Passages', *JBL* 86: 311–319

Williams, Ritva H. (1997), 'The Mother of Jesus at Cana: A Social-Science Interpretation of John 2:1–12', *CBQ* 59: 679–692

Wills, Lawrence M. (1997), *The Quest of the Historical Gospel: Mark, John, and the Origins of the Gospel Genre*, London: Routledge

Wilson, Jeffrey (1981), 'The Integrity of John 3:22–36', *JSNT* 10: 34–41

Winandy, Jacques (1998), 'Le disciple que Jésus aimait: pour une vision élargie du problème', *RB* 105: 70–75

Windisch, Hans (1926), *Johannes und die Synoptiker*, Leipzig: Heinrichs

Wink, Walter (1968), *John the Baptist in the Gospel Tradition*, Cambridge: Cambridge University Press

Winter, Martin (1994), *Das Vermächtnis Jesu und die Abschiedsworte der Vater*, Göttingen: Vandenhoeck & Ruprecht

Winter, Paul (1974), *On the Trial of Jesus*, Berlin: de Gruyter

Witherington, Ben, III (1984), *Women in the Ministry of Jesus*, Cambridge: Cambridge University Press

—— (1990), *The Christology of Jesus*, Minneapolis: Fortress

—— (1995), *John's Wisdom: A Commentary on the Fourth Gospel*, Louisville: Westminster John Knox

—— (1998), *The Acts of the Apostles: A Socio-Rhetorical Commentary*, Grand Rapids: Eerdmans; Carlisle: Paternoster

Witkamp, L. T. (1985), 'The Use of Traditions in John 5.1–18', *JSNT* 25: 19–47

—— (1996), 'Jesus' Thirst in John 19:28–30: Literal or Figurative?' *JBL* 115: 489–510

Wojciechowski, Michal (1987), 'Le don de l'Esprit Saint dans Jean 20.22 selon Tg. Gn. 2.7', *NTS* 33: 289–292

—— (1988), 'La Source de Jean 13.1–20', NTS 34: 135–141

Woll, D. Bruce (1980), 'The Departure of "The Way": The First Farewell Discourse in the Gospel of John', *JBL* 99: 225–239

—— (1981), *Johannine Christianity in Conflict: Authority, Rank, and Succession in the First Farewell Discourse*, Chico: Scholars

Wright, Nicholas T. (1996), *Jesus and the Victory of God*, London: SPCK; Minneapolis: Fortress

Wyatt, Nicolas (1990), '"Supposing Him to be the Gardener" (John 20,15): A Study of the Paradise Motif in John', *ZNW* 81: 21–38

Yadin, Yigael (1961), 'More on the Letters of Bar Kochba', *BA* 24: 86–95

Young, Brad H. (1995), '"Save the Adulteress!": Ancient Jewish *Responsa* in the Gospels?' *NTS* 41: 59–70

Zeller, Dieter (1993), 'Jesus und die Philosophen vor dem Richter (zu Joh 19,8–11)', *BZ* 37: 88–92

Zumstein, Jean (1997), 'Johannes 19,25–27', *ZTK* 94: 131–154

INDEX OF NAMES

SCRIPTURE INDEX